Stephen Watts Kearny, *SOLDIER OF THE WEST*

Stephen Watts Kearny

SOLDIER OF THE WEST

DWIGHT L. CLARKE

UNIVERSITY OF OKLAHOMA PRESS

NORMAN

Library of Congress Catalog Card Number: 61–15148

Copyright 1961 by the University of Oklahoma Press,
Publishing Division of the University.
Composed and printed at Norman, Oklahoma, U.S.A.,
by the University of Oklahoma Press.
First edition.

TO EDNA AND EDMUND

My dear wife and son

Introduction

FEW AMERICAN SOLDIERS have suffered the historical eclipse that shadows the memory of General Stephen Watts Kearny. Until I read Bernard De Voto's *The Year of Decision—1846*, I thought of him merely as one of the many officers who appeared on the western scene during the Mexican War. Other writers had repeatedly asserted that there was something equivocal about Kearny's conduct toward John C. Frémont. His personality had often been described as forbidding. References in De Voto's book led me to read further, and I soon became convinced that Kearny had received very unfair treatment from biographers of Frémont and many writers on the Mexican War.

Why were there at least fifteen complete biographies of John C. Frémont? Why had Frémont and his colorful wife furnished the favorite theme for several novelists, while General Kearny had not merited one full-length biography?

Two answers suggested themselves. First, John C. Frémont possessed graphic powers of description and narration. He made a great contribution to the cartography of western America and popularized knowledge of the lands beyond the Shining Mountains. As he excited the imagination of his fellow Americans, a hero myth developed around his name. That the Pathfinder "found" trails that had already been trod by less articulate predecessors, that his record showed seamier sides—these actualities had become obscured. When

Kearny, the superior officer of such a figure, displayed the moral courage necessary to call Frémont to account for his insubordination, his admirers suffered a violent shock. The man who brought such charges inevitably incurred unpopularity.

Second, we must allot to Senator Thomas H. Benton a full share of responsibility for the prejudice and neglect shown General Kearny. Benton was a great leader in the Senate, the prophet of Manifest Destiny, and a roaring lion in controversy. He adored his daughter Jessie, Frémont's beautiful and imperious wife. Her slightest wish was her father's law. When General Kearny found it his unpleasant duty "to reduce John C. Frémont's heroic dislocations," to quote De Voto, he kindled the rage of the fiery warrior.

In the winter of 1847–48, the court-martial of Lieutenant Frémont was held as a result of General Kearny's charges. The defendant had the full benefit of his father-in-law's prestige as well as his skill as a trial lawyer. A few months later, Kearny's nomination for a brevet major general's commission was submitted to the United States Senate. For thirteen days, Benton bitterly fought its confirmation.

Ultimately, Frémont stood convicted, and General Kearny's promotion was confirmed. These were the facts, but a large segment of the public never accepted them. A study of the treatment accorded Kearny and Frémont forces one to conclude that virtue must indeed be its own reward. My research has convinced me that Americans need to be reminded that Stephen Kearny, before he entered California in November, 1846, was considered one of the ablest officers in the United States Army and a recognized authority on Indian affairs and frontier conditions. Kearny did not just ride out of the morning mists into the deadly lances of the Californios at San Pasqual, then engage in a hot dispute with Stockton and Frémont, and eventually prove a rather awkward witness at a court-martial. He cannot be made to disappear thereafter like the dehumanized figure some writers have contrived. Had he drowned while fording the Colorado on that memorable march from Santa Fe or even died of his wounds at San Pasqual, history would perforce have acclaimed his many achievements.

What irony then that events between November, 1846, and June,

1847, could have almost blotted out recollection of thirty-six years of devoted service in many areas of America. Regardless of the pros and cons of his dispute with Frémont, Kearny's brief administration of California was wise and beneficial. That makes the widespread ignorance of General Kearny's contribution to our history all the more unwarranted. "Historical eclipse" does not seem too sweeping a term for it.

One factor that has contributed to this eclipse is Kearny's own taciturnity. He was laconic in speech and correspondence. He was no showman and would have been the despair of a modern press agent. Apparently it never occurred to him to explain or defend his actions in speech or through letters to the press.

The record abundantly confirms De Voto's comment on the innumerable misstatements about Kearny of which so many writers have been guilty. To a bewildering degree they have misspelled and mispronounced his name, confused dates and details about his ancestry, birth, education, career, and death. When these errors are added to the malice stemming from Frémont's and Benton's attacks upon him, small wonder if the average reader has acquired a distorted image of Stephen Watts Kearny.

To bring him into sharper focus I started as any biographer must, to search for concrete facts—the whens, wheres, whats, and whys of one man's life. The end of the task leaves me with the feeling that I actually knew Stephen Watts Kearny. As the acquaintance matured my respect for the man, his essential integrity and dedication to America became more obvious to me.

The primary sources studied include General Kearny's letter and order books, his diaries, journals, and personal correspondence, his family Bible, and letters of members of both General and Mrs. Kearny's families. These last are obviously incomplete; no letters by Mrs. Kearny herself have come to light, although mentioned several times in correspondence of others. (A story has come down in the Kearny family that long ago a trunkful of the General's papers was destroyed.) Letters, diaries, and journals of officers and enlisted men serving under General Kearny and of the public officials with whom he came in contact more often rounded out and confirmed the official reports than conflicted with them. There is much material in the War Records Division of the National Archives, the *Congressional Globe* and the *Congressional Record*, and *American State Papers*. There are only a few important gaps in the records which, considering the lapse of more than a century, is not surprising.

Newspapers published in many eastern cities, New Mexico, and California carried abundant references to our subject. These had to be checked against other sources for frequent contradictions even where too obvious bias was not involved.

Secondary sources comprise about every written history covering the years of Stephen Kearny's active life, as well as biographies of related lives and local chronicles of the regions of his activities. Many of the best of these sources have been published in journals of historical societies.

Abundant footnotes were originally made, but the reader is spared their inclusion by a method of substantiation pioneered in two excellent books published by the University of Oklahoma Press; namely, Madeleine B. Stern's *Louisa Mae Alcott* (Norman, 1950), and John Paul Pritchard's *Criticism in America* (Norman, 1956). Basically, it provides bibliographical annotation by chapter section as each chapter is advanced (see Notes on Sources, pages 401–26).

It is impossible to list all who have been helpful in my research, but my sincere thanks go to each one.

First, there are members of the Kearny family who have helped me. A cousin of my wife, Warren Kearny Watters of New Orleans, first put me in touch with his distant cousin, Mr. Philip J. Kearny of New York City and New Haven, Connecticut (a grandson of Stephen Kearny's eldest brother, John Watts Kearny). Like Abou ben Adhem, his name leads all the rest of the wide-flung Kearny clan in the interest and helpfulness he displayed.[1]

Another Philip Kearny (descended from General Phil Kearny) and his wife Elaine of Palos Verdes Estates, California, have been most helpful and put me in touch with a wide circle of Kearny relatives. In several cases this produced invaluable material.

Thanks go also to Mr. Cresson Kearny of Montrose, Colorado;

[1] Philip J. Kearny died on July 31, 1958.

also to Mrs. Richard Arthur Bullock of St. Louis and Mrs. Jerry Mihm of Clayton, Missouri (both great-granddaughters of the General) for family letters and newspaper clippings that have been most helpful. In addition, they unearthed Stephen Kearny's will. Professor W. Samuel Howell of Princeton University courteously aided me in locating these ladies. The number of other direct and collateral descendants of the General who have been co-operative is almost legion. The same is true of members of the Radford family (Mrs. Kearny's relatives). My thanks to all of them.

Personal friends for whose aid I am grateful include Mrs. Arthur Doran of Los Angeles and Mrs. Ruth Hayburn Cisek of San Francisco. Ward S. Parker of Creve Coeur, Missouri, generously furnished copies of some of the General's letters.

I have drawn liberally on libraries and historical societies, starting with my very good friend Dr. Lawrence Clark Powell, librarian of the University of California at Los Angeles. His constant interest and encouragement will always be gratefully remembered. Numerous members of his staff gave courteous help; especially Wilbur Smith and James Mink. The Missouri Historical Society in St. Louis generously made available much essential material. Its former archivist, Mrs. Frances Biese, and the present manuscripts librarian, Mrs. Frances H. Stadler, aided me greatly. Similarly, fine treatment was accorded me by the staffs of the Huntington Library at San Marino, California, the Southwest Museum in Los Angeles, and its director, Carl Dentzel, and the Bancroft Library at Berkeley. Mr. George P. Hammond, director of the latter, was particularly helpful in making available the Thomas O. Larkin papers, many of which are still unpublished. Another member of the Bancroft staff, Dr. Dale L. Morgan, outstanding authority on the West, was generous with advice. I shall always feel indebted to Allen R. Ottley of the California State Library for bringing the Samuel F. Du Pont Journal-Letters to my attention. The San Diego Historical Society made available some unpublished diaries. Its former president, Colonel George Ruhlen, U.S.A. ret., gave generous advice together with numerous maps, photographs, and military details. The librarian of the Museum at Santa Fe, Miss Gertrude Hill, has been a helpful correspondent, as have the officials of the National Archives and

Library of Congress. Colonel Frederick P. Todd, director of the Museum of the United States Military Academy at West Point, helped with a critical report of the early oil portrait of Lieutenant Kearny. Milton Halsey Thomas, curator at the Low Memorial Library of Columbia University, courteously supplied data regarding Stephen Kearny's stay at Columbia.

Other historical writers have been co-operative. Among them I am glad to list Mrs. Mary Rockwood Peet of Escondido, California; Otis E. Young of Peoria, Illinois; Elliott Arnold of Beverly Hills, California; John Bloom of Falls Church, Virginia; Captain Fred Blackburn Rogers of San Francisco; and my friend, William W. Robinson, who was of particular assistance in locating the site of the battle of the Rio San Gabriel.

Grateful acknowledgment is also due the painstaking labors of my secretary of many years, Miss Catherine Mon, in deciphering and transcribing my manuscript. Lastly, I am happy to record my gratitude to my dear wife, Edna, for her constant interest in reading each chapter as it came from my pen. She brought to this task the great advantage of her discriminating taste, as well as the fresh point of

DWIGHT L. CLARKE

Los Angeles, California
September 5, 1961

Table of Contents

Illustrations

Stephen Watts Kearny, *SOLDIER OF THE WEST*

1. *Birth—Ancestry—School Days*

A BATTLE AND A BIRTH that occurred in August, 1794, while wholly unconnected, can in the light of history seem coincidental. On the twentieth of that month at the Battle of Fallen Timbers, General Anthony Wayne broke the power of the fierce tribes north of the Ohio River. Ten days later a few hundred miles eastward a boy was born who was to become another successful general. Just as Wayne had secured our frontiers in the old Northwest Territory, this future general greatly extended them in a different direction. He proved himself one of the ablest administrators of our Indian problems in that vastly wider west that was not even American at his birth.

Stephen Watts Kearny was born on August 30, 1794, in his father's house in Newark, New Jersey. The large frame structure with two wings occupied a fifteen-acre estate on the west bank of the Passaic River and faced the road from Newark to Belleville.

Little Stephen's arrival probably created no great excitement. In the twenty-four years of their marriage, his mother, Susanna Watts Kearny, had already presented her husband, Philip, with fourteen children. To these parents, another birth must have seemed only a routine event. The latest born was to remain the youngest of the family. He is said to be named for a kinsman, Etienne de Lancey.

It is doubtful if the boy retained much recollection of his father, for less than four years after Stephen's birth—on June 17, 1798—

Philip Kearny III died in Newark. In the family records he is usually designated by the three numerals to distinguish him from his father and a great-uncle who bore the same name. Susanna Kearny was spared for many more years, dying in Newark on May 6, 1823, at the age of seventy-six. Both she and her husband are buried in Trinity Churchyard, New York City.

In the paternal line, the emigrant ancestor of the Kearnys of Newark was Michael Kearny, born in Ireland in 1669. The family there can be traced to an Edmund Kearny in 1506. It had its crest and motto, "Semper Fidelis." Reputedly the name meant "warrior" or "victorious" in the old Irish tongue and was once "O'Kearny." In every record examined, including photographs of centuries-old family tombstones in Ireland, the name has been invariably spelled "Kearny." (Yet the United States government, when it named an army post in Nebraska for General Kearny, misspelled it Fort Kearney. The same unwarranted extra "e" appears many times in midwestern place names honoring the General. Invariably also, this family pronounces its name "Carney," even though San Franciscans persist in referring to their thoroughfare, named for the General in 1847, as "Curney" Street.)

The Kearnys owned large holdings near Garrettstown, County Cork, in southern Ireland. They were noted for their tolerance in a day when that virtue was rare. For several generations, the men married Anglo-Norman wives. The date of Michael Kearny's emigration to America is usually given as 1704, but some evidence indicates an earlier date. He probably first settled in Philadelphia, but lived for a time in New York City and Virginia. His second wife, Elizabeth Brittin, was of a Pennsylvania Quaker family. Their son, Philip II, was born May 18, 1704. Michael moved to Perth Amboy, New Jersey, in 1720, and held various important public offices in that colony. He was also a warden and vestryman of St. Peters (Protestant Episcopal) Church in Perth Amboy.

(While the name Kearny is admittedly Irish, few other surnames in Stephen Kearny's ancestry are recognizable as Irish. There is an unusually complete record of his forebears for many generations and Dutch, French-Huguenot, English, and Scottish names predominate. Some writers in championing Frémont in his famous con-

4

troversy with General Kearny have referred in less than complimentary manner to the latter's Irish blood and temper. For two
or more generations all of his ancestors were born in America, so
why should we now call Stephen Kearny anything but an American?)

Philip Kearny II was a wealthy lawyer and an extensive land-
owner. He, too, occupied a number of public offices in New Jersey.
He was an able and popular lawyer and practiced in the courts of
the province for many years. He married a widow of French-Huguenot ancestry, Susannah Ravaud Burley. They were the parents of
Philip Kearny III, father of our subject. This Philip III was born
in 1733 at Perth Amboy.

On July 4, 1770, Philip Kearny III married Susanna Watts, the
daughter of John Watts Sr. of New York City. Watts was the last
royal recorder of the Province of New York, member of the King's
Council, one of the founders of the New York Public Library, and
the first president of the New York Hospital. He was the son of
Robert Watts, a native of Edinburgh, and belonged to a family
long distinguished in Scotland. The name was spelled Watt before
his emigration. (For some unaccountable reason, a few writers have
stated that "Stephen Kearny was the son of Philip Kearny and Lady
Barney Dexter (Ravaud) Kearny, his wife." I have searched unsuccessfully for Lady Barney Dexter through extensive records.)

In 1776, because of his Loyalist views, Philip III was obliged to
leave his native town, and later was imprisoned. His subsequent
parole was conditioned upon his remaining within a limited area then
remote from the British. When the King's troops occupied the Jer-
seys, he joined them and returned to his home in Perth Amboy, only
to find redcoats quartered there. Later when the British evacuated
the town, Philip Kearny accompanied them to New York City, ultimately becoming an officer in the city's militia. During this period
he knew the adversity of exile and declared he "lived there on his
own money until all was spent." In time he was granted a pension
and ultimately collected some indemnity from the British Loyalist
Claim Commission for his lost property. Philip's father-in-law, John
Watts Sr., was also a Loyalist and suffered similar confiscation of his
large estates. He died soon afterward.

Revolutionary history is full of cases of colonials who remained loyal to the British Crown and went into exile because of the failure of their cause. Either there were extenuating circumstances in Philip Kearny's case or he was personally highly regarded, for we find him settled in Newark, New Jersey, immediately after the advent of peace. He once more established himself as a wine merchant. His wife did not lose her inheritance because of her father's attainder by the New York Legislature, but was allowed to recover nearly all of her extensive properties for a nominal consideration. Soon after the Revolution, Philip III acquired the Kearny homestead at Newark, which remained in the family for a century and a half. He left a substantial estate on his death.

Through his grandfather, John Watts Sr., and his wife, Ann de Lancey, Stephen Kearny was descended from a host of New York City's pioneers. The names were variously English, French, Dutch, and Scottish; mostly persons of prominence, judges, provincial officeholders, and lords of manor lands.

The erosion of time has deprived us of all but a few details concerning the early life of Stephen Watts Kearny. It is recorded that he attended the common schools of Newark. Beyond that, we have only scant fragments concerning his formative years. These consist of a few letters from Stephen to his brother Ravaud. Though brief, they bring to life a lively lad. The first is dated "Wednesday morning 1807" and is reproduced with the original spelling, punctuation, and capitalization:

> I have not received a letter from you my Dear Brother I don't know when & I hope you are not a going to stop. I want to know if you will with me kill of[f] all the bantoms & I will send John's down pretty soon then we will have some fine fowels, Jame Plat's cock and Sidmans fight like the duce & neither one will not give up yesterday they got at it but parted them I wish you would let me know if you will do that & if you will I will buy some fowels & let mama have these.
> I remain to be yours,
>
> S W K

The second communication is undated and breaks off in the middle

6

of a sentence. One can tell from the context that it was probably written soon after the letter just quoted. Its martial references are faintly prophetic:

Dear Brother:

I take the present opportunity of letting you know of the Great Battle that has been fought this side of the Pasaik this morning at half Past ten I armed General white with an intention of driving Major Red off these plains.   they engaged, a small skirmish ensued in which the Gen. was victorious (like the never failing Sir W. Wallace he drives all before) no great loss on either side the Major retreated—afterwards your little ensign had a most terrible engagement with the Genl which would have proved fatal to one side or the other, had not my all powerful arm as Lord Randolf in the engagement between Douglas & Glenalvon drew the sword & swore "he that struck the next blow should be *my enemy*"[.] at this word they halted I took the Gen & put him in close confinement for having engaged with such superior force—It is expected that the next time they engage, it will be a most desperate battle, both armies are in good repair waiting for an attack—if you give this to Lang & Turner it may be important to some People who deal in feathers because both sides were almost stript . . . once more . . .

When we come to the third letter, we find its adolescent writer had shifted his interest from cockfighting to the maidens of his acquaintance. It bears no date or postmark but is endorsed "S. W. Kearny 1809 or 10 N.ark [Newark] merry letter:"

We all were very much disappointed at your not coming up the other day for the Party at Dy—— which you promised me you would—however none of the girls were pleased but I really was delighted we had the all accomplished Miss Eliza Macomb there and if you knew what an impression she has on me I know you would pity me but I am born to trouble—I must sigh & bless her but never expect more, I resign all pretences to Miss D—— therefore *now you may have her*   Mother is well and all the family—I salute you with distinction.

S. W. Kearny

Remember me to all the

GALS

Hanc litteram flammis uve.

7

Stephen might as well have omitted his Latin. Ravaud failed to heed the request, so 150 years later we find this evidence of puppy love preserved like papers of state in a historical collection. Except for these boyish relics, I have found none of those homely, human details about the young Stephen that would help us better to understand the adult man.

We are on a little firmer ground as to his higher education. The records of Columbia University show that he entered King's College (later to become Columbia) in 1808 as a member of the class of 1812. He was registered for the freshman and sophomore years only. In those days Columbia's first-year curriculum leaned heavily to Latin (Cicero, Sallust, Horace, and Lucian) with some Greek, and English grammar and declamations. Geography and Euclid were included. What a coincidence to find that Xenophon—leader of one of the most memorable marches in ancient history—was the Greek author studied by the future commander of some of the longest and most important marches in the annals of the United States.

Columbia's sophomores in Kearny's time also spent many hours with Latin authors—Virgil, Livy, and more of Horace—and had to declaim in Latin as well as English. The second year curriculum was heavier in Greek—Demosthenes, Homer, and Herodotus. English, algebra, plane trigonometry, and geography filled out the prescribed studies. The record shows that Stephen Kearny was a member of Philolexian, a literary and debating society then in existence at Columbia.

In 1847, a contemporary of Kearny wrote of his college days, "he much endeared himself to his classmates and companions, always punctiliously respectful and courteous in his deportment; he never wounded the feelings of others while the serenity and equableness of his temper joined to his unpretending modesty, stern integrity and cool and resolute determination of character won the highest respect of all his acquaintances. In fact he possessed in himself and in his nature so much of high and chivalrous feeling that he may be almost said to have been born a soldier."

There is no record at Columbia of his presence in the student body after 1810, and this casts doubt on the oft-repeated story that Stephen Kearny left college a few weeks before graduation to enlist for the War of 1812. We can only speculate as to what may have moved this sixteen-year-old student to abandon his college career. His brothers, John Watts and Philip, were then operating a large shipping firm in New York City. There is one report that Stephen worked in some capacity for this firm before he entered the army. Definite evidence on the point is lacking.

Several writers have stated that Kearny attended Princeton, but Princeton has no evidence of his presence there (a fire long ago destroyed its early records). Some commentators have added that Stephen's interruption of his college career to enlist met with strong objections from his family. His persistence in carrying out his plans in the face of opposition is cited as an early example of his strong will and firmness of purpose. Nothing about the family's attitude, however, appears in the record.

One further evidence of Kearny's collegiate career merits attention. The final accounting of his father's estate was not made until after Stephen's mother died in 1823. This account states that Stephen's share was debited for "Four years in college, yearly $400.— for years 1809, 10, 11 & 12. . . . Entered army in 1812." While this does not prove that the young man attended Columbia for two years more than the records of the college show, it rather positively establishes that he had four years of college education *somewhere*. In 1823, Kearny, then in his twenty-ninth year, and an officer of the regular army, would have been likely to protest this charge of $1,600 against his patrimony if it had been erroneous.

More than one historical writer has referred to Stephen Kearny as a West Pointer. It seems proper to conclude these details regarding his formal education by a refutation of the term. There is not an iota of evidence that he ever was a student at the Military Academy. Nor did he, himself, ever make such a claim.

9

2. *The School of the Soldier*

THE NEXT CERTAIN RECORD we have of Kearny is on April 24, 1810, when Governor Tompkins of New York commissioned him an ensign (that day's equivalent of a second lieutenant) of a company of the Fifth Regiment of the First Brigade of Militia of the City and County of New York. The commission enjoined "you are to take said company into your charge and care as Ensign thereof and duly to exercise the officers and soldiers of the company in arms, who are hereby commanded to obey you as their Ensign." In peacetime, that could hardly have been a full-time occupation. On April 18, 1811, Governor Tompkins made him a full lieutenant of the same regiment.

On March 12, 1812, Stephen Kearny was appointed a first lieutenant of infantry in the United States Army. Then truly began the career of military service that was to cease only with his death over thirty-six years later. War with Great Britain was not actually declared until June 18, 1812, but for more than a year preparations for the conflict had been multiplying. Unfortunately these preparations leaned more to bombastic oratory than to expert planning. On July 23 of the same year, Kearny was assigned to the Thirteenth Infantry Regiment.

The next few months taught the young lieutenant many lessons in military affairs, of which fighting was a relatively small part. He quickly learned the unreliability of untrained militia and found little to choose between raw militiamen and regular army recruits. He must have rejoiced that he now held a regular commission when he saw militia officers obsequious to the privates who had elected them. If in later years Stephen Kearny was considered a strict disciplinarian, perhaps it was because this early service so emphatically taught him the importance of discipline. Nearly everything that happened in that campaign was an excellent example of how not to fight a war.

At long last, General Dearborn managed to assemble a small and poorly equipped army in upstate New York and was ordered by the President to invade Canada. By the end of August his army began to move to Plattsburg. New York militiamen were scattered for two hundred miles along the St. Lawrence, and made some forays across the river which only succeeded in antagonizing the Canadians. Dearborn's regulars encamped at Buffalo, while the main militia concentration was at Lewistown, New York, about midway between Niagara Falls and Lake Ontario.

Major General Van Rensselaer commanded the New York Volunteers in this sector. A kinsman of the same name was a colonel serving under him. The officer in command of the regulars at Buffalo was Brigadier General Alex Smyth, inspector general of the United States Army. He held all militia officers in such contempt that when the Van Rensselaers sought a conference with him about their invasion plans, he disdained to reply. Terrain that included two great lakes and Niagara Falls created a knotty enough problem for any council of war.

General Brock, the able British commander, had his headquarters at Fort George on the Niagara River. He had built substantial barracks and expected the attack would be made there. Seven miles upstream a portion of his forces were entrenched on Queenston Heights —1,200 British regulars and militia including the famous Forty-Ninth Regiment of veterans of the Peninsula War and 250 Mohawks under their chief, Joseph Brant. The Niagara River at Queenston Heights was about 200 yards wide with bluffs rising 230 feet above the water. It was a strong location, but the Van Rensselaers chose it as the place to launch the invasion.

Among Smyth's 1,650 regulars idling in camp near Buffalo was

Lieutenant Colonel Winfield Scott. From a chance encounter with a militia officer he learned of the Van Rensselaer plan. Scott thought he saw the opportunity for the action he desired. Without seeking Smyth's consent, he marched his forces on a stormy night to join the New Yorkers.

At three o'clock in the morning of October 13, 1812, Colonel Van Rensselaer ordered the first of the invasion forces to cross the river. It consisted of three hundred militia and an equal number of Lieutenant Colonel John Chrystie's regulars. The Thirteenth Infantry's new lieutenant, Stephen W. Kearny, was about to receive his baptism of fire. Chrystie, himself, was one of the first of the invaders to be wounded. This left the senior regular officer on the Canadian shore a twenty-five-year-old Captain named John E. Wool.

General Van Rensselaer had remained on the American side of the Niagara to give fire support to the landing party. Scott and his regulars had reached Van Rensselaer's position by the waterside just after the first Americans had crossed the river. A heavy rainstorm, almost complete darkness, and the swiftly running river all heightened the tumult and confusion.

General Brock, when surprised at Fort George by the sound of heavy firing, hastened to the heights with reinforcements. Even though his men were stubbornly defending their position with musket fire aided by a three pounder, the Americans were pressing the attack and showed every sign of holding the riverbank. Captain Wool's offensive was so spirited that at last the British fell back. As daylight disclosed the state of affairs, Colonel Van Rensselaer ordered the young captain to storm the heights. Dauntlessly Wool, gallantly aided by Lieutenant Kearny and a second lieutenant, led his men up a precipitous path which the defenders believed unscalable. The attackers were only able to surmount it by pulling themselves up on rocks and bushes.

This ascent drew a withering fire from the British. In a few minutes almost every commissioned officer near Kearny had been killed or wounded. Eighteen years later, General Winfield Scott still recalled that wild morning with kindling enthusiasm when he met Stephen's nephew, Philip. In telling him of the storming of Queenston Heights, Scott said, "undaunted, Kearny went on resolutely at the head of his company and gained the peak of the hill, the objective, and drove the enemy from the field. It was one of the most brilliant engagements of the war." In admiration of his young subaltern's gallantry, the wounded Chrystie, before he was ferried across the river, sent Stephen Kearny his own sword.

Wool's forces gained the rear of the enemy's fortifications a few moments after the British commander reached the spot with reinforcements. The Americans narrowly missed capturing Brock and his entire staff. Despite this newly arrived aid, the British were routed and forced to retreat to Queenston village. Wool raised the American flag over the redoubt on the heights. The guns that the Thirteenth Regiment captured in this assault were the first trophies taken by American troops in this war. In the heavy fighting of the final assault, Colonel Van Rensselaer was severely wounded. He bled profusely and had to be borne down the bluffs to a boat. Captain Wool, too, was wounded and was carried across the river. A few minutes later, both General Brock and his adjutant were killed. This loss further demoralized the British and there was a lull in the fighting.

At ten in the morning, General Van Rensselaer crossed the river to survey the battlefield. He quickly perceived that the small band of victors would face a difficult situation should the British bring up reinforcements. While the nominal command was held by Brigadier General Wadsworth of the New York Militia, the most active senior officer was now Lieutenant Colonel Scott. He prevailed on Van Rensselaer to let him cross over and take charge of the fighting units as a volunteer officer.

Brant's Mohawks were the first of the foe to resume the attack. Scott's defense beat them off. Then new troops from Fort George under General Sheaffe succeeded in reaching the rear of the Americans and joined with the Canadian militia and Mohawks near Chippewa. Sheaffe now commanded a force of about a thousand men. Van Rensselaer saw the hard-won victory slipping from his grasp and hastily recrossed the river for reinforcements. Perhaps the most disgraceful incident in American military history followed. It was bad enough that General Smyth, with a considerable body of regulars, continued, like Achilles, to sulk in his tent, and never moved a man to assist his fellow countrymen who were fighting and dying a few miles away. But right in sight across the river hundreds of militiamen watched the boats return with the wounded. The spectacle so chilled their ardor that they absolutely refused to enter the boats. To Van Rensselaer's frenzied commands and expostulations, their answer was that they had not enlisted to serve outside their home state of New York. All the exasperated general could do was to send over fresh ammunition for the hard-pressed fighters on the heights.

In shining contrast to the cowardice of Smyth and the militiamen was Colonel Scott's Second United States Infantry. They were ready and eager to join the fray, but the civilian boatmen who had been engaged to ferry the soldiers declared the crossing too hazardous, and fled the scene. To heighten the frustration and despair at American headquarters, the camp was a quagmire from the heavy storm that had raged for twenty-eight hours. From the standpoint of logistics, it is sad to note that of the more than 6,000 regulars and militia immediately adjacent to the point of invasion, only 1,100 ever participated in the fighting. Some of them had clung to their foothold on Canadian soil for over 12 hours when General Sheaffe opened his counterattack. About 350 Americans were then fighting on the heights and about 250 along the bluffs and in the nearby town of Queenston. Outnumbered and with no relief at hand, the Americans quickly fell back. Sheaffe threw his entire command upon them. The men on the heights were overwhelmed and retreated down the bluffs. Many were killed and wounded by the galling fire.

General Wadsworth saw that the day was lost and sent Sheaffe a white flag. The Indians cut off its bearer and the slaughter continued. At last, Colonel Scott stuck a white rag on the point of his sword and forced his way back to Queenston village. Sheaffe accepted the capitulation at sunset. Wadsworth's surrendered forces numbered some nine hundred Americans; more, it was claimed, than the total British detachment that captured them. Of all the men who had crossed the Niagara nearly every one had been killed or made prisoner. Ninety Americans died at Queenston Heights and a hundred were wounded—a heavy percentage of casualties out of the small total of eleven hundred engaged in the battle. Only the cowardice of some of their own commanders and the white feather displayed by the militia deprived the Americans of a victory that would have carried far-reaching benefits for the United States. Subsequent operations along the Canadian border would have been a different story. But if a disaster in most ways, Queenston Heights held some solace for the Americans. Despite the small number of combatants, it provided the first real taste of powder to three young officers who were to play decisive roles in the war with Mexico years later—Winfield Scott, John Wool, and Stephen Kearny.

Lieutenant Kearny was among the hundred wounded, though not seriously, and was one of the little band of survivors who were taken prisoner when General Sheaffe accepted General Wadsworth's surrender. Most of the prisoners were started overland to Montreal. En route they encountered black looks from the Canadians they passed. A few months earlier, this same population had dreaded being overwhelmed by the armies massing to the south. Now they remembered nuisance raids on their soil and glared scornfully at the straggling line of dispirited captives. The militia officers were soon paroled, but Colonel Scott and his regulars were ordered to the Quebec Citadel. They formed a most unhappy band of officers. It was bad enough to have been defeated and captured in battle. But not long before, the British authorities had suspended all exchanges of regular officers. Scott, Lieutenant Kearny, and the rest faced an indefinite prison confinement. Along the way, Scott narrowly escaped murder by two Indians who thought all prisoners of war were fair targets.

Soon afterward, the Americans were placed on board a vessel bound for Quebec. Disgusted at their prospects, Scott and Kearny studied the chances for escape. Their British guards seemed careless, and the two plotted to overpower their captors, seize the vessel, and carry them to the nearest American post on the frontier. Before they could execute their scheme, a change in the personnel of the guard forced them to abandon it. Shortly thereafter they arrived at Quebec and were securely lodged in the old French citadel.

Most accounts of this period assert that Scott and his fellow prisoners were subjected to numerous indignities. In one instance, Colonel Scott, abetted by Lieutenant Kearny, vigorously protested

15

the treatment accorded some Irish captives. Evidently, the British considered them traitorous subjects of the crown rather than prisoners of war. Their brogue was all the proof required to send them to England for trial. Twenty-three had been so condemned when Scott and Kearny appeared on the scene and sternly ordered the prisoners to refrain from all speech. Despite the protests, the British commander persisted in his course, and the unfortunate men were transported. However, Scott had returned to the States before any executions were carried out and notified the London authorities that he would hold as hostages an equal number of British soldiers captured at Fort George until the Irish prisoners were released. These hostages would receive whatever punishment the British dealt the Irish. This vigorous action probably saved the lives of the twenty-three.

Another incident makes a more dramatic story. Sometimes it has been told with Kearny as its hero. Certainly he was present, and the incident is in character with what we know of his youthful exploits. Yet honesty forces us to record a doubt as to the identity of the courageous American who rose to the challenge. It could have been either Stephen Kearny or Mann Page Lomax, a lieutenant in the artillery also present at Quebec.

Apparently their status as officers entitled the Americans to dine in the room used by the British staff. Subalterns of whatever race have always been noted for their hot blood, and the British officers at Quebec were no exception. On one occasion, a young Englishman rose and loudly proposed a toast, "Mr. Madison, dead or alive!" Instantly, an American lieutenant jumped to his feet and in a bland manner thanked his enemy for thus reminding him of the chief magistrate of his country, although not for his toast. In return he wished to propose a toast to His Royal Highness, "The Prince of Wales, drunk or sober!" All the British sprang from their chairs with roars of indignation. A hand-to-hand collision seemed inevitable, but the commanding officer calmed the assemblage by ordering the arrest of the young Britisher who had offered the first toast.

Possibly their captors were just as pleased as the prisoners when orders came early in 1813 to load the latter on a cartel ship for Boston to await exchange. Recent American victories had resulted in the capture of many British officers, so that now His Majesty's government looked with favor on the exchange of prisoners. Lieutenant Kearny, while his ship lay off New York, asked the Adjutant General to intercede in his behalf so that he might resume active duty. This effort met with only qualified success. He was to be released from the cartel ship, but limited thereafter to recruiting duty without the right to return to service in the field. This was little to Kearny's taste; recruiting duty has never attracted young officers of energy and ambition. In respectful terms he let the Adjutant General know of his feeling.

A week later he received from the War Department the welcome news that he had been made a captain of the Thirteenth Infantry. Some references to this promotion base it on his gallantry at Queenston Heights. Oddly enough his formal commission as captain, signed by President Monroe, though effective from April 1, 1813, was not issued until January 20, 1817. Even his captaincy could not offset Kearny's dislike for recruiting duty. Once more he respectfully addressed the Secretary of War to protest being passed over.

Although the war went on for nearly two years after Stephen Kearny's exchange, there is no clear record that he actually engaged in further combat with the enemy. Incidental references indicate that he did. One writer, typical of several others, says, "After he was exchanged he served with honor through the war and acquired such distinction as to retain his rank of captain during the army's reductions of 1815 and 1821."

His first assignment after his release took him to Sackets Harbor. Soon after we find him at Plattsburg Barracks, and in the next few years he seems to have moved frequently between these two posts. At these frontier stations he quickly acquired the reputation for good discipline and soldierly demeanor that marked the rest of his career. Soon after the war he was transferred to the Second Infantry, then located at Sackets Harbor, and later moved to Plattsburg.

During Kearny's wartime stay at Sackets Harbor, the American and British were maneuvering for the control of Lake Ontario. Commodore Chauncey commanded the few vessels the Americans owned in those waters, while Sir James Yoe led the enemy's forces.

With the limited facilities available to either side, the element of surprise and a shift in the wind or weather could suddenly alter the advantage. On one occasion when Sir James temporarily had the upper hand, he appeared in front of Sackets Harbor and challenged Chauncey to come out and fight. The American commander refused on the ground that he had no marines available for his ships. In the close hand-to-hand naval fighting of 1813, marines aboard a ship of war were as essential as sails, cannon, shot, and powder. Captain Kearny and another officer, hearing of this dilemma, hastened to Commodore Chauncey and offered to serve as marines with any force that could be secured. Both young men were much chagrined when the Commodore declined their services. Probably such displays of zeal and courage were the reasons why Kearny retained his active status of captain on the conclusion of peace. The American army was then drastically reduced to a mere skeleton force. The few officers who remained on active duty were necessarily men who had distinguished themselves for both ability and gallantry.

It is in this period that we find evidences of Captain Kearny's activity in fields outside of the military. In 1819, the speaker selected to address an Independence Day celebration was unable to appear. Kearny was chosen to act in his place. A formal dinner was attended by some fifty persons, including several titled ladies from Europe. Then Kearny's regiment was paraded, and he delivered his speech. In writing Ravaud about this occasion, Stephen revealed modest pride when he remarked that in "the expressed opinion of others [my] effort was well received."

Later that same year, Captain Kearny and a detachment of the Sixth Infantry were ordered from Plattsburg to Council Bluffs on the Missouri, first of many long peacetime journeys he was to make. In 1819, when much of the distance had to be covered on foot and the rest by every sort of river craft, a writer who termed it "a long and fatiguing journey" was undoubtedly not indulging in overstatement.

For Captain Kearny, this transfer from the settled East to the Far West actually marked a turning point in more than just his military service. Even his wartime duties had not taken him far afield, and he had continued to consider Newark his home. (To

18

the end of his days Kearny regarded Newark as his real place of residence.) He could not realize it when the detail marched out of Plattsburg; but henceforth, this scion of New Jersey and New York was to become almost a stranger in the lands of his fathers. Save for a few trips eastward (and one longer detail of duty in New York in 1832), the plains, mountains, and frontier posts of the West were to be his home for all his remaining years. Stephen Kearny was not merely going west; he was about to become a westerner.

Following its acquisition by the United States in 1803, Louisiana Territory experienced few changes until 1819. American garrisons had replaced Spanish soldiers in a few cantonments. (Spaniards had continued to occupy these even after the land had been ceded to France.) Americans also established some new posts along the middle and lower Mississippi. In the greater Northwest, which Lewis and Clark had explored for Thomas Jefferson, little had changed. British fur traders continued to operate. The purchase by the United States had made slight impression on them or the Indian population. After 1783, Great Britain had been slow in surrendering many of the frontier forts and when war broke out in 1812, these had been quickly reoccupied by their former owners. The administration in Washington, hard pressed by the campaign along the Niagara frontier, was forced to neglect everything beyond the Mississippi. Settlers along the river had to protect themselves, and the portion of the fur trade that had fallen into American hands was soon lost to the enemy. The war delayed for several years both exploration and military occupation of the lands acquired from France. Even with the coming of peace, American authority was reasserted slowly (for example, Prairie du Chien was not reoccupied until June, 1816). The army had been all but disbanded after the Treaty of Ghent and was in poor position to defend the territory.

On the other hand, the energy of the new nation created an ever rising tide of westward migration that pressed harder on the retreating aborigines. Innumerable treaties with tribe after tribe caused the relinquishment of eastern lands as the Indians moved west. In a short time their new ground was similarly coveted by another wave of pioneers. Aggression brought retaliation, and both spelled trouble along the frontier. By 1818, President Monroe's administration determined to send two expeditions into this new northwest, both to impress the Indians with the power of the United States and to curb the British influence with fur traders and savages. The first of these was called the Yellowstone Expedition, because its destination was the confluence of the Yellowstone and Missouri rivers. If this proved impracticable, the Mandan villages were planned as the alternative objective. A second force was to occupy the headwaters of the Mississippi. This command of over four hundred men under Lieutenant Colonel Henry Leavenworth commenced their journey about the same time as the Yellowstone Expedition. They started from Fort Bellefontaine, a post that was a short distance above the mouth of the Missouri on its south bank. This force proceeded to the confluence of the St. Peters (now the Minnesota) and Mississippi rivers and erected barracks at present-day Mendota, Minnesota. Soon afterward, this post was moved across the St. Peters to the site of present Fort Snelling.

In their tasks these two expeditions developed a type of service destined to characterize the American army for many years. Hard experience resulted in methods of operation that finally appreciably influenced all modern armies. This fact lends added significance to the little group of American officers who led these first commands through the trans-Mississippi region.

Colonel Henry Atkinson, commander of the Yellowstone Expedition, was an able officer but the War Department thwarted his efforts from the outset by assuming charge of all preparations down to the smallest detail. Atkinson could undoubtedly have reached the Yellowstone during 1819. He would have used keelboats, a type of craft that had long successfully operated in the treacherous and shifting currents of the Missouri. No steamboat had ever ascended that river, but Washington chose this way of transporting over eleven hundred men with all their equipment and supplies.

Officialdom compounded the mistake by making a loose contract with a builder to construct the vessels for an exorbitant price. Large sums were wasted before the five steamboats left St. Louis in the summer of 1819. Two never reached the Missouri, and a third went but a little way upstream after months of costly repairs. The two sturdier craft went only as far as the mouth of the Kansas, wintered there, and returned the next spring to St. Louis.

Colonel Atkinson, in desperation, devised a contraption to work a paddle wheel by hand. Manned by some of his soldiers, the vessels so equipped made snail-like progress up the Missouri. Because of these blunders, the Commander was forced to seek winter quarters when less than halfway to his goal. Marching most of his troops overland, Council Bluffs was reached on September 26. One historian succinctly declared that "the whole enterprise has been smothered in an elaboration of method."

This winter camp was on the Nebraska shore of the river some miles above the present Iowa city of the same name. The first arrivals called it Camp Missouri, sometimes Camp Atkinson. Fort Calhoun, Nebraska, now occupies the site. The War Department considered the location important because it was about halfway between St. Louis and the Mandan villages. Also, it was not far beyond the frontier settlements and in the midst of the most powerful and numerous Indian tribes west of the Mississippi. Strategy, too, was served, because at this point the Missouri most nearly approaches the upper Mississippi, where Leavenworth was constructing a post. In an emergency the two forts, three hundred miles apart, could aid one another.

The dispatch of the Sixth Infantry with Captain Kearny to Council Bluffs formed part of the preparation for the Yellowstone Expedition. Colonel Atkinson's forces did not depart in a single body, for we know Kearny was still at Sackets Harbor as late as July 8, 1819. Moreover, Atkinson noted the arrival at Fort Bellefontaine of 90 officers and enlisted men destined for Council Bluffs in June. We do not know when Captain Kearny reached Bellefontaine, nor whether he underwent the trying steamboat experience. It seems probable that he traveled to Council Bluffs by both keelboat and overland marches. The force that reached Council Bluffs in September, 1819, consisted of Colonel Atkinson's Sixth Infantry and a United States rifle regiment, totaling 1,126 men. During at least a part of the stay there, Kearny served as Atkinson's adjutant.

Even though Atkinson lacked the means to reach his original

objective, he had not forgotten the desirability of establishing communication between Camp Missouri and Colonel Leavenworth's new post on the upper Mississippi. A trail across country seemed preferable to twelve hundred laborious miles of river travel on undependable craft. An exploration party must be sent to find the most practical route to the mouth of the St. Peters. Captain Matthew J. Magee of the rifle regiment was to command it. Four other officers, fifteen soldiers, four servants, and an Indian guide completed the detail. The guide brought along his wife and infant papoose. Eight mules and seven horses were provided for the outfit. Stephen Kearny was one of the four officers. He kept a journal of the entire trip that furnishes our best record of it. It was not published until eighty-eight years later. The journal is a clear and simple narrative. While setting forth many details that an exploring party must report, it still makes interesting reading.

3. The Yellowstone Expeditions—1819–25

THE MAGEE PARTY left Camp Missouri early on July 2, 1820, crossing the river and taking a northeasterly course through well-timbered country. On the Fourth, an extra gill of whisky was issued each man, and at a dinner of pork and biscuits all drank mint juleps to "the memory of our forefathers." The twenty-six-year-old captain, undergoing his first experience with the real wilderness, writes vividly of the journey. One senses his exhilaration at the far sweep of the horizon, and the wild scents and fresh winds of the prairie. Despite the sting of wasps and attacks by mosquitoes he could admire the horsemanship of the Indian woman and the affection shown her and the papoose by her mate.

Much game was sighted—deer, elk, and badger—and some of it killed for food. The young lieutenant tried to write casually about his first taste of buffalo—better than common beef. Soon he was referring to five thousand of these animals as "a small drove." When they came to a lake, Kearny almost waxed poetic, "Its banks are gently sloping and covered with sand and pebbles; and a thin growth of timber with the reflection of the sun on the water and the knowledge of our being so far separated from our friends and civilized society irresistibly enforce upon us an impression of gloomy beauty."

On the other hand, danger lurked on the lovely prairie; rattlesnakes slid through the long grass. After two weeks, the guide lost his way, and to make matters worse, provisions were nearly exhausted. Magee was about to order one of the mules killed for food when from the crest of a high ridge the Mississippi was sighted far to the east. When they reached its banks in southeastern Minnesota, food was obtained in barter with friendly Indians. Two days later, Kearny had his first view of an Indian village. The old Sioux chieftain proved a generous host.

On July 25, the explorers reached Camp Coldwater, Colonel Leavenworth's new post near the mouth of the St. Peters. "They were a little astonished at the sight of us," wrote Kearny, "we being the first whites that ever crossed at such a distance from the Missouri to the Mississippi." The next few days provided entertainment and rest for the wanderers. This included attendance at probably the first marriage of whites within the present state of Minnesota, with Colonel Leavenworth officiating. A visit to the Falls of St. Anthony followed. A long, labored sentence in Kearny's journal described the falls as disappointing.

On July 29, Kearny, with a few other officers, began the descent of the Mississippi by boat. (The soldiers returned overland to Council Bluffs with the stock.) This was another excursion into a strange, new world—a beautiful cave, curious mineral specimens, and oddities of nature. Another chieftain was visited and the Captain had his first lesson in Indian oratory and treaty making. The voyager wrote enthusiastically of the rich and beautiful country despite the intense heat experienced. At Sac and Fox villages fresh scalps dangled outside the lodges. Yet when some of the braves dined with the officers at Fort Armstrong, their polite table manners amazed the Captain.

Leaving some of the party here, Kearny, with two other officers and two Negroes, continued the journey in a canoe purchased for six bottles of whisky. Presently they encountered the curious vessel "Western Engineer." Its steam escape pipe was fashioned like a huge serpent with its head protruding at the bow. In motion, the monster wheezed loudly and appeared to churn the waters at the stern paddle wheels. Transferring to this craft, they tied their canoe to its stern and prepared to enjoy easier travel. Too soon, the steamboat grounded on a sand bar and the Kearny party returned to the canoe. They reached St. Louis on August 19. In three weeks they had descended nine hundred miles of the Mississippi. In about seven weeks, Stephen Kearny had covered wide stretches of the West on horseback and by motley river craft. He had seen considerable parts of what are today six populous states of the Union, and had come to know the land and many of its aboriginal inhabitants. Now he was truly a westerner.

Unfortunately, Stephen Kearny did not continue his diary after his return to St. Louis. Our only knowledge of his next tour of duty derives from another man's journal.

Sometime in September he was sent to Fort Smith, Arkansas, as inspector and paymaster. His arrival there closely coincided with that of Major Stephen H. Long and his expedition, who were returning from an exploration of the Rocky Mountain region. They arrived at Fort Smith in September, 1820, and there found Captain Kearny. On the twentieth, Kearny, in company with two of Long's officers, started down the Arkansas to visit the Cherokee Agency and then go on to what is now the famous Arkansas Hot Springs, which they reached on the twenty-eighth. They were "royally treated" at several settlements visited, including Little Rock, then "a village of some six or eight houses." At one of these they feasted on "Corn bread—bear's meat and coffee—a treat worthy the attention of an epicure."

They tarried at Little Rock until October 3, then started for Cape Girardeau in Missouri. The three-hundred-mile ride was accomplished in nine days. At the Cape, they met the steamer "Western Engineer." When Major Long arrived, he and Captain Kearny started up the river for St. Louis, but at Saint Genevieve both fell victims of intermittent fever. In Kearny's case the illness proved serious, and he was confined to his bed for some weeks. Soon after his recovery he read of a staff vacancy in the army. The young captain was ambitious. He applied for the position the next day; but, although he solicited the aid of military friends, did not receive the coveted appointment.

During the next few years, Kearny continued to live a wandering life with frequent moves from one army post to another. On June 1, 1821, he was transferred to the Third Infantry, commanded by Colonel Leavenworth, then stationed at Detroit. Probably he left

Detroit shortly, as he was soon transferred to the First Infantry, whose headquarters were in Baton Rouge. He apparently remained at the latter post until sometime in 1823. Also in April of that year he was brevetted a major "for ten years of faithful service in same grade." Shortly after this recognition, his mother passed away in Newark on May 6. Kearny was absent on furlough during the last half of 1823. On his return to Bellefontaine near St. Louis he took command of four companies of the First Infantry.

Despite the failure of the First Yellowstone Expedition, the War Department had not abandoned its plans. Recent serious Indian disorders along the Missouri had alarmed the administration. Both the Arickaras and Blackfeet had committed outrages against the fur traders, and detachments under Colonel Leavenworth had engaged in indecisive warfare. The government resolved on more effective measures to curb the hostility. Congress authorized the making of treaties with the river tribes, and appointed Atkinson, now a brigadier general, and Major Benjamin O'Fallon, Indian agent, as commissioners to visit the Indians and negotiate treaties. Atkinson was again placed in command, but given a free rein in planning the operation and equipping the expedition. Paddle wheels operated by hand, with which the General had experimented in 1819, were again installed on keelboats to supplement the sails, poles, and cordelles traditionally used in river navigation.

Major Kearny and his four companies of the First Infantry were to be sent that fall to await the main party at Council Bluffs. This marked another milestone in Kearny's career. It would be the first of his many long wilderness journeys in command of a military force. Once more we owe most of the story of this preliminary stage of the Second Yellowstone Expedition to Kearny's own diary. Of a size to fit his pocket, the small notebooks in his neat handwriting have been preserved though never published. Kearny's diary noted the state of the winds and weather, the strength of the river's current, departures and arrivals, distances traveled, and observations on the geography and wild life of the country. But his is certainly the bare bones of the diarist's art, laconic and factual without emotion. Because of these notebooks, we know quite well where Kearny

26

was on certain dates—providing he was in motion. To him, a diary was not a repository for speculative musings. Whenever he was on prolonged duty at some cantonment, the diary abruptly ends.

Major Kearny's command left St. Louis on Friday morning, September 17, 1824. A considerable crowd lined the riverbanks to indulge their curiosity as to how this new attempt to navigate the unruly Missouri would succeed. The onlookers knew the expedition planned to go far up the river but in view of the 1819 steamboat fiasco, there seemed grounds for skepticism. Kearny's four keelboats were commanded by Lieutenant Harney, Captain Spencer, Lieutenant Guyer, and Captain Mason. By dark, they were two miles below the Missouri and tied up for the night. The next morning the bugle roused them for an early breakfast, and the expedition entered the Missouri just as the sun rose. At Fort Bellefontaine, they took on sixty recruits for the Sixth Infantry. Some freight was unloaded to make room for "considerable pork and whiskey." General Atkinson, in company with Senator Benton of Missouri, greeted their arrival at St. Charles. (It is quite possible that this encounter was Stephen Kearny's first meeting with Thomas H. Benton, an acquaintance destined to ripen into warm friendship, yet to end in one of the most tragic enmities in American history.)

For the next six weeks, life for Kearny and his expedition became a succession of crises and near disasters. Machinery constantly broke down. Snags, sawyers, and sand bars continually disputed passage up the treacherous river. Storms and caving banks lent variety. Every few days men deserted. Major Kearny sent detachments to scour the country and bring back the offenders. One of these slit his throat when retaken. Death of a soldier aboard a keelboat forced a pause for burial with the honors of war.

Sometimes trips ashore resulted in serious complications. Hunters in search of game frequently were lost in the thickets and timber along the Missouri. More than once when the boats had gone on without the hunters, death from starvation and exposure was narrowly averted. The necessity of bargaining for pork and other provisions at the infrequent and scantily stocked trading posts was a problem added to mechanical and navigation difficulties. Exciting events like near shipwreck in a storm, a man overboard, and the birth of a girl baby to one of the camp women are compressed into two sentences of the diary.

Sheer necessity seems to have made a mechanic and boat builder out of Stephen Kearny. He must have possessed considerable practical ingenuity and soon became as accustomed to the anvil, hammer, and chisel as to the saber and carbine on the parade ground. Now and then, bands of Indians were encountered and treated to feasts. Occasionally, a passing keelboat brought scraps of news from Council Bluffs and carried soldiers' mail to St. Louis. By late October, snow fell and ice appeared along the riverbanks. A soldier fell overboard and drowned immediately in the icy water. General Atkinson had ridden across country and beat the keelboats into Council Bluffs so that he could greet Major Kearny when he disembarked shortly after noon on November 1. The Major had completed his first independent mission.

Kearny and his command wintered at Council Bluffs. The following spring, General Atkinson and his fellow commissioner, Major O'Fallon, came up the river in eight keelboats. They left St. Louis about March 20, 1825, and arrived at Council Bluffs on April 19. It seems probable that Major Kearny had taken a sizable force with him in the fall. Nowhere does his diary give the total number, but General Atkinson in his report says that 476 men formed the escort that set out from Council Bluffs (now known as Fort Atkinson) in May. Among them were Colonel Leavenworth, Major Kearny, some 15 other officers, and a physician.

Major Kearny did not start upriver until May 16, when he resumed his diary. He left early in the morning with his detachment in four keelboats. Five more carried General Atkinson and the Sixth Infantry.

Atkinson's report and Kearny's diary contain surprisingly little repetition. The General wrote a formal account of stops made, tribes visited, councils held, and treaties executed. One has to read the diary to appreciate the daily struggle of the men in the keelboats against the shifting currents, driftwood and caving banks, the sawyers and sand bars, and above all, with the frail and cranky machinery of the boats. Certainly these early voyagers up the Missouri were learning the hard way that its "navigability" was at best a euphemism.

General Atkinson quickly discovered that Major Kearny was the best qualified of the party to repair damages to the boats. Navigational difficulties were likewise entrusted to him to solve. This left the commander free for his many councils with the Indians and the overall direction of the expedition. Although Kearny was constantly employed in this manner throughout the long journey, one looks in vain in his diary for any claim to credit for such skillful labor. Neither is there evidence that he ever complained about such strange tasks for an army officer. Apparently he and his men accepted as their duty whatever circumstances exacted of them.

On June 9, the commissioners held their first council with the Ponca tribe three hundred miles above Fort Atkinson. Despite the oppressive heat, the Indians were entertained by a military parade. A satisfactory treaty resulted, and after the Poncas put on a dance the trip was resumed. Soon the Great Bend was reached where the Missouri made almost a complete circle upon itself. Here, Kearny added something to the growing knowledge of the geography of the Missouri. The Big Bend had been laid down from north to south on all maps of the region up to this time. Kearny correctly noted that the true course of the river at this point was from east to west.

Every few days new Indians were encountered and more councils held with virtually every tribe of the northwestern plains. Each tribe held solemn councils with the white men and made grave, dignified speeches and stately promises. Presents were exchanged and lasting friendships pledged. We can question how much sincerity there was on either side, but for the time being, the prospects for peace in the Northwest were enhanced. The Indians had never seen so many soldiers. To heighten their amazement, six rounds were fired from a howitzer on one occasion. "They exploded handsomely and made a deep impression on the savages." So much display put on by so large an expedition was costly, but nothing compared to the expense of widespread Indian warfare.

Independence Day was celebrated in a manner that the Dakota prairies have never seen repeated. Early on the Fourth, a few of the officers visited a prairie-dog village and tried unsuccessfully to shoot some of its citizens. At noon an extra gill of whisky was served to each soldier to drink to the anniversary. Then national salutes were fired from the six pounder and the howitzers. Some Cheyenne chieftains were formally received—Kearny described them as the finest-looking Indians yet seen. In the afternoon, the commissioners and the officers visited the camp of the Oglala tribe. Their hospitable hosts had boiled thirteen dogs almost to shreds. As drink for such a feast, Missouri River water was brought to the board in the paunches of buffalo. The taste is said to have lingered, but not pleasantly! General Atkinson, Major Kearny, and the rest must have been a hardy lot. After the aforementioned delicacies, they returned to their own camp and partook of wine and fruit "in commemoration of the day."

The weather was now very hot, with temperatures as high as 106°. Some of a mounted party fainted while out on the prairie. Mosquitoes were a constant trial. On July 26 they reached the Mandan villages, near present Bismarck, North Dakota. Here the expedition came the closest to active hostilities. On August 4, a council was held and a treaty signed with the Crows, who had shown a decided reluctance to accept the commissioners' invitation to a council. During the speeches and pipe smoking that followed, some of the Indians had stealthily tampered with the army's field pieces and then became boisterous and insolent. In attempting to quell them, Major O'Fallon struck three or four with the butt end of his pistol, one so severely that the blood ran freely down his face. The interpreter, too, laid vigorously about him with his rifle as a club. An ominous roar went up as the redskins fixed arrows to their bows. The drums rolled the assembly and the soldiers fell into ranks on the double with their guns ready.

Major Kearny and two or three other officers found themselves nearly surrounded by scowling Indians and momentarily expected an attack. At one time, Kearny writes, "peace or war was as uncertain as in throwing up a copper, whether it comes, head or tail." By much exertion, General Atkinson effected a partial reconciliation. According to a private letter written by one of Major O'Fallon's clerks, this was not the only time that O'Fallon caused trouble on the expedition. The writer accused him of being "vain, overbearing and jealous of anyone who seemed to be thought to stand as high as he in the judgment of Indian character." The letter said O'Fallon interfered with General Atkinson's command of the expedition. Their relations were so strained that during part of the journey they did not speak to each other, and narrowly avoided blows.

Anxious to meet the Assiniboines and Blackfeet and include them in the tribes with whom treaties were being made, the expedition moved up the river on August 6. On the seventeenth, the men who had fought the river so long and endured so much had the satisfaction of reaching their destination, where the Yellowstone flows into the Missouri. Two days later, Kearny's diary records a welcome encounter. "General Ashley and his party arrived today about noon with a hundred packs of beaver skins, from the mountains. He left Council Bluffs last November and wintered near the headwaters of the Platte. Has met with several nations of Indians and had his horses stolen and his party fired on by the Blackfeet. . . ." This was William Ashley, brigadier general of the Missouri Militia, and one of the great leaders of the fur trade. His party had just descended the Yellowstone in skin canoes and brought news that the Blackfeet must be above the Falls of the Missouri, rather certainly beyond the reach of the commissioners. However, Ashley thought there was a good chance of finding the Assiniboines closer at hand. The fur trader was glad to have the protection of General Atkinson's military escort, and it was agreed that his party would wait at the confluence of the rivers until Atkinson's return from his hunt for the Assiniboines.

The commissioners, with some 350 of their escort, went on up the Missouri in 5 of the keelboats on the twentieth. Major Kearny was one of this party. Hunting was even better above the Yellowstone, but there was no fresh sign of Indians and the General reluctantly resolved to end their search at the Porcupine River, 120 miles above the Yellowstone. The weather was warm and the river dropped rapidly. Further ascent might find them stranded in a trickling stream. They were back at the mouth of the Yellowstone on August 26, where General Ashley and his men with their beaver packs were taken aboard and the entire party commenced the return trip.

Descent of the Missouri was a different business than the long crawl upstream. Generally, the miles slipped past with only slight incident. At the mouth of the Cheyenne, the expedition had a demonstration of the workings of the grapevine telegraph. Here some Sioux warriors were awaiting the General, already aware of the clash with the Crows, and anxious to hear a firsthand account. On September 19, the boats tied up to the bank at Council Bluffs. How wondrous the forces of gravity and falling water—the journey that had taken one hundred hard, gruelling days to accomplish upstream had been completed with far greater ease on the descent in only twenty-six!

Major Kearny noted in his diary that the party had returned to Fort Atkinson a month earlier than they had expected. He estimated that in a little over four months the detachment had traveled more than twenty-seven hundred miles and held satisfactory councils with all the tribes encountered. He shared the pride expressed later by General Atkinson in his report that no lives had been lost nor serious accident sustained.

Ashley and his mountain men pressed on downstream to St. Louis in a few days, while the commissioners and a small military escort embarked on October 7 for St. Louis. General Atkinson's report of the expedition discussed the pros and cons of a military post near the Mandan tribes, or at the mouth of the Yellowstone. To protect the fur trade properly, a military post somewhere near the three forks of the Missouri might seem desirable. However, Atkinson emphasized that such a garrison could not subsist unaided on game in the region. It would be expensive to send considerable supplies so far, and therefore he felt it was inexpedient to establish more posts above Fort Atkinson. It appealed to him as more practicable to send a strong force of three or four hundred men every few years as high as the Falls of the Missouri. Such a demonstration would impress the Indians more strongly than a permanent fort in their midst. This was a forerunner of arguments in which Stephen Kearny was to participate years later.

The Second Yellowstone Expedition was a success. A powerful segment of the Indian population had had firsthand evidence of both the friendship and might of the government. British interference with the Indians of the Northwest had been shown to have little present basis in fact. Best of all, no blood of friend or foe had been shed to accomplish these results. Altogether, the Second Yellowstone Expedition reflected lasting credit on its leaders.

4. *The Winnebago War and Fort Crawford*

MAJOR KEARNY'S DETACHMENT was left at Council Bluffs when General Atkinson departed. The accommodations being inadequate, the General had directed Kearny to construct winter quarters. In less than four weeks, the Major had completed a new post called Cantonment Barbour eight miles downstream from Fort Atkinson. Here, he and his men spent the winter of 1825–26. Though isolated, the garrisons of the two posts enjoyed a surprisingly gay social season. In the sutler's journal of dinners and dances, Stephen Kearny's name appears frequently as a guest and at least once as the host.

On May 1, 1826, he received orders to move his command to Fort Bellefontaine. With characteristic dispatch he embarked it by eight the next morning. Passage down the river was reminiscent of earlier struggles with the Big Muddy—stormy weather, tricky currents, leaky boats, and dreary camp sites on flooded banks where rattlesnakes sometimes enlivened the arrival. Bellefontaine was reached in time for breakfast on May 10. Kearny found that cantonment in a decayed state, but the buildings seemed comfortable quarters to men who had just endured nearly a week of rain in open boats and wet overnight camps.

His forces remained at Bellefontaine for exactly two months. They then moved down the Mississippi, encamped about four miles below Carondelet, and started work on another construction project destined to become one of the most famous army posts in America—

Jefferson Barracks. With the statement that "the Third Infantry arrived here from Green Bay [Wisconsin] in September," Kearny's diary abruptly closes.

The building of Jefferson Barracks started the day Kearny arrived, July 10, 1826. For the second time within a few months he found himself superintending a construction job. Even though he was not an engineer nor a member of the Engineer Corps, his superiors must have considered him well qualified for such responsibilities. In the next few years he was to supervise the erection of numerous forts and barracks in the Midwest.

Stephen Kearny not only constructed the early buildings but was the first commander of Jefferson Barracks. Because of its central location, it immediately became the army's regional depot for the Mississippi Valley.

Before its completion he laid aside his building activities to participate in what has been dignified by the name of "The Winnebago War," though it would be more exact to call it an incident.

Many of the northwestern tribes, when not in open conflict with the whites, warred with each other. These internecine feuds were deep seated, though their cause was obscure to Americans. In the first quarter of the nineteenth century, the unrest ordinarily existing was heightened by the development of rich lead mines around Galena on lands which were unquestionably within the territory reserved to the aborigines by treaties solemnly made by the federal government. Rough adventurers, excited by mining fever, had little regard for Indian rights.

By the summer of 1826, the smouldering resentment of the Winnebagos was ready to burst into flame. That tribe inhabited present-day Wisconsin from around Green Bay to the neighborhood of Prairie du Chien. The authorities in Washington chose this particular time to order the abandonment of Fort Crawford near Prairie du Chien. Its garrison was transferred to Fort Snelling in October, 1826. The savages believed the troops had fled because of fear of them. A family near Prairie du Chien was massacred early the following year. Travelers on the Mississippi were attacked with fatalities on both sides. The white settlers became panicky and appealed for help to the miners at Galena and the commander of Fort

Snelling. A hundred volunteers soon came up from Galena and four companies of regulars were dispatched from Fort Snelling.

General Cass, governor of Michigan Territory, which then included present Wisconsin, rushed to St. Louis and appealed for help. General Atkinson quickly led the entire First Infantry to Prairie du Chien. Major Kearny, as the commander of one of its battalions, dropped his construction work and went along.

On Atkinson's arrival in the trouble zone, many more volunteers joined him from Galena. Soon afterward, when he marched to the portage of the Wisconsin River, his force was strong enough to overpower any resistance from the many Winnebagos concentrated there. Atkinson was ready for war and made that plain in the demands he sent to the redskins. He gave them, however, one last chance for peace. If they would surrender the warriors who had terrorized the region, he promised they would receive fair trials. The innocent members of the tribe would not be harmed if they remained quietly at home. In a few days, the Winnebagos bowed to the inevitable and four of the outlaws gave themselves up to the military.

The tribe was cowed and although their basic grievances were not satisfied, the Winnebago War came to an end. General Atkinson, before returning to St. Louis, took the wise step of regarrisoning Fort Crawford with two companies of regulars. Trespasses by the lead miners continued to plague the land and cropped up again in a few years as the more serious Black Hawk War, which Stephen Kearny was to miss.

By the end of September, 1827, Major Kearny and the First Infantry were back at Jefferson Barracks. The interrupted building work was resumed. General Gaines soon arrived on his annual tour of inspection. His report of his visit is unusually enthusiastic. Drill and discipline were termed "unexceptionable and exemplary." The General found the officers of the First Infantry so well versed in their duties that he was ready to vouch they would make excellent artillerists, dragoons, and riflemen. This regiment was "the best light infantry I have ever seen. I know of no officer of the regiment who is not possessed of some peculiar fitness for his station. The regiment is greatly indebted to the talents and steady vigilance of Major Twiggs and Kearny for the present excellence of its character." (He noted in this connection that both its Colonel McNeil and Lieutenant Colonel Taylor had not been with the regiment for some time.) General Gaines believed the First Infantry could safely have its formal instruction terminated and be assigned other duties, except that it provided such a good model for other regiments to emulate. He recommended its ultimate conversion to a dragoon or artillery regiment. This was probably the genesis of the idea that bore fruit over five years later in the organization of the First United States Dragoons.

The General commented, too, on the fact that although the men of the First had been kept so busy constructing Jefferson Barracks, this had not been at the expense of drill and proficiency in arms. A proper balance had been maintained by their commanding officers in pointed contrast to some other posts. While mentioning discipline as maintained by Stephen Kearny, one is struck by its steady, consistent character. In every report of various army inspectors who visited his commands, we find the same praise for the morale of men and officers.

John McNeil was colonel of this regiment but absent in the East at the time of the Winnebago Expedition. In writing to the Colonel after his return from Prairie du Chien, Kearny expressed admiration for General Atkinson. "The General," he wrote, "in the management of this affair displayed much good judgment combined with his usual military firmness, both of which were very necessary in consequence of the peculiar situation we were in towards the Winnebagoes. . . ."

It is possible that the young major modeled his own later conduct on that of General Atkinson. The General's handling of the Winnebagos reads much like some of Stephen Kearny's subsequent dealings with various Indian tribes. The avoidance of warfare as long as possible, and a display of sufficient force to impress the chieftains that the army meant business—these were the bases on which their policy was built. At the same time compassion for the innocent and helpless and a willingness to hear grievances—this was the unwritten code of conduct pursued by both Atkinson and Kearny in all their dealings with the western tribes. In both men there was an absence of swash-buckling. They were not theatrical nor glamorous but some pages of our Indian history are brighter because of their contribution.

In mid-October of 1827, Major Kearny obtained a sixty-day leave of absence with permission to apply for its extension for six months. This gave him the welcome opportunity to visit his family for the first time in many years. In Colonel McNeil's absence he had been temporarily in command of the First Infantry.

Kearny's letter to Colonel McNeil is interesting too for the light it throws on his powers of observation in the political field and the soundness of his judgment in a realm so remote from his own pro-fession. Written a whole year before the presidential contest of 1828, he commented on the election which had just been held for members of the New York Legislature, ". . . the leading question agitated and that upon which the election hinged was relating to the General Command, whether Jackson or the administration party should predominate. Jackson members have been run in by large majorities. The friends of the administration [i.e., President John Quincy Adams] say that the election must not be considered as showing how the state will vote next fall for President but I must confess it appears to me very much like it and unless Clinton and Van Buren should change (of which you will suppose there is no probability) this state may be fairly calculated upon as being in favor of Jackson." While not a Democrat, events a year later proved the young major a good prophet. New York was one of the states that elected Old Hickory.

On October 12, Kearny left St. Louis in company with General Edmund P. Gaines en route to New York. By mid-November, Kearny was in Albany, going on to New York City soon afterward. We do not know whether his leave was extended or when he re-turned to the Midwest. Presumably, Stephen Kearny had been back at Jefferson Barracks for some time when in the late summer of 1828 he was assigned to command Fort Crawford. Major Kearny arrived at Prairie du Chien on September 10, 1828. Four companies of the First Infantry, totaling a little under two hundred men, formed the garrison.

Kearny found the buildings dilapidated, the location generally unhealthy, and morale low. In fact, the surgeon on duty at Fort Crawford a short time before Kearny arrived reported that not only the soldiers but the inhabitants of adjacent Prairie du Chien and the Indians in the vicinity were all subject to intermittent fevers, dysenteries, and diarrheas.

Soon after Kearny assumed command, a new medical officer was assigned to the post, Dr. William Beaumont, noted in early nineteenth-century medical history as a pioneer in the study of stomach disorders and the role played by the gastric juices. The new commander must have worked a minor miracle, for a few months after Dr. Beaumont's arrival the surgeon commented in the most glowing terms on "the healthfulness and efficiency of the troops at this post ... unprecedented within the limits of my recollection." He credited the transformation to the effective measures undertaken by Major Kearny and the strict but salutary discipline exacted. Dr. Beaumont further observed that the men were kept too busy with drill and the necessary routine of garrison duty to indulge bad habits or develop discontent.

Shortly after Major Kearny took command at Fort Crawford, its garrison witnessed a most tragic breach of discipline. One of the soldiers, a young man named Reneka, had enlisted for adventure. Possessed of a good education, he performed his duties in exemplary fashion and was a favorite with both officers and men. While off duty he went on a drinking party and not being used to alcohol, completely lost control of himself. Staggering into the barracks he grabbed a rifle and rushed out on the parade ground swinging it like a maniac. The officer of the day ordered a corporal to arrest the drunken man. At this, Reneka fired the rifle at the lieutenant, killing him instantly. Following his conviction at a court-martial, a gallows was erected and he was hanged. Before the trap was sprung, the unfortunate young man made a touching speech, imploring his comrades to avoid the liquor that had brought about his downfall.

Kearny had it practically demonstrated the winter after his arrival that the way of the peacemaker is often hard. The Indian Agent at Prairie du Chien, Joseph M. Street, was striving to keep trespassers off the lands reserved for the Indians. Miners and settlers were continually invading the reservation to cut timber. This served to fan the hostility of the restless Winnebagos. On one occasion, a party headed by a man named Brunet was cutting such timber. Major Kearny, at Street's insistence, arrested them and, confiscating the lumber they had sawed, hauled it into the fort to be used in the new construction. Brunet obtained a writ of replevin for the lumber. Major Kearny would not allow the sheriff to execute it. For this, the local justice had Kearny arrested for resisting the civil authorities. (This justice was one John Marsh, later a pioneer California doctor.) Brunet promptly sued both Kearny and Street for false imprisonment and damages. The local court decided that the Indian Agent and military had exceeded their authority and entered judgment in favor of Brunet for over thirteen hundred dollars. More than three years later, Congress passed a bill to reimburse the defendants but they remained permanently out of pocket for the costs they had incurred to defend themselves.

One of Major Kearny's first tasks at Fort Crawford was another building project. The flooding Mississippi had badly damaged the old barracks and the site was too subject to overflow. On Kearny's recommendation, Washington authorized selection of a new location and erection of suitable buildings. It complicated his problem by issuing conflicting instructions which made both Kearny and his quartermaster responsible for the same duties. Despite some inevitable friction both men made commendable progress, but because of lack of competent artisans and available material the work dragged. As a precaution, the Major made emergency repairs to the old quarters so that they would be habitable for one more winter. Kearny apparently displayed so much energy that the quartermaster in his own report admitted he could not keep up with him.

About this time, Kearny was advised by the War Department that he had been advanced to a full majority as of May 1, 1829, and could drop "brevet" from his title of major. In connection with the new structures the War Department asked Kearny to suggest changes and additions but he declined to do so as he had just learned that he was to be superseded as commanding officer.

In July, 1829, Lieutenant Colonel Zachary Taylor arrived at Fort Crawford and assumed command. It is odd to find at this small, remote frontier post at one time so many men destined for larger roles in the epic of America. While Colonel Taylor was in command, a certain Lieutenant Jefferson Davis reported for duty. In due course he was to court and a few years later marry Sarah Knox Taylor, daughter of the commander. Fate was to lead the father to the White House, while the groom was to become best known to history as the president of the Southern Confederacy. In a few weeks after their marriage his little bride was dead, a victim of malaria.

There may be details about the rebuilding of Fort Crawford, the replacement of Stephen Kearny by Zachary Taylor—and perhaps the relations between the two officers—that would make interesting reading. Kearny's refusal to suggest changes in the plans because he knew he was to be replaced arouses our curiosity. This is sharpened by a letter written by Zachary Taylor to his brother long afterward in which he expressed an unfavorable opinion of Stephen Kearny. Apparently, Major Kearny returned to Jefferson Barracks soon after Taylor's assumption of the command.

Peace did not long prevail in the Wisconsin region. In May of 1830, on an island in the Mississippi below Prairie du Chien, a superior force of Sioux and Menominees surprised a small band of Fox Indians camped on the island, killing nearly half of them. This affair was known as the Fox or Kettle massacre. Soon after, because of the mounting tension, General Atkinson ordered Major Kearny to take four companies of infantry from Jefferson Barracks to reinforce Fort Crawford. En route north he stopped at Dubuque, and evicted lead miners who had intruded on lands of the Fox Indians. Leaving a few men to police the Dubuque region, he went on to report to Colonel Morgan, now in command of Fort Crawford. (Zachary Taylor had received a two-year leave in 1830.)

The crisis on the upper Mississippi had become so intense that the "Great Red-headed Father," General William Clark, of Lewis and Clark fame, now superintendent of Indian Affairs, went up from St. Louis to attempt a pacification. He and Colonel Morgan as Indian commissioners were to hold another council with the unruly redskins. Because of this duty assigned to Colonel Morgan, Kearny as the ranking officer at Fort Crawford found himself once more its commander.

41

The commissioners felt it important to include the Sioux in the council they planned to hold with their allies, the Winnebagos. Major Kearny was therefore asked to take a detachment to meet the Sioux chiefs and escort them to Prairie du Chien. Otherwise, it seemed only too likely that they would be attacked en route by the Foxes, still smarting from the Kettle massacre. Kearny and his soldiers, with the Sioux chieftains, joined the commissioners without a shot fired, though they rode through a country where hatred and blood lust lurked behind every rock and tree. From the negotiations at the ensuing council valuable concessions were wrung from the Indians and another Winnebago treaty concluded with them on August 1. Upon Morgan's release from his special duties he resumed command of Fort Crawford, and Kearny returned once more to Jefferson Barracks.

While stationed there an incident occurred that was often retold as characteristic of Kearny's military spirit. He was drilling a brigade near the post. The maneuver was the simple exercise of marching in line to the front. Kearny was an excellent horseman and rode a perfectly trained mount. As the line advanced he sat facing it, with his horse slowly backing in the direction taken by the brigade. Suddenly the animal missed his footing and fell, pinning his rider under him. Kearny had drilled these companies so long and so well that not one of its soldiers wavered or moved out of place to assist him. The marching men had approached to within ten feet of their prone commander when in a loud, distinct voice as calmly as if he were still in the saddle, he commanded, "Fourth Company, obstacle, march." The captain of this company wheeled his men to the rear of the next company. When the line had passed on, leaving Kearny behind them, he again commanded: "Fourth Company, into line—march." Fortunately, he was not seriously injured. Extricating himself from under the horse, he remounted, rode around to the front of the brigade, and executed the next maneuver as if nothing had happened.

5. *The Course of True Love*

In the early years of the nineteenth century, St. Louis was noted for its distinctive society. The old French families and the merchants interested in the thriving fur trade furnished its solid core. Isolated from the rest of America, these townspeople developed a close-knit circle renowned for its hospitality and lavish entertainment. The small group of army officers stationed at Bellefontaine and later at Jefferson Barracks was a welcome addition to this society. Entry to the well-appointed homes of St. Louis must have seemed a heaven-sent contrast to garrison duty and the hardships of remote frontier posts.

Major Kearny, a member of a highly-connected Eastern family, well educated, unmarried, and in his early thirties, undoubtedly found many doors open to him in these charmed circles. Both private and official correspondence of this period characterize him as "gallant, intelligent and energetic." His trim, erect figure set off his soldierly bearing and his piercing eye commanded and held respect. We have seen how the performance of his field duties also brought him in contact with leaders of the civic and business life of the city such as Senator Thomas Hart Benton and General William Clark. Kearny was certainly in close association with the latter at the time of the Winnebago Treaty of August, 1830. Entries in the great explorer's diaries refer incidentally to Major Kearny as far back as May 10, 1826.

43

We know that when Kearny returned from the Wisconsin country in the summer of 1830 more than merely military duties quickened his pace. He was already a frequent visitor at the large, imposing home at Main and Vine streets, where Clark kept open house for all the visiting Indian chieftains and virtually every distinguished visitor to St. Louis. William Clark's household in those years included his second wife, Harriet Kennerly Radford Clark, and the children both of that marriage and of his earlier union with Julia Hancock Clark. Four children were born of the first marriage and two of the second. Harriet Clark, a widow when the General married her, brought to his home two children of her first marriage, Mary and John Radford. (A third son, William, continued to live with his maternal uncle.) Apparently this was a happy family. General Clark's and Harriet Clark's older children were actually related because the General's two wives were first cousins. Readers of the Lewis and Clark epic will recall the romantic story about William Clark going to the aid of two young girls who were having difficulty with a balky horse on a Virginia road. There is a family tradition that when Julia Clark lay dying in 1820, she whispered to her husband that if he thought of remarrying he "bear in mind" her cousin Harriet (the other girl he had met in the long ago by the roadside in Virginia).

Apparently every one in both the Clark home and in the numerous circle of their friends made much of the General's stepdaughter, Mary Radford. In a letter to his son, Meriwether, in January, 1830, William Clark reported fondly, "Mary is highly respected and has been a good deal envied by some of the contending young ladies of the city and vicinity. To show her disregard to the contending parties she gave a great party at which she had all concerned and near two hundred other persons." For a young lady not quite eighteen, Mary Radford must indeed have been something of a belle. That was the opinion held of her by a young cousin who wrote many years later, "Mary Radford was a great beauty, very intelligent and accomplished." The officers at Jefferson Barracks among whom Stephen Kearny figured prominently, as well as the young bachelors of St. Louis, seem to have crowded the Clark house as they vied for her favor. One other aspirant for Mary's affections evidently believed himself on the inside track. This was none other than her second cousin and stepbrother, Meriwether Lewis Clark.

The Redheaded Chief was undoubtedly a great explorer. He knew the American Indian as well as any man then living. Yet he apparently was less than astute where the love affairs of youth were concerned. Else how could he have written his son in the language quoted above and not have expected to promote the romance budding under his nose? About a year before, the son, then a West Point cadet, had written to his father for advice. William Clark replied "if it is Love which requires counsel, let me advise you to divert your reflections on that subject, or at least untill you complete your education. You will be in no danger of delay if the object is worthy of you even several years delay in your addresses to an object of true worth would be commendable."

Then the sage counsellor proceeds to inflame the absent lover's imagination by stressing Mary's growing popularity. Small wonder that Meriwether chafed and grew homesick. He had been Mary's constant escort and many in their circle considered them almost engaged. Under parental urging, Meriwether eventually returned to West Point. But a great-granddaughter of Mary Radford still cherishes two souvenirs that indicate the young man's thoughts were not solely on his studies. He made a tiny oil painting of his place of exile and also a miniature pen and ink sketch of West Point which he sent back to Mary.

Meanwhile the dashing Major Kearny from Jefferson Barracks became an even more frequent caller at General Clark's. One commentator said that "when he entered a ballroom all feminine hearts were aflutter." Evidently he had eyes for only Mary. Since a soldier's time for courtship is subject to unexpected interruptions, he soon requested permission of General Clark to propose to her. This certainly put the older man in an embarrassing position since he knew how deeply his own son loved her. Yet it was like his honest nature to interpose no obstacles but let Mary herself decide. The young lady at first demurred and asked for more time to make up her mind. But Kearny must have laid heavy siege for soon she consented to set the wedding date. It was predicted that this wedding would be one of the most brilliant social events St. Louis had ever seen. Nearly every one expected to attend. The Clark house was beautifully decorated with flowers. The best caterers had been engaged to serve the supper.

At West Point, neither studies nor paternal advice had curbed Meriwether's restless spirits. Doubtless he inherited a love of adventure from his famous father, and when opportunity offered he joined a party of hunters bound for the West. One night while they were camped on the prairies, some travelers from St. Louis stopped to share the evening meal. A casual inquiry as to news from that city brought forth the remark that the beautiful Mary Radford was shortly to be married to Major Stephen Kearny. Springing to his feet Meriwether exclaimed: "By gad, she's *not*," and in an instant had saddled his horse and galloped at top speed for home. By hard riding he managed to reach it on the day set for the wedding.

The guests were already crowding the large rooms lighted by myriads of candles. The wine was iced and the wedding cake ready for the Major's sharp sword. An orchestra screened by flowers and shrubs awaited the signal to burst into the wedding march. Many of the guests had seen the groom and his groomsmen enter, all in full military dress. They waited now at attention in a side room, gazing expectantly at the broad stairway, but no bride descended. The musicians improvised some incidental music as the guests began to whisper nervously. Something was amiss, but what?

Upstairs the unexpected late arrival was pleading his case. He, Meriwether, was surely her own true love! The poor bride promptly fainted and when she was revived seemed uncertain as to which gentleman she wished to marry. Meanwhile, Stephen Kearny paced the hall, beset by fears and embarrassment. General Clark and his wife shared his feelings, while Mary, herself, probably thought she was the most unhappy creature living. Writing long after the event, Mary's cousin recalled the day vividly. She was only a child at the time, and described herself as "the go-between and messenger" for the distraught lovers. "Lewis distracted, Kearny distracted! What was to be done? Everybody there and the rooms full, wondering why the bride did not make her appearance. Father and mother distracted and minister talking first to Mary and then to Kearny and Lewis Clark. General Atkinson's anger at the insult to his favorite officer. He swore. I heard him and child as I was did not wonder or blame him, such an insult was enough." At last the guests were told the bride was ill and the wedding had been postponed to the next day. Flowers, music, wedding supper all prepared for naught; it must have been a crestfallen crowd of guests who at last filed out of the Clark house. "Kearny broken-hearted returned to the Barracks," the little cousin recalled.

St. Louis seethed with conjecture and rumors. Mary was spirited out of town for a few days. General Clark and his wife knew how to keep their own counsel, so society waited in vain for explanations. The first positive news they received was that a few days later Mary Radford married Major Stephen Watts Kearny at William Clark's country place, "Maracastor" (the Beaver Pond). In Kearny's own handwriting in his bible we can still read the entry, "September 5th, 1830. S. W. Kearny and Mary Radford married near St. Louis, Mo. by Rev. Mr. Horrell."

The unsuccessful suitor dropped out of sight for some time. Four years later he married Miss Abigail Churchill in Kentucky. Their union was a happy one. The two rivals in love were to become fast friends, and we shall meet Meriwether Clark more than once in the story of Stephen Kearny's life.

An earlier chapter described how the United States Army was all but disbanded after the War of 1812. Despite the steady westward advance of the nation in the ensuing years, the small size of its regular armed forces astounds one. It speaks eloquently of the enterprise and self-reliance of the pioneers of the early nineteenth century. Nowhere is the antimilitaristic instinct of the young republic better revealed. American frontiersmen would keep a musket or rifle over their cabin doors (and use them effectively on innumerable occasions) rather than follow the conventional pattern of the Old World where defense was left to the professional soldier.

Although the slowly retreating red men were an ever potential menace, by 1830 the regular army had an authorized strength of only six thousand officers and men. Its effective numbers were chronically reduced by heavy desertions and delays in recruiting. Seven regiments of infantry and four of artillery encircled the inhabited

47

portions of the United States, a circumference of some six thousand miles. The nation then contained about one-and-three-quarter-million square miles with a population of close to thirteen million.

Such a nominal force had to be widely scattered. Undoubtedly large areas of the country never saw a man in uniform. The militia existed largely on paper and was usually seen only at turkey shoots or in response to Indian alarms. Nearly half of the entire military establishment, or 2,555 men, made up of 56 companies, were stationed in 16 separate posts that comprised the Western Department of the army. By 1830, 7 of these establishments formed the real line of frontier defense in the West. Roughly this line extended from Fort Snelling in Minnesota to Cantonment Gibson in Arkansas Territory near present-day Muskogee, Oklahoma. This frontier usually lay well to the west of the populated areas of the States, although emigration into the border zone behind it was constantly increasing. Just as steadily the region of Indian occupancy was being pressed farther westward.

The handful of officers of so small an army had many diverse problems to solve. Discipline, vigilance, swift marches, and a firm demeanor had to take the place of superior numbers. Rough, practical engineering that could build a blockhouse, locate a water supply, and preserve the health of the garrison rated higher than precision on the parade ground or military etiquette. The captains of the frontier had to be as good diplomats as they were disciplinarians. A shrewd judgment of men and, above everything else, hard common sense could often outweigh nonexistent regiments in reserve. The author of a recent biography of another soldier of this period appropriately points out that too much of the qualities and achievements of these pioneer officers was forgotten in the giant upheaval of the Civil War, because, as one critic complained, "They know everything about handling fifty dragoons and nothing about handling fifty thousand men." The retort might well be made that what this little corps of officers did with "fifty dragoons" on innumerable occasions forms one of the amazing chapters of American history.

The furthermost of these outposts in 1830 was Fort Leavenworth, established in 1827 by Colonel Henry Leavenworth to protect traders along the Santa Fe Trail. Here, Major Kearny brought his bride immediately after their wedding. The records examined by the writer do not state when Kearny was transferred to Fort Leavenworth. One source indicates it was prior to his marriage. If so, he could not have been there long before the wedding.

The bride's stepfather gave the newlyweds a Negro maid and her husband as a wedding gift. The maid rode with Mrs. Kearny in the carriage to Leavenworth while the man trailed the Major on horseback. The Kearnys had not merely acquired two good servants. From the outset they inspired in this Negro couple a loyal devotion that was to play an important role in the Kearny family for many years.

It was well for the young bride that she had this faithful maid near her, for she was about to experience as great a change in her environment as any newly married woman has ever known. Fort Leavenworth was as rough and remote a frontier post as then existed. Outside its own garrison the only humans likely to be encountered were Indians, grizzled mountain men, and teamsters and traders bound to and from Santa Fe. Indian and Negro women were to be found near the fort, but Mrs. Kearny was the only white woman within many miles. One writer has emphasized her isolation by saying she did not lay eyes on another white woman for over two years, but that is an exaggeration. Mary Kearny apparently left no letters that could tell us her reaction to this life of exile in a primitive society, alleviated only by the companionship of a devoted husband.

Extended field duty did not affect the Kearny's domestic life until March, 1831. Then another long river journey preceded one more fort-building assignment. In May, 1824, the army had established Fort Towson near the confluence of the Red and Kiamichi rivers. Soon after its establishment, the garrison became involved in difficulties with both neighboring white settlers and the Arkansas authorities. It was decided to abandon the post despite the strong objections of Colonel George Croghan, the inspector general of the army. The garrison was removed in the summer of 1829, and to insure that the soldiers would not return, the settlers soon afterward burned all the buildings.

By 1830 the national administration had resolved to remove the Indian tribes of the Southeast to new lands west of the Mississippi in what is now Oklahoma. These Choctaws, Cherokees, Creeks, Chickasaws, and Seminoles numbered about sixty thousand. They were peaceful, industrious people following a settled, pastoral life. They had a simple form of government and were little disposed to resist the national authority. On the other hand, their enforced removal created problems. They were not prepared to live as neighbors with the predatory tribes that roamed the southwestern plains. The Pawnees, Comanches, and Kiowas viewed this emigration policy as an unwarranted invasion of their ancestral hunting grounds.

Washington, therefore, was forced to strengthen its southwestern frontier, not so much to protect nearby white settlers as to guard the transported Choctaws, Cherokees, and Creeks from hostile Indians of the plains. Major Kearny's orders to reoccupy and rebuild Fort Towson was one of the first steps taken to carry out this policy.

Other accounts exist of this particular expedition, but an unpublished diary kept by Stephen Kearny is our best source for his part in it. It is difficult to lay aside this 1831 diary. While still terse and strictly factual, Kearny's style has grown more vivid. It reveals a greater consciousness of the wilderness—cypress swamps, distant pine-clad hills, wild fowl overhead, even the magic of moonlight. Nevertheless Kearny had yet to depart from the laconic and impersonal. Entries for each day, for example, are set down for a full month without a hint of Mrs. Kearny's presence in the party. Then the husband of seven months casually notes that "Mary and myself walked . . . about two miles." The effect on the reader is as startling as if Mary had just dropped from a parachute.

Probably the expedition started from Jefferson Barracks, or Baton Rouge, on a steamboat that landed the troops at Grand Ecore on the Red River near Natchitoches, Louisiana. The diary does not say where Major Kearny and his wife joined the others. Its first entry is on March 10, 1831, when four companies of the Third Infantry, commanded by Major Kearny, left Grand Ecore in four keelboats. Over six weeks later, Kearny's battalion tied up at the old boat landing of Fort Towson. During the interim they had engaged in a never ceasing struggle with the Red River's strong and capricious current, fought their way by inches up winding bayous where the trees met overhead, only too often forced to back out of cul-de-sacs, lost themselves in chutes and channels, moored their boats night after night to cypress trees growing in the lakes and bayous, cordelled over innumerable sand bars and narrowly missed shipwreck from snags and log jams.

In the tedious ascent of the Red, the diary is reminiscent of Kearny's earlier pushes up the Missouri. The snail-like pace, the absence of dry camp grounds, the near disasters from broken masts, leaking hulls, and collisions—these made up the daily account, varied occasionally by an alligator scuttling off the bank at their approach. Much of the river was too deep for poling, many banks too matted with vegetation for cordelling. "Warping" and "bushwhacking" are two expressions Kearny frequently used to describe the method of progress. Several times the river broadened into lakes so that sweeps could be used. More rarely they were able to rig sails and take advantage of the wind. Often both lakes and bayous were so thickly set with cypress trees that the keelboats became wedged between their trunks. Fifteen miles a day was about the best progress made; more often only four. They were favored with some clear weather, but thunderstorms were more frequent.

The diary has a tragic entry on April 21:

> About an hour before daybreak as I lay in my cabin, doors and windows open, the weather threatening rain and the night intensely dark, I heard a splashing in the water opposite my cabin door, like a man falling in the river. I jumped up, it was too dark to see anything, got my candle which I had kept lighted but could not see more than the ruffling of the current. I missed my boy Jake from his sleeping place and was convinced it was him. Several of the men and Lieutenant Lupton endeavored to find him but without success. They dove to the bottom while we held candles to guide them, as to the places. After an hour's search we gave it up. Thus in a moment was a good, honest, faithful Negro who had lived with me, for ten years, & in the prime of manhood & good health, summoned away.

Guides who lost their way or failed to carry out instructions complicated the journey. Once across the Arkansas boundary the detachment found a more settled land with some prosperous plantations. Here lay debatable ground claimed by both Arkansas and Mexican authorities in nearby Texas. Some of the former vainly pleaded with Kearny to locate the new fort in their territory. At noon on April 26, 1831, the boats reached their destination. Kearny immediately established Camp Phoenix as a base during the rebuilding of Fort Towson. A less pleasant task was the eviction of an influential squatter who had begun to improve the site. He continued to agitate against the project in every way possible, and was abetted by a number of white neighbors. Kearny, therefore, issued an order prohibiting either whites or Indians from building within three miles of the fort. The Major again had to use his soldiers for construction workers. Material must be processed from raw sources. So lime was burned, coal was mined, trees felled, and a truck garden planted for the mess.

Word soon reached Kearny that a large band of Pawnees were raiding Choctaws near by, so he visited the latter's camp to reassure them. His diary preserves his speech to them:

Choctaws, I am glad to see you. I welcome you on your arrival to this country given you by your Great Father. This country is to be the permanent home of your nation. 'Tis here where your children are to be born and your old people to be buried. You see 'tis a far better one than that which you have left. In thus undertaking to settle the country 'tis necessary that you exercise great prudence. You are men and can understand what I say to you. I am sent here by your Great Father to protect you. I have just arrived. We have a cantonment to erect which will occupy us all summer. Every man of us is at work. Till this is finished, we can be of little service to you and you must depend on yourselves. You have lately lost one of your men by the Pawnees. That man belonged to your nation. The loss is a national one and not confined to his family. I understand some of you wish to avenge it. Let me advise you, by no means think of it. You have not strength to hunt your enemy in his own holes and then cope with him. Your young men wish to hunt; well let them do so and likewise let a party of fifty (you say you can spare them) make circuit around about your hunters to guard your frontier and give alarm if traces are seen. Let this party be cautious and not venture too far. A dozen of you are more than equal to twice your number of Pawnees, but they are too numerous for you at present to contend with. As I am here for your protection, your enemies are my enemies. I look upon you Choctaws as my brothers—and your women as my sisters. Be cautious for a while.

Soon afterward, Kearny was warned that some Choctaws were planning to steal horses from the Pawnees. The commander of Camp Phoenix quickly proved he could use sterner language. The ringleader received a message saying:

I understood he was going out with a party of men to steal horses from the Pawnees. *This I will not suffer.* The Choctaws have come here from east of the Mississippi to live in peace and quietness, and I will not suffer him and a few discontented men to embroil the whole people in constant wars and difficulties. I want him distinctly to understand that should his or any other party go out at any time to steal horses from the Pawnees or neighboring Indians or to get scalps from them, that I shall on their return, seize them, bring them to my garrison and shut them up in irons and on bread and water, till I can hear from their Great Father what more to do with them.

Independence Day provided a pleasant interlude. Kearny entertained all the officers (seventeen) at dinner in his new house. It was about nineteen feet square and had been finished a few weeks earlier. In the evening the noncommissioned officers gave a dance in the company quarters. It had now turned hot, with temperatures in the nineties.

Shortly after daybreak on August 31, Stephen Kearny left Camp Phoenix in his carriage. Characteristically, he has interpolated in this day's entry "having Mrs. Kearny with me." A soldier and a maid accompanied them on horseback. For the next nineteen days they made what must have been a gruelling drive of 596 miles to St. Louis. Even the diary changes its form. The preceding entries, including those written aboard the keelboat, are neatly done in ink.

53

During this carriage trip Kearny used a pencil, wrote in a larger, more scrawling hand—that of a man in great haste. Once, Kearny reported the road "tolerable," oftener "very bad." Wind, rain, thunder, and lightning tormented the travelers. Once the carriage actually overturned, although without injury (so Kearny thought) to its occupants.

Their course virtually bisected Arkansas diagonally from the southwest to the northeast, passing through Little Rock. The greatest distance covered in any day was forty-five miles, once they made only seven. Most of the time they ate and slept in private homes that served for boarding houses, usually run by widows. Occasionally, Kearny wrote "good house," but there are also entries like "rainy morning—house so bad determined to leave it, which we did at daybreak." Finally at five in the afternoon of September 19 they drove into St. Louis.

Nowhere does the diary hint at the reason for this trip. However, the explanation is to be found in Stephen Kearny's own handwriting in his family Bible. In eight words this entry tells of one of life's deepest sorrows. The nineteen-year-old wife so accustomed to the gay whirl of St. Louis society, removed for more than a year from Harriet Clark's experience and counsel, jolting and jouncing for nineteen days over execrable roads towards the tragic ending of the hopes and dreams in the heart of every expectant mother—all of that is in the Bible entry, "November 14, 1831, a daughter, born, died and buried in St. Louis."

Stephen Kearny remained with his wife for only a few weeks. Then, because his task at Fort Towson remained unfinished, he departed from St. Louis on horseback on October 11, and reached his post on the twenty-seventh. Construction was completed a few weeks later.

As soon as the Major learned of the tragic outcome of his wife's confinement, he obtained leave to rejoin her and left Towson on the last day of 1831. Unbeknown to him another shadow had already fallen over their household; Harriet Clark had died in St. Louis on Christmas Day. Kearny rode into the city on January 18, 1832. Here his diary abruptly breaks off for several years.

6. *The First Dragoons*

IN THE SPRING OF 1832 the War Department appointed Major Kearny superintendent of recruiting service with headquarters in New York City. As he was told this tour of duty was for two years, his wife accompanied him when he left St. Louis in mid-April. Except for this assignment, Kearny would undoubtedly have been one of the regular army detachment that went from Jefferson Barracks to participate in the Black Hawk War. Although disappointed at missing this active service, he was pleased that the transfer enabled him to present his wife to his brothers and sisters. Their letters reveal the affectionate interest with which they followed the adventures of their youngest kinsman. With some leave to his credit, Kearny considered traveling by way of Canada if weather and road conditions permitted. Two of his sisters resided in Montreal. Probably he had to abandon this plan, for a few weeks later a cholera epidemic forced him to postpone a visit to his brother Ravaud in upstate New York. We know little about the family reunions, but one sister wrote the following January that "the Major and his lady [are] enjoying themselves in New York."

Washington's view of the frontier was undergoing a change that would vitally affect Stephen Kearny's career. Infantrymen could garrison block houses, but "walk-a-heaps," as the Indians dubbed them, made a poor showing in the field against fleet-footed red men. This fact was finally recognized in a law signed by President Jackson on March 2, 1833, creating the First Regiment of United States Dragoons. Even though dragoons are not exactly synonymous with cavalrymen, their common mobility and tactics justify our terming this event the birth of the modern United States Cavalry.

Cavalry was a decisive factor in many American victories in the Mexican War and still a combat force as late as the Spanish-American conflict. Its apprenticeship on the high plains and in Mexico prepared it for its crucial role on many a battlefield of the Civil War. But for the tactics and techniques slowly and painfully worked out for the First Dragoons in the thirties and forties, the later military history of the nineteenth century would have been wholly different. Until the advent of the airplane, his cavalry was the eyes of an army commander. It not only gave him mobility and protection against flank attacks but was the sole safeguard to his lines of supply and communication. While many of the pioneer officers of the cavalry did not survive into its time of greatest effectiveness, they were as responsible for its later victories as those who actually won them.

The First Dragoon Regiment was created on a generous scale; 1,832 men to be ultimately enrolled. It constituted the elite corps of the army. Major Henry Dodge was named its colonel. Not a professional soldier, he was well known on the frontier for his role in the defeat administered to Black Hawk. The War Department planned to make the second ranking officer primarily responsible for drilling and training the regiment as well as its recruitment. His orders charged him to recruit "healthy, respectable men, native citizens not under twenty and not over thirty-five years of age, whose size, figures and early pursuits may best qualify them for mounted soldiers." Their enlistment was to be country wide to prevent sectional feeling. This second-in-command must not only be a proven administrator and drillmaster, but capable of evolving the tactics applicable to mounted troops. There being no American cavalry and few precedents applicable to the western frontier, this task called for imagination and creative ability in addition to practical experience. There was a dearth of such men in the army. When the lists were scanned it was soon realized that Stephen Watts Kearny appeared best fitted for the post. More than one writer has called him the father of the United States Cavalry.

Certainly, Kearny's new position entailed far more critical responsibilities than superintending recruiting in New York. Therefore,
long before the expiration of the two years of duty, Major Kearny
was recalled to service in the field. The order of the Secretary of
War dated March 4, 1833, directing him to "report to the General
in chief without unnecessary delay" also advised him of his appointment as lieutenant colonel of the First Dragoons. With the exception of an order he was to receive some thirteen years later, this was
undoubtedly the greatest recognition officially accorded Stephen
Kearny. Everything he had previously done was a preparation for
it. Everything that happened thereafter was its logical result. Students of military affairs have also felt this appointment was as
important to the First Dragoons as to Kearny personally. Albert
G. Brackett writes: "It proved a most admirable selection and the
high character which the regiment subsequently attained was mainly
due to him."

With the scanty evidence before us, it is difficult to follow Lieutenant Colonel Kearny with complete certainty during the year after
his promotion. Undoubtedly he went to Washington immediately
after receipt of Secretary Cass's order. It seems certain that he was
in St. Louis on June 27. Six days after her husband's promotion,
Mary Kearny gave birth to their first son, William, in New York
City—the only one of their family to be born in the East. The new
arrival was "christened near St. Louis" on June 27 according to
Kearny's own entry in his family Bible. It is reasonable to assume
that the child's father was present, since under travel conditions in
those days, Mrs. Kearny would scarcely have made the arduous
journey from New York with an infant a few months old unless
she was accompanied by her husband. Neither is it likely he would
have brought his wife and baby west unless he expected to spend
a considerable part of his time at the headquarters of the new regiment, Jefferson Barracks.

The complete roster of the regiment's officers in August, 1833,
shows Kearny at St. Louis, "superintending the recruiting service
for the regiment." Doubtless such duties took him to Louisville
where we find him that same August. Since the First Dragoons were
to be enlisted in various parts of the Union, Kearny must have made

many such journeys. One dragoon, writing from Jefferson Barracks several weeks after seeing Kearny in Louisville, commented that he had not yet joined the regiment and added "report speaks highly of his skill in tactics."

For an organization destined to become the pride of the army, the First Dragoons got off to a bad start. Some critics thought Colonel Dodge too lax, others believed Lieutenant Colonel Kearny too strict. Any blame for the frequent desertions and low morale must be laid at the door of those in the senior command who mobilized a new unit of such ambitious design without also promptly taking steps to mount, arm, and equip it. Many officers and recruits reached headquarters before either their barracks or stables were completed. Little equipment awaited them; arms, cartridge boxes, holsters, and saber belts were all missing, but worst of all for a mounted regiment, there were no horses! To increase dissatisfaction, men who had eagerly joined an elite regiment were put to work as laborers on the unfinished quarters.

Enough horses for three companies actually arrived in October. Eventually they were allotted according to their color, so that each company's horses were all bay, black, white, sorrel, gray, or cream. Drill went on week after week, and in November the regiment was paraded before the critical eyes of the Inspector General George Croghan. On November 10 he pronounced the men, their mounts, and equipment all in excellent order. Probably Colonel Dodge and Lieutenant Colonel Kearny felt their worst troubles were over. Their assurance was short lived. Suddenly they received orders to march all of the command then ready to distant Fort Gibson on the Arkansas River. As soon as the rest of the regiment had been concentrated at headquarters, it was to join Colonel Dodge. Like so many acts of government, the reasons for this untimely order were political rather than military. An economy-minded Congress wanted to see these dragoons in the field since protection of the frontier had been the purpose of their creation. The legislators overlooked the fact that the new regiment was not yet fully assembled, or equipped. They seemed equally unaware of the unseasonable time chosen for a five-hundred-mile march through sparsely settled country by men new to field service.

Since Kearny was busy elsewhere, he did not accompany the regiment to Fort Gibson. Therefore the details of that winter march are omitted. They form an epic of privation and suffering intensified by the uselessness of the march. On April 20, 1834, General Henry Leavenworth assumed command of the western division of the army and began preparations for an expedition among the wild Comanches and Pawnee Picts that roamed the plains between the Red River and the Rockies. These were tribes which had never recognized the authority of the federal government. In the same region, Osages were warring on Kiowas. The War Department decided that it must impress these savages with an imposing display of force. A secondary objective of the expedition was to attempt the recovery of both white and Indian victims of kidnapping raids by these redskins. A few days after General Leavenworth arrived at Fort Gibson, he reviewed all of the forces assembled there. Five additional companies of dragoons were en route from Jefferson Barracks. Lieutenant Colonel Kearny rode in on May 31, just ahead of two of these companies.

Two months earlier, Stephen Kearny had again become a father. Charles Kearny was born on March 7, 1834, at Jefferson Barracks.

A small group of civilians accompanied General Leavenworth. Best known of them was George Catlin, the artist whose sketches, made while with the expedition, contribute greatly to our knowledge of the Indians of the plains. Both by these pictures and his facile pen, Catlin preserved a much more vivid record of this calamitous summer than we would otherwise possess. A Prussian botanist, Carl Beyrich, was also at Fort Gibson, eager to study the flora of the Southwest. Another member was the Indian Commissioner, Montford Stokes. The force should have started not later than May 1, but late arrivals delayed departure. Colonel Dodge and part of his regiment got under way on June 15 but the main force, including the Seventh Infantry and General Leavenworth, did not leave until the twenty-first.

The first few days march was across the prairie to the Canadian River where lush wild flowers made a riot of color. Too soon a scorching sun turned them a somber brown with the temperature over

105° in the shade. It was not long before sick and unfit men began to straggle back to Fort Gibson.

When we read how the dragoons were uniformed, we wonder that any were able to continue their march. They wore a double-breasted, dark-blue cloth coat, with two rows of ten gilt buttons each, decorated cuffs and yellow collar framed with gold lace. Trousers were a blue-gray mixture, with two stripes of yellow cloth three-quarters of an inch in width on the outside seams. Their caps resembled an infantryman's, but included a silver eagle with gold cord and a gilt star in front, topped by a drooping white pompon of horsehair. They wore ankle-high boots with yellow spurs. Each bore a saber with a half-basket hilt in a steel scabbard. A sash of deep-orange silk net was tied to the right hip and worn with full dress, which required a black patent-leather belt and white gloves. As a concession to simplicity, their undress uniform had only nine buttons on each breast, one on each side of the collar, four on the cuffs and on the flaps of the coat, and two on the hips. An epaulette was strapped to each shoulder. To complete their discomfort in summer, each dragoon carried a blue-gray, double-breasted great-coat with a cape. After weighing himself down with the above impedimenta, he had to carry a rifle and supply of ammunition. The chief function of the gold buttons, stars, and net sashes was to catch in the underbrush through which their wearers had to ride day after day. Officers and recruits soon found their energy melting under the merciless sun. Bad water also speedily increased the sick rolls. Very soon, Surgeon Hailes was the hardest-worked man in the outfit. General Leavenworth assigned to Kearny the task of forming an encampment of the sick men and horses. This was originally located near the junction of the Canadian and Little rivers, close to the site of Holdenville, Oklahoma.

General Leavenworth halted his march at the False Washita River. Only half of his men were still on their feet. Catlin described their malady as "a slow and distressing bilious fever." The epidemic afflicting the soldiers had extended to their horses. Scanty feed aggravated their poor condition. Each day some of the mounts died. Grimly conscious of the evil consequences of abandoning the campaign, General Leavenworth ordered Colonel Dodge to press on with all the men and horses fit for travel to the Comanche and Pawnee villages. Dodge could only muster two hundred for this service. At their crossing of the Washita, his men used a canvas boat covered with an elastic gum, belonging to Kearny. It served excellently where streams could not be forded.

When the expedition entered the Cross Timbers, it encountered an additional and formidable obstacle. Hunters and trappers had so named an irregular strip of rough land fringing the great prairies. Post oaks, blackjacks, and some hickory and elm occasionally attained fair size, but more often constituted a dense scrub growth matted with grapevines and greenbriers. Frequent prairie fires had stunted most of the trees but enhanced the impenetrable undercover which made ideal hiding places for wild beasts and savages. Only arduous hacking with hand axes and sabers could cut a trail for the dragoons and their horses.

General Leavenworth, himself, moved slowly onward to the southwest. Unhappily, while hunting buffalo he was thrown from his horse. Already sick with the prevailing complaint, a burning fever ensued and on July 21, 1834, he died at the Cross Timbers. Command of the scattered forces now devolved on Colonel Dodge, although the news did not reach him for several days. Only 250 able-bodied men were still on duty out of about 500 dragoons and infantrymen who had marched out of Fort Gibson. Colonel Dodge, Lieutenant Colonel Kearny, Major Mason, and two lieutenants were the only officers still fit for service. The artist Catlin was now among the sick.

Shortly before his death, the General had placed Kearny in charge of another sick camp established in the Cross Timbers west of the Washita. The invalids at the post on the Canadian were moved to this new sick camp.

Colonel Dodge's smaller force, despite incredible hardships and a growing sick list, penetrated far into the lands of the Comanches and Pawnees. The expedition only escaped massacre because of the tact and vigilance of its commander. Dodge even succeeded in the rescue of some hostages. The able-bodied remnant of the expedition rode into Fort Gibson early in August.

Kearny's slower column of invalids and convalescents did not reach the post until August 24—"a pitiful caravan of sick men and worn out horses," one witness wrote, "those too sick to travel with the first contingent followed in wagons and litters." Previously, Dodge had ordered Kearny to transport his charges at the sick camp directly across the prairies to Fort Leavenworth, a distance of nearly four hundred miles. It was indeed fortunate for these sufferers that this directive was countermanded. Had Kearny been forced to obey the order it is doubtful if any of the invalids would have survived. In the great heat endured (on one day it was 114°) recourse had to be made to stagnant water. It was poisonous and promoted disorders of the liver.

Fort Gibson had become a charnel house with several deaths daily. Overworked Surgeon Hailes was now seriously ill. Repeatedly Catlin, burning with fever, listened to muffled drums and the mournful strains of "Roslin Castle" as burial parties passed his window. Beyrich, the botanist, was dead, as well as over a hundred dragoons and infantrymen. Even though ill, Catlin continued to take notes. In commenting on the vast cost of the expedition, the artist summarized it, "what the dragoon regiment has suffered since they started this summer campaign is incredible and unexampled, . . . to Colonel Dodge and Colonel Kearny, who so indefatigably led and encouraged the men through it, too much praise cannot be awarded." By the time he reached Fort Gibson, Stephen Kearny, too, was sick.

"Disastrous" is the word commonly applied to this expedition. Disastrous it certainly was in the high percentage of deaths and disabilities sustained. Many bloody frontier battles have shown fewer casualties. Yet more than one commentator has properly refuted the term "disaster" as applied to the expedition's outcome. It resulted in councils with wild tribes which for two years had refused to meet the Indian commissioners. One authority terms the council, held at Fort Gibson on September 2, "probably the most important conference with Indians ever held in the Southwest. It paved the way for agreements and treaties essential to the occupation of a vast country by one hundred thousand members of the Five Civilized Tribes immigrating from east of the Mississippi." It was the true start of settled Indian occupation of present Oklahoma. It contributed immeasurably to the security of settlers in a new country and to the development of the Southwest to the then limits of the United States. It facilitated the acquisition of the remaining lands stretching to the Pacific. Most important was the relative peace it brought to the Southwest at a time when the United States was unready for widespread Indian warfare. To accomplish this, eighty-eight of the First Dragoons had died. In consequence, valuable years were purchased to prepare for the all-important events of 1846–47. Ironically, those who died to pay the price never knew the importance of their sacrifice.

Colonel Dodge knew his frontier and apparently was the first official to propose the dispersal of the dragoon regiment at various strategic points in the West. Even before the summer campaign of 1834, he recommended that the First Dragoons be divided into three parts along lines similar to those that were carried out after the regiment straggled back to Fort Gibson. His plan was to leave three companies there to protect the far-western frontier, and to station the remainder at two convenient points on the Mississippi River. From such centers they could easily make a display of force and both prevent Indian encroachment on the settlers and protect the red men's lands from incursions by lawless whites. Such a post located in the upper-Mississippi country might also prevent open warfare between the powerful Sioux and Chippewa or Sac tribes.

As early as May 19, 1834, the War Department directed that during the following winter Lieutenant Colonel Kearny with 3 companies should occupy a new post to be built near the mouth of the Des Moines River. The other companies were divided between strategic locations on the frontier. Kearny delayed his departure to allow the sick to regain sufficient strength for the long march. On September 2, he wrote the Adjutant General's office to request that a name be given his new post. With the chronically short rations of the recent expedition fresh in his mind, he also asked that it be declared a "double-ration" post—a wise precaution in view of its remote and isolated location. With 3 companies totaling 113 men, the Lieutenant Colonel set forth on September 3. For 3 weeks they averaged 20 miles a day across the prairies, low-timbered hills, and farms of Missouri. Late in the evening of the twenty-fifth they drew rein at their new home.

It was near the present village of Montrose, Iowa, a few miles above the confluence of the Des Moines and Mississippi rivers. His first view of the spot did not arouse Kearny's enthusiasm. The low ground where Fort Des Moines stood possessed slight military value and was exposed to floods. The Quartermaster's Department was supposed to have erected proper barracks, but Kearny found both uncompleted work and poor construction. He advised the War Department that he and his men would do their best to finish the post. Once more he was called upon to erect a fort with poor material and unskilled workmen. Kearny had just undergone several months of gruelling service and had not fully recovered his health; small wonder that with a severe winter threatening, the prospect discouraged the Lieutenant Colonel. The Secretary of War advised that the post's official name was "Fort Des Moines, Michigan Territory." He acceded to the "double-ration" recommendation, but supplies continued to be scarce. Even when the fort was completed in November, the soldiers all suffered from the extreme cold.

Not long before the erection of Fort Des Moines, a few settlers built houses nearby. This hamlet became known as Nashville. Kearny, because of his experience at Fort Towson, did not favor close neighbors. Uncertain as to what authority he had to keep the settlers at a distance, he nevertheless moved vigorously to suppress a nuisance. Over thirty years later a pioneer of the region recalled that some of these settlers established saloons and retailed whisky to the soldiers. Some of them overindulged and caused disturbances. As a consequence, Lieutenant Colonel Kearny ordered the destruction of all the intoxicating liquor which his men found in the possession of citizens of Nashville. In Kearny's annual report of the regiment for 1836, mention is made of two members of Company I —"tried by the civil authorities for breaking open a house and destroying liquor of a troublesome citizen living in the immediate vicinity of Fort Des Moines. . . . in obedience to orders of the commanding officer of the post," i.e., Kearny himself. While the old settler still remembered these extreme measures, time had apparently mellowed his judgment. In speaking of Colonel Kearny and the officers who served under him at Fort Des Moines, he said, "they will ever be remembered by the surviving pioneers. . . . for it was through their vigilance that civilization here received its first impetus. Their bayonets taught us to respect the rights of others and from martial law we learned the necessity of a civil code."

The Leavenworth-Dodge Expedition had demonstrated the need for reorganizing the First Dragoons. Its overall usefulness was unquestioned, but tactics and administration were undergoing the acid test of experience. Practical, fundamental changes were in Stephen Kearny's particular field. His fellow officers looked to him for leadership in this respect. On his march from Fort Gibson, he had but little opportunity to ponder the problem. Probably the new system of dragoon drill and maneuvers which was to go into effect a little later had its inception at this time.

Poor quarters, insufficient arms and rations, troublesome neighbors, and drunken soldiers were not Kearny's only problems. In the course of the late winter more recruits and horses were sent to him, but he sadly lacked trained subordinates. By the spring he requested permission to take his men into the field for discipline and instruction. In asking for more officers he wrote, "it is absolutely necessary that officers who either know something of their duty or who are capable of learning it (all in the Regiment are not) should be with their companies." About then, Lieutenant Albert Miller Lea arrived most opportunely. The captain of Company I had gone to Illinois to purchase horses, so Lea replaced him. He found its men careless, undisciplined, and lacking stables for their mounts. He set up a whipsaw and when he found a soldier neglecting or abusing his horse, he made him cut lumber. This plan benefited all concerned —better-treated animals, more lumber for needed buildings, and better-disciplined men. The commander was so well pleased with his new subaltern's methods that he gave Captain Boone leave to visit his family and added his company to Lieutenant Lea's responsibilities. The medicine that had been so good for Company I might benefit Company H.

Before Kearny's letter about field service had time to reach its destination, instructions arrived that it had not been the department's intention to make Fort Des Moines a permanent post. It would provide winter quarters for dragoons who were to patrol the country. Eventually a permanent fort would be built at a more advanced spot.

The order directed Kearny to proceed with his command up the Des Moines River to its junction with the Raccoon and select the site for this military post. The detachment was also to pay a visit to Chief Wabasha at the Sioux villages near the highlands of the Mississippi.

The commander left Fort Des Moines on June 7 with 150 men, a surgeon, interpreter, and some Indian guides. During the next 12 weeks the detachment traversed much of present Iowa and southern Minnesota. Save for a few trappers, the region was entirely unoccupied by white settlers. Small bands of Indians roamed the country which abounded in game. After a 400-mile journey, Chief Wabasha's village was reached. It was located on the site of present Winona, Minnesota. The dragoons made a camp nearby and here they were visited by the Chief, his braves, and a train of women and children curious to eye the soldiers. A small deputation of Sacs also attended the council which Lieutenant Colonel Kearny held before his tent.

His manner was dignified and even deferential to the aged chieftain who had always shown himself friendly to the whites. Kearny urged the warring tribes to forget their feuds and live in peace, which would please their Great White Father. Two days were given over to speechmaking. Kearny proved himself adept at the formal oratory and figurative language of the red men. When they spoke of "keeping intentions warm under your arm" and of a peace pipe "without spot, without blood," he matched them with "the soaring eagle of Wabasha's fame" and his road between the hostile tribes on which "no wolf must howl." When all the speechmaking was ended, Wabasha and his Sioux, as well as the Sacs, made a treaty with Kearny and the council closed.

A biography of Stephen Kearny written shortly after his death includes a sentence that commands attention. I have not found the subject mentioned in any other account of this summer's tour of duty. The phrase reads: "He [Kearny] also made a long march to the headwaters of the Mississippi, visiting the village of Wabasha and *effecting a cessation of the trespassing of the British subjects, from the Earl of Selkirk's settlement at Pembina, on the territories of the*

66

United States." [The italics are mine to denote the unexplained language.]

Immediately after the War of 1812, the Earl of Selkirk, owner of a large land grant from the Hudson's Bay Company, promoted a colony on the Red River of the North. In 1818 a village and church were established at Pembina, on the west bank of the Red immediately south of the international boundary. (There is still a town of Pembina on the same site in North Dakota.) The boundary's exact location had not been defined at the time. In 1816, Congress had passed a law excluding all foreigners from the fur trade within the United States. Soon after Pembina was founded, the United States and Great Britain settled the long-standing dispute as to the boundary line by fixing it on the forty-ninth parallel. This rendered a large part of the Selkirk grant null and void.

Major Stephen H. Long conducted an expedition into the region in the summer of 1823 and reported that he found over three hundred persons living at Pembina. Long's astronomical observation located the forty-ninth parallel exactly and he had a wooden stake driven on the boundary line. His survey proved that all sixty houses in the village, with only one exception, were on American soil, "a discovery which appeared to be entirely to the satisfaction of the settlers," according to a footnote. While some references cast doubt on the reasons for the abandonment of the settlement, a historian of the region says, "In 1823 after five years' establishment the Selkirk settlers at Pembina, suspecting that they were located south of the boundary line, removed farther down the river [Red] to the mother colony. . . ." (Fort Garry or present-day Winnipeg.) It would seem that Major Long's survey prompted this move.

One's curiosity is aroused, however, as to why Stephen Kearny in the summer of 1835 was in any way concerned about Pembina. His report does not indicate that Kearny ever came closer to Pembina than southwestern Minnesota. Winona is far from being at "the headwaters of the Mississippi." The journals of the march nowhere indicate the detachment was ever farther northwest than Brown County, Minnesota, a good two hundred miles south of Lake Itasca, the true "headwaters" of the Mississippi. Pembina is about two hundred miles to the northwest of Itasca.

If representatives of the Pembina colony, Indian agents, or other officials visited Kearny anywhere along his route in connection with the alleged trespass, one would expect this fact to be mentioned in his report. Somewhere, sometime, a hidden letter or chronicle may come to light to explain this incident.

Kearny, after the council with Wabasha adjourned, marched westward, hoping to intercept the Des Moines River. Eventually his detachment swung south and reached the upper waters of its west fork. When they drew rein on August 8 on the site of the city of Des Moines, they were writing the first chapter in the history of Iowa's capitol. They camped here two days and surveyed the region for the proposed new post. Kearny later reported unfavorably on the military possibilities of the location. Since his force was now on short rations, the commander pressed forward on the tenth and returned with the dragoons to their base on August 19.

Kearny had the satisfaction of having led 150 men 1,100 miles without a casualty or serious illness. All the animals, wagons, and other equipment returned safely. Knowledge of the Iowa country had been greatly increased and the spectacle of such a well-equipped force moving easily through the heart of their country was bound to influence the Indians in preserving the peace.

An interesting commentary on Kearny as a disciplinarian was written during this expedition by a member of Company I (which had so recently undergone the whipsaw routine), "Colonel Kearny is very mild and the command is in good health and spirits. So much rain renders marching unpleasant. We have to encamp each evening in mud and water but still I am in better condition than when in quarters."

Despite the flimsy, drafty buildings at Fort Des Moines, we know Kearny had his family with him. Our knowledge springs from curious sources. In proceedings before the Iowa courts some years later, it was brought out that "in 1834 Colonel Kearny brought to . . . Fort Des Moines . . . a woman slave who remained in his household as long as they remained at the fort." Like a preface to the Dred Scott litigation, the Iowa tribunal ruled that slavery could

68

not be tolerated in its territory. The reference undoubtedly is to the Negro maid given the Kearnys by General Clark.

From another indirect source we know that the children also lived at Fort Des Moines. Whatever discomforts he and his family suffered, Kearny did not complain of them in his letters to his eastern relatives. On one occasion he must have accused himself of being a poor correspondent for his sister Ann wrote their brother Ravaud in 1835, "Even our Colonel begins to make his apologies and his wife Mary sometimes his substitute. He is stationed at present and has been there since October at Fort Des Moines, Missouri [*sic*] Happy with his wife and two little boys in a log house and it delights me to find how soon he can turn to all the duties of domestic life." The log house was soon more crowded, for on September 24, 1835, Harriet Kearny was born at Fort Des Moines. A few visitors relieved the monotony of life at the isolated post. George Catlin, the artist who had shared with Kearny the hard experiences of the 1834 campaign, called on him with an Indian agent.

The Kearnys had to endure one more winter at Fort Des Moines during which there was much sickness and many desertions. In the spring of 1836, Colonel Dodge resigned his army commission to become territorial governor of Wisconsin. Command of the First Dragoons devolved upon Kearny as the next ranking officer, and a little later General Atkinson ordered him to move to the regimental headquarters at Fort Leavenworth. Promotion quickly followed when on July 5, 1836, President Andrew Jackson signed a commission for Stephen Kearny as colonel of the First Dragoons from July 4 of that year.

7. Shonga Kahega Mahetonga

COLONEL KEARNY'S REMOVAL to Fort Leavenworth meant more than merely a pomotion in rank. He had previously exercised separate command, but always over a detachment of limited size. Henceforth, while the forces under him remained small, his responsibilities embraced a far-flung area with his regiment usually scattered. One of Kearny's first steps was to strengthen Fort Leavenworth's defenses. Several years before he took command, Colonel Croghan on a tour of inspection had criticized the haphazard construction of the post. When he again visited Leavenworth, a few weeks after Kearny's arrival, Croghan was glad to find that the new commander had started the erection of two blockhouses. He was also surprised by the improvement shown on the drill ground; "the maneuvers which I required were executed in a very creditable manner."

While subject to the general commanding the Western Department at Jefferson Barracks and to the War Department in Washington, Kearny at Fort Leavenworth was more removed from his superiors than the farthest arctic outpost of today. In every sudden emergency the decision had to be his. The reliability of informants had to be weighed, and solid facts sifted from rumor and exaggeration. Long marches that might entail needless hardship and expense depended on his judgment.

Primarily the Colonel's duty was to protect about 1,000 miles of frontier with a force that seldom exceeded 600 effective soldiers.

He had also to preserve the peace among the many Indian tribes who were constantly jealous and suspicious of each other. For 4 years commencing in 1837, the First Dragoons' regular task was not only to defend the frontier, but to escort to their new homes those Indians still east of the Mississippi who were to be transported westward. Their new reservations must also be policed. About 37,000 red men had agreed to emigrate. Within striking distance west of the frontier lived some 230,000 Indians indigenous to the region. Another 50,000 had already emigrated there. These 3 groups could account for roundly 67,000 warriors. Happily they were far from united, but they were still a menace to the handful of troops defending the western line of settlement. Kearny, himself, recommended that a definite limit should be fixed for the frontier. He believed its proper protection required a regiment of infantry or artillery and one of dragoons in each of three regions: between the Mississippi and Missouri, west of the Osage, and between the Osage and Red rivers. He was not the first army officer who had to carry on with far less than what he believed a safe minimum of strength.

For the decade preceding the outbreak of the Mexican War, Kearny's life was one long routine of training and drilling dragoons. It meant a constant succession of escorts, patrols, and expeditions through the Indian country. It was an unspectacular service. One of the historians of the period, while calling him "foremost of the winners of the Southwest," spares only one sentence for Kearny's services during the more than quarter of a century after the termination of the War of 1812, "he was stationed at various military posts in the regular service until he organized the Army of the West." Thus can a man suffer historical eclipse.

Stephen Kearny probably never heard the word "logistics," but he had certainly mastered its meaning. The forces at his command were always a mere fraction of their potential enemies. His actions proved that he believed that an idle dragoon was all but useless to the country. When not drilling, his men were deployed over the prairies on marches and patrols. Their constant mobility made up for their lack of strength. Repeatedly the roving tribes encountered a squadron of dragoons. With what must have been disconcerting frequency, these patrols had a way of riding between the roaming bands and their own villages. Indians bent on mischief were likely to think twice when they knew retreat was cut off. The soldiers never took the offensive unless a tribe provoked them. But when a savage heart was hot for scalps or plunder it was chilling to discover some of Kearny's dragoons hovering on the horizon. This ounce of prevention took the place of many pounds of military might. A constant show of force to impress the savages, coupled with persuasion and conciliation—these were always more desirable than a bloody fight.

A study of this period arouses amazement that so insignificant a military force successfully preserved the peace along the frontier. While many of the Plains Indians were not actively hostile to the whites, potentialities for trouble were never absent. The primary source of irritation was the savages' contact with traders and emigrants along the Santa Fe and Oregon trails. Also, the tribes which had been induced to cede their ancestral lands kept moving west. Their increased numbers disturbed old hunting grounds and produced new feuds. Under a rash or belligerent officer open warfare could easily have erupted many times in such a disturbed region. It was well for the army that the menace never became a reality, for the potential enemy consisted of superb horsemen. Their mobility matched their courage and equestrian prowess because their commissary roamed in the form of millions of buffalo across their trails. Their independence of bases and supplies exceeded the fondest dream of any army commander. Although the pressure of the westward tide of settlers increased, the towns and farms of midland America enjoyed tranquillity behind a line of defense inherently weak save for the training and discipline enforced by the Colonel of the First Dragoons. The absence of gory combat was unspectacular, but the growth and strength of America were better served by the courses pursued by Kearny. Residents along the frontier held him in high regard and felt secure in his protection. The very Indians whom he watched so warily also respected him, and his influence over them became marked. They trusted his promises and feared his wrath. In these years the prairie tribes named him "Shonga Kahega Mahetonga"—the Horse Chief of the Long Knives.

A historian of the American army in writing of Stephen Kearny said in appreciation of his service during this period, "he made himself the idol of the West, and devoting himself to his regiment, made its discipline perfect. . . . Bland in his manners, but of iron firmness, kind to his juniors, . . . requiring the strictest obedience, measuring his expectations by the rank of the officer, his conduct became proverbial. . . . His men looked on him as a protector. It is believed that during the whole time he commanded the First Dragoons no soldier ever received a blow except by the sentence of a general court-martial for the infamous crime of desertion. . . . though probably the strictest disciplinarian in the service, there was less punishment in his corps than any other."

A few years later an anecdote appeared in the press that is characteristic of Stephen Kearny's conception of military life. It seems that some subordinate addressed a military unit as "gentlemen." Kearny in correcting him said, "there are colonels, captains, lieutenants and soldiers in this command but no such persons as 'gentlemen.' " Yet a softer side to the man is revealed. Returning from a brief steamboat trip to St. Louis, with his wife and two younger children, his diary notes, "the soldiers who had collected on shore gave three loud cheers—not very military but certainly evincing a very good feeling towards their commander."

The diary, which was discontinued in January, 1832, was resumed on September 26, 1836. (Entries follow through March 22, 1838, when the diary ceases, until December 28, 1839. The entries begin again on December 28, 1839, and continue through January 15, 1842, when they suddenly end. So far as I have discovered, this was the last of his diaries.) The entries are still brief and factual. Temperatures and precipitation, and the rise and fall of the Missouri are repeatedly set down. The arrival of Sir William Drummond Stewart of the British Army was recorded on September 26. He and his hunting party, so often mentioned in western narratives, were returning from the Rockies. Kearny entertained Captain Stewart at dinner, who impressed him as being "an intelligent man." While Sir William was genuinely devoted to big-game hunting and life in the wilderness, there is an element of mystery about his long trips through the Rockies. Some suspect that he may even have been a British agent. The question of Oregon was unsettled and Sir William may have added international spying to his interest in the wilderness. The Colonel's duties covered a varied field: surveys of new military roads, rehabilitation of old posts, the location and improvement of new ones, peacemaking between quarreling tribes, payments of annuities due under Indian treaties, attendance at courts-martial, the dispatch of reinforcements for the Seminole War in distant Florida.

We have already noted that Kearny had long been studying a way to improve and standardize the drill and maneuvering of mounted troops. His labor now took tangible form in the preparation of a manual. On January 4, 1837, this was printed and distributed to the army under the direction of the commander in chief. It was a small, twenty-eight-page booklet of a size to fit the pocket entitled:

CARBINE MANUAL
or
Rules
for the
Exercise and Manoeuvers
for the
U. S. Dragoons.
Prepared by
Col. Stephen W. Kearny,
United States Army

———

War Department

———

Washington, D. C.
Printed at the Globe Office.

———

1837

Attached to it was General Order Number One enjoining that it be "observed and executed with exact precision." The manual described carbine exercises on foot, horseback, and dismounted service. It instructed the soldier in the manual of arms, loading, aiming and firing, and the use of the bayonet. As would be expected, it is a terse, impersonal work, but plainly that of a lover of horses. It reads, "He (the dragoon) must be made to know that kind and gentle treatment to his horse is the surest means by which he can be managed, or anything taught to him; that very great care is necessary that he at no time strike or touch the horse's head with the carbine; that in loading or firing, he must avoid altering (as far as possible) the usual feeling of the bridle in the horse's mouth, or his own seat and balance on his back, each tending to alarm the animal—a horse once rendered timid by accident, or the carelessness of his rider, in firing from his back, will make the practice of it afterwards difficult if not dangerous," and a few pages farther on, "the dragoon . . . should be very careful to avoid alarming or disturbing his horse; kind and gentle treatment and speaking to him in a low voice, if necessary, will keep most horses quiet and still; this treatment cannot be too strongly enjoined on the dragoon, who must see the advantage of obeying it."

A man so devoted to horses naturally enjoyed the occasional races between mounts of the different companies. Kearny was more at home on a horse than anywhere else and preferred a horse to a stagecoach or any other conveyance. His diary lists many purchases of mares and stallions to improve the strain, and occasionally a commission to a friend to find him another horse. Breeding and racing were among his few hobbies. Another time the diary noted proudly the corn harvested from Kearny's field which "begins to look like that of a farmer—large stacks of hay and fodder and many horses and cattle."

In a brief entry on October 25, 1836, we find the genesis of another great military career: "Wrote yesterday to my brother P. K. recommending that his son should apply for a 2d Lieut^c in the 1st Regt Dragoons." This son was Philip Kearny. His maternal grandfather had wanted to make young Philip a lawyer. The latter obediently pursued the necessary studies but when the old gentleman died, Philip followed his own inclinations. There were military heroes on both sides of his family, and he was fired by the tales about his Uncle Stephen told him by General Winfield Scott. The advice sought from that uncle had far-reaching historical consequences. On June 6, 1837, the steamboat "Kansas" arrived with sixty-two recruits in the charge of two lieutenants who had come from New York via New Orleans. One of them was Philip Kearny, who had

75

obtained his second lieutenant's commission on March 4. He rejoiced at the prospect of serving under his uncle. It was to prove a valuable tutelage. Another visitor that spring was Mrs. Kearny's elder brother, Lieutenant William Radford of the United States Navy. Later in the diary we read of Philip's popularity with his fellow officers and that he supplied the post with a billiard table.

A recital of all the dragoons' marches in this decade would be tedious. Kearny briefly lists them in his annual reports. Even when on some pacific errand, their commander frequently had a detachment detour through the lands of a nearby tribe just for the moral effect. On other occasions, intruders had to be herded off forbidden territory, murderers pursued and brought to justice, and prisoners taken in tribal raids rescued and escorted to their homes. In the one year, 1836, detachments of the First Dragoons were riding from as far south as Nacogdoches on the Texas border to Forts Crawford, Dearborn, Winnebago, and Howard (on Green Bay) in the north.

On January 17, 1837, the Kearnys' third son, George, was born at Fort Leavenworth, but died on October 6 of the same year.

During these years Kearny was thrifty in the management of his personal affairs. Mindful of his family responsibilities, he was saving his money and investing it at ten and twelve per cent in St. Louis with the aid of good friends like Captain Ethan Allen Hitchcock.

General Gaines arrived at Fort Leavenworth on a formal tour of inspection on July 9, 1837, and remained several days. In writing of the drill and parade conducted for the General, the Colonel said "I drilled it [the regiment] very much to the satisfaction of General Gaines." The General's official report was unusually enthusiastic, "the first Dragoons as drilled by Colonel Kearny are the best troops I have ever seen." In fact, the dragoons had become the model unit of the army, and even Kearny, exacting though he was, wrote in his diary when Company G, sixty-nine strong, rode out of Fort Leavenworth for Fort Gibson, "the company is as well mounted, armed and equipped as any I ever saw. Fine material to make good soldiers; many [are] recruits." Philip Kearny was one of the sixty-nine.

Despite its isolation on the frontier, life at Fort Leavenworth was far from dull. Dinner parties and dances occurred frequently, and theatrical companies surprisingly often disembarked from the river steamers to stage productions at the post. The Colonel and his lady were leaders in these entertainments. For one Washington's birthday celebration a number of civilians from the town of Liberty were guests and stayed over for a dance and theater party the following nights. Kearny's diary arouses one's curiosity about the dance on the last evening, "the ladies appeared much pleased and were more lively than on the 22nd." Sometimes the little theater did double-duty as a church when some clergyman visited Leavenworth. Another daughter, Mary, was born to the Kearnys at Fort Leavenworth on July 13, 1839. A more personal side of her father, rarely revealed, is displayed in his diary a year later. "This is the birthday of my little daughter, Mary, who is one year old. Walks very well, talks a little and is one of the finest children I ever knew."

In between patrols and Indian negotiations, Colonel Kearny found time to continue construction activities. During his years at Fort Leavenworth, a number of buildings were erected under his supervision, including a hospital and guardhouse. In 1836, Congress had authorized the erection of "advance military posts" for the better protection of the western frontier. Kearny and Captain Boone were appointed commissioners to survey and recommend a site. In April they went up the Missouri, explored the area below old Fort Atkinson, and selected a location adjacent to the powerful and warlike Pawnee nation, which would bear close watching. Troops based here would be favorably situated to guard the more advanced settlements. For some reason the War Department let the commissioners' recommendation go unheeded for another eight years. Two more advance patrol stations were built by Kearny in the summer of 1842. His concept of frontier strategy had not changed; the best way to keep a close watch on Indians was to stay as near them as possible. Settlers were forever moving westward. Fewer and fewer Indians remained east of the Mississippi. The first of these stations was on the Marmiton River, north of Fort Wayne. It was called Fort Scott, and the present Kansas city of that name occupies the site. This post was established in May by two companies of the First Dragoons. Another company set out from Fort Atkinson in September and built Fort Sandford near Fairfield in present Clay County, Nebraska.

In late October, 1839, reports of serious trouble in the Cherokee Nation caused Kearny to take a force of 250 dragoons to the scene. At the moment, his quartermaster was without funds to supply the expedition, but Kearny personally advanced the necessary amount. Kearny's investigation disclosed more peaceful conditions than he had feared. He penetrated the Cherokee country as far as Fort Wayne without finding cause for serious apprehension. But at that post, the contrast between the dragoons he had brought south and the garrison was striking. Men and mounts of the former were in fine condition; at Fort Wayne, the horses were all rough and un-curried and the soldiers dirty and slack in appearance. He was anxious, too, about Fort Leavenworth itself, most of whose garrison he had been forced to bring south. A long stretch of the frontier was temporarily without defense. He resolved to get back there as rapidly as possible, but decided also to exchange garrisons. The companies which rode with him to Fort Wayne were left there. He led its garrison to Fort Leavenworth to undergo better discipline and bring them up to the standard of the First Dragoons. He proudly noted in his report that on the return journey the detachment rode 300 miles in 9 days without injury to man or horse.

Lieutenant Colonel Richard B. Mason made a later visit to the Cherokees and also reported all quiet there. While on this duty, Mason and Captain Philip St. George Cooke became involved in a controversy that called for all of their commander's diplomacy. The difference concerned the regimental reports. Cooke was high spirited; Mason determined to bend him to his will, even if that required a court-martial. Both were able officers whom Kearny was most reluctant to lose, so he sent Cooke off to Kentucky on a recruiting trip. Mason was directed to select a healthier site for the garrison of Fort Wayne. By thus keeping these officers busy in separate spheres, Kearny bypassed a dispute that could have damaged every one concerned.

To recount all the incipient uprisings and depredations which Kearny arrested before real harm occurred would be monotonous.

Probably the full record of them has not been preserved. Occasionally more serious troubles were quashed in a manner that well illustrates his methods and explains how he kept the frontier peaceful for so long. On one occasion in 1839 he learned that the Otos were threatening their white neighbors and insulting their Indian agent. The Colonel, with two hundred of his dragoons, paid them a visit. Nearly a thousand Otos and other Missouri River Indians lived along the west side of that stream near the mouth of the Platte. Game was becoming scarce, and their cultivation of corn was not too successful. Whisky peddlers from Council Bluffs were busy among them. Kearny summoned the chiefs to a council on September 16. Contrary to their usual custom the Indians came fully armed. Kearny bluntly refused to speak to them while they bore weapons. He said he neither feared them nor wanted to fight. If they wished to talk to him they must deposit all weapons at a distance. Reluctantly, the Indians obeyed. Then the Colonel said while glad to see them he had heard of their bad conduct and demanded that they surrender the guilty men so that they could be publicly chastised. The chiefs surrendered three young braves whom they bitterly reproached for the mischief they had caused. They richly deserved a lashing, but the Indian agent requested that the prisoners not be publicly whipped. He promised he would be personally responsible for their good behavior. Kearny finally yielded to this plea, closed the council, and rode away with his dragoons. Another uprising had been scotched without bloodshed.

A more serious collision with another tribe in 1842 merits attention. The government was continuing to move Seminoles from Florida to a reservation on the Canadian River in Indian Territory. When three hundred of them reached the south bank of the Arkansas, they suddenly defied their escorts and crossed the river into the lands of the Cherokees. Word of this came to Fort Gibson while Kearny was there with five companies. While a heavy thunderstorm raged, Kearny marched them through rough country. When near the Seminoles on the second day, Kearny sent for their chief, Nacklemaha. When the latter appeared, he was proudly fingering a dirk he wore in a sash. (From its appearance, some of Kearny's officers suspected it had been taken from an officer killed in the Florida wars.)

79

Kearny demanded through an interpreter what the Seminole had to say for himself. Nacklemaha complained that his people had been promised they would be settled near Fort Gibson. Because that promise had been broken, declared the Chief, they would go there anyhow. They were looking for friends among the Indians north of the river. In Florida they had been treated with more friendship and consideration. The Chief was accustomed to sit when he had business to transact. Kearny ignored the broad hint about being seated. "If you received that promise, it was unauthorized. You shall *not* go! This day you shall recross the Arkansas and set out for your lands on the Canadian."

The Seminole reluctantly recognized that he had met his match. He endeavored to temporize, but Kearny stared him down. At last, Nacklemaha promised to obey. The Colonel dismissed him but immediately sent scouts to watch the Indians, as he had small faith in the Chief's promises. Soon the trumpets sounded "To horse." The Indians had not moved toward the river. Coolly, the Colonel ordered, "if we come to blows, put your sabers well in, but on no account strike a woman or child!" Captain Cooke's company led the march. In two miles they neared an Indian camp. A Seminole boy on a pony attempted to dash past the dragoons. Kearny himself grabbed the lad's reins and turned him over to two soldiers. He fought like a wildcat and slipped from their grasp. Although surrounded by mounted dragoons and flashing sabers, he continued his flight. Rather than see him cut down, Kearny ordered the soldiers to let him escape.

A little farther on a small band was captured and taken across the Arkansas in a flatboat. By evening the dragoons learned that nearly all of the Seminoles had escaped beyond the Illinois River. It was in flood and a hundred yards wide. Nevertheless, Kearny ordered Captain Cooke to cross it with two companies and pursue the fugitives. Cooke wrote later that if he had had time to think about it he would have pronounced the operation impractical. The banks of the river were vertical, there was only one small canoe at hand, and it was nearly dark. But, he said, "I had faith" and in half an hour he had crossed the Illinois with three-quarters of his men and half the horses. (Cooke not only "had faith," but he and

Courtesy Cresson H. Kearny, a grandson of General Kearny

Stephen Watts Kearny as a young officer. This unsigned oil portrait was done about 1812 or 1813.

From *The Valley of the Mississippi* by
J. C. Wild (St. Louis, 1841)
Courtesy Missouri Historical Society

Kearny superintended the construction of Jefferson Barracks in 1826. He was the first
commander of this post, which was to become the army's regional depot for the Mis-

his dragoons were accustomed to obeying Colonel Kearny's orders.) After many weary hours, most of the Seminoles were captured and herded across the Arkansas. Only one saber wound was administered in all the chase. Eventually, the whole band was forced back to the land designated for them on the Canadian. They made no further attempt to invade the Cherokee Nation.

Kearny was always quick to temper justice with mercy. He happened to visit the Potawatomis shortly after the Sioux had killed one of their braves. A Sioux family had just been captured by the Potawatomis and the tribe was about to kill these prisoners. Kearny insisted that they be sent back unharmed to their own people.

The winter of 1840–41 was unusually severe in the Missouri Valley. On January 8, Kearny noted a temperature of twenty-three degrees below zero. The ink froze on his pen while he wrote in his dining room. Guard was paraded on foot to spare the horses. A month later the thermometer was still hovering around zero. Then on March 9 it snowed all day to a depth of ten inches, and into this white world came another daughter of Stephen Kearny's, Louisa, "a fine girl" according to his diary.

One of the patrols made in 1842 was occasioned by an outrage committed upon traders over the Santa Fe Trail. This trade had become important to the many Missouri merchants engaged in it and to their associates in New Mexico. For much of its distance the trail was flanked by the new republic of Texas. Since the Alamo and San Jacinto, no love was lost between Texans and Mexicans. Border desperadoes claiming to hold Texas commissions viewed the Santa Fe caravans as fair game. That summer, word reached Kearny that such a gang headed by one "Captain" McDaniel had ridden out to plunder wagons along the trail. A troop of dragoons rode in hot haste, but failed to intercept it.

Meanwhile, Don Antonio José Chavez, a wealthy resident of Albuquerque, was en route to Independence with teams carrying bullion and furs. During bad weather, he lost some of his mules and finally made a forced camp in the vicinity of present-day Emporia, Kansas (far inside the boundaries of the United States). Here the McDaniel gang fell upon the Mexican, shot him down in cold blood, and plundered his train. Even though Mexicans were poorly regarded along the frontier, Chavez was well known and respected. His murder created great excitement and a widespread hunt ensued. Eventually the guilty band was captured by the dragoons. The leader and his brother were tried and hung and their companions imprisoned.

On all the patrols and expeditions of these later years, the story was different from the ordeals suffered during the First Dragoons' formative period. Celerity of movement and excellent condition of both the men and their mounts were almost taken for granted. One company that spent most of a summer on the upper Mississippi covered seventeen hundred miles without loss or material injury to a single horse. Even so, the service still encountered rough times. Three companies riding from Fort Wayne to Fort Leavenworth found the horse flies so troublesome that night marches had to be made to preserve the animals. Hard riding was still caused by false alarms or blunders of jumpy militia officers. Climate and terrain were unchanged but officers and men were far different. Training and discipline alone account for the transformation. Men took better care of themselves and their animals. That had been insisted upon until they were ready for any emergency.

By 1840, the Colonel could write Lieutenant Philip Kearny, now an observer with the French Army in Algeria, that although Americans could gain from studying the methods of such good soldiers as the French, units like his own First Dragoons had nothing to fear by comparison with the best.

By 1842 he felt that his regiment was also ready for whatever might befall the country. Though normally devoted to preserving the peace, he had become reconciled to—even anxious for—a war with Great Britain. The Northwestern boundary question and other grievances had angered both countries. In February he wrote to another nephew, "Although the signs of the times not long since were in favor of such a war, yet I regret to say that I no longer consider them so. I say 'regret' because I think war must ensue before our difficulties are settled, and I therefore think the sooner it comes the better! A war would tend to unite the feelings of our people and the public men would then be willing to put the country in a state of defense which they will not do in times of peace."

Kearny's judgment was only partly wrong. In 1842 the prospects of war with either Mexico or Great Britain—or both—seemed fairly certain. The joint occupation of the Oregon country by Britain and the United States, in force since 1818, was satisfactory to neither. While the clamor for the annexation of Texas was far stronger, expansionist sentiment, especially in the North Central States, was mounting for "all of Oregon." Southern politicians saw in it a means to offset Northern opposition to the annexation of Texas. A few years later the agitation gave birth to the slogan of "Fifty-four Forty or Fight." Kearny was merely wrong as to the outcome of the difficulty. Its settlement became imperative. By an uncomfortably close margin, diplomacy and compromise were to win out in the Northwest, while proving ineffectual in the Southwest. The letter just referred to gives one reason why we find so little personal correspondence of Stephen Kearny's. He urged his nephew to continue to write him but warned that he would not always send answers. So much official writing was incumbent on him that he confessed to an aversion to private correspondence.

For Kearny himself, the outstanding event of 1842 was another promotion. While his rank remained unchanged, he was placed in command of the Third Military Department of the army, with headquarters in St. Louis, succeeding Major General Gaines. On August 4, with his adjutant and staff he left Fort Leavenworth, reaching Jefferson Barracks a week later. He still remained colonel of the First Dragoons, but he was closing a chapter of seven busy and in some ways happy years when he left Fort Leavenworth. In that period he not only made important contributions to the nation, but shaped the course of his own later career.

In the process, Kearny had more than once overtaxed his strength. Three times during 1837 he mentioned personal illnesses in his diary. They were apparently all digestive disturbances. Several similar attacks confined him to his bed in following years. Modern diagnosis might ascribe a psychosomatic cause for these illnesses. In addition to strenuous duty with long hours in the saddle in all kinds of weather, the commander of the First Dragoons was subject to con-

83

stant tensions. Frustrating experiences with politicians and pompous superiors, clashes with civilians who had axes to grind at the army's expense—these would undermine the health of any conscientious officer.

8. *The Stirring of Manifest Destiny*

LIFE AT JEFFERSON BARRACKS meant enlarged responsibilities for Stephen Kearny. It also afforded a wider social horizon for his wife and children. Months before the move he had planned to send the two older boys to an eastern school the following year. It was easier to house his family in officer's quarters on the frontier. In St. Louis, where they had so many friends and relatives, Jefferson Barracks was scarcely a fitting residence for the family of the department commander. Ellen Kearny was born there on January 10, 1843. The Colonel would have to look for a house in the city for his growing family.

Soon after Kearny was transferred from Fort Leavenworth, he again had to intervene in behalf of a valued aide. Captain Cooke and Captain Trenor had quarreled about an administrative problem. During Kearny's absence, Trenor had Cooke arrested and insisted that he be court-martialed. The Colonel had no patience with such altercations. He diplomatically reprimanded Cooke, but followed it with a wink and advised Trenor to drop the matter. Trenor persisted in making a serious issue of the affair until Kearny had to tell him that if there was a court-martial, it would be told that Trenor had suppressed certain protests written by Cooke to regimental headquarters. Trenor subsided reluctantly. In one of the rare instances where we find Kearny discussing personalities, he commented on Trenor's unpopularity to a friend acquainted with both captains and added, "You know Captain Cooke, a gentlemanly clever fellow but has his faults—who has not." About this time pressure from the Santa Fe traders prompted an order to Kearny to send escorts to protect their caravans. Probably because he considered Cooke "a clever fellow," Kearny selected him for this duty. With four companies in the Fort Leavenworth area, he was to guard the traders from attacks by either Indians or highwaymen. Captain Boone with three companies was also sent from Fort Gibson on similar service.

These moves were preliminary to the outstanding event of 1843 on the prairies. Another force of Texas irregulars, 180 strong, adopted the name of the "Texas Invincibles." Their leader, Jacob Snively, secured a Texas commission that amounted to a letter of marque and reprisal. Under it, the Invincibles proposed to prey on Mexicans found on the prairies north of the Texas settlements. The republic was to receive half of any booty. Both the Santa Fe traders and the Mexican government became alarmed and complained to Washington. Snively's force rode north in April; Cooke's started west about five weeks later. Cooke's and Boone's commands converged about the middle of June. A large wagon train that relied on the dragoons for safety was approaching from the east. Snively's Invincibles were hovering nearby on the south bank of the river, evidently hunting for the caravan. Some of their scouts ran into one of Cooke's patrols. The main force of dragoons pursued them and soon discovered their camp across the river. Cooke sent an aide to demand the reason for their invasion of American territory.

A fine point of geography and international relations was involved. Since 1819 the western boundary of the United States had been the one-hundredth meridian from the Red River on the south to the Arkansas on the north. At the latter point, near present Dodge City, the boundary followed the meanderings of the Arkansas into the Rockies. Therefore, both sides of the Arkansas were American territory east of the one-hundredth meridian; west of it, only the north side was American. The dragoons and Invincibles had met at Jackson's Grove not far from Pawnee Rock, which is east of the one-hundredth meridian.

Captain Cooke demanded that Snively's outfit surrender all its arms because the Texans had trespassed on American territory. Snively stoutly asserted that as the boundary was unmarked, no one could be sure of its location. If they were actually west of the one-hundredth meridian, then he and his men were on land claimed by Texas. As the argument grew heated, Captain Cooke commented that a number of Texas horsemen had actually crossed to the north bank of the Arkansas. Regardless of their east and west position, that fact placed them within the United States. Cooke was no man to temporize. Spurring his horse, he led all the dragoon companies across the river, where they quickly surrounded the Invincibles and demanded their arms. Snively frantically protested that to leave his men without weapons on the prairies was to sign their death warrants. The Dragoon commander finally agreed that they could retain ten rifles and a few pistols. After some hours of wrangling, the guns were surrendered. The Snively party broke up. One group straggled off to hunt buffalo. The rest rode back to Texas. Several of them were killed by Indians en route, which gave point to Snively's protest. Meanwhile, the traders' caravan had moved on safely towards Santa Fe. Both the Americans and Mexicans engaged in the trade had an increased respect for the dragoons and, of course, for Cooke. The latter, however, had created a delicate international complication and won the undying enmity of Texans. He had also proved to Stephen Kearny that he was an officer who could be safely entrusted with independent command under the most trying circumstances, a fact that was to have a striking sequel three years later.

An incident that occurred in St. Louis that spring marks the first appearance in our narrative of John C. Frémont. The novelist Irving Stone in his *Immortal Wife* has magnified its significance. Novelists and dramatists certainly possess a license to embellish facts and fill in gaps in the record *provided* that their historical figure acts consistently with what is definitely known of his personality. No one has ever marked the precise point where such license is no longer valid. Therefore, novelists at times lose their bearings in the no-man's land between history and fiction. The St. Louis incident illustrates this problem. The known facts are that Frémont was then organizing his second Oregon expedition and expected to traverse

87

country inhabited by treacherous Indians. He and his father-in-law, Senator Benton, recalled that General Ashley had once provided a howitzer to a supply train for protection. Senator Benton and Colonel Kearny had long been good friends, and the latter had known Jessie Benton Frémont from her infancy. These warm ties made it easy for the young explorer to apply to the commander of the Third Military Department for the loan of a twelve-pound howitzer. Kearny promptly supplied the howitzer as well as some other arms from the St. Louis arsenal. Doubtless he was happy to oblige good friends and gave the matter little thought.

Part of the sequel is still in the realm of fact. When the War Department learned that Frémont was taking such a weapon on a supposedly scientific expedition, much alarm was felt. Relations with Great Britain were strained because of the Oregon controversy. The delicate balance of peace with some of the Indian tribes also seemed to be jeopardized. Rash use of the gun might provoke a crisis. Therefore, Colonel John J. Abert, who was in charge of the Topographical Engineers, hastily dispatched a message recalling Frémont. He was told to return instantly to Washington, and that another officer would replace him as head of the expedition. To insure delivery, two copies of the peremptory order were rushed west, one to Frémont's permanent address in St. Louis, the other to Kaw's Landing (present-day Kansas City) where the party was about to start across the plains. High-spirited Jessie Frémont received the first message. She knew what a tragedy it would be for her husband to abandon this long-dreamed-of journey. Her womanly intuition warned her that Abert might have dispatched a duplicate recall to Kaw's Landing. In a mood of indignant defiance, she suppressed the letter but rushed an envoy to her husband with a cryptic message to leave *at once* and trust all to her. Frémont obeyed, and departed from Kaw's Landing before Abert's second message arrived. Jessie Frémont had saved the second expedition but seriously compromised herself, and indirectly her husband. As soon as she knew that Frémont was safely on his way, the impulsive young lady wrote to Colonel Abert and frankly admitted what she had done. She assumed all blame and emphasized that her husband had left without knowing of the orders.

Now we enter the conjectural realm where novelist Stone takes over under his dramatic license. In *Immortal Wife*, Colonel Kearny calls in person on Jessie to tell her that Washington had upbraided *him* for lending Frémont the howitzer. When she tells him of her own part in the affair, the book has him lecture her severely for having presumed to interfere with the processes of government. In a strong and exciting scene, he all but convicts her of mutiny and foresees a dark future for her and her husband if they continue on such a course. Did it ever happen? I have never found any reference to the alleged reprimand. An examination of all letters sent to Colonel Kearny from May to December, 1843, by the Secretary of War, the Adjutant General, the Chief of Engineers, the Topographical Bureau, and the Chief of Ordnance failed to disclose such a reprimand. The record is equally silent as to the heated interview between Kearny and Mrs. Frémont. I am convinced the incident must be set down as a rather extreme example of the license sometimes taken by novelists. I cannot accept the relationship built by Mr. Stone between the borrowed howitzer and later events. He invests Kearny with surprising prescience when he talks to Jessie Frémont about her mutinous nature. Stone has the Colonel lay the groundwork at this point in the novel for the charge of mutiny he was forced to lodge against John C. Frémont over four years later. Stone implies that because of this incident, Kearny henceforth harbored a grudge against the Frémonts. That heightens the tension between his opposing figures, but I submit it is nothing but fiction. In my study of Kearny's statements and actions I have never found anything that remotely links the loan of the howitzer to the controversy in 1847. Readers of this chapter of *Immortal Wife* would almost certainly concur in Justin Smith's characterization of Kearny as harsh and domineering. Convinced as I am that the interview never occurred, such a portrayal of Kearny, regardless of dramatic license, strikes an entirely false note.

Despite all his administrative duties, Kearny found some time for the round of social activities for which St. Louis was famous. Mrs. Kearny, of course, was thoroughly at home here with her relatives in the Clark, Kennerly, and Radford families. In the late spring she and the Colonel, together with Meriwether Lewis Clark and his wife Abbey, went to Kaskaskia to attend the wedding of Mrs. Kearny's brother, John Desborough Radford, to Sophie Menard, daughter of Governor Menard of Illinois. This brother-in-law, John Radford, was something of a thorn in Kearny's flesh. Hunting and fishing were his main interests in life. The Colonel, in a letter to his other brother-in-law, William (whom he found far more congenial), unburdened himself, "John and his wife are now with us. She is a very fine woman with good sense and good ideas but not brought up to be a good manager. John has no vices but is the most indolent man and reflects less about the future maintenance of a family than any man of my acquaintance. In looking for a farm he is constantly talking about the *good hunting* and *fishing near it*. Perhaps when once settled he may begin to work."

William Radford was at this time a lieutenant on the U.S.S. "Savannah," about to depart on a three-year cruise of the Pacific. The letter last quoted contains a curious reference to Kearny's own future. After mentioning the travel in store for William, it says "If I am sent to the Columbia as Governor General of Oregon we shall have the pleasure of meeting." We do not know what made Kearny expect such an appointment nor why nothing came of it. Actually, Oregon was one of the few regions in the West which he never saw. How much the course of history might have been altered had he been governor of Oregon on the outbreak of the war with Mexico! Such speculation calls to mind another life whose course was nearly changed several years later by an appointment to the governorship of Oregon. He was a lawyer in Springfield, Illinois, named Abraham Lincoln.

Stephen Kearny in this letter also told of a visit to Jefferson Barracks by a famous Frenchman, Marshal Henri Gratien Bertrand, one of Napoleon's comrades in exile at St. Helena. General Bertrand, as he calls himself, was in St. Louis on September 22. He had with him a friend and also his son, a captain in the French Army. Colonel Kearny and Senator Benton drove the General and his companions to Jefferson Barracks the next evening. All the officers called upon Bertrand in dress uniforms, and the ladies of the garrison were formally presented. At ten o'clock the visitors embarked on a steamboat to visit Andrew Jackson at the Hermitage. "He is a very interesting old man," wrote Kearny, "and one whom all soldiers can delight in paying honors to."

On November 1, 1843, the headquarters of the Third Department were moved from Jefferson Barracks into St. Louis.

Captain Cooke had not heard the last of his brush with Colonel Snively and the Texas Invincibles. In November, 1843, Texas lodged a protest with the government at Washington. Texas soil had been outraged. Captain Cooke had behaved like a savage. Exception was taken to a letter General Gaines had written General Taylor upholding Cooke's conduct. In due course, the State Department replied that Cooke had acted in accordance with express instructions and had operated entirely within American territory. The United States would pay for the weapons confiscated and would also order a court of inquiry. Once more—doubtless to the secret delight of both officers—Kearny had to succor this Captain Cooke who had such a penchant for hot water. General Gaines appointed the Colonel to preside over the court of inquiry promised Texas. It was held at Fort Leavenworth on April 24, 1844. In due time it found, "that there was nothing in the conduct of Captain Cooke that was 'harsh and unbecoming' " (as had been charged). "The confidence reposed in him by his government was not in any degree misplaced."

Still another boy arrived in the Kearny family that summer. Clarence was born on September 5, 1844, at St. Louis.

During Kearny's St. Louis years, a new Fort Des Moines was built at the location the Colonel had surveyed in 1835. (The old post at the mouth of the Des Moines had been abandoned in 1837.) Although there was much routine activity, peace generally prevailed along the frontier.

By the end of 1844 it seemed as if Stephen Kearny's hopes and predictions of early 1842 were to be realized. Oregon loomed larger in the public eye. Its military occupation became a lively probability. Since British sea power had to be reckoned with, troop movement by land—even over a tremendous distance—seemed preferable. What better nucleus could the War Department want than the First Dragoons? Occupying an advanced base, trained in prairie marches, accustomed to the Indian problems likely to be encountered

—it was ready made for whatever occasion might arise. A general air of expectancy pervaded Fort Leavenworth and St. Louis.

In addition to the threat of war, the movement of emigrants over the Oregon Trail had assumed impressive proportions. They had to traverse a region of warlike and treacherous tribes. No better excuse was needed for sending a large military force towards Oregon, so on April 9, 1845, the commander of the Third Military Department was ordered to take five companies of the First Dragoons over the trail as far as the South Pass. This was only one demonstration of the working of "Manifest Destiny" in the Polk administration's western policy. Two other expeditions of the same period had the same origin: Lieutenant James Abert's march through the Texas Panhandle and western Oklahoma, and Captain John C. Frémont's topographical expedition to California.

The ninety-nine day expedition that ensued is one of the epic adventures of the American army. The results compare with many military campaigns in wartime. For Stephen Kearny it was a longer march by a larger force. In experience for his dragoons it was the curtain raiser for the Army of the West's greater trek the following year. For emigrants bound for Oregon it was an answer to prayers.

Kearny selected the best of the First Dragoons for the expedition —the 5-company garrison of Fort Leavenworth. On May 18 they trotted away from that post. Each company was 50 strong. Staff, artillerists, teamsters, and officers made the total 280 men. Each dragoon bore a saber, carbine and pistol. Two mountain howitzers trailed the column. Lieutenant Philip Kearny was one of the officers, as was Philip St. George Cooke. The guide was Thomas Fitzpatrick, famous "Broken Hand" or "White Head" of the mountain men. The Commander adopted the practical policy of living off the country so far as possible. Rations were cut to bare essentials. Only 30 beeves and a small flock of sheep were driven along. Like the Indians, Kearny depended on the buffalo they were bound to encounter.

On May 24 they reached the Oregon Trail near the Big Blue. As far as their eyes could see plodded the long line of ox-drawn covered wagons as well as the cattle, horses, and sheep of the settlers bound for Oregon. So many animals grazing as they moved were like a scorching fire to the feed along their route. The Colonel met this obstacle by ordering a forced march that placed the dragoons in front of the van of emigrants. It was a dry season, and forage at best remained scarce. Each day the expedition overtook other emigrants who welcomed the soldiers as deliverers because of the increasing number of Pawnees and Sioux lurking on every hillside. The soldiers were able to give much practical advice, for the majority of the drivers were ill prepared for the vicissitudes of the long journey. Around the forks of the Platte, buffalo were met in abundance. Stirring hunts and joyous feasting followed. For many more weeks this supply of meat remained available.

To the people in the covered wagons, Kearny and his men seemed like knights-errant. One young woman, later writing of life on the road to Oregon, told movingly of the wild cry of "Indians!" one night in her camp on the Platte:

> While under arms awaiting attack a regiment of U. S. soldiers commanded by Captain Kearney [*sic*] and Lieutenant Frémont [a lapse of memory, as he was not a member of this expedition] appeared. These gallant commanders . . . assured us that their . . . boys would perform guard duty at nightfall, that our stock should graze in peace and safety and that the weary teamsters might rest. . . . They had been sent by the government to escort emigrants across the plains. . . . The soldiers remained with us about ten days or so and then marched on to the foot of the Rocky Mountains . . . but their patrol service rendered our journey absolutely safe. . . . Captain Kearny gave us some useful instructions regarding our camp ground arrangements. We were to drive near enough together so we could lay the tongue of our wagon just back of the hind wheels of the one next in front, thus forming a perfect circle. . . . We were also instructed to build our fires outside the circle that our movements might be more hidden from enemies. The men were drilled as to their duty. . . . No Indian attack occurred.

This woman had had a demonstration of the value of discipline.

As they rode west, the dragoons passed villages of Sioux. Kearny invited their chiefs to attend the council he planned to hold at Fort Laramie. The Sioux promised but among themselves shook their heads in alarm; these were a new kind of white men—very powerful medicine! On June 14, Fort Laramie welcomed the expedition. The fort was a trading post of the American Fur Company, located at the mouth of the Laramie River. Nearby stood another post, Fort Platte, operated by a rival concern. The dragoon companies were the first American troops ever seen there. Here, where civilization and barbarism mingled so intimately, raw liquor, filth, and coarse habits made unlovely sights and smells. Captain Cooke summed up the contrast between the two "civilization furnishes house and clothing, barbarism children and fleas." The Colonel prudently chose a spot somewhat distant from both posts for the dragoon camp. That ensured better forage and some protection against contaminations of trading post life.

The council with the Sioux was held on June 16. The Colonel and some officers rode out with an escort to an open plain. Two American flags fluttered from lofty staffs, as well as a third banner of Indian design. Twelve hundred Indians of both sexes had gathered under them. The traders at the Platte post had provided chairs and benches for the officers, curtained with elk skin, and with buffalo robes for carpets. The Indian chiefs were squatted in a great semi-circle before the chairs. The Indian women and children were ranged behind them in a wider circle.

Through an interpreter, Kearny addressed the multitude:

> Sioux: I am glad to see you. Your Great Father has learned much of his red children and has sent me with a few braves to visit you. I am going to the waters which flow to the setting sun. I shall return to this place and then march to the Arkansas and home. I am opening a road for the white people and your Great Father directs that his red children shall not attempt to close it. There are many whites now coming on the road, moving to the other side of the mountains. They take with them their women, children and cattle. They all go to bury their bones there and never return. You must not disturb them in their persons or molest their property. Should you do so your Great Father would be very angry with you and cause you to be punished. Sioux: You have enemies about you but the greatest of them all is whiskey. I learn that some bad white men bring it here from Taos and sell it to you. Open your ears and listen to me.

It is contrary to the wishes of your Great Father that whiskey should be brought here and I advise you whenever you find it in your country, no matter in whose possession, to spill it all on the ground. The ground may drink it without injury but you cannot. I wish you Sioux to remember what I have now said to you. . . . Your Great Father is the friend of his red children and as long as they behave themselves properly will continue to be so. I have not come among you to bring you presents but your Great Father has sent a few things that you may remember what I have said to you.

A few Sioux chieftains replied with lofty speeches, and the Colonel ordered presents distributed—cloth, blankets, tobacco, knives, beads, and looking glasses. An Indian woman began a stately chant. The braves joined in the song. Its primitive music had a wild beauty. It was their thanks for the gifts and the visit. Before the council broke up, the Colonel ordered three shots fired from one of the howitzers. This caused great astonishment among the Indians. Kearny promised the Sioux that when night fell he would send up stars (rockets) to the heavens, "to tell the Great Spirit that they had listened to his words."

With one company left in charge of the camp, the westward march was resumed the next day. The country was more rugged, and rattlesnakes and grizzlies disputed the way. The ascent of the South Pass is gradual, thus the Colonel and his officers were puzzled to know the exact moment when they had reached their destination. They drank from a spring trickling westward to join the Colorado before they realized they had crossed the Continental Divide. To commemorate the occasion, the Colonel held a regimental muster at the summit, the first time American troops had ever been paraded on a Pacific watershed or a mile and a half above sea level.

The dragoons were 280 miles beyond Fort Laramie and 850 miles from Fort Leavenworth. This was the farthest west that Stephen Kearny had traveled thus far. No doubt he was as much stimulated by the magnitude of the land as by the rarity of the atmosphere on this continental ridgepole. He was within long range of Oregon itself. How long before he would be going on at the head of a larger expedition? Or would he be riding with a small escort to assume gubernatorial duties? In the midst of such reflections, he probably never looked to the south and southwest where destiny really beckoned. Captain Cooke poetically called this "the mountain edge of Oregon . . . the land of promise and fable," although the dragoons were kept busy by mosquitoes of marvelous size "who rejoice in blood." Bands of emigrants continued on down the trail as Kearny and his command rested in the pass. Later he reported that this season's travel had at that time totaled about 850 men, 475 women, and 1,000 children.

The four companies started their return to Fort Laramie on July 1. At their camp on the night of the third, an emigrant leader requested the Colonel to fire one of his "big guns" on the morning of the Fourth. "Do it and I will treat you all!" Kearny answered that he drank nothing but "Sweet Water" (not even *eau sucrée*). Captain Cooke's biographer thinks this was because the Colonel was a teetotaler. I find the evidence quite conclusive that Stephen Kearny was not a teetotaler. Many writers mention instances when he drank wine (seldom spirits) and always apparently in moderation. Remembering that this Fourth of July incident occurred on the banks of the Sweetwater River, we may perhaps accuse the Colonel of a pun. On Independence Day one of the howitzers made the mountains echo. Cheers went up and hats were tossed in the air from the covered-wagon train.

After a day's enforced rest because the Colonel and nearly all the command became suddenly ill, the camp near Fort Laramie was reached on July 13. All five companies set out on the fourteenth, leaving the Platte trail and heading up the Chugwater, a tributary of the Laramie. Their route roughly paralleled the front of the Rockies and ultimately led them to a Cheyenne village. It was well that Kearny's orders from Washington directed him to return via Bent's Fort and the Arkansas. Like a horde of locusts, the emigrants had consumed the forage over a wide swath along the Oregon Trail and were probably also responsible for the prairie fires that were destroying both the feed and the sparse but vital growth of firewood. Kearny held a council with the Cheyennes on July 16. The Colonel spoke in much the same vein as at Fort Laramie. Presents were again made before the council broke up.

As they moved on south they rode for six miles through the hushed, stately aisles of a pine forest, a novel experience for these prairie veterans. Then they camped close to the foot of Pike's Peak itself. The white summit challenged more than one stout heart but there was no time for mountain climbing. Grass was becoming scarce and their mounts more jaded. As they pressed on, other snowy ranges etched the blue skies. The lofty panorama of the Sangre de Cristos unfolded on their right hand, culminating in the breath-taking challenge of the Spanish Peaks. Exhilarated by the thin, crisp air and the dazzling light reflected from the heights, they at last reached the Arkansas River some sixty miles upstream from Bent's Fort.

In riding down the river, Kearny was not just returning home by a different route. He was close now to the northern border of Mexico. Since Congress voted favorably on the annexation of Texas on March 1, relations between the United States and Mexico had become strained. Even though the American army had an unquestioned right to patrol its own frontier, Washington had deliberately planned this display of force for its effect on Governor Armijo in Santa Fe and the authorities in Mexico City.

As the dragoons were seen approaching Bent's Fort, its small cannon fired a three-round salute in welcome. Charles Bent and Ceran St. Vrain were waiting at the sally port when Kearny alighted on July 29. To these plainsmen, the Colonel was an old acquaintance from the days in 1820 when they had all been at Fort Atkinson. This was a gala day, too, for Bent's Fort; no such cavalcade had ever visited that lonely trading post. The military character of the dragoon's visit was emphasized when they detained and questioned a dozen Mexican traders in the neighborhood.

On the evening of Kearny's arrival, Bent and St. Vrain entertained him and his officers at a sumptuous dinner. They were urged to make a longer visit but the Colonel ordered only an overnight camp. This allowed time for necessary reprovisioning. Three years earlier the army, with exceptional foresight, had sent reserve stocks of supplies to this post to be ready to meet any emergency. Kearny was gratified to find that the rice and hard bread had kept well in the dry mountain air, and that the supplies had been in the charge of such honest custodians. Over the dinner table, Bent told Kearny much of conditions beyond the southern mountain border. A year later, the Colonel would have ample reason to remember that conversation, and to ply the same informant with more questions about New Mexico.

Tom Fitzpatrick left the detachment at Bent's Fort. They no longer needed a guide on the plainly marked trail down the Arkansas which Kearny took a day later. Had Kearny been traveling less rapidly, he would probably have met Captain Frémont. The latter's expedition, soon to make so much history in California, started from Bent's Fort shortly after Kearny's departure. As they rode eastward, one incident afforded considerable satisfaction to both Kearny and Cooke. While they halted at Jackson's Grove, their engineer took careful observations of their longitude. He found it to be well east of the one-hundredth meridian. This proved that Colonel Snively and his Texans had been trespassers on American soil when Captain Cooke disarmed them on this spot in 1843.

Late in the afternoon of August 19 the weary companies reined their horses on the familiar parade ground of Fort Leavenworth. They remained at attention while their colonel commended them briefly for an arduous task well performed. In ninety-nine days they had marched twenty-two hundred miles. Every man had returned alive and well; the only serious casualty was a private who had lost an arm because of his own carelessness. What a contrast to the Leavenworth-Dodge expedition of eleven years before.

When General Winfield Scott transmitted Colonel Kearny's report to the War Department a few months later, he declared this tour of duty "has been made with extraordinary despatch and success . . . his [Kearny's] officers and men entered upon the expedition with spirit and conducted themselves throughout with credit. The great number of Indians passed must have been powerfully impressed with the vigor, alertness and fine appearance of the troops as well as by the wise and humane admonitions of their commander."

Kearny with his adjutant, Captain Turner, arrived at St. Louis on August 30. In the next two weeks they prepared the report of the expedition. Turner had kept a journal and the engineer had made a map of the regions visited. These were dispatched to Washington.

The reports described the country through which they had ridden with comments on the problems involved in its administration. Kearny ranged himself with men like General Atkinson who opposed the establishment of military posts far beyond the frontier. One near Fort Laramie had been suggested. Captain Cooke had selected a suitable site, but Kearny recommended against any such location. He believed the protection it would afford emigrants would not be commensurate with the enormous expense of its maintenance so far from any supply base. The alternative policy he favored was to send out military expeditions similar to the one he had just conducted every two or three years. Thus the Indians could be kept reminded of the ease and rapidity with which dragoons could move about the country whenever needed.

Kearny was certain a shorter route could be opened to the "Wilhamet," as he spelled it, than the present Oregon Trail. He believed it could be shortened four hundred miles. If a survey were deemed advisable he recommended Thomas Fitzpatrick, his recent guide, who "has been much west of the mountains and has as good if not better knowledge of that country than any other man in existence."

He denounced the purveyors of "Taos lightning" who infested the country between Bent's and Fort Laramie "bringing whiskey which they trade to the Indians, consequently causing much difficulty and doing much harm. This should be prevented and possibly might by the appoinment of a sub-agent who I recommend be located at Bent's Fort who . . . might put a stop to the traffic. . . . I cannot refrain from repeating in this place what I have for many years been convinced of—the good of the Indians would be much advanced and the peace of the country much more effectively secured if Congress would pass a law declaring the whole of the Indian country under martial law. The difficulty of taking persons accused of offenses in the Indian country with witnesses to the civil courts which are so remote and which sit only at stated periods in a year render much of the . . . law . . . inoperative and useless."

General Scott commented that legally there could not be martial law in the United States or its organized territories, but that Colonel Kearny's suggestion applied to the Indian country lying outside of the States and organized territories. Scott evidently favored Kearny's proposal of biennial or triennial cavalry expeditions rather than permanent forts at remote points. In view of the later conflict between Kearny and John C. Frémont, it is curious to note that the two men were already on opposite sides of a current topic in 1845. Frémont was on record as favoring the "forts" method of controlling the wild tribes beyond the frontier.

Kearny's family in the East took pride in the interest the public was showing in Stephen's expedition. His brother Philip wrote Mary Kearny: "am frequently asked is Colonel Kearny a relative of mine and I never fail to reply that he was my mother's baby." Then he gently chided his sister-in-law because none of Stephen's children had been named for Kearny ancestors or relatives. Philip was sure the English would not war with the United States "and I hope the Mexicans will have as much wit." But if Stephen and Mary were too heedless of family ties, one incident of the summer campaign must have pleased brother Philip profoundly. While the detachment tarried just beyond the summit of the South Pass, his son, Lieutenant Philip, filled a bottle with water from a westward-flowing rivulet. Later this water was used in the baptism of his own son, John Watts Kearny.

9. The Army of the West: Genesis

THE YEAR 1845 sharply changed American history. Some of its most important happenings occured while Stephen Kearny was conducting the summer campaign to the Rocky Mountains. Even though he was far from the scene, these events completely altered his future. Ever since Texas had won its independence in 1836, many citizens of both the United States and the Lone Star Republic had agitated for its annexation to the Union. This movement was strenuously resisted by Northern opponents of slavery. The slaveholding South just as strongly championed it. The Democratic party had elected James K. Polk to the presidency in 1844 on a platform that favored annexation. Just prior to his inauguration on March 4, 1845, Congress voted to invite Texas to become one of the United States. On July 4, Texas itself voted to enter the Union. There were details still to be negotiated, thus formal admission was not consummated until December 29 of that year.

Mexico had never recognized Texan independence. It viewed annexation by the United States as an act of war. There was still a faint chance that diplomacy might avert hostilities. The Polk administration—contrary to the belief of many Americans down to this day—seems to have tried sincerely to reach a peaceful agreement with its southern neighbor. In November, President Polk dispatched John Slidell as minister plenipotentiary to Mexico to discuss not only the matter of Texas but all questions in dispute. Slidell reached Mexico City in December but the administration there declined to deal with him about any subject except Texas. A sudden overthrow of government brought in a new president. In taking over the reins, he reasserted Mexico's claim to Texas and refused to receive Slidell on any basis whatsoever. Word of this unfriendly attitude reached Washington on January 12, 1846.

Troublesome boundary questions between the two countries at last provided the spark that ignited the flames of war. Texas claimed all territory down to the Río Grande. Mexico insisted that the boundary of the Mexican state of Texas had always been the Nueces River. The Polk administration adopted the Texan point of view, and the day after it learned of Slidell's rejection ordered General Zachary Taylor to occupy the disputed strip. Taylor's forces moved southward on March 8 and reached the Río Grande on the twenty-eighth. Meanwhile a Mexican detachment had crossed the river. A couple of skirmishes soon resulted and by the last week of April, several Americans had been killed. On receipt of this information the President notified Congress that American blood had been shed in defense of the country. On May 11, the House of Representatives voted a declaration of war by a heavy majority. All but two of the senators concurred, and on May 13, 1846, Polk signed the bill declaring that a state of war existed with Mexico.

(It is strange to note how fast important news could travel in those years before telegraph, telephone, and radio. Only four days after President Polk signed the declaration, Commodore John D. Sloat in faraway Mazatlan, Mexico, heard rumors that war had begun. Two weeks later he knew of the battles of Palo Alto and Resaca de la Palma.)

The year 1846 started quietly enough for Stephen Kearny. Generally, conditions were peaceful on the plains. In March, the War Department tardily revived plans for an advanced military post at the location Kearny had recommended in 1838. He was now ordered to establish such a post. His departure from St. Louis on this mission seemed just a routine errand, but he was not to see his home again for a year and a half. After arriving at Leavenworth, he sent a small detachment up the river to start the project.

From a letter the Colonel wrote his twelve-year-old son Charles, we know that Mary Kearny and the younger children accompanied him on the steamboat to Fort Leavenworth. The letter is interesting because of the light it throws on his relations with his children and his views on education and deportment:

Dear Charles:

A few days since I received your letter of the 23rd of April & was pleased to learn that you and William continued in good health & contented with your residence at the the University—To remain so, you should be good boys—study & learn your lessons—your teachers will then like you, & you will improve & become wiser, as you grow older—Now is your time to learn—if whilst you are Boys, you are idle & lazy, your habits will become fixed upon you, & you may remain so during the remainder of your lives—But if you are studious & learn, you will soon find the advantages of it—will be proud of your improvement, & may grow up ornaments of society, & an honor to your Country—You Boys should not be led astray by seeing some young men living idly, and doing nothing—they are not respected by any one—they are condemned by all—such young men may inherit Property from their fathers, & therefore there may be no necessity for them to labor to make enough for their subsistence— but this will not be the case with you & William. As I have often told you, I have money enough to give you boys the best education in the Country but when your education is finished, I shall have no money to give you, but you must then make what is necessary to feed & clothe & support you—If you do not study, so that you can make your living by some profession or business, you will be compelled to starve or gain your support by manual labor—you boys should reflect well on what I have now written for you.

We had a pleasant passage up here in 6 days from Saint Louis— We are all perfectly well—Your little brother & Sisters enjoy themselves much more than when in the city as here they have fine play ground on the Parade; the grass is well grown & if they fall on it, they cannot be hurt.

You must tell your brother William that I have not forgot how badly he behaved on board the Steam Boat just before he left it.—I had hoped, that he would have been sorry for it, & in his letter have asked for forgiveness—If he does not learn to control his temper, he will never come to any good—He should reflect upon that.

Your mama sends her love to both of you, in which I join & hope you will both be good Boys—We shall expect to see you up in the vacation, & if William & you will bring up a Medal or even a Ribbon given for good conduct I will consider it the handsomest present you can bring to me. Min, Lou, Pud & Dan are well & send their love to you both. Yours

S. W. Kearny

Accompanied by Brigadier General George M. Brooke, now in command of the Western Department, Kearny briefly visited the site that was eventually called "old" Fort Kearny. Leaving a detail to construct the post, they returned to Fort Leavenworth on May 26. A few hours later, Captain Turner arrived with startling dispatches from Washington. As Kearny read them he must have realized that he was suddenly facing the greatest challenge of his career. The contents included a copy of the Declaration of War, and his appointment to organize and lead an expedition over the Santa Fe Trail to invade and seize New Mexico. A copy of the President's communication to Governor John C. Edwards of Missouri asking him to call for volunteers was also included. From that moment, Kearny's days and nights were filled with preparations while messengers dashed in and out with urgent orders.

While the war was unpopular in the North, especially in New England, news of its declaration aroused much enthusiasm in the South and the trans-Mississippi country. These regions considered this cause peculiarly their own. The rest of the nation might make only halfhearted gestures but Missouri, Texas, Kentucky, and their neighbors fervently believed the hour of their destiny had struck. If the regular army was not equal to the task, the Middle Border folk would fight single-handed. St. Louis and other towns of Missouri had long enjoyed trade with Santa Fe and Chihuahua. Ever since the days of Lewis and Clark, trappers, mountain men, and explorers had kindled interest in the West. The midlands of America were the home of Manifest Destiny. Its finger pointed ever more clearly to the Pacific Coast. Oregon was in dispute with Great Britain. Of course, America must possess Oregon. But California was equally a part of that last Far West whither Manifest Destiny led. The British had not yet claimed California. It was a Mexican province and beyond Santa Fe. Seize the latter and go on from that goal to grasp the farther prize—so dreamed more than one statesman in Washington besides James K. Polk. And so dreamed many dwellers in the Mississippi Valley—merchants, fur traders, and plowboys.

Santa Fe was considered ripe for taking, especially in Missouri. It was common knowledge that a year before, the Mexican government had virtually abandoned northern New Mexico. It could no longer protect the populace from Indian raiders. Its poorly equipped and usually unpaid soldiery—were just as likely to prey upon their own people as to protect them. Exorbitant taxes were levied. Extortionate duties were charged the caravans that brought the only goods on which the region could count from the outside world. Rebellious mutterings had been in the air ever since neighboring Texas had revolted. The province had two sections: the Río Arriba, or upstream area around Santa Fe, and the Río Abajo, or lower portion that included Albuquerque. More than half of both the population and the wealth was in the latter district. The Río Arriba, east of the Río del Norte and farthest removed from the weak rule of Mexico City, was especially ready for conquest.

Santa Fe traders thought so and brought back sorry reports of Governor Armijo. By all accounts he was the classic example of a Latin American despot—venal, greedy, tyrannical, and with neither scruple nor courage. Of lowly birth, he had risen in the world by bluster and cunning. The ignorant population of Indians and mestizos was impressed by the flashy uniforms with which he adorned his obese figure. They did not recognize the crafty mind of an adventurer with a finger in many enterprises. He pursued devious schemes in which he used both the savage tribes of the province and the local priests to further his ends—whether prompted by revenge, lust, or avarice. Armijo's own favorite saying best revealed his true character, "it is better to be thought brave than to be so." Small wonder that the people of St. Louis favored an early advance on Santa Fe. Little wonder, too, that President Polk's advisers told him an American army would encounter slight resistance from such a ruler or the populace he oppressed.

Governor Edwards promptly called for volunteers to fill eight companies of mounted troops and two of light artillery. They were to report to Colonel Kearny at Fort Leavenworth as fast as they enlisted. All over Missouri the proclamation aroused great enthusiasm. Farm boys almost literally left their plows in the furrows and rode their horses to the nearest town to enlist. The success of the recruiting movement was assured from the moment the public learned that the commander of the expedition to Santa Fe would be Stephen Kearny. He had long been idolized by the frontiersmen. Now men all but fought for places in line at the enlistment booths. Manifest Destiny was not only on the march; it had a leader who inspired the highest confidence.

Raw recruits would soon pour into headquarters by the hundreds but Kearny knew he needed far more trained men than were available. Most essential of all was his nucleus of experienced dragoons. Three companies were at Fort Leavenworth and he ordered more to assemble there from outlying posts. Even before this concentration was completed, tasks confronted him requiring more than their total. Emergencies forced him to rush detachments over the Santa Fe Trail on imperative errands. One was a vain attempt to capture an ammunition train consigned to Armijo before the declaration of war. A prominent Santa Fe trader named Howard had to be escorted to the Mexican boundary on a secret mission for the Secretary of War. (Today we would call him a fifth columnist.) Many other caravans were hurrying westward in the hope of getting valuable merchandise past Mexican customs before hostilities barred traffic. These had to be intercepted lest the cargoes fall into enemy hands. Eventually the ammunition train escaped, but Captain Moore and his fast-riding companies stopped all but some two dozen of the wagons and forced over four hundred to await Kearny's pleasure at Bent's Fort.

In the midst of all this turmoil, the Kearnys must have felt the serene manner in which life's processes go on without regard to man's breathless concerns. On May 30, Mary Kearny gave birth to another boy, Henry Stephen, at Fort Leavenworth.

Colonel Kearny wished to add two companies of riflemen to his army, but he doubted that he could find enough volunteers who would march on foot to Santa Fe. General Brooke, on the other hand, advised him to increase his command by at least a thousand infantry. Kearny began to foresee a breakdown of supply and transport. How many shoes would a thousand infantry wear out marching nine hundred miles to Santa Fe? How many wagons would he need to haul those shoes—and blankets, tents, cooking gear, and rations? Could he rely on killing enough buffalo to feed them?

He answered Brooke that he was "as yet ignorant of the entire plan of campaign against Mexico and her dependencies adopted by the War Department but rely on the safety and correctness of it and as the number of troops for the expedition was decided upon by the Department I am unwilling at this time to follow your advice which might seem to imply on my part a distrust in the head of it, a feeling I do not entertain. I shall endeavor to do my duty, expecting those over as well as those under me will do theirs"—respectful enough, but still a rather firm negative.

Soon afterward, Kearny received new instructions from the Secretary of War dated June 3 that threw new light on his problem. He had indeed been "as yet ignorant of the entire plan of campaign . . . adopted by the War Department." This letter so vital to the later controversy over the "conflicting instructions" given both by Kearny and Commodore Stockton and so pregnant with meaning to the future of California is too long to give here in full.[1] Portions must be quoted now if we are to understand the preparation of the Army of the West for its task: "I herewith send you a copy of my letter to the governor of Missouri for an additional force of a thousand mounted men. The object of thus adding to the force under your command is not . . . fully set forth in that letter, for the reason that it is deemed prudent that it should not at this time become a matter of public notoriety. . . . It has been decided by the President to be of the greatest importance in the pending War with Mexico to take the earliest possession of Upper California. An expedition with that view is hereby ordered, and you are designated to command it." These additional troops were to follow Kearny to Santa Fe. He was also authorized to muster into service a group of Mormons, not to exceed a third of his total force. The closing paragraph

[1] See its text in Appendix A.

of this letter was calculated to warm Kearny's heart as he read it. "I am directed by the President to say that the rank of Brevet Brigadier General will be conferred on you as soon as you commence your movement towards California."

Thus in three weeks Manifest Destiny had enlarged its vision of what was expected of the Army of the West. Washington was catching up with public opinion in the Middle West. Kearny, using the discretion given him by these orders, now asked the Governor that eight hundred of the new quota should be enlisted as infantry. He gave the scarcity of forage around Santa Fe as a reason for so few mounted soldiers. (The nature of the country and forage *beyond* Santa Fe undoubtedly troubled Kearny, but he was too discreet to enlarge on that point to Governor Edwards.) The papers of the period were full of conjectures and rumors about when various contingents would depart for the front. A correspondent summed up the general ignorance when he wrote, "The Colonel does not tell anybody his mind," and reluctantly admitted, "which of course is the only proper way to do business." Instead of disclosing his plans for foot soldiers, Kearny wrote the Governor "we always look upon infantry with bayonets as the main pillar and strength of an army." The next day he wrote another correspondent that if he would send him four or five companies of infantry volunteers, he would accept them *at once*.

On June 16, Colonel Kearny appointed First Lieutenant Abraham R. Johnston as regimental adjutant; later the War Department promoted him to a captaincy. Transport and supply, regardless of the proportion of cavalry and infantry, were among the most serious problems confronting Kearny. He swiftly drafted every supply wagon and teamster in the region. Many of these drivers were green hands and hopelessly inefficient, but they had to suffice. In a little while 100 wagons had been commandeered and 800 beef cattle rounded up for meat to take along on the hoof. The Quartermaster's Department reported that it required 1,556 wagons and the services of 459 horses, 3,658 draft mules, and 516 pack mules to transport the men of the Army of the West and their materiel and to keep them supplied both on the way to Santa Fe and after their arrival there. The cattle and oxen used by the expedition reached the impressive total of 14,904. These figures point up one historian's comment that the real obstacle that had to be overcome in the bloodless conquest of Santa Fe was not the enemy but distance and terrain.

Kearny designated Bent's Fort as the point of rendezvous of all the component parts of his army. One historian terms this an "unauthorized appropriation." This seems to me too critical of Kearny. What alternative had the commander of the Army of the West? His orders were to invade an enemy neighbor across a wide expanse of uninhabited country. Bent's Fort possessed the sole facilities accessible to his route. If property was consumed or destroyed he knew his government would expect to compensate the owners. This seems a case where the common welfare must override private interests in time of war. Had Armijo's belligerency matched his speeches and he had assumed the offensive, it is easily imaginable that Bent's Fort would have suffered far more than the damage done it under Kearny's orders. Charles Bent and St. Vrain were traveling eastward over the Santa Fe Trail when they learned of the use proposed to be made of the post. According to Kearny's critic mentioned above, "there was nothing to do but acquiesce." There is some evidence that William Bent at least felt the firm had been badly treated as to compensation for considerable damage sustained.

Charles Bent saw the Colonel at Fort Leavenworth soon after the announcement and apparently lodged no protest. Their meeting was cordial, and Kearny urged that Bent return west from St. Louis as soon as possible. He foresaw he would have many problems en route to New Mexico and that Bent's counsel would prove invaluable.

At the time of the outbreak of the war, some of the First Dragoon companies had been detached from their regiment to reinforce General Wool. While assembling the Army of the West, Kearny learned that two more of his best companies were about to join General Taylor. Captain Cooke and another valued captain, Sumner, would be lost to him. Kearny deemed their presence with their excellent units absolutely essential to his success. On such an occasion, Kearny seemed surprisingly able to thread his way without disaster between the pitfall of a too abject acceptance of orders and a too offensive objection to them. His language in his protest to General Brooke was masterly: "I have now most respectfully to urge—to demand (the interest of the public service admits of strong and respectful terms) that the two companies of my regiment, Captain Sumner's and Captain Cooke's . . . may be ordered by *you* to repair forthwith to this post to follow me on my trail to Santa Fe." The firm protest retained these two companies with their regiment.

Volunteers began to file into Fort Leavenworth by June 5. There they were mustered into service and assigned to companies of the First Missouri Mounted Volunteers. These men hailed from the central Missouri valley of the state. At Fort Leavenworth, they had been told, they would be supplied with quarters, forage, mess kits, rations, sabers, guns, ammunition, and a year's allowance of money for clothing. (In many instances this was the last money these recruits were to see until released from service a year later.) By June 27, enough men had volunteered to form thirteen companies. These volunteers could ride and shoot; no one could teach them anything about horses or guns. But the officers of the First Dragoons were responsible for their learning the rudiments of military life and tactics, an easier task to assign than perform. Kearny and his subordinates found the recruits full of enthusiasm and thirsting for combat. The discipline and drill required of any soldier proved far less alluring. For twenty days they underwent long periods of rigid drill every morning and afternoon. The novelty soon wore off. These youths found it hard to understand how strict and prompt obedience and the monotonous repetition of drill could have anything to do with the wholesale destruction of everything Mexican for which they had rushed to enlist.

A lieutenant of the Laclede Rangers while watching some of the troops of the First Missouri observed, "I suppose that when they become disciplined—if they ever do become disciplined—they will make tolerably good soldiers. The raw material is good enough, but then it is, in truth, *very raw*." The record in the war with Mexico shows more than one American regiment made up of the same kind of volunteers that got completely out of hand. Probably their commanders did not practice as assiduously as Kearny a practical means of keeping recruits out of trouble which he had learned years before.

He knew that if he worked and drilled his men so hard and continuously that they lacked time for mischief, they would be too exhausted to go out hunting for it when off duty. That, plus their commander's saving grace of not taking himself too seriously, best explain the relatively better conduct of these unruly volunteers of the Army of the West.

De Voto repeats with gusto the story written by a St. Louis war correspondent about these days at Fort Leavenworth. The Colonel on boarding a steamboat directed the sentry at the gangplank to bar the volunteers from the boat. Nevertheless, a crowd of them brushed aside the perspiring guard and followed Kearny to the deck. One, by way of apology, slapped the Colonel on the back and offered him a drink. Most regular army officers would have thunderingly ordered the offender to the guard house. Kearny, however, after an unsuccessful attempt at gravity, had to laugh. He pushed away the proffered moonshine and invited the soldier to have a drink of wine with him. Better than most professional officers, he seems to have recognized the fundamental distinction between an enlistee for the regular army in time of peace and the raw, hastily recruited volunteer of a wartime emergency.

The Missouri authorities were nearly as exuberant as the volunteers. More than once, Kearny had to hold them to the letter of their instructions and reject many volunteers who plainly did not qualify. The enlistees selected their own officers at exciting elections. In at least one instance the men of the new First Missouri showed judgment worthy of far more experienced veterans. They chose as their colonel a private from Liberty in Clay County who had left his law office to volunteer. He was Alexander W. Doniphan, destined to leave a name that is remembered whenever America's wars are recalled.

By June 16, Kearny could inform the Adjutant General that he then had 700 mounted volunteers and 52 infantrymen at Fort Leavenworth. He was still without tents, camp kettles, and mess pans. Only one staff officer had reported, Captain Thomas Swords, who was to be the assistant quartermaster of the expedition. Kearny did not know yet when he could start his march. But he had learned that Governor Armijo was expecting an invasion and could put 5,000 men in the field. (Actually, over the border the feeble administration was at least talking defense. Mexico City had notified Armijo that it expected war and warned him to prepare his defenses. On June 26 a caravan arrived in Santa Fe with definite confirmation of previous rumors that an American army was about to invade the province. The United States Consul did his best to persuade the Governor that peaceful surrender would be best for him and his people. Many of his aides and advisers favored such a course but Armijo remained obdurate. Undoubtedly, he was counting on the arrival of the ammunition train en route from Independence.) Because so many of its units were serving elsewhere, the dragoons at Fort Leavenworth now numbered only 300. One volunteer group that arrived during the formation of the army was the Laclede Rangers from St. Louis under Captain Hudson. (After July 31 they were attached to the First Dragoons.) They numbered 107 men.

The Army of the West had to have a competent surgeon. Such a man was available in the experienced army doctor in charge of the post hospital at Fort Leavenworth—Assistant Surgeon John Strother Griffin, a Virginian by birth with six years of army experience behind him, some of it on the plains. His journals of the expedition are some of the best accounts of it, salty at times because a contemporary described the doctor as "the best, most unctious [*sic*] swearer I ever knew. His swearing was mellow and emphatic, strong adjectives, not profane." Another important addition to the rapidly forming army arrived on June 24. It was a party of Topographical Engineers headed by Lieutenant William Hensley Emory, a thirty-five-year-old Marylander. His party also included First Lieutenant Warner and Second Lieutenants Abert and Peck. In addition to field and topographical engineering duties assigned to this group, their orders included any military tasks which Colonel Kearny might designate. Emory proved an important member of the expedition. His report of the long journey from Leavenworth to Los Angeles via Santa Fe and San Diego is one of our most reliable sources. In addition to these formal components, Kearny had also secured as scouts and Indian interpreters some fifty Delaware and Shawnee Indians. He gladly accepted the services as guide and interpreter volunteered by Anthony Robidoux, a well-known "mountain man."

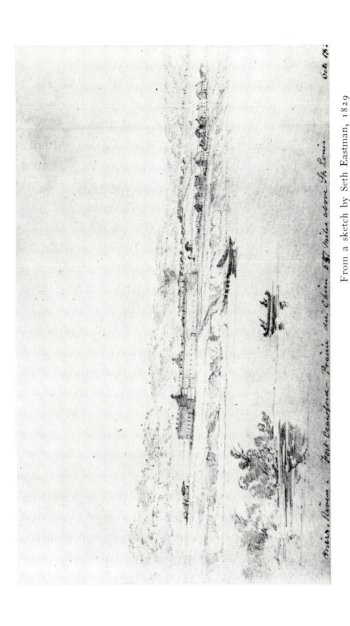

Prairie du Chien. Fort Crawford. Prairie du Chien 5[?] miles above St Louis. Oct 19:

From a sketch by Seth Eastman, 1829
Courtesy Peabody Museum, Harvard University

Assigned to command Fort Crawford in 1828, Kearny found the buildings dilapidated, the location generally unhealthy, the morale low. A few months later the post surgeon wrote that "the healthfulness and efficiency of the troops at this post . . . [is] unprecedented within the limits of my recollection."

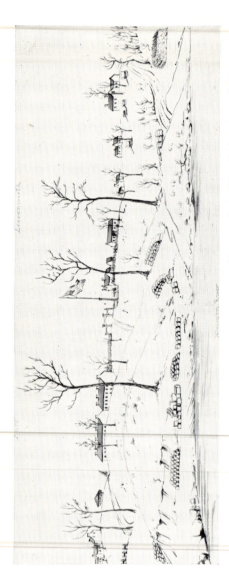

Leavenworth

Major Stephen Kearny brought his bride, Mary Radford, to Fort Leavenworth immediately after their wedding in 1830. Fort Leavenworth was "as rough and remote a frontier post as then existed."

The Colonel invited his good friend Lieutenant Colonel Ethan Allen Hitchcock to become his inspector general. Hitchcock was under medical treatment in St. Louis and had to decline. (Kearny in 1833 had tried to secure Hitchcock's transfer to the First Dragoons.)

Of all the Colonel's voluminous correspondence during June, 1846, the most important was a letter he wrote to Captain James Allen. It authorized him to raise a regiment of volunteers among the Mormons. He promised that they would be paid wages and at the end of twelve months service be released and permitted to retain the arms and accouterments furnished them. The Mexican War is marked by many picturesque episodes. None was more unique than the epic march of the Mormon Battalion set in motion by this letter.

Kearny planned to send forward various contingents of the army as fast as they were ready. Not only would this speed the advance, but forage and firewood along the way would be better conserved. As summer progressed, the problem of feeding the hundreds of animals was bound to become acute. With no enemy to fear for several hundred miles, there was no danger in dispersing his command. Two companies of the dragoons had started under Captain Moore on June 6. Lieutenant Noble had followed with another on the twelfth. Two companies of the First Missouri Mounted Regiment rode out on the sixteenth. Four more soon followed and Colonel Doniphan, himself, departed the next day with the two remaining companies. The First Missouri convoyed the wagon train and the cattle. The two infantry companies marched west a few hours in advance of Doniphan's detachment.

By the twenty-ninth, Kearny could write the Adjutant General "I have started fifteen hundred and twenty men from here on the Santa Fe Trail. I will leave tomorrow morning to overtake them and will concentrate the whole near the crossing of the Arkansas." The Colonel did not include in these figures his own party nor the two companies who were to follow him shortly. His little army totaled 1,658 men. Its light artillery's ordnance consisted of four 12-pound and twelve 6-pound howitzers. One member of the expedition gives the grand total as 1,701 but he took into account the teamsters, hunters, and traders who traveled with the army. (In faraway California they had not yet heard of the declaration of war, but startling things were happening there. At dawn on the fourteenth of that same June in the quiet village of Sonoma a group of armed American settlers routed General Mariano Vallejo from his bed and placed him under arrest. A few hours later they raised the hastily contrived standard of the so-called Bear Flag Republic. These Americans had recently conferred with Captain John C. Frémont, and though he was not present at Sonoma, what they did had his blessing. On June 24, some of these Bear Flaggers and a few Californians fought with each other the Battle of Olompali, between Sonoma and San Rafael, although neither side had learned of the outbreak of hostilities. Nor had sixty-one-year-old José Berryessa when he crossed San Pablo Bay in the daytime to visit his son, the Alcalde of Sonoma. In the boat with Berryessa were two De Haro brothers, carrying dispatches from General Castro, the Mexican commander at Monterey, to his lieutenant De la Torre. The De Haros had not heard of it either. But two days after Colonel Doniphan rode out of Fort Leavenworth, all three of them were shot down by Frémont's men without warning when they landed on the beach near San Rafael. Declaration or no declaration, that was real enough war to these luckless travelers.)

In his last official communication from Fort Leavenworth, Kearny relayed to Washington the news of the enemy he had just received from Bent and St. Vrain. They had left Santa Fe on May 27 and Taos on June 3. They had seen much of Governor Armijo. He had told them he was expecting from three to five thousand men from Mexico under General Urrea. Bent thought Armijo and Urrea were bound to be rivals if not open enemies. Armijo, he thought, could be won over and pitted against Urrea. Kearny reminded the War Department that the previous year he had recommended the establishment of an Indian agency at Bent's Fort. Such an establishment would have been of much use now in preserving peace on the American side of the border. Kearny also asked the department to send three hundred dragoon uniforms by the navy to Monterey, California.

About nine o'clock on the bright warm morning of June 30, Stephen Kearny, mounted on his sturdy bay, waved farewell to his wife and children gathered on the steps of his quarters, and rode away from Fort Leavenworth. One writer described him then as "tall, straight, bronzed, lean as a sea cusk." With him went his staff officers and the engineers. Next the light artillery clattered along with its fine brass cannon neatly polished for the occasion. Last came the remaining detachment of the First Dragoons at headquarters. Figuratively at least, all of the Army of the West was at last moving westward under the eyes of its commander.

The dragoons were more practically attired than they were in the terrible summer campaign of 1834, but still presented a very soldierly appearance. They wore broad-brimmed, low-crowned hats, with shirts and pantaloons of blue flannel. Bowie and hunting knives were buckled around the waist, and the ever ready carbine and a brace of pistols were slung in large holsters from the saddle. Each man carried a roll behind him in which he put his blouse and blanket. Deftly tucked into the roll were a metal plate, knife, fork, spoon, and drinking cup. At the head of the dragoons rode their standard-bearer, with the regiment's bugler beside him.

10. *The Army of the West: Exodus*

NUMEROUS JOURNALS were kept by officers and privates as the Army of the West toiled over the Santa Fe Trail. Since many miles separated the van of the column from the rear guard, each writer's chronicle varied as to incidents and mishaps. They told a common story however of the initiation given green volunteers on the long march across the prairies. Teams mired in soft earth and mud holes. Inexperienced drivers lashed their animals on upgrades until too soon they could not even drag their loads on the level stretches. Poorly fitted harness pulled over the collars or chafed the flesh of straining animals. Axles fashioned from green wood broke; later they dried out and fell apart. Bridges had to be built over streams.

Until the crossroad from Fort Leavenworth joined the Santa Fe Trail, many units lost their way. Some found themselves miles along the road to Oregon before friendly Indians set them right. One troop rode all the way eastward to Westport before it got its bearings. A persistent evil was the tendency of company commissaries to become separated from the men they were supposed to serve. Many a weary marcher rolled up in his blankets supperless in consequence. Heat, fatigue, and sparse grass took toll of both horses and cattle. Many times water was scanty, or when available warm and productive of violent cramps and retching. When nothing else plagued the exhausted soldier, he had to slap at swarms of mosquitoes and gnats.

Nearly every one in the rifle corps developed sore feet early in the march. These continued to torture the foot soldiers all the way to Santa Fe. Actually the first weeks provided a gigantic training program for the Missouri volunteers and teamsters. Kearny and his dragoons did not need this experience, but for the rest of his army it proved indispensable. Fortunately the enemy was still too distant to be a menace. Grueling lessons were being learned daily that would make soldiers out of these recruits.

The Colonel started with the rear guard but seldom traveled long with any one unit. Eying every detail, he had praise for some and admonitions for others. As a veteran horseman he was often aghast at the mishandling of the animals. Artillery officers had to be taught the fundamentals of caring for their horses. He became a familiar figure riding up and down the column, counseling, questioning, but always urging the army onward. Even the Fourth of July did not warrant a pause for any celebration—just a permission to the men to buy liquor from the sutler. Word passed from soldier to soldier that Colonel Kearny was hard to keep up with—"reputed one of the most expeditious travellers who ever crossed the plains."

One of the Laclede Rangers wrote "Colonel Kearney [*sic*] is still with us—or rather still has us with him. Nothing could exceed the confidence which every man seems to have in him. As a military man, we find him just strict enough to keep us all in order, but not in the least oppressive. He is, however, fond of rapid marching and keeps us at it steadily. Yesterday, for example, we made about thirty miles, and expect to make twenty-five tomorrow. These distances will not seem great to persons unaccustomed to military movements, but we find by experience that twenty miles a day is a good distance to move a camp. There is a great deal to be done—packing, loading the wagons, getting the horses ready—unloading, pitching tents, taking care of the horses, cooking, etc. etc. Every man in the company, from Captain down, is kept busily employed—so much so that I find the keeping of a diary, even with brief notes, quite an interference with other calls. . . . When all our camp gets in motion in the forenoon, our wagons, straggling horsemen and the companies spread over four or five miles of the prairies. We find it a great convenience to scatter along, as it leaves us all a better choice of the road, and keeps us clear of the dust." Later another soldier wrote home that the day before the men had marched thirty-four miles. Alternately, the privates exulted at these fast records or cursed President Polk, Colonel Kearny, and the nearest subaltern.

Once on the Santa Fe Trail, whose broad, well-marked roadway could not be missed by even a tenderfoot, the army frequently crossed small watercourses and Lieutenant Emory described the country as having the appearance of vast rolling fields enclosed with colossal hedges where trees lined the banks of streams. On the afternoon of July 7 the expanse of open prairie was a panorama of splendor under a gorgeous sunset. Spirits rose, the soldiers were nearing the "jumping off place," Council Grove. East of it lone travelers might still journey back to the settlements in safety; beyond lay a boundless expanse familiar only to the wild Indian and buffalo where possibilities for tragedy lurked in the smallest mischance. Officers enjoined greater caution; stragglers wandering any distance from the line of march would only too likely be murdered. Had there been a Francis Scott Key or a Julia Ward among these westward-toiling Americans, such a one might have seen a revelation in that sunset. The poet might have found apocalyptic reference to the nation's enlarging destiny because of events even then taking place beyond the glory in the West. On June 8, Commodore Sloat had quietly slipped out of Mazatlan and sailed north. He had not learned yet that war had been declared but he was determined not to let the British fleet steal a march on him. He reached Monterey on July 2. Still lacking confirmation of the events he strongly suspected, he was anxious not to repeat Thomas Ap Catesby Jones's embarrassing performance in 1842 when he had seized that same town of Monterey under the mistaken assumption that the United States and Mexico were then at war. Instead of overt action now, Sloat punctiliously offered to salute the Mexican flag. The honor was declined by the port authorities; not for any bellicose reasons but for want of powder to return the salute. For several days Sloat hesitated. The American consul, Thomas O. Larkin, added his cautions to Sloat's own prudence. But while they marked time, word began to circulate of the Bear Flag uprising at Sonoma. That almost surely would precipitate war. There was the off-chance that the British fleet might gamble boldly in such a crisis. So at last on July 7, Sloat landed a force of men, raised the American flag over the Monterey Customhouse and took formal possession of California for the United States.

"To make a war," Lieutenant Johnston confided to his diary, "the first thing to do is to be certain of filling your soldiers' bellies." Rations brought along from Fort Leavenworth had to feed the command until it reached the habitat of the buffalo. Other game and fish meanwhile were too meager to be dependable. The buffalo herds themselves did not graze very far east on the Santa Fe Trail. Moreover, in a column strung out for miles, distribution was a problem, if famine in one detachment and a feast in another were to be avoided. From Fort Leavenworth to California, this matter of rations constituted one of Colonel Kearny's most acute problems. When the expedition started he had given strict orders that after entering the buffalo country, no cattle were to be killed. The abundant wild game of the plains—elk, deer, and antelope as well as the buffalo—were to supply the meat. Tom Forsythe, a seasoned hunter, had been engaged to command a detachment of ten men from each company to serve as hunters. Forsythe had experienced packers and butchers with him. When in big-game country, the hunting party was to start ahead before midnight and reach the site of the next day's camp by dawn. By the time the army came up, they should have a plentiful supply of game.

When Pawnee Rock was reached, Forsythe led his hunters to its top where they saw what no mortal eye can ever again behold. As far as they could see the ground was covered with buffalo. Prepared as the soldiers were for the unusual, they were dumb with amazement. Finally one man asked how many animals were grazing before them. "At least a half million," the trapper replied. This was enough meat for the Army of the West—for all the armies of the world. But Kearny's orderly hunting plans had not taken into account the exuberance of the Missouri volunteers. Every one of them longed to kill his buffalo, or to draw a bead on one. Discipline was forgotten and the advance guard of troopers was transformed into a hallooing, galloping mob that fired at the startled herds and fired again as fast as they could reload. Many of the horses stampeded at the hubbub and order was only restored after hours of effort. The volunteers tardily learned also that a horse fed for days on grass cannot be suddenly raced for miles at breakneck speed without permanent damage. Many of the mounts hobbled into camp after the hunt, lame, badly winded, and with sore backs.

The Grim Reaper was never far away from the line of march. Several times soldiers were drowned when cloud bursts ravaged this semiarid land. A Missouri volunteer died suddenly one night. A dragoon was fatally stricken as his troop neared Bent's Fort; also a sergeant of the First Missouri succumbed to sudden illness the next day. In each case burial with the honors of war soon followed. The lighthearted, carefree volunteers found these ceremonies most melancholy. With a blanket for his coffin and the Stars and Stripes for his pall, the body of the deceased was borne on the shoulders of four men. Two others led his horse (if the dead man was a mounted soldier) with his arms on the saddle and the boots reversed in the stirrups. Five companies followed to the spot chosen for interment. An officer read a short service and prayer. Three volleys were fired over the lonely grave and when the earth was banked down solid and level with the prairie, the procession moved away. Rocks were mixed with the dirt to ward off the wolves, but no markers or gravestones were set. These would only have invited desecration by prowling savages. Yet long after the last dust of the Army of the West silently settled upon the trail, these hidden vestiges would remain at the heart of things as lasting evidence of its passing.

Occasionally the column overtook a caravan of Santa Fe traders who were glad to have the protection of the expedition. At one of these encounters a young Mexican walked over from the trader's wagons and asked permission to meet "El General." His name was J. Franco Chaves. He was returning to his home in Santa Fe from an academy in Fishkill-on-the-Hudson in New York. The Colonel was delighted to learn that the youth had been a schoolmate of his own sons, William and Charles. He invited Chaves to ride part of the way with him. It was good to be able to talk with a friend of his boys. Kearny recognized that young Chaves was intelligent and asked him "How would you like to interpret Spanish for me?" The lad, of course, felt complimented and gladly agreed. Fifty-seven years later, Colonel J. Franco Chaves was to recall this meeting and the resulting friendship when a portrait of General Kearny was unveiled in the courthouse at Santa Fe. The donor of the portrait, Mrs. Western Bascome (Ellen Kearny), a daughter of the General, was the honored guest of the city on that occasion.

At his evening camp site on July 19, Kearny met George T. Howard, who was returning from his mission to the Americans in Santa Fe. Howard reported that the common people of New Mexico were inclined to accept the peace terms Kearny had authorized Howard to disseminate among them—namely, lay down their arms and take an oath of allegiance to the United States. In return they would become American citizens and enjoy the rights and protection accorded all Americans. Howard was unable, however, to report any progress with the Mexican leaders. They were definitely hostile and preparing for war. Howard believed one force of twenty-three hundred was planning to defend Santa Fe, with another detachment forming around Taos.

The next morning the commander caused consternation among his staff. Lieutenant Abert recorded it, "This morning we had not marched far, when we saw General Kearny's guard stop and encamp. Soon Lieutenant Emory, who had crossed the river, rode over and informed us that General Kearny was very ill, and ordered one of our wagons to remain for the purpose of conveying the general on by easy stages; for our wagon was light and had good springs, while all the other wagons with the army were without springs and roughly built, like common Santa Fe trade wagons." Lieutenant Johnston referred to, "The sudden and violent illness of the Colonel commanding. The deep solicitude expressed by all showed how much interest the army felt in his being at the head of it." Lieutenant Abert's strictures on the unsuitability of the army wagons for ambulances were echoed by other members of this expedition. "A miserable, uncomfortable substitute for spring wagons" wrote one writer who declared that valuable lives had been lost because of this wretched equipment. This was only one of several ways in which army transportation miserably failed to render acceptable service to the extended expedition led by Stephen Kearny. To every one's relief the Colonel had sufficiently recovered by the next morning for the march to be resumed at an early hour. In a short time he and his escort reached the Cimarron crossing where they found the artillery and Laclede Rangers still camped. The staff officers rode two miles further and made camp in good grass. For the next few days the Colonel's progress was not as rapid as that of the rest of the column.

On July 21 heavy clouds darkened the western sky. Many of the marchers must have felt their hearts beat faster when under the black thunderheads they first beheld the striking and ethereal white beauty of Wah-to-yah (Wato-yah, Wattahyah) the Indian's way of expressing "the breasts of the world." Today we call them the Spanish Peaks. They were to loom as shining beacons before the Army of the West for many days; the first real mountains these Missouri farm boys had ever seen. Farther in the northwest, Pikes Peak reared its head. Without any command a loud shout went up from the ranks. These troops had advanced 566 miles in just 30 days. Even the regular officers could not bring themselves to rebuke these unmilitary cheers.

Rations were running short and most of the buffalo country was now behind them. The advance of so large a column must have frightened away any animals in the vicinity of the trail. The infantry had actually outwalked all the mounted units. Heat, half rations, scanty water of poor quality—despite all handicaps these foot soldiers were indeed proving themselves in Stephen Kearny's words "the main pillar and strength of an army." There were frequent showers with some lightning at night, so the country was ideal for marching, with flowers in abundance even though the grass was sparse and dried. Serpents still frequented paradise however; several rattlesnakes were killed about the various camp sites and many men were sick.

On July 28, Tom Fitzpatrick galloped up to the Colonel from Bent's Fort. He told Kearny that Armijo had summoned a council of the chief men of New Mexico to confer about the defense of Santa Fe, as well as other news of panic and hostile preparations going on over the mountains. The following day, Kearny advanced to within 10 miles of Bent's Fort. Most of his army was concentrated on the flat below it to the East where hundreds of traders' wagons were massed. The famous trading post was the only permanently occupied habitation between the Missouri settlements and those in New Mexico—an oasis of civilization (of sorts) in a wilderness of prairies and mountains, nearly 4,000 feet above sea level. Its adobe walls were 15 feet high, 4 feet thick, and strong enough to withstand any savage attack. It was built in a rough parallelogram 180 feet by 135. It had one main gate and over that a staff of ash from which floated a huge American flag that the marching soldiers had spied long before they reached it.

Colonel Kearny camped his First Dragoons with the artillery on the north side of the river east of the post. Doniphan and his volunteers were alloted a site on the opposite bank. Here the army paused briefly before the final push over Raton Pass into New Mexico. Colonel Doniphan ordered all the horses turned loose to graze. Shortly afterward at least four hundred of them stampeded. The wildest and most terrible confusion ensued. Most of the horses still had lariats about their necks, some that were still picketed broke loose. The lariats and iron picket posts served as flails to lash the frightened animals into greater frenzy. For hours they galloped over the plains and were only recaptured after the most arduous labor. Some were found fifty miles from the camp and thirty or more were never recovered. Private Edwards blamed Colonel Doniphan for the stampede since he had ordered the horses turned out to graze. Until his enlistment a few weeks previously, the eighteen-year-old private had been a clerk in a Missouri courthouse. Of such stuff are experts made.

Lieutenant Emory felt that the army's probationary period was behind it and wrote, "I would take occasion to speak of the excellent understanding which prevailed throughout between regulars and volunteers and the cheerfulness with which they came to each others' assistance. . . . The volunteers, . . . recently accustomed to the ease and comforts of smiling homes, bore up against fatigue, hunger and the vicissitudes of a long and tedious march, through unexplored regions, with a zeal, courage and devotion that would have graced time-worn veterans, and reflect the highest credit on their conduct as soldiers."

Captain Moore had captured three Mexicans. These were sent to Colonel Kearny's headquarters. They readily admitted they had crossed the Raton Pass to observe what they could report to Governor Armijo. Probably they were already resigned to their fate— a firing squad before one of the thick walls of Bent's Fort. But although the Colonel questioned them closely he had no intention of executing these men. Perhaps Kearny remembered his college classics and the advice given the Athenians by Pericles concerning their enemies, the Spartans: "We throw open our city to the world, and never by alien acts exclude foreigners from any opportunity of learning or observing, although the eyes of an enemy may occasionally profit by our liberality." Therefore he ordered that they be shown all the camps and particularly the artillery. Then they were to be set free to return to Santa Fe and report what they had seen. As they left on the thirty-first their leader exclaimed "My God! what is to become of our republic?" This proved to be one of Kearny's wisest moves in the conquest of New Mexico. The returning spies filled Santa Fe with exaggerated stories of the multitude of heavily armed warriors about to descend upon the province with unbelievably heavy cannon whose number grew with each telling. These live reporters helped the Americans infinitely more than a horde of dead spies.

On behalf of one of these Mexicans, a romantic plea in mitigation was entered. This man claimed he had come to Bent's Fort in pursuit of his wife. Several years before she had been taken prisoner by the Comanches, who later sold her to William Bent. Then the "bartered bride" had taken up with one of Bent's men by whom she had a child. The Mexican stoutly demanded the return of his wife. Colonel Kearny found himself almost in the role of King Solomon, and ruled that she go with her husband, provided she was willing. She assented and left the fort when the spies were liberated. Captain Turner concludes his journal entry of this affair with the terse sentence "A hot day." Presumably he referred to the weather.

The last day of July was a busy time at headquarters. While the last of the column was moving into camp, Kearny made another attempt at the peaceful conquest of New Mexico. One of the many traders immobilized at Bent's Fort by Captain Moore's embargo was Eugene Leitensdorfer. He was well recommended to the commander and told him he had great influence among the Pueblo Indians around Taos. Kearny detailed a squad of troopers to escort him to Taos. They carried with them a proclamation in which Kearny promised the Pueblos protection in their lives, properties, and rights if they would remain neutral and stay quietly in their homes. He further issued the following proclamation to the people of New Mexico, "The undersigned enters New Mexico with a large military force, for the purpose of seeking union with and ameliorating the condition of its inhabitants. This he does under instructions from his government, and with the assurances that he will be amply sustained in the accomplishment of this object. It is enjoined on the citizens of New Mexico to remain quietly at their homes and to pursue their peaceful avocations. So long as they continue in such pursuits, they will not be interfered with by the American army, but will be respected and protected in their rights both civil and religious. All who take up arms or encourage resistance against the government of the United States will be regarded as enemies and will be treated accordingly." Copies of this proclamation were also furnished the three spies when they were liberated.

(Two days after Commodore Sloat seized Monterey on July 7, Captain Montgomery hoisted Old Glory at Yerba Buena in California while one of his lieutenants performed the same act at Sonoma. A few days later there were similar flag raisings at Sutter's Fort and Bodega. Later that month, Sloat was succeeded by Commodore Robert F. Stockton. There was none of Sloat's hesitation in Stockton. Apparently not satisfied with his predecessor's annexation of California he issued another proclamation on July 23. It was much more belligerent in tone, called the Mexican authorities bad names, and all but invited them to fight. He also mustered into the naval service some of the former Bear Flaggers and American settlers under John C. Frémont—still a brevet captain of topographical engineers in the United States Army. Stockton, although a naval officer himself, commissioned Captain Frémont a major by an authority that has ever since tied in knots many an expert on military law. This irregular force was called the California Battalion of Mounted Riflemen. In order to seize possession of Southern California, Stockton had his new Battalion embark on the United States sloop "Cyane" on the twenty-sixth for San Diego. Stockton's occupation of Los Angeles in mid-August brought forth a proclamation in similar vein to that of July 23. Such bellicose utterances were at variance with the pacific policy advocated by the Polk administration to conciliate the Californians and secure possession of the region without conflict. These proclamations and the events flowing from them were to affect profoundly the conquest—not occupation—of California and Stephen Kearny's part in it six months later.)

Into the post on July 27 had driven nineteen-year-old Susan Magoffin, one of the few white women on the Santa Fe Trail that summer. Driving her wagon was Samuel Magoffin whom she had married eight months before. A few days behind them rode Samuel's brother and business partner, James. Because of letters to Colonel Kearny carried by James Magoffin, their party had been permitted to go over the trail as far as the Cimarron Crossing or Bent's Fort, as they chose, and there await Kearny's arrival. Even though it resembled bedlam, Bent's was a welcome haven for Susan. She was in poor condition after her long journey, and on the thirtieth was seized with labor pains. William Bent prepared an upstairs room for her, and on July 31 she suffered a miscarriage.

While Susan lay unconscious at Bent's Fort, brother-in-law James had arrived and was having an interesting conference with Stephen Kearny. Perhaps their meeting was more important to the destinies of both New Mexico and the United States than anything else that happened on that fateful July 31. Magoffin had long been interested in the trade with Santa Fe and Chihuahua. He spoke Spanish fluently and knew all the influential citizens of those areas. He was rich, generous, and patriotic. He was also well known to Senator Benton and through him met President Polk and Secretary of War Marcy. President Polk was most anxious to secure the northern provinces of Mexico without bloodshed, and James Magoffin seemed to promise the most effectual help in that direction. So when he sped west he bore letters from the President and Secretary of War to Colonel Kearny. He explained to the latter how he hoped to induce Governor Armijo and his officers by persuasion or bribery, or both, to submit peaceably to the occupation of their province. What he might not accomplish with Armijo perhaps he could effect through Colonel Diego Archuleta, the latter's assistant lieutenant governor. At the moment he needed an escort of dragoons to take him on in advance of the main army.

Kearny thought over the officers he had available for a dangerous and important mission. Captain Philip St. George Cooke had scarcely brushed off the dust of his long ride when Colonel Kearny concluded that he was his man. Bold, brave, and resourceful, he had the great advantage of being popular in New Mexico because of the Snively affair. Cooke was told as much as he needed to know of James Magoffin's role. Kearny asked him to take twelve dragoons under a flag of truce and conduct Magoffin to Armijo with a letter to the Governor. In it, Kearny would notify Armijo that the United States was annexing all of New Mexico east of the Río del Norte (Río Grande) because of the old claim Texas made to that river as its western boundary. He would warn Armijo that resistance would result only in needless sacrifice of life. If they did not oppose him, the people of New Mexico would be protected in their lives and property and their religion would be respected.

Cooke's biographer says, "he was mildly alarmed and somewhat downcast by this request. He had envisioned battle and promotion, not tame negotiation." But like Kearny he was a good soldier who put duty before everything else. Kearny once more was the diplomat, assuring Cooke he was the *one* man on whom he could rely for this task and that he had intended to halt the army's advance until Cooke's arrival for just this purpose. Captain Cooke promptly accepted the mission entrusted to him. The next day he and Magoffin set out for the Raton Pass with twelve dragoons.

On August 1, Kearny wrote the Adjutant General that he had received from James Magoffin the all-important instructions from the Secretary of War of June 18. "I desire you to say to him that no exertions will be wanting on my part to execute his instructions and the wishes of the President." Kearny fully and faithfully lived up to this promise.

11. *The Army of the West: Invasion*

W HEN S TEPHEN K EARNY ordered his expedition to advance from
Bent's Fort, far more was implicit than the march of an invading
army. Actually the tide of Hispanic dominance was being swept back
at the same moment that the loose hold of Mexico was broken. That
tide had reached its flood under Coronado three centuries before.
Even though his penetration of ancient Quivira in central Kansas
or Oklahoma had been slight and brief, it marked the earliest Euro-
pean claim to this region. Spain's short tenure of Louisiana after
peace was declared in 1763 was only a backwash rather than the new
thrust of an aggressive power. The French Revolution and Napoleon's sale of Louisiana to the United States in 1803 ended any
chance of Spain's remaining permanently in the region. Thus the
Arkansas River and later the hundredth meridian bounded the Spaniards on the northeast and afterward their successors in the new
nation of Mexico.

To the northwest the friction between Britons and Spaniards at
Nootka Sound had as long ago as 1790 reversed the tide there.
All along the vague northern boundaries this tide was receding.
Texas had broken away in 1836. At the other end of the frontier
no man knew where Mexican sovereignty ended. England claimed
the Oregon country, but who could say how far south her ambitions
might achieve sovereignty? Far enough certainly to make Mexico's

hold on California exceedingly weak. (The lack of powder at Monterey to return Sloat's salute was symptomatic of several things.)

Now on the center of the line could be heard the tramp of many feet as the young and vigorous forerunners of another breed marched to breach the walls. Though its members lacked discipline and military skill, they were imbued with zeal that ranked them with some of Israel's ancient hosts or Cromwell's Roundheads. Manifest Destiny—the expansion of America to the Pacific to give it room to grow and flex its muscles, as well as natural boundaries to buttress its unity —that and the Army of the West were not to be denied.

Now another tide, Anglo-Saxon in origin yet American-channeled, was sweeping up the Raton and the Sangre de Cristos, never to subside. Even as it was to take and hold the Southwest however, this wave would undergo modification and in its later stages acquire depths and shadings both aboriginal and Hispanic. Until 1846 no one conceived of an American Southwest; ever since it has remained a distinctive region that has changed and enriched the culture imposed upon it. Even in 1846 it was an ancient land that had known three centuries of white occupation. It was a land of wild mountains soaring above narrow river valleys, wide-stretching mesa lands browned by the sun most of the year, and a population that was small and scattered compared to its expanse. Authorities differ as to the population of New Mexico at the time of the American occupation. Lieutenant Emory credited the territory with a hundred thousand inhabitants but that is subject to question. The United States Census for 1850 only showed sixty-one thousand. This figure probably did not vary greatly from the total of four years earlier. Not the least of the reasons why the advance of the Army of the West was inexorable was the man who commanded it. Among Stephen Kearny's descendants, the tradition remains that "his life ambition was to further the westward expansion of our country!"

In New Mexico spies had been reporting Kearny's steady approach to Governor Armijo. On July 1 the Governor had appealed to the national government for help. The commander in Chihuahua encouraged him by replying that at a moment's notice he would start north with five hundred cavalry and an equal number of infantry. The governor of Durango also was ordered to aid the threatened province. Good words, brave words, but Armijo needed another kind of reinforcement.

Among Kearny's other concerns that busy last week of July, 1846, was the dispatch of scouts to reconnoiter the mountain passes in advance of his army. He asked William Bent to secure such a group for him without delay as he planned to march on August 2. Bent was still angry about the despoilation of his post, which looked to him as if a horde of locusts had descended upon it. In contrast to his brother Charles, William Bent seemed unable to get along with Colonel Kearny. He felt insulted by the modest compensation offered the scouts. Kearny had always shown a strict sense of stewardship where government funds were concerned. He may well have tried to drive too hard a bargain but he was in a poor position to haggle. He badly needed reliable information. The historian of Bent's Fort says he sent a peacemaker to settle his differences with William Bent. Lieutenant Johnston notes on August 1 that "the party of spies under Mr. Bent was . . . sent in advance today."

Some of Doniphan's regiment broke camp and began their march that same day. Leaving Dr. Vaughn at Bent's Fort with a small detail to care for the sick, Kearny and his staff rode out of camp at six o'clock on the morning of the second. Emory, awaiting their departure, first saw "a column of dust to the east, advancing with about the velocity of a fast walking horse—it was the Army of the West." As the column passed he took his place with the staff and all of them crossed the river. They were now invaders of Mexican soil. Like the march from Fort Leavenworth, the long ascent of Raton Pass produced a series of separate adventures and incidents as small groups toiled arduously upward in the heat with all too little grass and water. Generally the line of march for several days closely followed the present Santa Fe Railroad from La Junta to Raton Pass. By sunset on August 4 the Spanish Peaks again came suddenly into view as the column surmounted the ridge dividing the Timpas from the Purgatoire. In the light mountain air the snowy summits of the Sangre de Cristo Range were sharply etched against the deep turquoise of the evening sky. A little while earlier the men had passed their first scattered pine trees, as well as some piñons that were welcome because of their edible nuts.

A letter written by Captain Turner to his wife during this slow climb speaks eloquently of the fatigue of the soldiers and their declining morale:

> Camp at the Raton Mountains about one hundred miles from Bent's Fort, the St. Louis companies [Laclede Rangers] bear up tolerably well but Colonel Doniphan's regiment to a man is sick and tired of the business. Your *godfather* is wholly cast down and is about as fit to command a battalion of artillery as any *female* of your acquaintance. (don't repeat) But for the example set by the regulars I verily believe the volunteers would not reach Santa Fe.

(Major Meriwether Lewis Clark was the commander of the artillery battalion and without doubt the object of Captain Turner's unfavorable comment.)

The returning spies met Kearny not far below the summit and reported that all was clear ahead. Another two miles brought him to the crest. Despite his weariness he could enjoy the panorama of misty canyons and ridges stretching to infinity. Wah-to-yah loomed close in the northwest, and Pikes Peak and a galaxy of other snowy summits were visible to the north and south. The climbers were 7,500 feet above sea level, and the rarefied atmosphere was sweet with the perfume of thousands of wild flowers.

Descent of the Raton, being far more precipitous, proved a worse ordeal than the long climb. This was the poorest stretch of roadway yet encountered and barely passable for vehicles. Many wagons were smashed in the descent even though the men held them back with ropes. For hundreds of soldiers the most arduous toil netted only a half-mile of progress during a whole day. The dry grass created a grave fire hazard in addition and prompted one of Kearny's most peremptory orders to enforce caution.

The road swerved to the southwest several miles below the present town of Raton where it debouches on the plains. For a long distance thereafter the old trail ran considerably west of the present Santa Fe Railroad. (Trail and railroad do not converge again until

Watrous is reached.) Every soldier sensed that he was now in a different land as he gazed at the strange silhouettes of the mesas and cliffs sheered off abruptly as if their creation had been interrupted. Most of all, the red earth seemed strange. Nowhere in the midwest did the soil resemble this New Mexico dirt. Except for a few swift-running mountain streams, it even stained the creeks and rivers a turgid chocolate. No wonder the people of such a land dressed differently, spoke a strange tongue, and rode absurdly small donkeys!

Anyone with imagination would have been stirred by the mountains on their right—crest after crest clad in pines. Close at hand each tree was a grayish green, but in the distance the forested mountains turned to blue, with canyons deepening to purple. An air of mystery brooded over the ranges. Behind those ridges, said the mountain men, ancient villages nestled in folds of the hills. Some of them consisted of multistoried buildings unlike any structures American soldiers had ever seen. New Mexico even possessed a different sky. Except when heavy showers were falling, it was a dazzling blue. However, patches of fluffy white clouds always drifted lazily over the mountains to complete an atmosphere of enchantment.

An American trader from Taos met the column with a load of flour. Kearny was glad to buy it as his men were now on half-rations. The man said Armijo's proclamation had just reached Taos. It placed the whole country under martial law and called on all citizens to take up arms. His community was thoroughly aroused and belligerent. He reported that Armijo had assembled about two thousand Pueblo Indians and all other citizens capable of bearing arms. Three hundred Mexican dragoons had just arrived in Santa Fe; twelve hundred more were momentarily expected. According to this trader the Mexicans all wished to defend the province, but half of the Pueblos were lukewarm. However, they would be forced to fight. Interesting also, if true, was the man's statement that at a council in Santa Fe, Armijo had expressed himself as averse to resisting the invaders. But all the prominent men present had overruled him. The trader also reported that Armijo was using the priests to inflame the populace. He insisted that they tell their people of the horrors that the Americans would certainly inflict upon them. Despite short rations and the toils of the road, these predictions of battle raised the spirits of the Army of the West. They had traveled a long distance just to fight Mexicans, and it would be a shame not to come to grips with the enemy now.

More spies were captured and interviewed by the Colonel. Their stories varied but it seemed certain that Armijo would soon oppose the invaders. Just as at Bent's Fort, these spies were shown every detachment of the army. After a few hours' detention, they were set free to carry back exaggerated reports to lower Mexican morale. Kearny now commanded all units to close the gaps separating them and to march in close order. The slender stock of ammunition —only five rounds per man—had to be conserved as the expected supplies had failed to arrive. By August 14 the soldiers expected a clash with the enemy at any moment. Therefore they were not surprised to meet a Mexican lieutenant with three lancers who presented a letter to Colonel Kearny from General Armijo. It acknowledged the communication Cooke had brought and declared that the Governor could not recognize the Río del Norte as the United States boundary. The people of New Mexico had risen in arms, and the Governor was bound by duty and inclination to lead them. If Kearny would advance as far as Las Vegas, Armijo would meet him there and negotiate. There might be hidden irony in this suggestion of negotiation; at the very least there was ambiguity, thought Kearny. What kind of a reply should he send back by the lancer lieutenant? Since Captain Cooke was perhaps being held as a hostage, the return of the lancers assumed added importance. A sixteen-mile march brought Las Vegas in view. Kearny summoned the Mexican lieutenant: "The road to Santa Fe is now as free to you as to myself. Say to General Armijo I shall soon meet him, and I hope it will be as friends." The courtly lancer ceremoniously embraced the Colonel and two of his aides and then trotted away with his escort on the road to Las Vegas.

The American column followed closely behind until it reached some cornfields on the outskirts of the town and made camp. At a distance the low, flat-roofed adobes resembled a large brickkiln. For the first time in many weeks the Americans looked on the striking contrast of parched red earth beside green fields of waving corn.

Chocolate-colored irrigation ditches were full of water. No fences or hedges separated the camp and the cornfields. The prospect was overpoweringly pleasing to the weary marchers. Colonel Kearny immediately posted a chain of sentinels to keep both animals and men off the cultivated land. Strict orders warned that all private property must be respected. Neither corn nor any other possession of the inhabitants was to be taken unless first paid for. Any man whose horse got into the cornfields would have to walk the next day. The Colonel sent Captain Turner into the village to request the alcalde and his council to call upon him. This official promptly complied and told Kearny that as a Mexican he must obey his government but that he was pleased by the regard for the people of New Mexico displayed in the Colonel's proclamation.

The advance began early on August 15 because Bent's spies had brought word that six hundred men were holding a strong position in the Vegas Pass a few miles up the road to Santa Fe. Just at that moment, Major Swords and two other officers galloped in from Bent's Fort. They had heard the day before that the Army of the West was going into battle. They had ridden sixty miles during the night to arrive in time to take part in the fight. They had another reason for speed. They brought Stephen Kearny's commission as brigadier general to rank from June 30, 1846. Now he should be addressed as General Kearny.

When the headquarters staff reached the plaza of Las Vegas, the alcalde and a crowd of people met them. There was no sign of General Armijo. Kearny pointed to the flat roof of one of the buildings. "I want you to go up there with me," he told the alcalde, and from the roof he addressed the 150 people gathered in the plaza:

> Mr. Alcalde, and people of New Mexico: I have come amongst you by the orders of my government, to take possession of your country, and extend over it the laws of the United States. We consider it, and have done so for some time, a part of the territory of the United States. We come amongst you as friends—not as enemies; as protectors—not as conquerors. We come among you for your benefit—not for your injury.
>
> Henceforth I absolve you from all allegiance to the Mexican gov-

ernment, and from all obedience to General Armijo. He is no longer your governor; (great sensation). I am your governor. I shall not expect you to take up arms and follow me, to fight your own people, who may oppose me; but I now tell you, that those who remain peaceably at home, attending to their crops and their herds, shall be protected by me, in their property, their persons, and their religion; and not a pepper, not an onion, shall be disturbed or taken by my troops, without pay or by the consent of the owner. But listen! he who promises to be quiet, and is found in arms against me, I will hang!

From the Mexican government you have never received protection. The Apaches and the Navajoes come down from the mountains and carry off your sheep, and even your women, whenever they please. My government will correct all this. It will keep off the Indians, protect you in your persons and property; and, I repeat again, will protect you in your religion. I know you are all great Catholics; that some of your priests have told you all sorts of stories —that we should ill-treat your women, and brand them on the cheek as you do your mules on the hip. It is all false. My government respects your religion as much as the Protestant religion, and allows each man to worship his Creator as his heart tells him is best. Its laws protect the Catholic as well as the Protestant; the weak as well as the strong; the poor as well as the rich. I am not a Catholic myself—I was not brought up in that faith; but, at least one-third of my army are Catholics, and I respect a good Catholic as much as a good Protestant.

There goes my army—you see but a small portion of it; there are many more behind—resistance is useless.

Mr. Alcalde, and you two captains of militia, the laws of my country require that all men who hold office under it shall take the oath of allegiance. I do not wish, for the present, until affairs become more settled, to disturb your form of government. If you are prepared to take oaths of allegiance, I shall continue you in office, and support your authority.

It was, as Emory wrote, "a bitter pill" for the officials. In the hearing of all the crowd below, General Kearny admonished one of the militia captains, "Captain, look me in the face, while you repeat the oath of office." The man wavered, as did his brother officer and the alcalde, but under the General's unrelenting gaze they agreed to do his bidding. He required each man to raise his hand with thumb and finger crossed and to commence with "In the name of the Father and of the Son and of the Holy Ghost." After this formality was observed by each officer, Kearny and the others descended the ladder while the audience raised a faint shout. Perhaps the populace was relieved; in the change of masters they had little to lose.

Some critics have attacked this and similar acts of General Kearny in both New Mexico and California as unconstitutional. They can make quite a case on strictly legalistic grounds, but they overlook two important fundamentals. The first is that his orders of June 3, 1846, expressly directed him to require such oaths from the local officials in the country he occupied. Also, if the province he had orders to acquire could be taken without violence, any finespun technicalities about the steps involved would be avoided. He gambled and won on his invasion of New Mexico, and we may be certain he never lost sleep over the constitutional niceties he had disregarded. More than a century later the memory of his conciliatory policy is still cherished in New Mexico. So far as the people of that land are concerned, questions about the legality of his course have long since been forgotten.

As soon as the ceremonies in the plaza had been concluded, the army resumed its march. As they neared the defile every eye scanned it in vain for the six hundred defenders that had been so confidently predicted. Where was Armijo? The advance guard drew their sabers and spurred ahead. The pass was empty, and two miles farther they noticed that another narrow gorge was also deserted.

Stops were made for similar ceremonies at two more villages. At one of these villages, Captain Cooke rejoined the army with an American resident of Santa Fe whom Armijo had delegated to represent him. From them, Kearny learned of the all-important night session Magoffin and Cooke had had with Armijo and Colonel Archuleta in the Palace of the Governors on August 12.

Then, if not earlier, the Governor had decided not to defend Apache Pass. Not even Cooke was certain that Magoffin had bribed Armijo with gold, though he certainly suspected it. General Kearny could not be sure of the reasons for that momentous decision, and

136

we can only add our speculations to his. There is strong circumstantial evidence that bribery was used. Armijo's previous record of venality supports the suspicion, and his known cowardice does not weaken the case. Archuleta had proved more patriotic and argued against the course the Governor had chosen. Then the latter pointed out that they only had to give up the lands east of the Río Grande; the Río Abajo would remain Mexican. Archuleta, as the Governor's successor, could negotiate about that important territory to his own great advantage. Archuleta may have cherished selfish ambitions and was doubtless no angel, but at least he did not sell out. The Governor's argument mollified him, and he left the conference in the belief that only the upper province was to be abandoned. Later, Archuleta was bitter because he felt himself swindled. General Kearny's various proclamations, not only at Santa Fe but at the several towns en route, made no distinction regarding Arriba and Abajo. All of New Mexico was being declared American territory by seizure and annexation, so Archuleta found himself an acting governor of nothing. In fairness to all concerned, it appears that developing events rather than any individual "double-crossed" Archuleta.

While Magoffin himself brought to Kearny the important instructions of June 18, there is nothing to show that he knew the contents of the sealed packet he carried. Perhaps when Magoffin met with President Polk and Secretary Marcy, they doubted Kearny's ability to carry his conquest beyond Santa Fe (at that time few of his force had moved out of Fort Leavenworth). Santa Fe had been the first announced objective, and the Texas claim was consistent with that. Washington may have been willing (and so authorized Magoffin) to accept the eastern half of New Mexico temporarily and trust to later events to secure the western part. To accomplish this, the administration may have countermanded a negotiation with some Mexican official like Archuleta. If this could result in the peaceful occupation of the Santa Fe region by Kearny, Magoffin might have to allow such a man to govern the remainder of the province.

Kearny had the advantage of full knowledge of his instructions when he conferred with Magoffin at Bent's Fort. Even had he not been cautioned to secrecy about his ultimate destination, it was characteristic of him to tell Magoffin only as much as the latter had to know. Armijo could be bribed, bluffed, or threatened out of his strong position at his capitol without the American emissary's knowing any more than that which President Polk had told him. In fact, there was a real danger in letting James Magoffin know too much. He might inadvertently drop a hint about the march west from Santa Fe. That assignment was difficult enough without additional obstacles. Kearny's march to California must cross the lower, or Río Abajo, portion of New Mexico. It would certainly be dangerous, if not fatal, to find Colonel Archuleta disputing his passage. Any admission that he was not annexing the lands west of the Río Grande would invite such resistance. Kearny's letter to Governor Armijo that Magoffin and Cooke carried with them from Bent's Fort supports this explanation.

Two of John C. Frémont's biographers—Herbert Bashford and Harr Wagner—in discussing Magoffin's role in this conquest, state that Kearny did not seem to understand the situation—that is, the implied if not express agreement by Magoffin that American annexation would stop at the Río Grande. On the contrary, I am sure General Kearny understood it perfectly, better than Magoffin, Armijo, or Archuleta, because he knew all the facts. What was the "situation" Bashford and Wagner thought Stephen Kearny did not understand? Was it the agreement Magoffin probably made with Armijo and Archuleta that the United States halt its annexation at the Río Grande? Was he not and should he not have been far more concerned with occupying and holding *all* of New Mexico, peaceably if possible, and then continuing his march to California in accordance with the June 3 and June 18 orders from the President? Why was Magoffin there at all, and why did he propose anything to the Mexican officials? Was it not to aid General Kearny in successfully accomplishing the purposes of the administration? That being so, it was necessary that Kearny act in keeping with both the letter and the spirit of his instructions, rather than "understand" or carry out an agreement James Magoffin may have made. In whatever particular way in which Magoffin's undertaking ran counter to the orders given Kearny, the latter was forced to disregard or even to repudiate it.

A recent writer on Santa Fe adds the comment that after General Kearny's entrance into the city, Magoffin reminded him of the promises he, himself, had made Colonel Archuleta. Archuleta, argued Magoffin, must be given either the territory promised him or a position of authority under the new government. General Kearny was busy, says this commentator, and did not send for Archuleta.

Several years later, when everything connected with Stephen Kearny was anathema to Senator Benton, he put the worst possible construction on the General's actions in these matters. Benton not only gave Magoffin sole credit for the bloodless conquest of New Mexico but actually charged that the General's annexation of the whole province was a violation of Magoffin's agreement with Archuleta. He also criticized Kearny severely for not mentioning Magoffin's role in his official report. Benton was one of the foremost champions of the westward expansion of the United States. Yet rage and prejudice forced him into the inconsistent position of criticizing General Kearny for furthering that expansion.

Better than any man in Washington in 1846 (save the President and Secretary of War), Senator Benton knew everything about the orders sent to Kearny. In one place they read "in case you conquer Santa Fe (and with it will be included the department or State of New Mexico)." Yet Benton carefully omitted mentioning those orders when he criticized Kearny for following them. Benton laid the blame for the Taos uprising in the fall of 1846 on Kearny's failure to abide by Magoffin's agreement. (Kearny had left New Mexico before that occurrence, and Sterling Price had succeeded him as military governor. The insurrection was unquestionably a serious affair, but Archuleta's disappointment was only one of many things that provoked the outbreak.) Bashford and Wagner's comments illustrate how Benton influenced the points of view of later authors writing about this period.

Cooke's return was most opportune since he had just traversed the road over which the army would march into Santa Fe. He told General Kearny that even though Armijo and his regulars had fled to the south, the forces he had raised locally had previously been

139

sent out to defend Apache Pass and were perhaps as yet unaware of the Governor's desertion. For fear this militia might still carry out its orders to fight, Cooke's practiced eye had scouted out a more circuitous route over which the General might detour his command if the defenders still occupied the pass. Therefore, General Kearny placed Cooke in command of the advance guard.

On the sixteenth the column halted at San Miguel, the most populous place yet reached. Here the alcalde balked at taking the oath and appealed to the village priest for support. The General asked both men to accompany him onto a roof where he proposed to address the people in the same way he had at Las Vegas. The priest objected—he would not speak to the people in support of the invaders, no matter what force was used. The General assured him he need say nothing but merely accompany him to the roof. The priest complied in the presence of his flock, but continued to argue against the American invasion. Kearny admired the man's courage and allowed him to continue for a while. Finally he told him that his remarks were silly, that he and any of the clergy like him labored under a great misunderstanding of the intentions of the government of the United States. It did not propose to disturb the religion, churches, or priests of New Mexico. However, if any churchman stirred up the people to oppose the advance of the soldiers, his clerical robe would not protect him from punishment. This lecture was delivered before townspeople who had long been under the sway of this priest. When the padre saw that none of his arguments had any effect, he invited the American general to have a glass of Taos brandy with him.

After the alcalde had taken the oath of allegiance, Kearny joked with the padre over their brandy, and when he took his leave the priest cordially embraced him and they shook hands in a friendly farewell. More Mexicans met the Americans with predictions of fierce fighting; others contemptuously dismissed the idea or offered General Kearny unsolicited advice about how to vanquish the cowering Armijo. Kearny kept his own counsel and let the heralds and rumormongers do all the talking.

August 17 was an anticlimax to volunteers spoiling for battle, though not to veterans like General Kearny. By early forenoon rumors increased that quarrels had broken out among the Mexican officers and that the General himself had fled to Albuquerque. Passers-by reported that the Mexican regulars had marched south also and that the canyon had been deserted. Some miles back the trail had begun to draw away from the open prairie, as if to seek the shelter of a series of low, pine-covered hills. The trees were becoming taller and thicker. The stream beside their line of march sang more loudly as they climbed the mountain pass. At the upper edge of a forested amphitheater, the column paused before the ruins of Pecos. The amphitheater was admirably sheltered from gales by the hills half encircling it, yet it was airy and commanded a long view down the Pecos River to the wide plains. The largest building had long been a barbaric temple maintained, tradition said, by descendants of Montezuma. Until a few years previously, a sacred fire had burned there for unknown ages. A curious legend persisted that the ancient inhabitants had always looked for a miraculous return of Montezuma from the East. In some Indian villages, many of the more simple natives even saw Stephen Kearny's conquering arrival as the fulfillment of the ancient prophecy. He came from the east, and his conciliatory proclamations were in keeping with the release from bondage of the Spanish-Mexican oppression.

The morning of August 18 was rainy. Before the army started its march, General Order Thirteen was read at the head of the column. General Kearny declared the country annexed to the United States as a part of Texas and enjoined every American soldier to respect the persons and property of its inhabitants. Lieutenant Hammond and twenty dragoons reconnoitered the canyon ahead before the column moved forward. It was deep and narrow and surrounded by cliffs. Determined men could have safely hurled tons of rock on the invaders. Although an ideal spot for defense, no Mexican disputed its passage. On the contrary, evidence multiplied that even in preparing to defend Santa Fe, the enemy had gravely blundered. Instead of availing himself of the canyon's natural advantages, Armijo had clearly planned to fight in advance of that location— if at all. One hundred yards before its narrowest gateway, a not too formidable abatis had been constructed in more open and less easily defended ground. Even with artillery massed behind the abatis, the position could have been easily turned if not first reduced by the howitzers. Emory properly described Armijo's arrangement as "very stupid."

Kearny was determined to enter the capital before nightfall even though it was twenty-nine miles from his camp that morning. The road was bad, the horses were on their last legs, and the army was desperately short of supplies. However, Kearny knew the psychological advantage of pressing his success before mischance could intervene. A little after noon the vanguard met two Mexicans who had ridden out to meet the invaders. One was the acting secretary of state of New Mexico. This official brought General Kearny a letter from Juan Bautista Vigil y Alared, the lieutenant governor, which told of Armijo's flight. Vigil explained his readiness to receive the General in Santa Fe and extend him the hospitality of the city.

It was three in the afternoon when General Kearny and his staff caught their first view of Santa Fe. Like Las Vegas, it reminded the observers of a great brickyard. The rain ceased as the officers waited for the troops behind them to come up. About a quarter to five the bugles were blown for the advance. As the head of the column rounded the last turn and marched down San Miguel Street toward the plaza, the sun burst from under the clouds massed on the mountaintops. Ranks closed and every man straightened instinctively as the General led his three troops of dragoons, followed by the infantry, into the city. For men just finishing a nine-hundred-mile march they made a gallant appearance—the first troop mounted on black, the second on white, and the third on sorrel horses. Colonel Doniphan's regiment followed the infantry through the crowded streets. Every flag, banner, and pennon of the expedition was unfurled to wave proudly in the afternoon breeze. Even sullen onlookers were impressed.

The column marched around the plaza, and General Kearny and his staff at last halted before the main door of the ancient Palace of the Governors. There he dismounted and with outstretched hand advanced to the long covered porch of the Palace where Lieutenant Governor Vigil and a score of officials and townspeople awaited him. There was a ceremonial handshake. Vigil offered the American officers some wine and brandy. "We were too thirsty to judge of its merits," wrote Emory, "anything liquid and cool was palatable."

Even while the glasses were being filled and passed, General Kearny bade some of his dragoons rig up a temporary flagpole on the roof of the palace. As the sun sank behind the western mountains the Stars and Stripes fluttered out in the wind where all could see. The flag of the invaders waved peacefully at the end of the Santa Fe Trail. Drums rolled and bugles blared as the footsore infantrymen presented arms in the plaza. On the hills to the east one of the howitzers rent the air with a thirteen-gun salute.

Stepping out from the doorway, the General lifted his hand for silence, and declared in loud and deliberate tones:

> I, Stephen W. Kearny, General of the Army of the United States, have taken possession of the province of New Mexico in the name of the government of the United States, and in the name of that government do hereby advise and instruct the inhabitants of this country to deliver their arms and to surrender absolutely to the government of the United States in whose name I promise to this country and its people protection to their persons, lives and property, defending them in their homes and possessions against any savage tribe. For this government is very powerful to protect you in any untoward event, and in this manner I take this province of New Mexico for the benefit of the United States.

Governor Vigil and his fellow officials had surrendered with the best grace they could muster. There is a note of pathos in this portion of Vigil's response to the proclamation:

> It is not for us to determine the boundaries of nations. The cabinets of Mexico and Washington will arrange these differences. It is for us to obey and respect the established authorities, no matter what may be our private opinions. . . . No one in this world can successfully resist the power of him who is stronger. In the name of the entire department I swear obedience to the Northern Republic and I tender my respect to its laws and authority.

But among the little houses in the narrow streets fear and grief ruled those of the populace who had not fled to the hills. The poor and illiterate classes cowered in dread of being branded "U.S." on the cheeks as they had been told would happen. Women sobbed and covered their faces with *rebozos*, in shame and dread. The American soldiers would all be turned loose like wild animals to abuse them. Their churches, too, would be desecrated. Armijo and his minions had told them so.

Soon after the flag-raising, the American officers were escorted by Governor Vigil to the home of a Mexican official where dinner was served. The latest historian of Santa Fe gives a report of this occasion, which seems based on the tradition still lingering there of Stephen Kearny's conduct. The General's courtesy, says Mr. Horgan, was real and perfect. He could put himself in the place of others. The men he was talking with had surrendered their city and province to him, yet he made them feel like his hosts. He was at ease and so were they. Ever afterward the mountain air over the city would be colored by the stars and stripes of his flag. It was the greatest change that had yet befallen the ancient city of Santa Fe. At the dinner he wore his dress frock coat of blue with gold epaulettes, gold pipings, and gold buttons. Belt and saber were laid aside, but he strapped them on when dinner was over. Rising, he said that he and his officers were tired after the day's long march. Thanking his Mexican hosts, the General returned with his staff to the Palace of the Governors.

With growing wonder they strolled through the empty rooms. In Armijo's recent office they were amazed to find dried human ears tacked on the walls. How better could the absent Governor have impressed his personality on these men of another breed, come to replace him? The Palace made some barbaric pretensions to grandeur; it possessed a large ballroom—but its floor was of packed earth. Some of the inner doors were covered with buffalo hides painted to resemble grained wood. Decay was too evident but that was appropriate, for an old regime had just passed awayy.

Hours later, the worn-out mules of the wagon train were still dragging their loads over the rough roadway to the hilltops overlooking the fallen capital. It was so dark before the occupation was complete that some of the army pitched the few available tents in no formal order in the near-by fields and hills. There was no feed for the starving horses, and they had to be staked on barren sand. Nearly all the soldiers spent a supperless night. Many had no bedding or even tents because these were still on the wagons that did not arrive until well into the night. Kearny and some of his officers threw their blankets down on the floors of the Palace. These were hard beds, but repose in them was easier because of the comforting thought that a long, difficult, and dangerous mission had been successfully accomplished without the shedding of any man's blood. General Kearny had earned the right to slumber soundly on that momentous August 18.

12. Santa Fe

AUGUST IS A BEAUTIFUL MONTH in Santa Fe. At nearly seven thousand feet above sea level the nights are always crisp and the skies so clear a man can reach up and clutch a handful of stars. The days are warm in the sun, pleasantly cool in the shade, and nearly every afternoon brings a sudden downpour that ceases as quickly as it came. Only the dampened dust, the glistening leaves of the poplars around the plaza, and an acrid tang in the air remain to tell that it has rained at all.

August 19, 1846, was a typically fine day for the busy army. The first task was to find pasture for the starving livestock. Horses and cattle were driven to meadows on Galisteo Creek where there was good grass and plentiful water. In a few weeks the army should once more have serviceable mounts.

At nine o'clock in the morning the citizens of the city were summoned to the plaza, where General Kearny repeated his declaration of annexation and announced that he was governor of New Mexico. He emphasized the peaceful intentions of his government and stated that all existing civil officials would retain their offices for the time being, provided they took the oath of allegiance to the United States. The alcalde and other local dignitaries stepped forward, and the required oaths were administered. Many of the populace came up to shake hands with General Kearny, hailing him "Governor." One old man of ninety-two embraced him and wept as he stumbled away.

A hundred-foot flagpole was immediately constructed for the plaza. Kearny ordered a strong fortification erected as soon as possible for better defense of the city. His engineers selected a low hilltop not more than a third of a mile northeast of the plaza. As it commanded every part of the town and was itself beyond gunshot of the more distant hills, the General approved the location. It was mapped by the twenty-second. Within a week more than one hundred laborers were busily at work on what was to become Fort Marcy.

In the first few days after the occupation headmen of the Pueblo Indians began to slip in from their little villages in the hills. They were a fine, hardy-looking people, and while shy toward the strange officers, they were disposed to be friendly. They wanted to gaze upon this warrior who had come from the east and overthrown, as if by magic, the Spanish-Mexican rule they feared and despised. Yes, he was white as foretold, he had come with the rising sun, and Armijo and oppressors like him had fled. Gladly they made their submission and took the required oaths of allegiance. They were among the best and most peaceable inhabitants of the land. Their adherence to the American cause was a victory in the truest sense.

A different type of native also visited Santa Fe. These were the Navahos, dreaded both by Mexicans and Pueblos, who looked to their new rulers to protect them from the wilder tribes. "Naked, thin and savage looking fellows," wrote Emory, "dropped in . . . they ate, drank and slept all the time, noticing nothing." Emory was probably wrong here. The Navahos had heard that Kearny was going to enforce his laws against them—absurd laws to curb their time-honored right to raid, pillage, and kill Mexicans and Pueblos whenever they felt the urge. Doubtless they had come to size up the General's medicine and report how strong it looked.

Many of the townspeople who had fled began to straggle back as reports spread that the Americans were not mistreating the inhabitants. On the twentieth one of the returning fugitives was a leading priest of Santa Fe. A Missouri volunteer described him as "a fat, jolly fellow who bets high at monte, loves good liquor and attends all the fandangoes of respectable people." The padre called on General Kearny to explain that the women in his family had persuaded him to run away. The General sternly told him it would have been more in keeping with his office to have remained with his flock.

On August 22, General Kearny issued another proclamation. In addition to the conciliatory statements of his earlier address, he called on all residents who had not returned to their homes to do so at once under penalty of being considered enemies and having their possessions confiscated. He also promised to protect the inhabitants from the raids and seizures to which they had so long been subjected by their enemies, the Utes and the Navahos. This proclamation was signed by General Kearny as governor of New Mexico. Within the week he announced the annexation of the entire province. This disposed of the halfway measure involved in asserting only the claim of Texas to the lands east of the Río Grande. Probably Kearny decided this was the best way to end any secret claims Colonel Archuleta might make to western New Mexico. It was better that everyone know that the United States claimed and was exercising sovereignty over all the Southwest between Texas and California. This news was received quietly enough by the populace, but Archuleta and a few malcontents felt deeply aggrieved and bided their time.

General Kearny's first official letter after taking Santa Fe was to Brigadier General Wool at Chihuahua on August 22. It informed him of events in New Mexico and promised to send him all the men that could be spared as soon as Colonel Price with the Second Missouri Volunteers and Captain Allen and the Mormon Battalion arrived. The General expressed the opinion that the region about him was subdued and peaceably inclined and that he, himself, would be leaving for California quite soon. Someone brought word of an antiquated printing press at Taos. It was lugged down to Santa Fe so that copies of the proclamation might be struck off in large numbers and given wide distribution.

General Kearny accomplished much of importance during his six weeks as governor of New Mexico, but probably the most far-reaching achievement was an action set in motion a few days after his arrival. Colonel Doniphan and Willard P. Hall of the Missouri volunteers were summoned. Knowing they were lawyers, Kearny asked them to undertake a study of the laws of New Mexico, and to suggest whatever modifications were necessary to make them compatible with American institutions and the Constitution of the United States. For greater clarity and practical application, Doniphan and Hall were asked to codify these laws. Doniphan called in to aid them two other men of singularly varied talents. The first was Francis P. Blair, Jr., one of the scouts hired by William Bent to spy out the army's advance. He, too, was a lawyer. The second, another member of his own regiment and destined to be its historian, was John T. Hughes.

Here we find Stephen Kearny rising above the plane of mere military command to the stature of statesmanship. Though the subject matter was dry enough, there is both drama and excitement in this work of Doniphan and his associates. This applies even to their backgrounds. Hall was only twenty-six years old and a private in Colonel Doniphan's regiment. In this task they shared the labors and responsibilities as equals—an example of democracy at its finest. During this same August, 1846, Hall was elected to Congress from his district in Missouri. It is a tribute to their versatility that these men could readily lay aside military duties to undertake such a juridical assignment. They brought it to completion swiftly and so successfully that over one hundred years later their labors still form the basis of the laws of New Mexico. When these fighting Missourians, suddenly turned lawmakers, delivered their finished report to General Kearny, he proclaimed it the basic law of New Mexico on September 22. Ever since it has been known as the Kearny Code.

On September 22, General Kearny also issued a bill of rights for the territory of New Mexico based on the Kearny Code. It consists of thirteen sections and is clearly derived from both the Declaration of Independence and the American Bill of Rights. In some phrases the altered language was especially designed to fit local conditions, especially the thirteenth clause—"no priest . . . shall ever be compelled to bear arms, or to serve on juries, work on roads or perform military duty." Since we shall later find one or two associates of Stephen Kearny berating him for not recognizing their part in some of his accomplishments, it is important to note here a striking instance to the contrary. General Kearny gave full credit to Alexander

Doniphan and Willard Hall for their work as lawmakers. His was the mind that saw the need for the task and selected experts most capable of executing it, but theirs were the intellects and the crowded hours of its accomplishment.

The best Spanish scholar in the entire Army of the West was Captain David Waldo of that versatile First Missouri. The General entrusted him with the task of translating the Kearny Code into Spanish together with the Constitution of the United States. These documents were immediately printed in both Spanish and English and widely distributed.

Although out of its chronological order, it is proper to note here that on January 11, 1847, Secretary of War Marcy in a letter to Kearny mildly rebuked him for the Kearny Code, with a reminder that only Congress could confer civil rights on the people of New Mexico. Kearny was informed that the President had not approved this Code and that it was not to be carried into effect. On the other hand, wrote Marcy, he was upheld for setting up a civil government in New Mexico as the necessary sequence of his conquest of the country. (Marcy's own instructions of June 3, 1846, expressly directed Kearny to do that very thing.) Long afterward, a historian of the Mexican War quoted one of General Kearny's proclamations in California, "Americans and Californians are now one people." He echoed Secretary Marcy's criticism by commenting "with the same exaggeration of his authority as at Santa Fe." I have found no record of Kearny's own reaction to Marcy's criticism. At the time it was written the General was already in California and in no position to do anything about New Mexico. It is more important that the Kearny Code has continued as the basis of the laws of that state to this very day in the mode of thought, legal practice, and customs of the people of the area. To borrow from the language of today's sociological jurisprudence, the survival of the Kearny Code despite the disapproval of the Polk administration and Congress is a happy example of how "living law" so often prevails over "positive law."

As a tactful gesture to the prevailing faith of the country, General Kearny (himself an Episcopalian) attended Mass at St. Francis Church near the plaza on Sunday, August 23. All of his staff accompanied him. He carefully observed this practice as long as he was in New Mexico. On one occasion he and his officers carried candles in a religious procession, although he later told Susan Magoffin he felt he was "making a fool of himself." One Sunday, Kearny paid a sick call at Dr. Griffin's improvised hospital. A staff officer was ill with tuberculosis, and in a manner both confident and fatherly Kearny encouraged the young man to hope for a speedy recovery. He told him of his experience at the church and that the musicians played the same tunes at the services as for the dancing though in a different tempo. The General was in fine spirits and left the patient greatly cheered.

On the night of August 27, General Kearny gave a large ball at the Palace of the Governors as a part of his policy of conciliation. It was a new experience for most of the common people to see the interior of the Palace, so four or five hundred persons eagerly flocked there. It was a motley throng; American army officers in gold-braided dress uniforms, dignified Spanish and Mexican dons in picturesque contrast, sturdy traders in ill-fitting "store clothes." Then there were the gamblers—female as well as male—ready to lure customers to their tables down the street. On display was a mural painted by a local artist. It showed General Kearny bestowing a scroll on a peasant on which the word "Liberated" was inscribed. A plow, cross, and cannon filled the background.

The ballroom was hung with all the flags and banners of the Army of the West. The *señors* and *señoritas* of Santa Fe studied with interest the handwork of the women of Missouri who had sewed and embroidered the company pennons of the First Missouri. The General paid marked attention to the senior priest among the guests. Dancing was alternately American and Spanish, with even some Indian numbers performed. Each race found interest in the steps and movements of the others. Not everyone present fully enjoyed the occasion. Captain Turner did not approve the universal habit of smoking by both men and women. He wrote that among the numerous Americans at the ball were "several genteel men and many rowdies." Probably because of the thick cloud of smoke, thought Turner, General Kearny became ill and had to go to bed.

Friendly gestures like this ball helped win over the populace. One of the soldiers writing home summed it up: "General Kearny is fast reaping for himself a crown of unfading laurels for his affable and kind treatment of the people and the wise and statesmanlike policies which he pursues." Even his attitude toward the fleeing Armijo won him friends. A few days after Kearny's arrival the former governor sent a message indicating that he wished to return and wanted to know on what terms he could do so. Soon afterward it appeared that Don Manuel had merely used this ruse to gain more time for his flight. Evidence accumulated that Armijo had disregarded many opportunities to put up a good defense. Reinforcements were en route to Santa Fe from El Paso del Norte. All counted for naught so long as the former governor lacked the will and the courage to fight. The townspeople soon came to have the heartiest contempt for him. Nevertheless, General Kearny wisely adopted a policy of forbearance toward his fallen foe. In referring to Armijo in one of his speeches he declared: "His power is departed but he will return and be as one of you. When he shall return you are not to molest him. I am your governor, henceforth look to me for protection."

Kearny's conciliatory policy was not unanimously approved by his soldiers. Many believed the Mexicans treacherous. More than one American grumbled that their general would punish a volunteer for offenses which were excused when committed by the Mexicans.

The General's gubernatorial duties were varied. Monthly license fees were fixed for the merchants, a treasurer and collector were appointed for the city, and more important, a burdensome stamp tax on all legal documents was abolished.

Brief mention has been made of Susan Magoffin at Bent's Fort. She and her husband drove into Santa Fe on August 30—the first American woman to arrive after the conquest—and established their home near the church. There General Kearny called upon them, and there began that charming interlude between the nineteen-year-old matron and the General that lightened the few remaining weeks before he departed for California.

Susan adored her vigorous young husband, but she quickly found in General Kearny a most agreeable and fatherly friend. No doubt she was flattered by the concern and gentle raillery with which he treated her. Undoubtedly his few hours in her company were to him like an oasis in this desert of soldiers, officials, patient staring natives, and the incessant demands all of them made. He had long known the gay social life of St. Louis. Something of that atmosphere had been retained in the more modest round of entertaining and theater parties he and Mrs. Kearny enjoyed at Fort Leavenworth. Forced to spend most of his time on the problems of a rough frontier, Stephen Kearny welcomed the contrast offered by the refinements and amenities that only flourish where ladies are a part of existence. Fortunately, Susan Magoffin faithfully entered in her diary everything that happened and what she heard or observed. Because of this, we have more details of Stephen Kearny's life during those few weeks of September, 1846, than for almost any other period of his fifty-four years.

Of their first meeting in Santa Fe she wrote: "I had made up my mind that the General was quite a different man in every respect . . . [he is] very agreeable in conversation and manners, conducts himself with ease, can receive and return compliments, a few of which I gave him." Like the other residents of Santa Fe, Mrs. Magoffin heard "constant rhumours [sic] that Gen. Armijo had raised a large fource [sic] of some five or six thousand men . . . and is on the march to retake his kingdom. . . . The Navajos have petitioned him (General Kearny) to make a treaty with them . . . as they deem the Gen. something superhuman since he has walked in so quietly and taken possession of the pallace of the Great Armijo, their former fear."

What seemed reliable reports reached General Kearny that Armijo and a Mexican officer named Ugarte had united their forces 150 miles to the south. Ugarte was said to have five hundred regulars and some artillery from Mexico. Armijo was supposed to be heading north with a considerable army that was being augmented in the towns along his line of march. The stories were too persistent to disregard, so the General decided to investigate. A force of over seven hundred men was quickly organized. Kearny's staff and escort totaled another twenty-five men. Colonel Doniphan was charged with the command of all the forces remaining in Santa Fe.

The twelve-day tour that started on September 2 took the detachment down the Río del Norte as far as San Tomé. Every town and pueblo en route was visited, and a large part of the province's population was given a close view of the new Governor and his troops. Armijo, the primary target of the expedition, was nowhere to be found, but the psychological results of the expedition were most beneficial to the American cause. Several incidents enlivened the tour. One has been often repeated to General Kearny's disadvantage. While preparing the second day's start, the General rode along the lines. The air was hot and dry. He noticed that most of the volunteers were in shirt sleeves. Sternly he ordered every man to don his coat or be dismissed from the service. This produced surprised scowls and mutterings, but all obeyed until Kearny reached a Captain Reid's command and saw that Reid had not heeded his orders. "Captain," he demanded, "have your men no coats?" "Some of them have and some of them have not," Reid replied. "Make all of your men wear them," the General insisted. "The Government has paid them liberally for their clothing and they must wear them."

Unabashed, Reid retorted, "They have not one received a dollar from the government and what money they could raise or clothing they could spare, has been expended for bread." One volunteer added in his diary that Reid told General Kearny that his men had come here not to dress but to fight, and had had to buy bread while on half-rations because of the neglect of Kearny's commissary. As to dismissal, they were not fighting for wages and if there was no place for them in the army, they would provide for themselves and fight the enemy where they found him. The writer said that General Kearny bit his lip and rode off to give the order for the day's march. Another account makes it appear that Kearny had to be reminded that the men's pay was in arrears. This report is a little hard to credit. (Back at Fort Leavenworth he and his paymaster had studied the matter of money supply. In comparative ignorance both of his ultimate destination and the size of his army, Kearny had advised the paymaster as best he could. The funds available to them were undoubtedly quite limited.)

The fullest chronicle of the expedition closes this episode with both praise and criticism of General Kearny. He was "a skillful, able and sagacious officer well fitted for the command of veteran troops, and the receipt of his commission as brigadier general gave general satisfaction. His greatest error was to force on volunteers the same discipline and austere treatment he would accord regulars under his command. The former are bred to freedom, the latter trained to obedience." The writer commented that it was an error common among regular army officers in command of volunteer troops. Three-quarters of Kearny's command were volunteers. The incident of September 3 is undoubtedly responsible in part for the epithet "harsh disciplinarian" so often fastened on Kearny. Probably in this case he feared the effect a tatterdemalion cavalcade would have on the populace of the towns through which they were about to ride. None of these communities had ever laid eyes on an American soldier. It was natural for a veteran commander to want his units to present a soldierly appearance. The threats of dismissal from the service sounded harsh. More than once we have seen Kearny exhibit a better understanding of human nature and the make-up of a volunteer. If he was censurable in this instance, we can recall some other great American commanders who went even farther under provocations; General George Patton comes to mind for one.

A more pleasant episode was the visit Kearny and some of his officers paid to the pueblo of Santo Domingo. Here the chieftains had their young men decked in war regalia and put on a spirited exhibition of horsemanship and a sham battle. Later a repast was served in the parlor of the village priest.

The whole valley of the Río Grande presented the same picture of green fields and irrigation ditches, and every few miles could be seen the little villages of low, flat-roofed adobe houses so strange to the eyes of the Americans. Wild, craggy, treeless mountains were on either hand, and the valley contained red earth, brown adobes, and brown-skinned villagers. In every hamlet the natives stared curiously at the soldiers. Each race found the other equally strange. Sometimes the townspeople even smiled at the Americans; at least they showed no hostility, not even fear. The Pueblos knew the difference between raiding Navahos, plundering Mexican soldiery, and these strange-tongued white men who paid cash for one's melons and grapes, eggs and chickens.

Between Padilla and Peralta stood the home of the Chavez family. Here young Franco Chavez took leave of the General after proudly presenting him to his kinfolk. In the private chapel of Don José, the officers attended Mass. After the service the priest surprised the visitors by delivering an eloquent speech in praise of the power and justice of the United States.

On General Kearny's return to Santa Fe, a formal flag-raising was held at the two-hundred-foot staff just erected. The pole was the loftiest object in all Santa Fe, and townspeople joined the soldiers in cheers as the Stars and Stripes were run up. The tang of fall was now in the air. Both days and nights were growing cooler. The high mountains were splashed with gold of quaking aspens touched by autumnal frosts. Within a week newly fallen snow would be sighted on some of the loftier peaks. Heavier dews lay on the brown meadows in the morning. It was time for men who must ride far into the unknown to bestir themselves—time to spur on to California for their rendezvous with Manifest Destiny.

General Kearny wrote the Adjutant General that he planned to leave Santa Fe about September 25 for California. He was taking with him Major Sumner and three hundred of the First Dragoons. He proposed to descend the Río Grande some two hundred miles, thence to the headwaters of the Gila, down it to the Colorado, and crossing that river, continue to the Pacific Ocean. Once there he planned to march north to Monterey. He hoped to reach California by the end of November. One request in this letter deserves attention, "in the event of our getting possession of Upper California, of establishing civil government there, securing peace and quiet among the inhabitants and precluding the possibility of the Mexicans again having control there, that I may be permitted to leave there next summer with the First Dragoons, and march them back to Fort Leavenworth."

When this letter was written, most of the important towns along the seacoast of California had been captured by the United States Navy and Frémont's Battalion of Mounted Riflemen. Kearny, of course, had no knowledge of those facts, and was only to learn them from Kit Carson at Socorro on October 6. The Mexicans *were* again "to have control there" (over considerable areas at least). But is it not strange that Kearny mentioned such future happenings as possibilities on September 16 in New Mexico? This must be set down as either a striking coincidence or a remarkable example of prescience. It is hard to recall any historical parallel. General Kearny also reported that Fort Marcy had been completed and could now accommodate a garrison of one thousand soldiers.

Questions involving the medical corps arose in the last weeks of General Kearny's administration. Dr. Vaughn had recently arrived from Bent's Fort with the soldiers who had recovered their health. Complaints of inattention to the sick and neglect of duty were so persistent that the surgeon requested a court of inquiry into his conduct. This body censured Dr. Vaughn. Opinion was sharply divided on this subject. Apparently the primary cause for criticism was the inadequacy of medical supplies. Probably no one with the Army of the West was responsible for that fact. However, General Kearny upheld the court's finding. One unfriendly critic blamed him and not the medical officer.

With characteristic speed and energy General Kearny pushed preparations for the California adventure. By present-day standards, the efforts made could hardly qualify as preparations. The Quartermaster's and Commissary Departments were just as backward and inefficient as the demonstration they had given on the long trek from Fort Leavenworth. Even while the Quartermaster's officers pleaded their inability to furnish teams, fine specimens of mules were publicly sold in Santa Fe at a higher price than the military would pay. For the thousand-mile ordeal awaiting the expedition to California, the best could not be good enough. The economies thus practiced were to be paid for at a usurious rate in the blood and suffering of brave men.

The authorities responsible for feeding the army seem to have operated on the time-honored principle that "anything is good enough" for soldiers. "Anything" too often was eaten as an alternative to starvation, so Taos flour and salt pork were standard supplies that, according to critics, required a good appetite to relish. Such a situation in a country where cattle and sheep roamed in goodly numbers was inexcusable. The Paymaster Department was even more lacking in meeting its responsibilities. If soldiers are not adequately fed they will of necessity augment their rations by their own purchases. However, a necessary corollary is that they be paid promptly in something that will serve as money. Apparently Washington never calculated the need of supplying seventeen hundred men with a practical medium of exchange. Except for the limited funds carried by the Paymaster from Fort Leavenworth, no cash was furnished the army. Nearly every soldier's pay was now far in arrears. With no cash available, brass buttons cut from their uniforms began to circulate at twenty-five cents a button. Ingenious soldiers managed to carve wooden buttons as substitutes, less handy ones used wooden pins, and even twigs and thorns. General Kearny could hardly purchase supplies for the trip to California in such a currency. Drafts on banks in Missouri or the national treasury were almost impossible to negotiate in Santa Fe, and entirely out of the question in the smaller towns. It seems almost a miracle that the General and his staff ever completed preparations for their departure.

Even while planning the journey, local problems still demanded attention. The Utes and Navahos continued to menace the more civilized population. On September 15, General Kearny ordered Colonel Doniphan to send two of his companies into the Ute country as a warning, and three more to patrol the region beyond Albuquerque where the Navahos were threatening. A week later the General bluntly warned some visiting Utes that they must behave or expect unpleasant consequences.

The critical Private Edwards was continuing his caustic comments, but now they were directed at General Kearny. While enduring hardships in the campaign against the elusive Navahos, he wrote:

General Kearny has taken the treacherous population of New Mexico under his fatherly care and protection; and looking with an eye of pity upon the bold aggressions of those adventurous savages, he has concluded to send parties out for the purpose of bringing the aggressors to justice or to make a treaty of peace with them and seal it with hostages, if thought necessary.

Immediately after the General had departed for California the same youth wrote home that the General had become unpopular with the American settlers in Santa Fe and declared the reason a "very just one." Those Americans who believed the only good Indian a dead one probably agreed. It seems that Indians had stolen horses and cattle from a certain American. The injured party proposed to hire men to pursue and punish the marauders. He asked Kearny's approval of a deal whereby this private posse would be paid by all the plunder they could take. As an alternative he proposed that Kearny pay wages to his men for such services. The General told him that the men he wanted to hire made their living by plundering Indians. Kearny would let him off that time but said that if he ever repeated such tactics he would cut off his ears.

On September 19, General Kearny attended a dinner party in his honor. We are indebted to Susan Magoffin for the menu and other details. Four young Indian girls served the courses. The first was a thin soup with noodles, followed by another thick soup containing bits of meat and vegetables and boiled rice thickened with butter and covered by slices of hard-boiled eggs. The meat was roasted, boiled, chopped, and stewed with a gravy of hot red peppers. The appearance of champagne gave General Kearny the opportunity to toast the company. "The United States and Mexico," he proposed, "they are now united, may no one ever think of parting." The brother of the hostess responded and the New Mexicans present shouted "Viva, viva." Then desserts were brought on. The guests were offered boiled custard seasoned with cinnamon and nutmeg, cake pudding, and luscious grapes. Susan observed that "the Gen. drank and enjoyed the Champain, he has been under the Doctor for some days past and consequently could now do justice to the dishes before him after his fast." Susan did not add that Dr. Griffin's office was overcrowded the next day, but that seems a reasonable assumption.

General Kearny's last days in Santa Fe were crowded with official tasks. On September 22 he set up the government which was to carry on after both he and Colonel Doniphan departed. These appointments marked the true beginning of American civil government in New Mexico. Both the new American influence and the old regime were represented. The choice of Charles Bent as the first

American governor was a particularly happy one. Although an American and popular with both fur trappers and Santa Fe traders, his wife was a member of a leading New Mexican family and he was widely known and trusted in native circles. His murder by the Taos insurgents in January, 1847, was as much of a loss to the Mexican population as to the American conquerors. Other appointees of General Kearny also rendered distinguished service. Francis P. Blair, Jr., the new district attorney, was destined for a career in which light and shadow were strangely mingled. Some of Kearny's other appointees bore names that recur frequently in the later history of New Mexico. The caliber of these officeholders is another evidence of the statesmanship exhibited by Stephen Kearny.

Undoubtedly many citizens of the territory were sincere in their cheerful acceptance of the change of sovereignty. They were disgusted with Armijo's misrule and looked forward to greater freedom and security under the American flag. Others who at heart were less friendly dissembled their feelings. Probably both sentiments moved the signers of a memorial to the President of the United States that was circulated just as General Kearny prepared to depart. It recited former Governor Armijo's conduct prior to the occupation and extolled the patriotism of the signers and their willingness to resist the invaders. Armijo, the memorial stated, had been shifty and irresolute in his course and had insultingly refused their assistance. With more emphasis than grammar it concluded, "Mr. Armijo done nothing and can say that 'I have lost all including honor.'" Many of the signers occupied positions under the new government. Attached to the memorial was a copy of Colonel Archuleta's report to the President of Mexico about his own efforts to resist. On the night of the twenty-third local merchants and the newly appointed officials gave a farewell ball at the Palace in honor of the departing General. Susan Magoffin was the belle of the occasion. It was her last meeting with General Kearny.

On September 24 the General officially advised Washington that he would "take off" for California the next day. He again mentioned the orders he was leaving for the Mormon Battalion and California Rangers to follow him. (He had recently authorized the organization of the latter.) The General by now had received a letter from Colonel Price written twelve miles west of the Arkansas River crossing on August 10. He had petitioned Kearny to send him supplies (again the Commissary Department had fallen short of its obligations). The General had arranged for provisions to be sent back from wagon trains then en route to Santa Fe from Bent's Fort. He had instructed Colonel Doniphan to leave for Chihuahua as soon as Colonel Price's forces marched in. His letter told of an important change in the General's plans. He had become convinced that horses were not well adapted to service in this southwestern country and that his expedition could not possibly reach California on horseback. Therefore he had required the Quartermaster to remount the dragoons on mules and had ordered the horses returned to Fort Leavenworth for service elsewhere. He would try to reach Monterey by December 12.

Then by midday on the twenty-fifth, General Kearny and his staff assembled in the plaza; Major Swords, Captain Turner, Captain Johnston, Dr. Griffin, and Lieutenants Emory and Warner of the Engineer Corps were on hand. The engineers had just added a draughtsman, the artist John Mix Stanley. Most of the drawings that we have of the country traversed by the expedition are his work. Some miles down the road five companies of dragoons awaited them —all that now remained of the diminished Army of the West. As Captain Cooke later expressed it, they were about to take "a leap in the dark of a thousand miles of wild plain and mountain." The thought exhilarated both officers and men. Every one believed this march would offer one more chance at the Mexicans. For once they were to be proved right; for a number of them it would also be their last chance to serve their country. But that risk always awaits a soldier, and they could not be expected to think much about it when the bugles sounded the advance. Probably they were more conscious that they were parting from comrades of long weeks and longer miles on the trail from Leavenworth—they to take their "thousand mile leap," and Doniphan's men soon to go on to hardship, peril, and glory in Mexico. Colonel Doniphan and his command would no longer have the benefit of General Kearny's observing eye and wise judgment. However, the General had helped in the hardening process that left Doniphan and his men better fitted for their tasks.

161

A little after midday, as the General raised his hand in salute, they trotted out of the plaza onto the road to Albuquerque. He had been there only five weeks, but all Santa Fe turned out with universal regret to see him leave. One must search the pages of history long and carefully to find another conqueror whose brief stay left such an enduring memory.

That sentiment was still uppermost in the minds of the citizens of New Mexico when in 1947 they held a Stephen Watts Kearny Centenary. One of the speakers praised the military speed and precision with which General Kearny undertook the organization of a government for New Mexico and had it completed by September 22, 1846. He closed with this tribute:

> The name of Stephen Watts Kearny is recalled with sentiment and gratitude by the people of New Mexico today. General Kearny was the brave and honorable leader in New Mexico's first test under the Stars and Stripes. We can say today as one of his close friends said when he died in St. Louis ninety-eight years ago . . ."If ever there was a man whom I consider really chivalrous, in fact a *man* in all that noble term conveys, that national soldier and gentleman was Stephen Watts Kearny."

13. *A Fateful Meeting*

FINE WEATHER PREVAILED as the expedition moved down the Río Grande Valley past Albuquerque. General Kearny had been forced to start without the aid of a single map. Fortunately, Broken Hand soon overtook the column. His knowledge and counsel as a guide were excellent substitutes. The old bugaboo of transportation recurred to plague the command. Buying and trading of livestock became the chief concern of the officers, but usually the guileless natives outsmarted them. The poor, half-starved animals never missed a chance to trespass on the roadside cornfields. General Kearny sternly protected the rights of the farmers against his own dragoons and made them pay damages if they permitted their mounts to stray.

A worse problem was the Navaho menace. On Kearny's previous march through this region these savages had boldly attacked villages close to the soldiers. Now the raiders caused widespread ruin a few miles ahead of the expedition. The General ordered a company of dragoons to give chase, but the marauders escaped by a narrow margin. Viewing the damage committed, Kearny authorized the injured Pueblos to send a punitive expedition after the Navahos. However, with characteristic compassion he warned the villagers not to harm any of the aged or women and children of the enemy. He also sent back orders to Colonel Doniphan to delay his regiment's departure long enough to march through the Navaho country and thoroughly subdue them.

Some anecdotes of General Kearny's conquest of New Mexico, though quite picturesque, do not ring true. A biographer of James Beckwourth, the famous mulatto mountain man, claims that the latter joined Kearny's forces somewhere along the Arkansas River after raiding Southern California ranches and driving off some eighteen hundred horses. Allegedly he herded a good part of this booty as far as the Arkansas and there met Kearny. The latter, according to Beckwourth, so admired his audacity that he urged him to dispose of his horses and join him in the advance on Santa Fe. The mulatto said that he did so and accompanied the Army of the West. Leroy Hafen sagely comments that Beckwourth was never unduly modest and that the tale should be seasoned with a pinch of salt. Two other doubts suggest themselves. Kearny's army needed horses desperately. Why would its commander have Beckwourth dispose of his animals elsewhere? Moreover, none of the numerous diarists of the expedition mentions Beckwourth's presence with it, a strange omission where so picturesque a character is involved.

Another apocryphal story tells of a board dug up by a grading crew in the Pecos Valley in the 1890's. Burned on it with a branding iron was "Here lies the bones of Sancho Pedro, the only d——n decent greaser I ever knew. Killed by Apache Indians 1846. Gen. S. W. K. U.S.A." The grandfather of one of the workmen claimed he knew Sancho to have been Kearny's hostler for years and that Apaches had killed him during a skirmish. Truly a picturesque tale, but Kearny had no brush with Indians in the Pecos Valley and none anywhere with Apaches. It does not sound like Kearny to call Mexicans "greasers," still less to make a permanent record of his own profanity, especially when placing a headboard over a faithful servant's grave. If Sancho Pedro was the General's hostler for years, he must have served at Fort Leavenworth or St. Louis, strange places for Mexican stablemen in the 1830's and 1840's.

On the evening of October 2 an express brought news that Colonel Price and part of his regiment had just arrived at Santa Fe. Save for a letter the General had received a few days earlier, Price had not kept Kearny informed of his progress. Through his adjutant's reply, the General administered the chilling rebuke he could direct at non-co-operative subordinates: "The General directs me to add that had you complied with the last paragraph of the Secretary of War's letter to you of June 3rd and not observed an apparent studied silence, the public interest would have been advanced and he would not have been subjected to embarrassment in relation to you and your command."

The same express of October 2 brought confirmation of Lieutenant Colonel Allen's death, which had previously been rumored. Pursuant to Kearny's orders, Allen had taken charge of the Mormon Battalion at Council Bluffs while the Army of the West was en route to Santa Fe. Allen marched the battalion to Fort Leavenworth. Soon after most of Price's regiment had taken the trail west, Allen ordered his command to march. He had become ill but hoped to overtake his recruits shortly. Instead in a few days they received word of his death. The War Department attempted to replace him but this officer never caught up with the Mormons. In the emergency the commander at Fort Leavenworth rushed Lieutenant Andrew J. Smith to lead them to Santa Fe. Technically the battalion was a part of General Kearny's army, but he was only now learning of these happenings. Who was to command the battalion—and how— had become a military conundrum. The Mormons had almost reached Santa Fe before Kearny was confronted with this question (they marched into Santa Fe on October 9). The General's orderly soul revolted at the thought of the type of officer the Mormons would select if accorded the privilege. Quickly he sent for Captain Cooke and asked him to return immediately to Santa Fe to take command of the Mormon Battalion on its arrival and also of Captain Hudson's newly organized California Rangers. The General told Cooke he was making him a volunteer lieutenant colonel for this assignment.

Neither officer was aware that this was a historic moment. For General Kearny it was merely the logical solution of one more of his problems. Captain Cooke's first reaction was probably disappointment because once again General Kearny's orders seemed likely to deprive him of chances for glory on the battlefield. The General was not trying to reward a favorite but only to get the battalion to the Pacific as fast as possible. Yet because of his action, the new

Lieutenant Colonel's name would forever emblazon the pages of history as the leader of one of the epic marches of all time. The hidden yet great potential in the battalion needed only the right commander to crown it with success. On October 3, Cooke started back to Santa Fe.

The column, between brushes with Navahos, was enjoying Indian summer days and crisp nights. The cottonwoods along the river blazed with gold. It was time to quit the valley and head west toward the Gila. A new difficulty interposed. The Mexican teamsters who had been engaged all refused to enter the hills, claiming that they were afraid of the Apaches. Emory shrewdly guessed their real motive was to extort higher compensation. Neither persuasion nor argument could move them, so at last Major Swords, as quartermaster, seized what he needed and paid the owners a liberal price. Much to the American's surprise, the teamsters were delighted.

The events now to unroll recall an ancient myth. Clotho, Lachesis, and Atropos—the Fates who spin the thread of human destiny—were quietly waiting three miles south of Socorro for Stephen Kearny on that October day. He and his men saw only a little cloud of dust in the distance. Out of it a small band of horsemen emerged and galloped toward them with wild halloos. They reined up suddenly, and Broken Hand recognized in the leader his fellow mountain man, Kit Carson. Kearny later described it as "Carson with a party of sixteen men." Swiftly, Kit told his story. He had left Los Angeles twenty-six days before and was carrying dispatches to Washington from Commodore Stockton and Lieutenant Colonel Frémont. They had made him a lieutenant of volunteers just before he left. He had covered eight hundred miles thus far and had nearly starved, but he had promised to deliver the dispatches in sixty days. Those dispatches were most important. He let General Kearny read them. The navy under the Commodore and a volunteer battalion under Frémont had conquered all of California. Mexican rule was a thing of the past. Peace now reigned on the Pacific Coast. Quickly, Kearny realized that this was important news. It called for a swift reappraisal of all his arrangements.

He knew that the problem of transporting and feeding his three

hundred dragoons and staff across the hundreds of miles of uninhabited mountains and deserts was a most critical one. His orders
plainly required that he go on, but now he needed only an escort
sufficient to cope with wandering Indians or bandits. A smaller party
could accomplish the passage more rapidly and with much less cost
in men, transportation, and subsistence. Moreover, Colonel Doniphan certainly should have all available men to subdue the Navahos.
If the General now sent back two hundred of his veterans, Doniphan
could finish that task and be able to march to Chihuahua sooner.
The favorable news from the West Coast had come most opportunely for the challenges facing the Army in both New Mexico
and Chihuahua. Since Kearny lacked maps of the region, he felt
fortunate in meeting Kit Carson. This experienced scout had just
blazed a trail over which he could easily guide the General. Fitzpatrick was a veteran mountain man but no one else could do the
job as well as Carson. The important dispatches to Washington
would have to be rushed along, but Tom Fitzpatrick would be ideal
for that task. To General Kearny, it seemed a practical solution of
several problems to substitute one man for the other.

The General told Carson that he wanted him to turn back and
guide the Army of the West. What followed can best be told in
General Kearny's own testimony at the court-martial of Colonel
Frémont:

Question: [by Frémont himself] Did the express [i.e., Kit Carson]
remonstrate against being turned back and did you insist and assert
the right to order him back?
Answer: Carson was at first very unwilling to turn back, being
desirous of proceeding to Washington to convey letters and communications to that place which he had received from Commodore
Stockton and Colonel Frémont. He told me he had pledged himself
that they would be received in Washington. At last I persuaded him
to return with me by telling him I would send in his place as dispatch bearer Mr. Fitzpatrick who was an old friend of Colonel Frémont and had traveled a great deal with him. Carson was perfectly
satisfied with that and so told me.
Question: Did he not tell you he was to carry back dispatches from
Washington to Commodore Stockton and Colonel Frémont?

167

Answer: No, he said they had asked him to return but he had not consented to and has since told me that he would not have done so.

While the General discussed with Kit Carson the details of the latter's news and debated what should be done, the column moved ten miles farther down the river. Camp was made in a beautiful grove of cottonwoods. Here the various orders were issued to govern the future movements of each unit.

Few chance meetings in history have proved more fateful—to the future of California, to Stockton, to Frémont, and most of all to Stephen Kearny. The decisions reached by General Kearny after reading Commodore Stockton's dispatches formed one of the chief points in the bitter criticism of the General by both Frémont and Benton. Yet long study of the evidence convinces us that they formed no tenable grounds for any criticism. Kit Carson's service as a guide for the American forces was to prove invaluable. Except for that immediate advantage, the heat engendered about the meeting at Socorro—both at Frémont's court-martial and by many later writers —could make us wish that Kit Carson had followed another route and missed General Kearny entirely. Not only would the course of history have been altered—in some respects for the better—but a deal of unfortunate controversy would have been avoided.

Criticism of Kearny for the Socorro episode falls into two categories: first, his alleged breach of Kit Carson's trust concerning the dispatches and the new assignment pressed upon the guide; second, the measures pursued thereafter by Kearny in the light of the news brought by Carson.

What occurred near Socorro to stir up criticism or controversy? Besides the conversation just covered by the General's testimony, what was said or noted by eyewitnesses as well as principals? In this connection it is important to consider whether such reports were written at that time or later, when contention may have warped men's memories or colored their testimony. About 1856, Carson gave two of his biographers his story of the meeting. Although this was a fine opportunity for him to unburden himself, he virtually omitted any mention of his reluctance to go back with Kearny. Kit Carson has had an abundance of biographers. Several of them give substantially the same account of the interview with General Kearny, without mentioning Kit's resistance or resentment.

The account of the same incident by Broken Hand's biographer is quite different—written, it should be remembered, eighty-five years after it occurred:

> When Kearny ordered Carson to retrace his steps to California as guide to his army (letting Fitzpatrick take the dispatches East) Carson protested against this staggering order. For more than a year he had been absent from his home in Taos and now asked to be gone another year! In his anger and indignation he would, it is said, have deserted but a good friend persuaded him against so rash an act, and with sullen resignation he turned again to the west.

Stanley Vestal goes farther than any other latter-day writer on this theme. He openly charges that Kearny bore enmity toward Kit Carson at Socorro because "the West Pointers did not not love Frémont," and that Kearny's dislike for Frémont probably extended to his right-hand man Kit Carson. It hardly seems necessary to point out, first, that Stephen Kearny was not a West Pointer, and secondly, that there was not a hint of enmity between Kearny and Frémont until some months later. On the contrary, both men and their relatives mingled on most friendly terms in the same social circles in St. Louis.

What do we learn from General Kearny's officers who kept journals? Dr. Griffin's entry for October 6 and 7, made a few hours later, seems picturesque and unstudied:

> Some eight or nine men came charging up to us with an Indian yell. These turned out to be (Kit) Carson, the celebrated mountain man and his party on his way to Washington with an express from Capt [sic] Stockton of the Navy and Col. Frémont announcing that they had taken California & that the latter was to be governor of the same. This created considerable sensation in our party, but the general feeling (was) one of disappointment and regret—most of us hoped on leaving Santa Fé that we might have a little kick-up with the good people of California but this totally blasted all our hopes, and reduced our expedition to one of mere escort duty—the Genl taking the same view of the matter took only two Companies C & K 1st Drags, and left the remaining three in New Mexico. . . . Dr. Simpson & myself drew straws to see who should go to California, and I won. . . . Mr. Fitzpatrick took Carson's mail and left for

169

Washington October 7th . . . we put out, with merry hearts & light packs on our long march—Carson as guide, every man feeling renewed confidence in consequence of having such a guide. . . . From the way the Genl marched today, I should say he was on his way in Earnest.

Here are many details of the new arrangement, but not a word about any argument with the man whose arrival caused the change.

Lieutenant Emory is a less important witness as he was not present at the moment of meeting:

Came into camp late and found Carson with an express from California, bearing intelligence that that country had surrendered without a blow, and that the American flag floated in every port. . . . October 7th. Yesterday's news caused some changes in our camp; one hundred dragoons, officered by Captain Moore and Lieutenants Hammond and Davidson, with General Kearny's personal staff . . . Messrs. Carson and Robideaux [*sic*] my own party . . . and a few hunters . . . formed the party for California. Major Sumner, with the dragoons, was ordered to retrace his steps. Many friends here parted that were never to meet again; some fell in California, some in New Mexico and some at Cerro Gordo.

In his *Thirty Years' View*, Senator Benton charged that Emory edited his journal after the controversy with Frémont so as to omit the fact that Frémont was governor of California. Emory certainly made no secret of having written parts of his journal later, as his sentence about the parting of friends plainly reveals. Probably Benton would have explained away Emory's failure to record Carson's indignant protests on the same grounds. Benton went on to make the point that Captain Johnston's journal did refer to Frémont as governor, and that his journal could not have been altered to fit changed circumstances because of his death in battle at San Pasqual on December 6 before the controversy arose. This reasoning should apply both ways, however. If Johnston's journal is reliable when it contains a reference pleasing to Senator Benton, it should carry equal weight when it testifies against his contention that General Kearny and Kit Carson clashed seriously.

Here is Johnston's entry for October 6:

The general told him (Carson) that he had just passed over the country which we were to traverse and he wanted him to go back with him as a guide; he replied that he had pledged himself to go to Washington, and he could not think of not fulfilling his promise. The general told him he would relieve him of all responsibility, and place the mail in the hands of a safe person to carry it on; he finally consented and turned his face to the west again, just as he was on the eve of entering the settlements, after his arduous trip and when he had set his hopes on seeing his family. It requires a brave man to give up his private feelings thus for the public good; but Carson is one such! honor to him for it.

Since the mention—or omission—of Frémont's governorship was so important a test of a diarist's reliability in Benton's eyes, it should be noted that Dr. Griffin also referred to Frémont as likely to be governor of California.

It is interesting to read Senator Benton's report of what Kit Carson said happened at Socorro, especially in juxtaposition with Johnston's journal (called reliable and unaltered by Benton) and the various versions given by Carson's many biographers. Here it is from his *Thirty Years' View*:

I met General Kearny with his troops . . . below Santa Fé. I had heard of their coming and when I met them first thing I told them was that they were 'too late'—that California was conquered and the United States flag raised in all parts of the country. But General Kearny said he would go on and said something about going to establish a civil government. I told him a civil government was already established and Colonel Frémont appointed Governor to commence as soon as he returned from the North some time in this very month (October). General Kearny said that made no difference, that he was a friend of Colonel Frémont and he would make him governor himself. He began from the first to insist on my turning back to guide him to California. I told him I could not turn back, that I had pledged myself to Commodore Stockton and Colonel Frémont to take their dispatches to Washington City and to return with dispatches as far as New Mexico where my family lived and to carry them all the way back if I did not find some one in Santa Fé that I could trust as well as I could myself; that I had promised them that I would reach Washington in sixty days and that they should have the return dispatches from the government in a hundred and twenty days. . . . General Kearny would not hear of my going on, told me he was a friend of Colonel Frémont and Colonel Benton and all the family and would send on the dispatches. Fitzpatrick who had been with Frémont in his exploring party and was a good friend to him would take the dispatches through. . . . When he could not persuade me to turn back he then told me he had the right to make me go on with him and insisted on his right and I did not consent to turn back till he had made me believe he had the right to order me and then as Fitzpatrick was going on with the dispatches and Kearny seemed to be such a good friend of the Colonel I let him take me back and I guided him through but went with great hesitation and had prepared everything to escape the night before they started and made known my intention to Maxwell who urged me not to do so. More than twenty times on the road Kearny told me about his being a friend of Benton and Frémont and all the family and that he intended to make Frémont governor of California and all that of his own accord as we traveled along or in camp and without my asking a word about it. I say more than twenty times because I cannot remember how many times, it was such a common thing for him to talk about it.

One's surprise at the elaborations and embellishments of this Carson-via-Benton version when contrasted with the others is only equaled by amazement at the unrecognizable Kearny here portrayed. Nowhere else have I found this reserved, laconic officer so loquacious, so repetitious, so familiar, and so condescending to a subordinate. We suddenly behold a two-dimensional figure labeled General Kearny but bearing no other resemblance to the real man. Two joint biographers of Frémont follow Senator Benton verbatim as just quoted, but then add words under the same quotation marks as if uttered by Carson: "This statement I make at the request of Senator Benton but had much rather be examined in a court of justice face to face with General Kearny and there tell at once all that I know about General Kearny's battles and his conduct in California." This statement is not contained in Benton's own account of the incident. Charles L. Camp, in repeating the version of the meeting given by Bashford and Wagner, said that Carson gave Senator Benton a long statement of his grievance two years later. The language is virtually that in the last quoted paragraph.

Bashford and Wagner, with indignation borrowed from Old Bullion, complain that while Fitzpatrick was a man who could be trusted to deliver the dispatches, he could not give the verbal information that Carson would have done, "to whom many things had been told. . . . It was presumptuous in General Kearny to turn back one who had been specially commissioned by high authority to perform a certain act. This made the Colonel and Commodore very angry and was really the beginning of their trouble with Kearny." These writers repeat, too, the bitterness expressed by Frémont in his *Memoirs*. There he made much of the note written by General Kearny to Commodore Stockton from Warner's Ranch. In it, Kearny merely stated he had met Carson en route west, but omitted any details of the meeting. Frémont termed this "duplicity," saying "it showed with the clearness of light the quality which was at the root of his character—a falseness which contaminated every other quality." Even Frederick S. Dellenbaugh in his biography of Frémont calls this resentment "trivial." He admits there was no justice in the contention that Kearny endangered the safe delivery of the dispatches by entrusting them to Fitzpatrick. Dellenbaugh recognizes that the latter was just as trustworthy and experienced on the frontier as Carson. (This condemnation by Frémont ignores the fact that Kearny's note to Stockton from Warner's Ranch was written by a weary man at the end of a grueling journey of many weeks. There was no necessity for a full and formal report but merely a note scribbled hastily to let the Commodore know the General and his force were near at hand. Such a message surely called for only bare essentials.)

A question constantly recurs as the above record is studied. Why was Kit Carson not called as a witness by the defense at Colonel Frémont's court-martial? That would have put the story of General Kearny's alleged high-handed conduct before both Frémont's judges and the public. Carson was admittedly on good terms with the Pathfinder and his family. His story as we have it from Frémont's champions would have been damaging to the prosecution's case. The defense was resourceful, energetic, and bent on leaving no stone unturned to vindicate John C. Frémont. Allan Nevins, probably the best living authority on Frémont, was asked this question, and he replied that he believed it was because Carson was not readily available. Against this must be weighed the fact that Kit carried other dispatches to Washington at Frémont's bidding a few months before the trial, and journeyed there again in the summer after its conclusion. To a man of his energy a trip to attend the court-martial would not have been too formidable an undertaking. We have been told that he longed to tell what he knew, yet the defense did not call on Carson to testify. Any trial lawyer might be pardoned if he made significant deductions from the failure of the defense to do so.

One other omission is important. It seems never to have occurred to the many shouting and perspiring critics to note that the dispatches got to Washington under Fitzpatrick's competent care just as safely and promptly as if borne by Kit Carson. The promise Kearny had given him at Socorro was carried out to the letter. At Socorro, Kearny believed that the safe and speedy arrival of a military force carrying out the urgent orders of the President of the United States should take precedence over the question of who carried a parcel of official dispatches. For this decision, General Kearny's name has been besmirched for over a century.

Let us look now at the remaining criticisms leveled at Kearny for the steps taken after meeting Kit Carson. It will be recalled that his orders of June 3, 1846, had said, "A large discretionary power is invested in you in regard to these matters as well as all others in relation to the expedition," and:

> Should the President be disappointed in his cherished hope that you will be able to reach the interior of Upper California before winter, you are then desired to make the best arrangements you can for sustaining your forces during the winter and for an early movement in the spring. Though it is very desirable that the expedition should reach California this season (and the President does not doubt you will make every possible effort to accomplish this object), yet, if in

your judgment it cannot be undertaken, with a reasonable prospect
of success, you will defer it as above suggested, until spring. You are
left unembarrassed by any specific directions in the matter.

The impartial student of today may interpolate this comment
to mean that he was "unembarrassed" by President Polk or Secretary of War Marcy, although for generations critics of every
variety led by John C. Frémont have pursued General Kearny's
memory with after-the-event restrictions and limitations on his discretion. In effect they have said: his march disregarded conditions
contained in his orders; he did not take a large enough force with
him; he did not leave a large enough force in New Mexico; he
went to conquer a land already conquered; he arrived in the "conquered" land with too small a force to oppose the "conquered" inhabitants whom he found in arms against him; there was no need
for his going to California at all!

This summarizes the contradictions and illogic of the charges
made against General Kearny by a motley host, wise after the event.
Some of them have actually directed every one of the above criticisms at Kearny with a charming disregard for consistency. All this
time the true and only answer to their comments could be found
in a careful rereading of the famous orders of June 3 and 18, 1846.
Obedience to them underlay every thought and action of Kearny's
from the time he marched out of Santa Fe until he started back
across the Sierra Nevada the next summer.

We have reached a fitting place to consider again some parallel
dates—deadly parallels now as well as coincidences. On October 6,
while Kit Carson was assuring General Kearny that California was
conquered and at peace, what were the conditions there? On September 15, Kit and his Delawares had ridden out of Los Angeles.
Captain Gillespie of the Marine Corps was commander at the pueblo under Commodore Stockton's orders. On September 23, Gillespie and his garrison of fifty were attacked by a force of Californians and for several days besieged behind entrenchments. At
the same time another group of Americans had surrendered after a
skirmish at Chino. With no relief in sight, Gillespie was forced to

abandon Los Angeles, though allowed to retire under a flag of truce to San Pedro where he embarked on the *Vandalia*. Soon afterward the Americans were also driven out of Santa Barbara.

On that same October 6, Captain Mervine of the *U.S.S. Savannah*, together with Gillespie's men from the *Vandalia*, landed forces at San Pedro in an attempt to recapture Los Angeles. Two days later they battled the insurgents at the Dominguez Rancho south of the pueblo. The foot soldiers could not gain ground against the superbly mounted Californians and had to retreat to their ships. All of coastal California south of Monterey had been recaptured from the Americans with the sole exception of San Diego, which lay under the guns of Stockton's small fleet. Frémont was in the north raising a force among the American residents to march to Stockton's assistance.

Thomas O. Larkin, the United States consul at Monterey, gave the best explanation of this insurrection. Larkin, better than any other American in California, knew the conciliatory policy his government wanted used toward the people of California. In a letter written from Los Angeles a few months after the revolt started, he said:

> I hear from many of the people of the country that had . . . any proper and prudent person been left here by the Commodore, all this disturbance would not have happened. It appears even from the Americans that Captain A. H. G. punished, fined and imprisoned who and when he pleased without any hearing.—I always told the Commodore he should have granted the Mexican officers their request to be sent to Mexico. He would not then and his cheap way of conducting with Captain G's harshness has brought the country to its present pass. . . . In May or June I saw that trouble was coming on California by that bad acted affair at Sonoma, began and ended in wrong.

Another particularly irritating measure instituted by Stockton was a curfew, effective from ten o'clock at night until sunrise. No such restriction had ever been placed on the high-spirited Californians. Its enforcement produced much the same reactions as hobbles and checkreins on their unbroken mustangs.

From a water color by Alfred Jacob Miller
Courtesy Walters Art Gallery

Two Indian scouts sight a fur boat on the Platte River, and the warriors of the tribe prepare to attack it. With a force that seldom exceeded 600 soldiers, Colonel Kearny had to protect about 1,000 miles of Western frontier from such menaces.

From the oil painting by Leon Pomarede
Courtesy the City Art Museum and
the Piaget Studio, St. Louis

In 1843 headquarters of the Third Military Department were moved to St. Louis, and the city became the home of Stephen Kearny and his growing family.

Neither Carson nor Kearny knew of these events. But, say the critics, Kearny should have turned back on hearing Carson's news since the latter made his instructions obsolete. In view of the explicit and urgent language in which his orders were couched, General Kearny did what any reasonable and experienced officer would have done (and what President Polk and Secretary Marcy approved when they later learned of it). He used the wide discretion invested in him to reduce the size of his force by two-thirds. With the remainder of his command he pressed forward to California. Had Kearny done what his latter-day critics would have had him do, what would have happened to the rest of the American occupation forces in California? If he had abandoned his own journey, consistency would have required him to cancel Cooke's orders to march the Mormon Battalion to the Pacific. Not a solitary American soldier would have arrived to reinforce Stockton and Frémont before Colonel Stevenson and part of his Seventh New York Volunteers reached San Francisco on March 5, 1847. One thing seems certain; there would have been a different court-martial, in which General Kearny would have been charged with plain disobedience to the orders of the President.

Another subject requires attention for a proper understanding of General Kearny's march from Socorro. It is a question of cartography and involves some more of the confusion and errors that have clouded General Kearny's memory. We today must guard against the natural assumption that the Upper California referred to in 1846 was identical with the present state of California. Note that in the first sentence of Secretary Marcy's letter of June 3, 1846, the term "Upper California" appears repeatedly. The famous orders to Commodore Sloat from Secretary of the Navy Bancroft also mention "Upper California." What area was meant by those words in 1846? Commander Wilkes's map of the Oregon Territory, 1841, shows Upper California extending continuously along Oregon's southern boundary from the Pacific Ocean to a point east of longitude 110° west. That brings its northeast corner nearly due south of South Pass (in Wyoming) and many degrees east of Great Salt Lake. It is most interesting to read on this map the legend that its eastern part contains information developed by Lieutenant Frémont's United States topographical engineers' exploration on the eastern side of the Rocky Mountains.

Best authority of all appears to be J. Disturnell's Map of Mexico (revised edition of 1847), the map that was used by the makers of the Treaty of Guadalupe Hidalgo to end hostilities between the United States and Mexico. True, that is a year later than Kearny's march, but I have found no cartographic or documentary evidence to indicate that there had been any material change in the boundaries of Upper California between the time of the Wilkes Map of 1841 and the Disturnell Map of 1847. Disturnell shows Alta (Upper) California colored in buff from the Pacific, south of the Oregon line and easterly to nearly 250 miles east of Great Salt Lake. On this map the eastern boundary of Alta California roughly parallels the upper courses of the Río Grande from north of Taos to the latitude of El Paso del Norte, with Chihuahua bounding it on the southeast. "Nueva Mejico" is shown as a long strip about 100 miles in width. Both the towns of Santa Fe and Albuquerque appear just east of it in a differently tinted territory labeled "Santa Fé." The headwaters of the Gila and virtually all the other tributaries of the mighty Colorado are within Alta California. In other words, the enemy country which General Kearny had orders to occupy and govern consisted of the present states of California, Nevada, Utah, and Arizona, and portions of Colorado and New Mexico. Of course, those orders specifically named New Mexico as well as Upper California.

Only when we consider Upper California in this enlarged compass do some of Kearny's instructions appear in their true light. When Marcy hoped the General would be able to reach "the interior of Upper California" before winter, we know he was not thinking of the San Joaquin or Sacramento valleys. It was a different task to "sustain your forces during the winter" in the vastly larger area actually referred to. "An early movement in the spring" could have been a long and tedious march, perhaps from the interior of Arizona, and not just a short jaunt through one of the coast range passes.

Much has been made by Kearny's critics of the fact that Stockton in October, 1846, supposedly held the ports from San Francisco south through San Diego. Granted that he did (and had not quickly lost some of them), viewed in the light of the true boundaries of Upper California, only a trifling (though important) part of the territory was held by the Americans. Kearny's orders certainly required him to go on from Socorro to take military possession of the country.

For centuries the Spaniards and Mexicans between them had maintained missions and forts at various points in present-day Arizona. Kearny had to safeguard the Americans west of the Colorado from an attack on their rear or their flank. A few weeks after General Kearny's march, Lieutenant Colonel Cooke, commanding the Mormon Battalion, followed him to California, although taking a somewhat more southerly route. The Mormon Battalion, though detached from him, was under Kearny's orders and as such included in the execution of President Polk's orders to the General. It is interesting to note that Cooke's forces encountered the garrison of four Mexican presidios that had been concentrated at Tucson. Cooke's battalion drove this garrison out of Tucson with all their artillery. Then this part of the Army of the West occupied and marched through that town—"taking military possession of the country" (even though temporarily), as contemplated in the orders of June 18.

The astonishing feature about the foregoing is that any student of history and military affairs can find in General Kearny's conduct a basis for criticizing the commander of a small expedition in a savage wilderness, hundreds of miles from his base and cut off from all means of quick communication. Everything he did under these circumstances was in direct obedience to explicit orders, and later fully approved by his superiors.

14. *The Thousand-Mile Leap*

THE REORGANIZED EXPEDITION started early on October 7, with four young Apaches as guides, but made discouraging progress. It left the main Chihuahua road where the latter crossed to the east bank of the Río Grande. Thereafter the route became a dim trail through thorny brush. The mules could pull the wagons only at a snail's pace. Several gave out on the first day. Carson said it would take over four months to reach California with the wagons and warned that far rougher country lay before them. Pack mules seemed the only practical method of increasing speed. Because the government wished him to establish a wagon road, General Kearny was reluctant to abandon the vehicles as long as a chance remained of getting them over the mountains. Writers like Stanley Vestal call his perseverance stubborn and blundering and seem to overlook the instructions given Kearny.

At a council on the night of the ninth it was finally decided to abandon the wagons and rush back orders to Major Sumner to obtain pack saddles. The wagons could be reclaimed later. Carving out a wagon route would have to be left to Cooke and the Mormon Battalion. Vestal gives entire credit for this very practical step to Kit Carson. He makes it appear that Kearny had never thought of using pack saddles. He pictures the General as a man unable to meet the challenges of the wilds. In refutation one has only to remember the success of the expedition to the South Pass and the rapid advance from Fort Leavenworth to Santa Fe when Carson had not been present. Kit was undoubtedly one of the finest scouts that the American frontier ever produced. But he can be accorded all the praise due him without belittling Kearny. In Vestal's eyes the latter could not possibly do anything right because he was an army officer.

In strong contrast is the comment Bernard De Voto made about this march:

> As for Kearny he was only a reliable officer of Dragoons doing a job set for him by a President who understood nothing whatever about it. He did the job so well that it has never had much comment by anyone. . . . What is remarkable in Kearny's march from here on is only the absence of remarkable events. Good management of expeditions, we are told, forestalls adventures. Kearny was a master of frontier craft and he had his own Dragoons, not only professional soldiers but veterans of the West. His one hard problem was how to maintain them as cavalry.

No assertion could be truer than De Voto's last sentence. Transport was not only Kearny's "one hard problem"; it was first in importance of the many confronting him. The thousand-mile journey to California all but dismounted every man in his command. We will grant that horses and mules of the proper kind were a very scarce commodity throughout the Southwest. But the government's niggardliness in not supplying sufficient funds for Kearny and his quartermaster almost defeated his final objective—arrival in California in condition to campaign effectively. For that very close brush with failure, the heaviest share of the responsibility rests with the administration in Washington.

More thrilling melodrama can be woven from the story of a Custer's Last Stand, or an ill-conceived undertaking like Frémont's Fourth Expedition in the winter of 1848. There, however, the suspense and excitement of the reader arise from the lack of cool, careful planning and sober calculation of risks. Kearny did not leave as rich a legacy to seekers for thrills and romance as the leaders of such ill-starred struggles. What irony that the one occasion (to be related in our next chapter) when so many feel that he, too, was

181

rash and hasty has caused the critics to judge his whole career by the events of a few hours. In his case that tragic happening has nearly obscured the record of a third of a century of uniform success.

While the column remained in camp awaiting the pack saddles, baggage and supplies were prepared for their use. Deer and quail swelled the larder, and the men enjoyed a brief rest. Indian summer was nearing its end; the days were warm until late afternoon with nights so frosty that once Captain Turner noted ice the thickness of a silver dollar at daybreak. It was high time to get across those forbidding mountains to the west. On the thirteenth not only the pack saddles but a full mail arrived. Letters from home revived everyone's spirit. According to Captain Johnston's journal, many "wrote to friends and closed the door to future communication with the States, as we will now pass into the Apache country, where it is probable no one will dare follow us." He, as well as several of his companions, was in truth passing into a country far beyond the Apaches, where none of this earth could follow.

The first day's march with the pack animals made eighteen miles to the last camp on the Río Grande, very near the site of the Elephant Butte Dam and today's town with the remarkable name of Truth or Consequences. Two miles farther down the river on the fifteenth, the soldiers picked up an ancient trail to the copper mines. Carson had not exaggerated the roughness of the route. Even pack mules made progress with the greatest difficulty. Over rolling slopes wooded with live oak, ash, and walnut, they had begun the ascent of the lofty Mimbres Range. Autumn's finger had gilded the aspens on the higher peaks. Cacti strange to middlewesterners appeared more frequently.

General Kearny sent Captain Turner ahead with a small escort to try to contact the Apaches living in these mountains. He was anxious to assure them of his pacific intentions and feared the sudden appearance of the whole cavalcade might alarm them. Turner could not find any trace of Indians but caught a large string of trout from the Mimbres River while he waited for the column. Since no Apaches had been found, the Indian guides sent up smoke signals to alert the natives of their presence and invite them to visit the soldiers. The dragoons had reached the extensive mineral zone of present-day Sierra and Grant counties, New Mexico. Copper and gold deposits had been worked there intermittently ever since the old Spanish times, but the mines were now deserted because of Apache raids.

This region was the scene of an altercation between the commander and his adjutant. The latter had hurried ahead of the column to examine the copper mines, but had not felt it necessary to ask permission of General Kearny. When the command overtook him, "I received from him [Kearny] a severe rebuke, which I thought so uncalled for, that I spoke to him on the subject after getting into camp. . . . he gave me no satisfaction, whereupon I made an official application to him to be relieved from duty on his staff and to be permitted to join my company now with General Wool. He has not yet given me an answer." Although this journal continues with daily entries through the fourth of the following December, the incident is nowhere again mentioned. Perhaps Kearny denied the request because it would have been almost impossible for Captain Turner to make his way alone to General Wool's army. The adjutant may even have withdrawn his application. We do not have the General's side of the story but whatever the estrangement between the two men, we find Turner loyally supporting his commander through all his later ordeals.

On October 19 the column crossed the Continental Divide and camped that night on the headwaters of the Río Gila in rough, broken country. They rejoiced in the fresh mountain air and balmy weather.

Before the expedition started on the twentieth, Mangas Coloradas or Red Sleeves, chief of the Mimbres Apaches, rode into camp accompanied by twenty warriors and women. All were mounted on small but mettlesome horses. Red Sleeves professed friendship for all Americans and promised to send some of his young men to show Lieutenant Cooke a good route for his battalion and wagons to the Gila. Kearny had Captain Turner write Cooke to treat these Apaches well and use their services. The Indians would deliver the note in person. None of them could speak either English or Spanish, but the General relied upon Cooke's ability to communicate with them by sign language. He gave presents to the chief and his men and also a paper to Red Sleeves setting forth their mutual pledge of friendship.

The Apaches assured the officers that one, two, or three white men could pass safely through their country. If they needed food or animals to ride, the Indians would supply them. Carson with a twinkle in his keen hazel eye said he would not trust one of them. These Apaches proved to be shrewd traders. After most tedious bargaining only a few mules could be had from them. Mangas Coloradas was visibly impressed by Kearny's soldierly bearing and the discipline of his dragoons. The Apaches knew of the General's capture of Santa Fe and proposed that he make common cause with them and take Chihuahua, Durango, and Sonora, killing all the Mexicans encountered. They found it hard to understand Kearny's polite rejection of the idea.

Recital of the toiling descent of each succeeding day would make monotonous reading. Only the details differed from mile to mile: rough, rocky trail, scant grass of poor quality, frequent dusty stretches in the powdery soil resembling cold ashes rather than earth. Here the mules sank ankle deep at every step. The strain on them was terrific. On a single day a dozen or more dropped in their tracks and had to be abandoned. Carson grimly warned that a little later the grass would be even scarcer and less nutritious. To deepen the gloom, he said that every party which made the trip through the Gila's canyons had emerged in a starving condition. For the greater part of the journey from the Continental Divide to Warner's Ranch the dragoons marched afoot to spare the animals. Sickness alone warranted a man in keeping the saddle.

One entry in Captain Turner's journal speaks for a multitude of the unsung, unknown heroes of America's western advance:

What difficulties do we have to encounter, we who perform marches in such a country—how little do those who sit in their easy chairs in Washington think or know of the privations, the difficulties we are daily, hourly subjected to. Even our anxious friends at home can form no idea of the trials and fatigue that we undergo each hour in the day—wading streams, clambering over rocks and precipitous mountains or laboring through the valleys of streams where the loose earth or sand cause our animals to sink up to their knees at almost every step. Then our frugal meals, hard bed and perhaps wet blankets. This is soldier's fare but I am sick of it and have no longer to endure it willingly, particularly when we get no credit for it. Unless we are fortunate enough to get into a fight before reaching California, and be successful in it too, our laborious service in marching over this country will never be appreciated. I hope, however, to get the approbation of my own conscience and the satisfaction resulting there from—the happy reflection of having performed all my duties faithfully.

Kearny's own reactions to these strange scenes are recorded in a long letter to his wife, written after his arrival in San Diego:

We had a very long and tiresome march of it from Santa Fe. We came down Del Norte 230 miles—then to river Gila. . . . We marched 500 miles down that river, having most of the way a bridle path, but over a very rough and barren country. It surprised me to see so much land that can never be of any use to man or beast. We traveled many days without seeing a spear of grass, and no vegetation excepting a species of the Fremontia, and the mesquite tree, something like our thorn, and which our mules eat, thorn and branches to keep them alive.

Infrequently more mules were obtained from Indians, but always these were poor, half-starved animals of slight value.

On November 8 the column entered Pimaland. Here lived the most civilized Indians the command had ever seen. Except for the color of their skin and their garb, they were wholly unlike any natives yet encountered. In manners, too, they did not in the least resemble other Indians. When Carson tried to bargain for provisions, he was told, "bread is to eat, not to sell; take what you want." Near the Pima village, the soldiers passed a large adobe ruin, quite the most imposing structure since the ruins of Pecos. Kearny questioned a Pima and was told it was the *casa* of Montezuma. The man related an ancient legend concerning its builders, but could not decipher the hieroglyphics for the General.

As word spread of the arrival of the Americans, Pimas and some

185

neighboring Maricopas hurried in to see them, bringing corn, beans, honey, and watermelons. These Indians showed neither fear nor suspicion of the soldiers. They were all honest, friendly, and generous. Despite the swarm of visitors—men, women and children—not the smallest article belonging to the expedition was pilfered. This was indeed a new experience. While the natives brought many gifts, they also wanted to trade, and Major Swords did a brisk business. However, the commodity most greatly desired—mules—was disappointingly scarce. Some of the officers rode through the Pimas' farms. The tribe practiced a high order of agriculture. Irrigation and drainage were expertly managed. Crops of corn, wheat, and cotton had been harvested, but the stubble showed them to have been bountiful.

The visit with the hospitable Pimas was like an oasis in the desert. When the expedition was ready to move on, the General gave the village governor a letter testifying to the good character of his tribe. All United States troops that might later pass this way were enjoined to respect the chief, his people, and their property. Two days later the column reached one of the Maricopa villages lower on the Gila. An old chief of this tribe traveled many miles to assure General Kearny of his friendship. From these Indians he learned that a Mexican frontier garrison was located at Tucson, about one hundred miles away. Several days earlier, while they were in the mountains, a searching view to the south showed the rather level area through which Colonel Cooke was soon to march the Mormon Battalion and its wagons. It seemed apparent to the commander that the battalion must pass near Tucson.

On November 22, Carson told them they were nearing the mouth of the Gila. The remaining mules were reduced to eating canebrake and the bark and leaves of willow and cottonwood. Kearny's own noble bay had endured so much that at last it gave out, and he was obliged to mount his mule. Most of the men were now afoot, strung out in single file for a considerable distance behind the staff on their mules. Men and animals struggled through the dust in oppressive heat. Suddenly the foremost rider reined up sharply. He had ridden into a lately abandoned camp. As many perhaps as a thousand horses and their herders had left it that morning. Had

General Castro really come back from Sonora? How close ahead were the unknown travelers? Carson believed the recent campers were probably only ten miles away at the crossing of the Colorado.

Military alertness immediately resumed sway. General Kearny ordered the long file of dragoons to advance on the double quick and the howitzers brought up as fast as possible. His party totaled only 110 men, too few in the General's opinion to await an attack. If Castro's camp could be found, Kearny would take the offensive as soon as darkness fell. Only by so bold a course could he prevent the Mexicans from learning the weakness of his own force. Suddenly a mounted Mexican was seen on a near-by butte. He was quite evidently surveying the expedition and soon disappeared. The General immediately ordered the camp arranged for defense and posted sentinels on the surrounding sand hills. Carson was sent forward to scout the crossing. "Find the enemy, Carson," Kearny told him, "and we will fight them tonight."

The guide soon located a half dozen recently extinguished camp-fires, scattered along the river bottom in unmilitary fashion; also a horse trail leading to the main crossing that looked like the track of loose animals. Only a few human footprints showed, one or two those of women. Lastly Kit saw two or three men at a distance. Lieutenant Hammond finally rode in with the howitzers at nine o'clock. He had seen large fires at some distance north of the Gila. Lieutenant Emory was dispatched with fifteen dragoons to reconnoiter the entire region. It was a bushwhacking job through the mesquite and willow jungle. They soon heard neighing. Investigation surprised a camp of Mexicans in charge of a large band of horses. Emory quickly decided this was no part of an army but the herdsmen of a *caballada* of maybe five hundred horses being driven from California to Sonora, presumably for General Castro's benefit. Emory posted a guard about the camp and took four herders back to Kearny. Each of the prisoners was interrogated separately. Four different stories about the ownership and destination of the horses were told. It was too late and too dark for a thorough reconnaissance, so the soldiers were bivouacked with every man ordered to sleep with his loaded gun at his side.

The dragoons remained in camp the next day to check the horses for remounts, as well as to rest the overworked mules. At least one of the Mexicans proved truthful. He gave Kearny the very important information that the Californians had revolted and driven Gillespie out of Los Angeles. Mervine's defeat by General Flores was also reported. Carson and some of the officers were incredulous, especially about the battle on the Dominguez Rancho. Carson had been very confident that the Californians would never fight. However, it soon became evident that the Americans had suffered some kind of reverse. Emory arrested a dispatch bearer carrying messages from California to General Castro and others. General Kearny found that the intercepted letters confirmed the bad news. Only San Diego remained in possession of the Americans. Three ships of the line kept the American flag flying at this one point in all of southern California.

With what seems exemplary conduct toward a wartime adversary, General Kearny paid a fair price for the twenty-five half-broken horses and a few mules seized from the Mexicans. Cash and some of the command's old worn-out mules were given in payment. While the tales told by the four captives varied widely, all agreed that at least *some* of the horses belonged to Castro himself. Actually two bands of horses and their herders had just encountered each other when Emory made his night reconnaissance. One was in charge of an officer of the Mexican forces. The other was a small group of Sonorans who had stolen a herd belonging to the Californians. Naturally the thieves were amazed to be paid by Kearny for part of their plunder. The Mexicans had very scant provisions of *pinole* and corn mush and no shelter at their camp on the river bottoms. Here on the night of the twenty-third one of their women gave birth to a child. The American officers made up a gift of tea, sugar, and coffee from their own meager store and sent it to the mother. When camp was finally broken, the General let the Mexicans leave with the balance of their stock. The expedition went on down the Colorado to the ford.

Kit Carson warned that no more feed could be found across the river. Therefore the General had every animal loaded with as much grass and other forage as it could carry. Many of the animals were hitched to the bushes, and the soldiers noticed how eagerly the mules and horses devoured the mesquite pods. It was a valuable discovery. Some of the mesquite was carried along. Later both men and animals found its beans quite palatable. Carson also pointed out that there would be practically no water anywhere until the coastal mountains were reached, ninety miles away. It was a grim prospect.

General Kearny's reflections were especially somber. He was certain that there had been a counterrevolution on the coast (as he had uncannily foretold in August). If he could only recall the dragoons sent back to Santa Fe, he could advance with more confidence. The intercepted letters had borne dates around mid-October. Since then the tide might have turned in favor of the Americans—or it might having further receded! To resolve these uncertainties and do what he could to retrieve the situation, only one course was open—to push on as rapidly as possible, desert or no desert. That after all was an old habit of Stephen Kearny's.

The Colorado, about one-third of a mile wide with four feet of water in the shifting channel, was forded on November 25. No one in the expedition would ever forget the week that followed. The route lay very close to the present international boundary and gradually swung north and west across the southern edge of today's Imperial Valley. In 1846 only a waste of sand dazzled the eye of the luckless wayfarer. Two days out from the Colorado, a small amount of precious water was laboriously scooped from holes in a gully at the Alamo. That was a lifesaver for some, although in the next few hours many horses and mules dropped dead.

The toiling men were enveloped in a heavy fog as they entered a mountain gap on the twenty-eighth. The desert had been crossed, its heat replaced by chill winds sweeping down from snowy summits. Neither water nor feed could be found for the starving animals. Many of the soldiers were down to their last ration. At Vallecitos packs of wolves hovered near by as the column shivered during a necessary rest. An inspection was held at this bleak camp. "Poor fellows," wrote Captain Johnston, "they are well-nigh naked—some of them barefoot—a sorry looking set," and closed his comment with a true prophecy (the last he was ever to make): "They will be ready for their hour when it comes."

On December 2 the expedition met some Mexicans fleeing to Sonora. The General let them pass as many were women and children. They said a war was on. It seemed likely the Americans might meet the enemy. Apparently no large armed forces were in the field. Guerrilla warfare with ranchers might be expected rather than pitched battles. Warner's Ranch, sixty miles from San Diego, was reached the same day. The man in charge, an American named Marshall, told the General that the Mexicans held all the country except the ports of San Diego, Monterey, and San Francisco. The Army of the West was now squarely astride the pass by which communication was maintained with Mexico. Marshall thought an Englishman named Stokes, who lived at Santa Ysabel fifteen miles away, might know about conditions in the country. He was immediately sent for.

For the moment news and dangerous location mattered little; food was the paramount consideration. Seven men ate a fat sheep at one meal. The rest of the command made heavy inroads on Warner's plentiful supply of beef and mutton as well as dried grapes and melons. The few surviving horses and mules must have thought the lush pastures under the oaks a veritable heaven after the torments of the desert.

When Edward Stokes arrived, he confirmed all that Kearny had learned from the intercepted letters. He was going to San Diego the next day (December 3) and although a neutral offered to carry any dispatches the Americans wished to send. Kearny gladly embraced this opportunity to get word to Commodore Stockton. He immediately dashed off this letter:

> I this afternoon reached here, escorted by a party of the 1st regiment dragoons. I come by orders from the President of the United States. We left Santa Fé on the 25th September, having taken possession of New Mexico, annexed it to the United States, established a civil government in that territory, and secured order, peace and quietness there.
>
> If you can send a party to open communication with us on the route to this place, and to inform me of the state of affairs in California, I wish you would do so, and as quickly as possible.

The fear of this letter falling into Mexican hands prevents me from writing more.

Your express by Mr. Carson was met on the Del Norte; and your mail must have reached Washington at least ten days since.

(The last sentence is the passage to which John C. Frémont took such violent exception, because it did not say that General Kearny had brought Carson back to California.)

About the time Stokes arrived at Warner's Ranch, word was received that a band of horses and mules belonging to the Mexicans was pastured some fifteen miles to the northwest. Despite their weariness, the General immediately sent Lieutenant Davidson and Kit Carson with a detail of dragoons to seize them. These animals were involved in an interesting episode. Don Antonio Coronel, one of General Flores' insurgents, had some days before started for Sonora with a *caballada* of one hundred horses. When he reached the Colorado, he learned from the Yuma Indians of the proximity of the Army of the West. Coronel was carrying dispatches from Flores to the Sonora authorities. The Americans might easily capture so small a party with a large *caballada* (and with them the letters) where a lone rider had a better chance of escape. Therefore, Coronel entrusted the dispatches to the man whom Lieutenant Emory intercepted on November 23. Coronel and the rest of his party turned back with the horses across the desert in advance of Kearny. He sent his horses ahead to Aguanga, some distance on the road to Los Angeles from Warner's. He had one of his Indians speed on to advise General Flores of the coming of the Americans. Coronel himself kept a close eye on the enemy's straggling approach. They were quite unaware of his existence. Coronel arrived at Aguanga on the cold, wet night of December 3, just a short time before Davidson's troop. Rain had been falling all day and he was drenched to the skin. He found shelter in the Indian huts nestled in a tangle of rocky hills and brushy hollows under the northern slopes of Palomar Mountain.

Coronel had just removed his outer garments when the Americans rode in to search for his horses. He escaped capture only by fleeing across country in his shirt. The dragoons seized Coronel's personal effects and about one hundred young mules and horses. Some had been broken and were fine animals, but the majority were of scant value.

The expedition resumed its march on the morning of the fourth in a cold, drizzling rain, going fifteen miles to Stokes' ranch at Santa Ysabel. Close to Stokes' headquarters a small band of Diegueño Indians had a rancheria. Its headman presented himself to General Kearny and declared his people did not want to take part in the war. They felt friendly to the Americans but wished to stay at home and work their farms. The General assured them that they could remain neutral and go about their daily tasks without fear of ill treatment.

In Stokes' absence, the major-domo at Santa Ysabel, generally known as Sailor Bill, was most hospitable and provided a bountiful dinner of mutton, *tortillas*, and grapes. However, Dr. Griffin pronounced the wine "abomnible." One newspaper writer many years later blamed the wine for the losses sustained on December 6, at San Pasqual. Archibald Gillespie hotly denied this in the next issue of the same paper. He certainly must be accepted as a reliable witness so far as this wine story is concerned.

The next morning as General Kearny plodded along with his column in a heavy downpour, a sudden flash of color under the oaks ahead thrilled every man indescribably. The Stars and Stripes fluttered bravely about a little group of horsemen. No such sight had so cheered them in a thousand miles. Speeding eagerly forward, the leading dragoons greeted the advance guard of a force that swiftly closed in behind the flag bearer. The commander was Captain Archibald Gillespie of the Marine Corps. Gillespie and his thirty-nine men and a small brass fourpounder (the famous Sutter gun) had been sent out from San Diego by Commodore Stockton when he received General Kearny's note of December 2. As Gillespie later reported the meeting: "Our flag was immediately given to the breeze and displayed for the first time upon those distant mountains, cheering the wayworn soldiers with a sight of the Stars and Stripes where they least expected to meet them." Soon afterward Gillespie met General Kearny and was received "with great kindness by himself and his officers." This picturesque incident took place close to the present hamlet of Ballena near Witch Creek.

As Gillespie's force had ridden north across Mission Valley in the moonlight, dwellers in the adobe houses watched them pass. One of these unseen witnesses, a sister of Andrés Pico, scribbled a note to her brother and rushed it to him. The hated Señor Gillespie was sallying forth to join another band of the wretched Americanos back in the mountains. Indians brought similar word of Gillespie's movements to Pico where he was camped ten miles north of San Diego. Pico disbelieved the story because he was sure all the Americans were safely besieged in San Diego. Gillespie was just on a raid for cattle and sheep to feed the starving Americans. The commander of the Californians resolved to ride out behind him and ambush the raiders when they returned with their booty. So that night Andrés Pico and a numerous company also rode as far as the little Indian village of San Pasqual. They took shelter in the brush and adobe huts and turned their horses out to graze in the northern end of the valley.

It is hard to explain Pico's apathetic reception of these warnings. Some weeks earlier word had reached General Flores from Sonora that a large body of men had been seen on the Gila. Flores reasoned correctly about their identity and sent Pico south with one hundred men to reinforce Don Leonardo Cota. The latter was hovering in the outskirts of San Diego to see that the Americans there did not break out. Pico was also directed to oppose any force that might try to reinforce the Americans in San Diego.

Captain Gillespie gave General Kearny a letter from Commodore Stockton: "Have this evening received information by two deserters of the arrival of an additional force of about a hundred men which in addition to the force previously here makes about a hundred and fifty. I send with Captain Gillespie as a guide one of these deserters that you may make inquiry of him and if you see fit endeavor to surprise them." Gillespie also had been instructed to tell Kearny that Pico with about one hundred men was at San Pasqual, and that if the General thought it advisable, he "should beat up the camp."

This information was received by Kearny and his officers "with

193

great pleasure . . . particularly by Captain Benjamin D. Moore of the First Dragoons who was extraordinarily desirous to meet the enemy as soon as possible." The contingent from San Diego, from the commander down, was gladdened by this attitude. They had a poor opinion of the valor of the Californians and vowed they would not fight.

Water and pasturage were scant, so the two forces camped some distance apart. Cold rain drenched the weary marchers, who once more rolled into wet blankets for the night without any supper. A few miles to the west Andrés Pico and his *caballeros* rested more warmly and better fed in the Indian huts. And somewhere among the mist-shrouded granite bosses of the Mesa Grande or the dripping snow-powdered pines of the Cuyamacas those three fateful sisters were looking down on both camps and once more busily weaving strange, dire threads of destiny for many brave men on the morrow.

15. San Pasqual

FEW MINOR ENGAGEMENTS have received as much attention from historians as those fought at San Pasqual, California, on December 6 and 7, 1846. On the scale of warfare they were only skirmishes. Notwithstanding this concentrated study, writers do not even agree about who was the victor! Almost every detail has aroused controversy. Admittedly there was genuine ground for doubt about what transpired. The fight began before dawn of a dark and misty day. Much of the action was not visible to the major portion of the Americans, since those actually in combat were widely scattered. Moreover, the leaders of the first charge were killed early in the conflict or so badly wounded as to render them poor witnesses.

This natural confusion has been heightened by the intense partisan clamor later raised against General Kearny. While this had nothing to do with the battle, Senator Benton and Colonel Frémont at the time of the latter's court-martial seized upon every conceivable charge against their opponent. When a student of the 1840's now studies San Pasqual, he must not merely search for the facts but separate them from a vast accumulation of error, conflicting testimony, prejudice, and distortion.

There are comparatively few primary sources for our knowledge of the event. These are official reports and diaries and letters of actual participants, written at the time or very shortly thereafter. They are supplemented by some secondary authorities. One of them merits almost as much credence as those in the primary category. These are accounts of participants and eyewitnesses as reported to others. Some were dictated or written long subsequent to the events described. Where this is apparent, both bias and failing memory must be weighed against their credibility. Ranking after these are a host of writers. Many have been honest seekers of the truth who sifted the evidence. Others have merely repeated what earlier writers said—without judgment of their own. In many cases they reflect the venomous prejudice of the Benton school. For any impartial reader, their versions both of San Pasqual and of other happenings in California during the Mexican War engender more heat than light.

With such a controversial subject it is advisable to lean heavily on the basic sources—first, General Kearny's official reports to the Adjutant General. These are supplemented by his letter to his wife written from San Diego on December 19, 1846. Allowing for the natural bias of any commander reporting his own actions, the impartial course is to accept at their face value only such parts of General Kearny's account as are confirmed by other participants.

One source that has had scant attention (probably because it has never been published) is Captain Archibald H. Gillespie's report to Commodore Stockton. No one is likely to accuse Gillespie of partiality toward Kearny. Yet oddly enough, the Marine officer in some respects presents the General more favorably than many of the latter's critics who were never near the scene. Gillespie's letter to the Secretary of the Navy written on February 16, 1847, tells of the fighting on December 6 and 7 with less detail but complete in most essentials. The two reports while not duplicates are in substantial agreement.

Lieutenant Emory took part in the fighting and gives a brief account in his *Notes*. So does Dr. John S. Griffin, who was the only surgeon present on the battlefield. His diary was written hastily on each of the critical days. In at least one respect to be later mentioned, it seems to me that Dr. Griffin's diary has not been sufficiently appreciated as basic evidence. Apparently Captain Turner did not resume his journal until several months after San Pasqual. A letter he wrote his wife two weeks after the battle is factual, but brief.

In the secondary sources on San Pasqual, we encounter a great variety of evidence. Several written accounts directly or indirectly report the experiences of participants or eyewitnesses. Some of these are of Californian and Indian origin. Later writers have drawn freely upon them. Arthur Woodward in the footnotes to his *Lances at San Pascual* indicates he had access to all that I have found, with one important exception. So far as my studies disclose, none of the writers on the history of this period has ever mentioned the source to which I refer. For nearly three quarters of a century its very existence seemed unknown. Men intensely interested in its subject matter, like Bancroft, Winsor, Larned, Royce, Cowan—and quite probably De Voto and Hanna—died without ever having heard of the *Private Journal—Letters of Captain S. F. Du Pont*, commanding the *Cyane* during the War with Mexico.

The Captain arrived in San Diego Harbor from San Francisco in command of the *Cyane* on December 26, 1846. Nearing Point Loma, someone hailed him from the small boat carrying the pilot. The voice was that of Lieutenant Edward F. Beale, U.S.N. Beale bore orders from Commodore Stockton for Du Pont to send ashore a contingent of the *Cyane's* crew to form part of the expedition about to march against Flores and Pico. Beale was evidently an old friend of Captain du Pont. While the pilot was bringing in the *Cyane*, he briefed her commander on all the latest happenings in southern California. The Captain on January 1, 1847, wrote in his journal:

> . . . the leading item of Beale's news was the arrival of General Kearney. (*sic*) I had been long wishing for him that things might resume their proper place; the army in the interior and at the posts, *we* on the coast and in the harbors. That some regular troops were so much wanted to keep order and be able thus to dispense with Frémont's irregular and vagabond force. One of the last persons I left in San Francisco was Lieutenant Radford, General Kearny's brother-in-law, who told me he had been overhauling the papers brought by the "Dale" and he did not believe the general was coming. He has come however but such a reception no man ever had. Somewhere in New Mexico he meets Kit Carson, the bearer of the Commodore's despatches from the Pueblo. Carson tells the General all is quiet in California, an election ordered, Commodore Stockton

197

had left the capitol, etc. That very circumstance had been greatly feared at the North and I was asked a dozen times if Carson's absurd despatches would not affect the General's movements. They did fatally—he sends back to Santa Fé two hundred of his three hundred dragoons under Major Sumner and comes on with the remaining hundred. He enters California at Warner's Pass, then encamps at San Pasqual, thirty-five miles from this place. There they heard that the enemy was in their neighborhood. I should have stated that before this at Stokes' rancho, they heard of the change of circumstances.

Captain du Pont then interrupted the narrative to explain how Beale was in a position to tell him about it:

> I forgot to mention that information had previously reached San Diego about General Kearny's approach and Gillespie and some thirty-five men with Beale . . . had been sent. . . . They had joined the detachment and were in camp.

With this background I feel we are justified in viewing the entry in Du Pont's journal as Lieutenant Beale's story of what he saw, heard, and did at San Pasqual. It must be borne in mind that his account was all written by Du Pont before the historic controversy arose to color anyone's views.

It is time to return to the two camps in the Santa Maria Valley, not far from the site of Ramona, where the dragoons and the contingent from San Diego spent the wet night of December 5. Early that evening Captain Johnston called on Captain Gillespie with General Kearny's request for the services of Rafael Machado, the deserter from the Californian forces whom Stockton sent with Gillespie as a guide. Kearny held a council of war. The General proposed an immediate reconnaissance of the enemy's position. With the information thus obtained they could better plan an attack on the morrow. Captain Moore opposed this. He was sure any movement by American scouts would be detected and thus the advantage of surprise would be lost. Pico's forces were superb horsemen on the best of animals, he argued, and the starved, worn-out mounts of the Americans would be no match for them. Moore preferred to have the whole column advance at once; then they would very likely catch the enemy dismounted and get his horses too—"To dismount them is to whip them." His objections were overruled.

Rafael Machado had been brought to the dragoon's camp. Beale and Alex Godey (one of the volunteers) had accompanied him there to report the General's intentions to Gillespie. Kearny ordered Lieutenant Hammond to take Machado as a guide on his reconnaissance. In both his reports Gillespie narrates the all-important occurrences between Machado's departure to join Hammond and his return with Beale and Godey a few hours later. Since Machado then told Gillespie what had happened, this is the most direct evidence we have of the reconnaissance. Beale, having returned with Machado, doubtless heard him report to Gillespie. Hammond did not live to give his account, and probably no other member of the scouting party left a record of it. Gillespie wrote to Bancroft:

> . . . the reconnoitering party composed of Lt. Hammond and Six Dragoons arrived at the base of the mountain, half a mile from the Indian village where the enemy were lying, halted and sent him (Rafael) forward to bring out an Indian to obtain the necessary information. Rafael went into the midst of the Enemy where they were sleeping, pulled out an Indian and ascertained that Andrés Pico was there with one hundred men. The Dragoons thinking he remained a long time dashed forward and passed the village, the clang of the heavy Dragoons swords awaking the sleepers, who came out, crying, "Viva California, abajo Los Americanos" and a great variety of abuse.

The dramatic details added in Beale's vertification of the adventure suggest the inevitability of fate. Du Pont writes:

> . . . a reconnaissance was ordered and Lieutenant Hammond and three dragoons left the camp for the purpose. After descending a long hill they turned around and came upon an Indian wigwam. The guide, an Indian, crawled in and soon discovered the whole party distributed in the huts, their horses at some distance, the packs and saddles off and nearby. The spy in the dark discovers a brother

Indian who beckons silence and tells him that Andreas (*sic*) Pico was among the sleepers and commanding about a hundred men. The Indians are very inimical to the Californians and always ready to betray them. The guide and spy was about retiring to rejoin Hammond when the latter, growing impatient, must ride up, his sword making a great noise which alarmed the sentinels. If he had brought twenty men he would only have had to place himself between the enemy and the horses and called out to them. They would all have come out, made a low bow and given themselves up in the most genteel manner in the world. They would have marched them to the tent in their front, retired and got their fine horses and saddles and very different would have been the entrance into San Diego.

It is not certain that the first noise made by Hammond would have aroused the party for the Indian sentries would not have told them but so soon as the dragoons heard the state of affairs, off they started and their swords were heard for a quarter of an hour ascending the long hill and the clattering of the horses' feet. That aroused the Californians, they caught their horses, saddled and mounted in a twinkling.

Gillespie's report gave the number of Hammond's dragoons as six; Beale's, as three. Otherwise the stories tally. (Years later Kearny's orderly reported Hammond had eleven men.)

One reads both narratives with a sense of mounting tension and the hand of destiny in the clang of the impatient Hammond's sword. Without that interruption the two Indians plotting in the darkness might have succeeded in betraying the sleeping Californians. It was neither the first nor the last time on that cold December night that the lives of many brave men, as well as much of Stephen Kearny's fame, would hang on a hair. Even his dragoons shared Hammond's impatience, and a last favorable chance was lost. Captain Gillespie must have sensed this when he wrote: "Thus the Californians were warned of the proximity of the Americans. The blunder by Hammond lost for Kearny the powerful advantage of surprise."

Most writers seem not to have recognized how narrowly this reconnaissance missed being a signal success. There is small point in dwelling on missed opportunity. Yet one senses the Benton-Frémont bias. Anything that even slightly mitigated one of their counts against Kearny was no grist for their mill. So Hammond's impatience and clanging sword, though reported by one of their own principal witnesses, were lightly passed over in 1847 and ever since.

The enemy camp was also not free from blunders. Andrés Pico seemed to be both stupid and stubborn. He had started with the conviction that all the American forces were confined to San Diego. The detested Gillespie was at large, but Pico reasoned that he was merely on a foraging expedition. The well-mounted Californians would easily ride him down and cut him to pieces when he drove back his ill-gotten booty. The warning letter from Pico's sister and the reports of his scouts were disregarded. Even his own men were alarmed by his failure to take precautions. They suspected the loyalty of their Indian companions and did not like to sleep so far from their horses.

The approach of Hammond's dragoons aroused a dog in the village. Scenting strangers, he barked. Pico sent an aide to investigate. One of the Mexican sentries challenged Machado as he slipped away, and by that time the clangor of the departing horsemen aroused the camp. Although a patrol reported seeing the intruders, Pico still would not believe they were Americans. He even refused ammunition to some of his force who were unarmed. At length the patrol returned with an army blanket stamped "U.S." and a dragoon's jacket that had been dropped in the Americans' flight. This evidence was a little too much even for Pico and belatedly he gave orders to round up the horses. Each man was to saddle and mount the first animal he caught.

Hammond and his noisy detail reached Kearny's headquarters a little before midnight. When the General learned that the enemy was alerted, he resolved on an immediate advance. It was so cold that according to most accounts the bugler could not blow reveille. The men had to be awakened by shouts. It had rained all night and everything was wet and the blankets frozen stiff. Word of the march having been sent to Captain Gillespie by Beale and Godey, the two forces moved westward on the trail to San Pasqual and united a little before three on the morning of the sixth. Significantly enough, Du Pont adds, "there was a good deal of excitement and desire for a brush and all pushed forward."

Much to his disappointment, Gillespie was first ordered by General Kearny to take his command to the rear and protect the baggage. The marine officer protested and pointed out that his brass four-pounder was an excellent piece and that his volunteer artillerists were well trained. On the other hand it seemed to him that the dragoons' two howitzers were in poor shape after their arduous journey and would fall apart at their first discharge. Whether because he sensed insubordination or presumption, the General curtly commanded, "Order that gun to the rear, sir!" Gillespie immediately obeyed. Just as he was taking the position directed, Kearney countermanded the order and bade him place his men on the left rear flank of the main body of dragoons commanded by Captain Moore. Gillespie straightway complied and the whole force moved on toward San Pasqual.

The weather had momentarily cleared and the moon, close to its setting, shone brightly. The north wind, blowing from the snow-covered heights, pierced everyone to the marrow. The men's hands were so stiff that they could scarcely grasp their bridles. The animals, too, were numb, sore, and weak from scanty, indifferent provender. While, as just noted, the bugler's lips were too chilled to blow a note, Pearce, the General's orderly, years later said the bugle sounded "Boots and Saddles" to start the column. For good measure, he added that when the valley floor was reached, "Charge as Foragers" was blown. That meant each member of the force was to select an opponent and vanquish as many as he could in his own way.

That is hard to reconcile with what next appears in most accounts. At the crest of the ridge between Santa Maria and San Pasqual, Kearny halted the column and gave his final orders. Enjoining implicit obedience, he said their country expected each of them to make the best effort in his power. He told them to surround the village and capture the Californians alive if possible. There was to be no unnecessary killing. "But," he closed in his old First Dragoons mood, "remember that one point of the saber is far more effective than any number of thrusts."

The expedition then descended the brushy trail by twos. This strung out the column in a long line with frequent gaps caused by the weaker animals. Gillespie and his volunteers followed Captain

Moore's command. While it had been clearer on the heights, the low-hanging clouds and fog still blanketed the valley. As they neared the Indian huts, the next tragic mistake of that dark morning climaxed the errors of judgment and missed opportunities. Most accounts say that as the valley floor was reached the order to "Trot!" was given but misunderstood by Johnston, who while still three-quarters of a mile from Pico's encampment, drew his sword and shouted "Charge!" Du Pont wrote:

> Those which were passably mounted naturally got ahead and they of course were mostly officers with the best of the dragoons, corporals and sergeants, men who had taken most care of their animals and very soon this advance guard to the number of about forty got far ahead—one and a half mile at least—of the main body while the howitzer was drawn by wild mules. In the gray of morning the enemy was discovered keeping ahead and with no intention of attacking but their superior horses and horsemanship made it mere play to keep themselves where they pleased. They also began to discover the miserable condition of their foes, some on mules and some on lean and lame horses, men and mules worn out by a long march with dead mules for subsistence.
>
> General Kearny who was with all his officers and of course Beale among the advanced body gave orders to "Trot" but his aide, Captain Johnston, mistook him and gave the order to "Charge" which in cavalry tactics means full speed. The General exclaimed, "O heavens! I did not mean that!" but it was too late and on they went at a gallop. Here again began a second separation from the disparity of the animals. There was no order—all straggling and about twenty-seven or twenty-eight out of the forty were alone in advance.

Military experts are better qualified than historians to debate why General Kearny decided to attack Pico in the pre-dawn fog of December 6. That is one of the most controversial points in his whole career. It would be a disservice to his memory to assume an attitude of uncompromising defense. In that easiest of all mental exercises—judgment after the event—one can list many reasons why Kearny should have chosen a different course. His men and animals were in the poorest possible condition for combat. The small escort Gillespie had led from San Diego did not add sufficient numbers of either men or fresh mounts to tip the scales materially. The carbines were well-nigh useless because of wet weather and sodden ammunition. The General knew little of the enemy's strength or available weapons (actually he overestimated their number). Another, though rougher and possibly a little longer, route to San Diego could have been taken from Santa Maria. Probably there were few if any enemy forces in position to dispute its passage. Finally, the dragoons were handicapped by their complete ignorance of the terrain and the poor visibility which made it hard to distinguish friend from foe.

Arthur Woodward expresses the opinion that "Kearny, having made one of the longest marches in the history of the United States Army, was spoiling for a fight and intended to have it." That seems entirely out of character with the man. The Kearny of Queenston Heights or Sackets Harbor might have so reacted; but not the veteran who had so many times shown forbearance when he could have picked up the Indians' gage of battle. Despite allowances for Hammond's lost opportunity and Johnston's mistake, Kearny as the commander must still shoulder the chief responsibility for the consequences.

We must remember that for two months he had been associated with Kit Carson. Knowing the latter's reputation, Kearny must have respected his judgment. Carson entertained a low opinion of Mexicans as fighters. He had expressed incredulity near Yuma when the first rumors reached the Americans of the reverses suffered in southern California. He apparently identified the native Californians with the unwarlike Mexicans he knew in New Mexico. The scout was still ruffled because his much-vaunted announcement of the American conquest had misfired. That must have made him sympathetic to Gillespie's burning desire for revenge because of his unceremonious expulsion from Los Angeles. Captain du Pont's journal had mentioned the early apprehension among Americans in California about the effect "Carson's absurd despatches" would have on the success of Kearny's expedition.

One badly wounded veteran of San Pasqual often told in later years of the reason for the battle: "Kearny intended avoiding them (i.e. the Californians under Pico) and passing on to San Diego but

Kit Carson assured Kearny that the Californians would not stand and *that it was a good opportunity to supply themselves with fresh horses.*" This is borne out by a statement of Carson quoted by Charles L. Camp. After briefly mentioning the return of Lieutenant Hammond "with three or four Dragoons," Carson said the General then determined to attack the enemy, *"the chief object was to get the Californians' animals."* [The italics in the last two quoted passages are mine.]

In the same article Camp notes that even the historian Bancroft was inclined to blame Carson for the misfortunes at San Pasqual. He mentions a letter in the Bancroft archives written by John M. Swan in 1875. Swan said Carson:

> . . . according to report told the officers under General Kearny that the native Californians would not fight but that all the Americans had to do was to yell, make a rush and the Californians would run away. Misled by these reports Kearny left two hundred of his dragoons behind in New Mexico. . . . I have no doubt of the truth of it and it was but too common among foreigners, both Americans and others, to talk the same way.

Camp disbelieved the story because Lieutenant Emory's report of events on October 6 and 7 (when Kearny met Carson at Socorro) makes no mention of such talk by the scout. That seems negative proof. Emory's *Notes* on October 6 said he "came into camp late and found Carson with an express from California, etc." Carson *could* have made these remarks prior to Emory's arrival.

It is unfair to blame Stockton for the message he sent urging Kearny to "beat up their camp." The Commodore qualified that advice with "if the general thought it advisable." An officer of General Kearny's rank would be expected to make his own decisions, regardless of the suggestions of others. Yet we cannot entirely overlook the cumulative effect of such a message when delivered by an officer like Gillespie to a man who had been listening to Kit Carson for so many weeks. Captain Gillespie had never concealed his contemptuous opinion of the Californians. The preceding April he had written the Secretary of the Navy: ". . . Californians of Spanish blood . . . have a holy horror of the American rifle, and will never expose themselves to make an attack."

Since the General knew that the enemy was aroused and awaiting him, why did he not delay the attack until daybreak? Surprise being ruled out, darkness could only favor the side more familiar with the ground. Kearny may also have realized that daylight would disclose his small numbers and their weakened condition. It is an old strategic trick to mask weakness by a bold demeanor. I believe we have the key to the riddle in the italicized quotations in the preceding paragraphs. Stephen Kearny was above all else a cavalryman. The scrawny, starved animals of his command must have aroused in him emotions of horror and dismay. His orders were not merely to reach San Diego. He must occupy and hold all of California. He had written Washington that he would proceed to Monterey. Now everything south of that town (excepting San Diego) was held by the enemy. Lacking anything like an intelligence service, he could only vaguely guess the strength and resources of his opponents. A march, with probable fighting, up hundreds of miles of hostile coast required all the horses and mules he could possibly seize. For that reason, despite his weak forces, he had raided the *caballada* at the mouth of the Gila. From the same motives he had ordered his desperately fatigued dragoons to ride through the cold, wet night to seize Coronel's livestock. The objectives of those two sorties had been attained without a battle so they are almost forgotten. But here, close at hand, Andrés Pico had maybe two hundred good horses, more precious than gold to Kearny at the moment. The importance he attached to these animals is further borne out by his official report after the battle. It contained rather few details, but there was one circumstance he felt it necessary to include: ". . . having learned from Captain Gillespie . . . that there was an armed party of Californians with a number of extra horses at San Pasqual. . . ." It seemed again a time to mask his weakness by a bold offense. In so deciding, General Kearny unquestionably erred. This was undoubtedly his "off day"; other and very successful generals have had them too. One recalls Stonewall Jackson's "lost day" at White Oak Swamp; that seems hard to explain until it is weighed in the

balance with Jackson's memorable achievements. We must never forget that a man's record is the sum of all his days.

While the majority of critics so definitely condemn Kearny on
this issue, it is curious to find that one of Kit Carson's ablest biographers upholds the General's conduct:

> Not realizing the fight was with free Californians accustomed to
> more initiative than the New Mexicans and *influenced by the con-
> tempt of Gillespie and Carson,* General Kearny's council decided
> to push on for San Diego and attack the enemy if they were opposed.
> In that plan was sound military sense. Boldness would win the way
> whereas hesitancy might result in a little force being shut off from
> the sea and all supplies and by a constantly increasing foe, confined
> helplessly inland while their chances grew less. [The italics are
> mine.]

One notes, too, that the General's officers were in accord with his
plan to attack, even though Captain Moore entertained misgivings.
The common inclination to advance boldly is in line with Gillespie's
statement of the enthusiasm for the offensive which he had found
when he first met Kearny's force near Witch Creek.

Returning to the moment when Captain Johnston made the fatal
mistake of shouting "Charge!" Du Pont comments that those who
were the best mounted inevitably drew away from the others. Johnston led the advance guard of twelve dragoons, all riding the pick
of the horses. Captain Moore followed with about fifty more dragoons, mostly on worn-out mules. As they galloped across the valley,
Johnston and his small band rapidly increased the gap between
themselves and the following troop. Kit Carson spurred on not far
behind.

The Indian village of San Pasqual occupied a tongue of high
ground jutting out from the hills. In a gully before the hamlet,
Pico's men were biding their time. As the first Americans rushed
furiously upon them, the Californians wheeled and discharged the
few firearms they possessed. One of the very first shots pierced Cap-

tain Johnston's forehead and killed him instantly. "One shot and the lance!" was the order given by Pico's lieutenant. Waving their swords and discharging what carbines were usable, the dragoons came on undaunted. When almost upon the Californians, the latter suddenly broke their line and galloped westward down the stream. For a moment it seemed they were retreating; for many of them the flight was probably genuine. Their course continued around the point of a rocky knoll thrust out from the north slope of the valley. Now the Americans had their first chance to observe their opponents' amazing horsemanship. (General Kearny later wrote: "They are admirably mounted and the very best riders in the world; hardly one that is not fit for the circus.")

Captain Moore undoubtedly believed the enemy in retreat and ordered a second charge. For a mile and a half his little detachment pursued the enemy, drawing farther away from their comrades who were still slowly feeling their way down the mountain. The retreating Californians now noted the scattered, irregular order of their pursuers and their small numbers. As suddenly as they had disappeared, they wheeled and galloped back with lances poised for attack. They scattered enough to outflank the oncoming column, much as they might encircle a herd of cattle. Soon Moore found himself alone in the lead, confronting General Pico. He fired his pistol and missed, then charged the General with his saber. The Mexican parried the blow and made a counterthrust with his own sword. Simultaneously two of his men pierced Moore with their lances. He toppled from his horse and a fourth Californian pistoled him as he lay prone. As the Captain fell his sword broke close to the hilt. When his body was later recovered, his hand still gripped the shattered blade. He had been wounded sixteen times.

Though other dragoons overtook their stricken Captain, their water-soaked carbines and pistols snapped ineffectively. In desperation they had to use their guns as clubs or rely on their sabers. In hand-to-hand combat the lances greatly outreached the swords and guns. Every one killed or wounded in this melee was lanced—an average of three "slots" in each man, Dr. Griffin reported. A number of the Americans were jerked from their mounts by *reatas* whirled about them by the Californians. Most of these lance thrusts

From a water color by Alfred Jacob Miller
Courtesy Walters Art Gallery

During the summer of 1845, Colonel Kearny and his First Dragoons journeyed to the Rocky Mountains and held impressive and beneficial councils with the Indians.

From a painting by Gerald Cassidy,
in possession of the New Mexico Historical Society
Courtesy Museum of New Mexico

On August 18, 1846, as American drums rolled and bugles blared in the plaza of Santa Fe, Stephen Kearny stood in the doorway of the Palace of Governors (pictured at right) and took possession of the province of New Mexico in the name of the government of the United States.

came from the rear where the better-mounted Californians closed at will on the dragoons as they rushed past. Those on the mules were especially vulnerable; a mule is reluctant to wheel.

By now indescribable confusion reigned. Men, mules, dragoons, and lancers milled about; some toppled to the ground. Shouts and curses mingled with the frantic neighing of the horses. A dozen hand-to-hand conflicts raged; men could scarcely distinguish friend from foe. In the poor light some of the mountain men, whose garb resembled that of the *caballeros,* narrowly escaped death at the hands of their own compatriots. Lieutenant Hammond, Moore's brother-in-law, seeing him unhorsed, rushed to his aid. He was heard to cry out to the dragoons behind him: "For God's sake, men, come up!" Just then a lance was driven deeply into his side and he fell from his horse. These brother officers were struck down close to each other near a lone willow tree. Moore died instantly but Hammond lingered two hours.

In the meantime Captain Gillespie, who had also raced to Moore's assistance, perceived the enemy's encircling movement. He feared an attack on the rear guard and ordered his men to dismount and drive the Californians out of the brush and cane along the river bottom. In the process they captured Pablo Vejar, second in command to Pico.

Most of the enemy had now charged back with wild halloos upon the little group of dragoons still fighting around Moore's body. Here their sharp lances wrought ghastly havoc. Nearly every one of the dragoons in the vanguard was either killed or wounded within a few minutes. Gillespie, sword in hand, dashed among them crying, "Rally, men, for God's sake, rally! Show a front, don't turn your backs. Face them, face them! Follow me."

His impassioned plea was probably unheard above the din of battle. These men were outnumbered, chilled to the bone, and exhausted from fierce fighting; they could do no more. All of a sudden a number of the Californians who had hated Gillespie in Los Angeles recognized him and set up a wild yell: "*Ya es Gillespie, adventro hombres, adventro!*" A horde of them rushed upon the marine, colliding with each other in their fierce desire to wreak vengeance on the hapless man. Somehow he successfully parried the first four

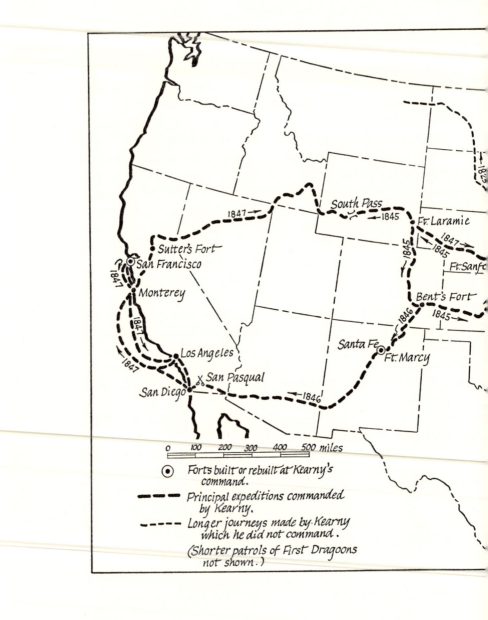

South Pass
1847 →
← 1845
Ft. Laramie
1847
1845
1845
Ft. Sanf
Sutter's Fort
San Francisco
1847
Monterey
1847
1847
Bent's Fort
1845 →
1846
Los Angeles
Santa Fe
Ft. Marcy
X San Pasqual
San Diego
← 1846

0   100   200   300   400   500 miles

⊙   Forts built or rebuilt at Kearny's
      command.

━ ━ ━   Principal expeditions commanded
          by Kearny.

- - - - -   Longer journeys made by Kearny
              which he did not command.

(Shorter patrols of First Dragoons
 not shown.)

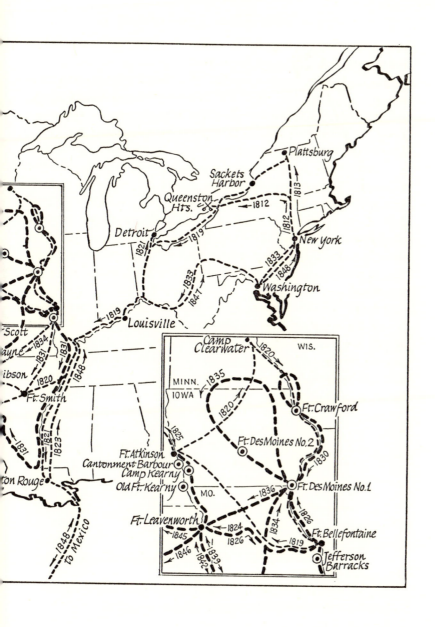

lance thrusts but as he tried to dodge the next, was struck on the back of his neck. The blow threw him from his horse, and he went down with his saber pinned beneath him. Another lance pierced him over the heart and penetrated to his lungs. As he turned to face this latest assailant, another Mexican charged him at full speed, aiming at Gillespie's face. The weapon cut his upper lip, broke a front tooth, and threw him upon his back just as his horse regained his feet and jumped over him. In some fashion Gillespie managed to rise and, recovering his saber, slashed his way out of the confused throng toward one of the howitzers where the scattered Americans were beginning to rally. (For years a legend persisted around San Pasqual that when Gillespie was dismounted a number of his enemies abandoned the fight to pursue his fine horse. According to this tale, so many *caballeros* galloped after the horse as to start a general retreat.)

One of the incidents about which accounts differ is the part played by the two howitzers and the Sutter gun at San Pasqual. Even Gillespie's two versions are contradictory on this point. The above narrative of his participation in the battle and of the wounds he sustained is in virtually his own words from his report to Commodore Stockton. But in writing the Secretary of the Navy less than two months later, he said:

> . . . in passing to the rear I came upon one of the howitzers without a person near it—I called to several as they passed to stand by me by the gun, but no attention was paid and becoming more faint every moment I left the howitzer and moved towards the second, about which the force had begun to rally. On passing it, I heard the cry "Where is the match?" "There is none" was the reply. I instantly struck fire to my machero (a wick lit by flint and steel) and fired the gun, which decided the action. I could stand no longer. Lieutenant Beale took command of my men . . . and Midshipman Duncan coming up with the carbineers and the field piece (this must have been the Sutter gun) he fired a shot at the enemy which drove them from the field.

We know that in bringing the two howitzers to the battleground, one of the mules became unmanageable and, despite the driver's frantic efforts to rein him, dashed toward the enemy dragging the howitzer after him. Two of the lancers rushed at the gun. The unlucky driver sought refuge under the carriage but was killed by the lancers. One of the Mexicans shot the mule and the two dragged the howitzer away with their *reatas*. They could not use the gun. At least one of the dragoons said its capture was the reason why the Californians galloped away so madly; the taking of the howitzer was in itself a victory! He added that the loss of the gun probably saved the lives of a number of the Americans. Many of the lancers who would otherwise have continued their deadly work were busy removing the fieldpiece. Long afterward the loss and recapture of the howitzer were to give John C. Frémont equally useless grounds for recrimination against General Kearny.

We have just read Captain Gillespie's statement that two cannon shots were fired—one by him from the howitzer and one by Midshipman Duncan from the Sutter gun. General Kearny has been criticized for saying in his report, "Our howitzers were not brought into the action, but coming to the front at the close of it, before they were turned as to admit of being fired upon the retreating enemy, the two mules before one of them got alarmed . . ." then repeating the story of the loss of the gun to the enemy. Certainly he leads us to believe the cannon shots were not fired. Later we shall see why he may have known little about that stage of the conflict. Arthur Woodward interprets Gillespie's report to the Secretary of the Navy as referring to the Sutter gun. Lancey in his *Cruise of the Dale* has Gillespie fire the howitzer before Duncan discharged the Sutter gun—as related here. Woodward thinks that either Gillespie or Lancey or both were confused over who fired which cannon. (For a man with all the wounds Gillespie had just received, that seems a reasonable assumption.) Bancroft does not believe any cannon was fired at San Pasqual.

I feel sure that one, and quite likely two, cannon shots were fired that morning. That helps to explain the retreat of the Californians. Artillery fire was a new and unpleasant experience to lancers who had been riding and spearing their opponents almost at will. Without waiting for any more cannon fire, most of Pico's force retired down the valley. Gillespie always claimed it was his burst of grapeshot that turned the scales.

While following Johnston, Moore, and Hammond to their deaths and watching Gillespie's hairbreadth escapes, we have lost sight of General Kearny and the rest of his command. When he realized how Captain Johnston had misunderstood his orders and that it was too late to stop the charge, the General spurred his jaded horse in support of the vanguard. Close by rode Captain Turner, Lieutenants Emory and Warner, and Dr. Griffin. Next came the volunteers under Captains Gillespie and Gibson, followed by the howitzers whose action we have just noted. Major Swords and the baggage train were still some distance to the rear. Despite these efforts, the General and those with him were more than a mile behind Johnston and Moore when they first clashed with Pico's forces. In the fog they could see little of the contest, but the outcries and rattle of weapons and equipment were plainly heard. When they arrived on the field of battle the Californians were making their countercharge, and soon all of the officers were in the thick of the fray, parrying lance thrusts and slashing at their stabbing foemen with their swords. "The old general defended himself valiantly," Beale told Du Pont, "and was as calm as a clock." As Kearny fenced with a lancer in front of him, another struck him from behind. Kearny would undoubtedly have suffered a fatal wound except for the valor of Lieutenant Emory. Rushing in, Emory drove the assailant away with his sword. Even so the General had been wounded in three places and was bleeding freely. Captain Turner, although in the thick of the fray, seems to have borne a charmed life. Lances cut his jacket in several places and one penetrated just far enough to scratch his skin.

With General Kearny disabled, Turner now took command. Pearce, the orderly, was within a few feet of him when Kearny was wounded. Years afterward he claimed that the General ordered a retreat but that Captain Turner cried out: "No, never, men! Never turn your backs on these men, or you will all be cut down. Dismount!" By this time Lieutenant Warner and Captain Gibson had also been painfully lanced as well as the scout Roubidoux. From Gillespie's reports it appears that the cannons were fired after General Kearny received his wounds. That may explain why he stated they did not take part in the battle.

Kit Carson rode at Captain Johnston's heels in the first charge. Perhaps that burst of speed was responsible for saving his life. Just before the two forces clashed, Carson's horse stumbled and threw him to the ground. In the fall his rifle was broken. The scout was barely able to roll out of the way of the flying hooves. When he could rise he found himself bruised but unhurt. He had to run a hundred yards to rejoin the others. Here he took a carbine and cartridge box from a dead dragoon just as Captain Moore and his column smothered him in its dust. When the Californians wheeled and charged back, Kit took cover in the rocks of the hillside and fired at the darting lancers whenever they came in range. Later he assisted at the night burial.

As more of his column continued to arrive on the floor of the valley, Kearny wished to attempt another charge. Captain Turner and the few officers still capable of taking the offensive dissuaded him. With so small a number of able-bodied men left, it seemed unwise to resume the battle. The wounded men must be given prompt attention. Across the valley a large group of horsemen were visible. The General feared they would attack Major Swords and the baggage train. He directed Lieutenant Emory to take a detachment and go to the Major's relief. Emory's party met the baggage train just coming into the valley. As the combined force returned, Captain Johnston's body was discovered and carried back for burial. It had already been plundered. He and one dragoon were the only Americans killed by gunfire. All other casualties, both the dead and wounded, were due to the murderous lances.

Dr. Griffin's diary gives the most accurate report of the wounded. As the surgeon hurried to the aid of Lieutenant Hammond, he saw the General lying near by with blood flowing freely from his wounds. Before he could attend to either, a lancer nearly speared the surgeon. He drove him off by snapping an unloaded pistol in his assailant's face. Gillespie, covered with blood, reeled by him; he seemed in critical need and Dr. Griffin set about dressing his wounds. As he worked, Captain Gibson cried out for his services. Griffin knew

Kearny required quick attention and turned to help him but the General, looking slowly at the dead and disabled, said, "First, go and dress the wounds of the soldiers who require more attention than I do and when you have done that, come to me." While the doctor was busy carrying out this order he looked in Kearny's direction and saw him fall in a faint. Griffin ran to his side, stopped the hemorrhage, dressed his wounds, and restored him to consciousness. Several officers and soldiers near him thought he was dying. One lance thrust cut his arm in several places. More serious was a deep gash in the buttocks. This made it extremely painful for him to ride his horse for many days.

It is shocking to read in notes made by one of the dragoons some years later that "many of the men said (regarding Kearny's wounds) it was a d——d good thing, it would have been well, if they had killed him . . . it was a disgrace because if he had waited for daylight, no man would have suffered; they would have seen how to defend themselves." This makes strange reading when one remembers the *esprit de corps* of the First Dragoons—even sadder reading when we recall the General's direction to Dr. Griffin to attend the other wounded ahead of himself.

Whatever the real reason for their flight, Pico's men had at last retreated, and the Americans remained in possession of the battlefield. After such a mauling they were glad to make camp for the night near the scene of the second charge. The abundance of rocks and cacti made a poor resting place and hampered the treatment of the wounded. However, the sloping ground commanded a view to the south and west and insured the soldiers from a surprise attack. The present-day battle monument marks this campsite of December 6.

In studying San Pasqual we have the testimony of a neutral eyewitness. Felicita, the daughter of Pontho, chieftain of the San Pasqual Indians, told her story years afterward to a local white woman. It is subject to the inherent weakness of all accounts committed to writing long after the event. On some moot points it bears out the versions of the affair given by Gillespie and Beale and not available to earlier historians:

. . . one morning we heard the sound of voices shouting on the mountain side towards Santa Maria. Clouds hung low so at first we could see nothing but some figures of men like shadows came riding down the mountain. They were soldiers wearing coats of blue. . . . The Mexican soldiers were sitting on their horses holding their long lances in their hands. They now rode swiftly to meet the soldiers in blue and soon there came the sound of battle. The Indians in great fear fled to the mountains. We hid behind brush and rocks and watched. One of our men who had lived at the Mission told us that the strange soldiers from the hills were Americans and that they were fighting to take the land away from the Mexicans. The Mexicans had not been good to the Indians so we were not sorry to see the new soldiers come against them. At first there were only a few of the American soldiers who came down the mountain and there were many Mexicans so the battle went hard. Some of the Americans were killed and some wounded. Then more of their men came from the mountain and the Mexicans were driven away. We saw them ride down the valley and wait behind a hill. Soon we saw the Americans moving down the valley. When they came near the place where the Mexicans were hiding there was more fighting and we trembled as we watched. The Americans did not shoot their gun many times. Perhaps rain had made the powder wet. They struck with their guns and used the sword while the Mexicans used the long lances and their reatas. The mules that the Americans rode were frightened and ran all through the willows by the river. After them rode the Mexicans on their swift horses, striking with the lances and lassooing with the reata. It was a very terrible thing. As the hours passed we crept nearer and nearer to the valley. There was little shooting so we were not afraid of the bullets. . . . Towards evening another company of Americans that must have been far behind came to the fighting place [probably the rear guard with the baggage train]. Then the Mexicans rode away and the American soldiers had time to look for their dead and wounded.

Dr. Griffin observed that Kearny's command suffered thirty-five killed and wounded, and yet not more than fifty men of the command had seen the enemy! (Gillespie's estimate was a maximum of forty-five). Few engagements can exceed San Pasqual's record for the deadliness of the combat. Since several reports assert that

217

about seventy of Pico's men actually fought, it is apparent that the Americans were considerably outnumbered as well as outclassed in mounts and usable weapons. This further testifies to the sheer courage and fighting spirit displayed by Kearny's little force, despite all the conditions militating against its success.

Gillespie's first report to Commodore Stockton said the American losses were twenty-one killed and twenty-three wounded. In the second he reduced the total to thirty-eight. Griffin's total of thirty-five included seventeen killed. One man later died of his wounds in San Diego. The official roster of all the American dead as finally prepared by Dr. Griffin and listed by Arthur Woodward totals twenty-one. General Kearny's report to the War Department lists nineteen dead (but one of the wounded died a week after the report was written). I believe twenty-two is the correct number.

While there were minor discrepancies about the American casualties, when we attempt to report Pico's losses we encounter real difficulty. General Kearny has been criticized for reporting that he thought the Californians lost a large number of killed and wounded. Yet he frankly added that he had no way of determining the number. Gillespie at first claimed the enemy's total was twenty-seven. His overenthusiastic volunteers said they were certain of eighteen, and he pointed out that the dragoons reported from ten to twelve in addition. Later Gillespie said that an Indian at the San Bernardo rancho (west of San Pasqual) told him the Californians brought fifteen or eighteen wounded men to the ranch, one of them nearly dead.

Dr. Griffin said the Americans took two prisoners. Like Kearny he thought "the enemy must have suffered as much as we did." Pico would only admit to one man killed and twelve wounded. Too little attention has been paid to one entry in Dr. Griffin's journal. Local authorities like Judge Benjamin Hayes gave it enough credence to mention many years later. To quote Dr. Griffin on December 20, 1846:

> A report reached our camp the other day that the Indians had killed eleven Mexicans—that these fellows had first attacked the Indians, taken their cattle and horses and killed some five or six

218

Indians—that at night the Indians had surrounded their camp, taken the party prisoners—then took them off to some distance and shot them to death with arrows. All tell the same story as regards the number killed but vary as to the manner. *Those best versed in California affairs believe these men were killed in the action of the 6th* (i.e., Battle of San Pasqual) *and that the Mexicans complain of the redskins to conceal their own loss.* They acknowledge one killed and fourteen desperately wounded. After the action of San Bernardo (December 7–10, 1846) I sent word to Pico that I would be most happy to attend to his wounded. He replied that he had none. It is now said that his men are in the greatest state of excitement against him for not accepting my services.

The italics are mine and relate to the so-called Massacre of Pauma by San Luis Rey Indians sometime between December 6 and 12, 1846. (Pauma is a small valley in the western foothills of Palomar Mountain.) The coincidence of the dates of the Pauma Massacre with the Battle of San Pasqual is striking and deepens one's uncertainty over just how lightly Pico's forces emerged from the fray.

Lieutenant Emory's *Notes* also indicate that the Californians suffered heavier casualties than are usually stated. While at San Juan Capistrano on January 5, 1847, Emory was "attracted by a house having a brush fence round the door, as if to keep out intruders. I was told there were four men within, in the agonies of death, from wounds received at the battle of San Pasqual." Also Consul Thomas O. Larkin wrote on January 11 that it was believed in Los Angeles that the Californians had lost more than they themselves knew.

The battered Army of the West faced the melancholy task of burying its dead. It was first planned to carry them to San Diego for interment. A quick survey disclosed, however, that not enough strong pack animals remained to convey both dead and wounded. The badly injured required some form of ambulance. Therefore it was determined to inter all the dead in one grave when night fell. Emory's lines are too eloquent to shorten:

When night closed in, the bodies of the dead were buried under a willow to the east of our camp, with no other accompaniment than the howling of myriads of wolves, attracted by the smell. Thus were put to rest together and forever, a band of brave and heroic men. The long march of 2,000 miles had brought our little command, both officers and men, to know each other well. Community of hardships, dangers, and privations, had produced relations of mutual regard which caused their loss to sink deeply in our memories.

(One of the members of Gillespie's party wrote Hubert Howe Bancroft long afterward that six enemy dead were buried in the same pit as the Americans, but confirmation from any other source seems lacking.)

Kearny's own reflections at this somber hour were vividly recalled when he wrote his wife about San Pasqual after arriving in San Diego:

> We gained a victory over the enemy, but paid most dearly for it. . . . The loss of our killed is deeply felt by all, particularly by myself who very much miss my aide Johnston who was a most excellent & talented soldier & Capt. Moore who displayed great courage & chivalry in the fight, as did Lieut. Hammond. . . ."

But what of the living? Provisions were exhausted; the horses, dead; and the mules, nearly so. Even the men who had escaped wounds were ragged, half-starved, and worn by fatigue and exertion. Conveyance of the wounded was the first pressing problem. Gillespie and Beale told Captain Turner that sufficient wheeled vehicles could be had in San Diego. Turner, by the light of the camp-fire, wrote a brief account of the engagement and of their plight to Commodore Stockton, together with an appeal to send help. He urged that if possible carts to transport the wounded and provisions to relieve their starving condition be provided. The Captain read the letter to the General as he lay exhausted on the ground after his wounds had been dressed. Kearny approved its contents. Early on the morning of the seventh, Alex Godey and some picked men took a circuitous trail over the southern hills to carry Turner's letter to San Diego. (Actually, Stokes, the English rancher from Santa Ysabel, brought Stockton the news of the fighting at San Pasqual.

Apparently he reached San Diego about the same time as the Godey party.)

As the day wore on, some of Pico's forces came into view down the valley. Dr. Griffin was making surprising progress with his patients. General Kearny was able to mount his horse and resume command. The remaining dragoons were consolidated into one company under Captain Turner. It was decided to move once more against the enemy. The remaining mountain men had contrived some rude horse litters, "travois" they called them. Willow poles were cut and dragged like sleds with one end trailing on the ground. Buffalo robes were lashed between the poles and the wounded laid on them. With these litters and the packs in the center, the march was resumed toward San Diego. The column drew away from the river for the security of the hills to the north. The route corresponded roughly with present Highway 78 from San Pasqual to Escondido. The Californians retired before the Americans' advance but hovered in sight. (Here one of Kit Carson's biographers departs from the usual account of this march and says Kit was in command of the advance guard on the march to San Bernardo.)

One hundred years ago what is today known as the "San Dieguito River" was called the "San Bernardo." A few miles southwest of the battle monument where the Americans camped on the night of December 6, the San Bernardo flows through a low gorge between the hills. San Bernardo Mountain and the lower rocky hills to its east form the northwest wall of the valley here, while the steep conical peak called "Battle Mountain" bounds it on the south side. Like all southern California streams, the San Bernardo is usually dry, and this was apparently the case in December, 1846. However, the sandy river bed through the narrow pass was well lined with brush and small timber. After a few miles' progress the guides had General Kearny swing sharply to the left to avoid the higher hills in front. The most direct route to San Diego passed to the south.

It was not long before the rancheria of San Bernardo was reached. This belonged to a widow named Snook, but except for a few Indians, it was deserted when Kearny's force arrived. On their way over the hills the column had rounded up a considerable herd of cattle. At the rancheria, too, they were glad to catch some chickens for the sick. By the time Kearny's column had reached Snook's, the Californians had circled around the dragoons and were hovering to their north, west, and southeast.

About a half-mile southeast of Snook's lie several low, boulder-strewn hills, thick with cactus and brush. One hill commands the passage up and down the river. As General Kearny resumed the advance from the ranch house, driving the cattle before him, a band of the Californians suddenly galloped out from the shelter of these hills. As the Americans came within range, they opened fire. No one was hit, but Emory and a small detail were ordered to charge the lancers and seize the hill commanding the narrows. The Californians had already occupied its summit and greatly outnumbered their opponents. Many had dismounted and were firing from behind the boulders, while the Americans had to advance upon them in the open. They made it in a headlong dash for the crest and the fight was soon over. It was not a place where the lance could be used to advantage, and the Californians quickly broke and fled. In his report General Kearny said his men killed and wounded five of the enemy without themselves suffering any casualties.

A much more serious result of this scrimmage was the loss of all the cattle. There were no horses left capable of pursuing them. To make matters worse, most of the chickens, too, had vanished. The entire force was now virtually without rations of any kind. "It was then," Captain du Pont writes, "that they wanted the other two hundred dragoons which those wretched dispatches had turned back."

Eying the rougher terrain ahead and the hovering enemy, General Kearny decided it unwise to attempt to advance under the handicap of the wounded and the baggage train. He ordered camp made for the night upon the hill. This allowed Dr. Griffin to redress the wounded, whose condition he reported as discouraging. Probably the detachment would have to cut its way to San Diego the next day. While the position was defensible, the prospects looked grim. With food gone and the river dry, even water was a problem. But the streams of this region maintain an underground flow even when dry on the surface. Therefore sufficient water was finally obtained by digging holes in the sandy bottoms below the hill. At the most it was a muddy and meager supply. For food the fattest of the mules provided the only answer. The best of these were little better than skin and bones. But they warded off starvation and gave the low eminence its name of Mule Hill. Gillespie even reported that the men each day improved in strength and spirits under this diet of mule meat. The neighborhood was strewn with boulders of all sizes. The General had the men build battlements of these rocks, with the smaller ones wedged into the crannies between the larger. Over one hundred years later this rock fortification still stands on Mule Hill as a rude monument to those beleaguered and starving men.

While they anxiously watched for a relief party on the morning of the eighth, a commotion some distance across the plain caught the soldiers' attention. A disappointing explanation arrived in the form of a flag of truce from General Pico with a request to exchange prisoners. Lieutenant Emory was sent to treat with Pico; he took with him Vejar, the one prisoner held by the Americans. His parley with the commander of the Californians was brief. Pico had four prisoners, just captured, and demanded four of his own men as an even exchange. Emory was in a poor trading position. For Vejar, General Pico would only release Burgess, one of Godey's companions. Emory had no choice but to accept him.

(Senator Benton in his long philippic against General Kearny in the Senate tells a different story of this incident. Emory's statement that *he* was sent to meet Andrés Pico could not be more unequivocal. However, Benton, and later Frémont in his memoirs, gave a highly circumstantial account in which Lieutenant Beale was the emissary who parleyed with the Californian commander. One could infer that they obtained the story from Beale himself. However, it seems very strange that Du Pont, in writing at length of Beale's adventures soon afterward, includes none of their picturesque details. One of these described Beale as "dashing" through the Río San Bernardo on his way to meet Pico without pausing to drink or water his mount; this was the same river in whose dry bed the Americans on Mule Hill had just dug holes for water! Such discrepancies in the Benton-Frémont annals are bound to cast a doubt on any of their unsupported assertions.)

223

With Castilian courtesy, General Pico also used the flag of truce to send to Captain Gillespie some food and clothing which the captured men had been bringing to him from friends in San Diego. Burgess explained how the entire party had been taken prisoners a little earlier that morning. As they came in sight of Mule Hill, the Californians had swooped down on them. This was the disturbance which Kearny's men had observed. Godey and the others had successfully reached San Diego and delivered Captain Turner's letter to Commodore Stockton. They had carried back his reply but for fear of being captured had cached it in a tree. (When the march to San Diego was resumed, investigation disclosed that the letter had been removed from its hiding place.) Burgess knew the contents of the message; the Commodore refused to send reinforcements!

This negative answer forced General Kearny to decide upon extreme measures. His position, with no prospect for relief, was hopeless; better therefore at any hazard to march on in the chance that they might cut their way through. In this crisis, the officers held a council and the navy's representatives pledged themselves most strongly that Stockton would send relief. Dr. Griffin felt removal of the wounded at the moment would be extremely hazardous. Therefore General Kearny agreed to wait a little longer.

Lieutenant Beale and Kit Carson volunteered to slip out that night and take word of their desperate plight to Stockton. The General objected that he would need Carson's services in case they had to cut their way through. But Beale represented that Kit's company would greatly increase the prospects of his eluding the besiegers. (An inspection plainly revealed three lines of sentries maintained by the well-mounted Californians.) Kit said it was certainly a forlorn hope but with the General's permission he would chance it as he hated to let the boy (Beale) go alone. Kearny finally yielded to these arguments, and plans were made for them to leave after nightfall with an Indian as a guide. For a long time this Indian remained anonymous. In recent years research by various writers and publication of a century-old nautical journal have supplied him with an embarrassing surplus of names. *Che-muc-tah*, the name used by the sailor from the *Portsmouth,* while not necessarily correct, will be used hereafter.

As Beale prepared to leave on the night of the eighth, General Kearny had his orderly bake the remaining handful of flour into a small loaf for the Lieutenant. The latter refused the loaf because it was more needed on Mule Hill. After darkness fell, Carson, Beale, and *Che-muc-tah* crawled through the rocks and cacti to elude Pico's sentries. Their shoes made too much noise on the loose stones, so Carson and Beale removed and tied them to their belts. In the arduous task of tiptoeing and creeping through the brush, they lost the shoes. The journey in bare feet over cacti and sharp rocks was a torturing ordeal. *Che-muc-tah* was the first to reach San Diego at six o'clock on the evening of the ninth. Beale staggered in four hours behind him, almost delirious from fatigue and pain. Kit had bravely chosen the most dangerous route, which was also the longest, so he did not arrive until the morning of the tenth. By the time Carson came in, the long-delayed relief party had already started for San Bernardo.

The dispatch of this expedition under Lieutenant Andrew F. V. Gray of the *U.S.S. Congress* involves another of the innumerable controversies about San Pasqual. The more extreme Stockton-Frémont partisans even assert that there never was any refusal to send the relief party nor any undue delay in its marching. But the stubborn record remains in Dr. Griffin's diary that Burgess verbally gave Kearny the message contained in Stockton's missing letter: "Commodore Stockton refused to send us a reinforcement." Men in the dire peril besetting the defenders of Mule Hill do not misunderstand messages of that sort.

Confirmation is to be found in an unpublished manuscript of General Flores' in the Bancroft collections; a letter from Flores to General Andrés Pico dated December 10, 1846, told him to press his attacks on General Kearny because Stockton's captured dispatches had disclosed that he could not send a force to relieve General Kearny. Is this not the answer to why Stockton's letter cached in the tree by Godey and his companions was missing when the column searched for it? The best proof of all arises from the fact that the officers on

225

the hill considered it necessary after Burgess' arrival to send another appeal to Stockton. Knowing that such a messenger would be in sore peril of his life, no one would have volunteered to attempt the mission nor would General Kearny have permitted it except for the unfavorable answer from Stockton.

Unquestionably the Commodore was hard-pressed for horses, supplies, and even men. It would not have been easy to answer Captain Turner's appeal with reinforcements and the needed carts, provisions, and medical supplies. The refusal had been dispatched on the seventh.

At Frémont's court-martial Commodore Stockton testified that, as soon as he learned of the grave condition of General Kearny's men, he felt he must immediately send his whole force to their rescue. He was vague about dates, said he gave orders to prepare two days' provisions and to assemble some artillery pieces, and immediately ordered his aide-de-camp to proceed with a body of troops to the Mission of San Diego where the Commodore planned to join Gray "the next morning." That sounds like the morning of December 8. Yet he added that when Beale arrived on the evening of the ninth, the troops under Gray were nearly ready to *start* for the Mission. *Now* the Commodore was going to join Gray there on the morning of the tenth. He directed Gray to hide his forces in the daytime so that they could make a night march, which would have brought them to San Bernardo by the morning of the twelfth. All this time the wounded lacked adequate care, and all the men on Mule Hill were barely sustaining life. All this time Pico's well-mounted lancers were closely hemming in Stockton's fellow countrymen and restraining them not only from escape but even from a successful foraging raid. With San Bernardo only twenty-nine miles away, why the idle hours on the seventh, eighth, and ninth? Surely here it could be said that "he gives twice who gives quickly." Perhaps Commodore Stockton felt twinges of conscience after sending the letter refusing aid. Perhaps he began to worry that his own reputation might suffer if the worst befell the beleaguered men. Whatever his reasoning, we do know that preparations for an expedition had been started before *Che-muc-tah* drew his first long breath after arrival. Lieutenant Gray in fact marched that same night for the

Mission. A line in Captain Gillespie's report to the Secretary of the Navy offers a clue to what happened at Stockton's headquarters: "the credit of the march is due to Capt. (Jacob) Zeilin of the Marines, without whom the force would have been in a sad condition."

In the meantime what was happening on Mule Hill? Everyone there realized the heavy odds against them. Probably the three messengers would not get through. Even if they did, Stockton might again refuse aid. Still hoping, they prepared for the worst. On the morning of the ninth, Kearny ordered the destruction of all non-essential property. He was not going to give Pico any booty. All through that day and another night the grim vigil continued, "the enemy . . . constantly hanging around us but are very careful not to come within gun shot. Sergeant Cox died on the 10th." That evening Pico's men drove a band of their own horses and mules among the few scrawny animals left to the Americans in an attempt to stampede them. The alert soldiers saved their own stock and dispersed the advancing herd by a missile from the Sutter gun. Several fat mules dashed too close, and bullets from the hill's defenders augmented their meat supply.

Later that day Dr. Griffin reassured the General that all but two of the wounded could now safely keep their saddles. So that night General Kearny quietly passed the word that everything be readied for an early-morning march. Some two hours after midnight, the weary sentinels heard the tramp of many feet to the southwest. Their challenging "Who goes there?" brought the most welcome of hails from the darkness—"Americans."

The suddenly awakened men behind the rocky breastworks beheld what seemed a miracle. In solid formation 80 marines and 120 sailors advanced up the slope. A few hails of greeting swelled to cheers and excited interchanges. The newcomers passed out clothing, tobacco, jerked beef, and hardtack. They themselves were tired, cold, and hungry and the men on the hill treated them to hot mule soup. Kearny's men gave up their cramped sleeping places and blankets to their rescuers, who had earned a few hours' slumber. Mule Hill's garrison was too excited for further sleep. They eagerly awaited dawn to finish their march to the sea. While they were chatting about their good fortune, one lone musket ball whistled harmlessly through the camp—a last, mournful shot of disappointment from an enemy robbed of its prey.

On their march to San Bernardo, the relief party had captured one of Pico's men. He disclosed that his commander had 160 men at the San Pasqual fight. One hundred of these had been sent from Los Angeles. A few days later authentic sources reported Pico's total on the sixth had been 180 men and that one hundred reinforcements had reached him on the seventh. This amply accounted for the tight ring he had thrown around Mule Hill. By daybreak on the eleventh most of the foemen had vanished; only a few horsemen hovered around Snook's rancho. So sudden had been their flight that most of their cattle had been left behind. These were rounded up by the Americans and driven along when they left Mule Hill. The journey was started at an early hour. Through the hills to the south they marched without incident. The enemy carefully kept out of sight. Camp was made that night at the rancho of one of their foemen. This made the soldiers the more eager to help themselves freely to his cattle and sheep, pigs and chickens, and even some wine to cheer the wounded. One of the sailors wrote in his journal: "The two hundred and forty hungry American soldiers left that ranch and house as clean as only a swarm of locusts ever did."

Lieutenant Gray was a stricter disciplinarian than General Kearny. Such wholesale looting of even an enemy's house went decidedly against his grain. He could restrain his own relief contingent but had no authority over the dragoons or volunteers. He appealed to General Kearny to stop the raiders. His only reply was a quizzical smile and "Yes, yes—I know—the poor fellows are half starved—let 'em run—they won't kill any more than they can eat." Another sailor wrote that Gray retired in disgust, "but many an honest heart blessed the old General for his kind heart and in the same breath d——d Lieut. Gray for a fool." Thanks to the involuntary hospitality of the absent ranchero and the tolerance of General Kearny, the devoted little band that had accompanied him all the way from Santa Fe rolled into their blankets that night with full stomachs for the first time in many weeks of torment.

At four o'clock the next afternoon, the whole command marched into San Diego in a pouring rain. Commodore Stockton had not joined Lieutenant Gray but now went on foot to the edge of town to offer formal welcome to General Kearny. He and the officers of the *Congress* and *Portsmouth* extended hospitality. The Commodore offered his own quarters to the General. He accepted them until he could find other space. The march had been a grim ordeal for some of the wounded. Two of them had traveled all the way on the same rude travois constructed on the battlefield. One died a few days after reaching San Diego.

General Kearny himself was ragged, begrimed, and weary to the very marrow. The worst of his wounds was not healing and this last horseback ride had been torture. He and the merest remnant of the force that had bravely headed west from Fort Leavenworth had finally reached the Pacific! The march just completed, like all those led by Stephen Kearny, had been marked by the absence of any mishap to the personnel, if we except the battle casualties. He was doubtless too ill and exhausted to feel elated over what had been accomplished. His expedition had just completed one of the longest and most difficult marches in human history. This man had conquered a forbidding wilderness, hunger, thirst, pitiless heat, and numbing cold and had at last fought the enemies of his country. Only an amazing courage and dogged determination had brought his forces to their journey's end.

The record of this march must be weighed in the scales when we ponder whether San Pasqual was an American victory or defeat. What is victory? May we not define it as the successful attainment of the objective in a battle or campaign. That may be the lifting of a siege, the cutting of communications, or the capture or destruction of enemy forces. When we study this December fighting, we must remember that Kearny's primary purpose was to reach the Pacific as ordered, establish contact with the navy, and complete the conquest of California. If the Americans after fighting a battle were barred from those objectives, everyone would agree that they were defeated. But if after fighting the battle they attained those further ends, just how can we refuse to credit them with a victory—even if a costly and desperate one?

General Kearny's tactics on the night of December 5–6 were at fault. "Blunders" is one word applied to them with reason. He should have known that his dragoons' carbines were useless because of wet ammunition. Some accounts say many of the sabers were rusted in the scabbards from long disuse. If that was true, he should have known and corrected it; he should have realized that because of the deplorable condition of his animals, he could not effectively execute the rapid advance dictated by his strategy. We have already noted arguments that he exercised sound strategy in pushing on from Santa Maria. But the line between strategy and tactics is sometimes difficult to draw. Strategy is most likely to be successful when implemented by sound tactics. Napoleon said the art of war consists in always having larger forces than the enemy at the point of attack—or defense. To do this, rapidity of movement is essential; or in General Nathan Forrest's words, "get there fustest with the mostest."

Captain Moore showed he recognized the force of this when he argued for an immediate surprise attack. With the enemy dismounted and asleep at some distance from their horses, the Americans would have momentarily possessed the superior forces at the point of attack. With surprise ruled out, they lost not only that advantage of superior numbers, but because of their inferior mounts, that of rapidity of movement as well. Doctor Griffin put it less technically when he wrote "this was an action where decidedly more courage than conduct was showed." But poor tactics and defeat are not synonymous. Victories have more than once been won in spite of bad tactics. Historians have never agreed over who was victorious at San Pasqual. There is a formidable roster of those who write it off as a defeat.

Senator Benton and, of course, John C. Frémont were the first to stigmatize it as such. Commodore Stockton agreed with them. Starting with Hubert Howe Bancroft down to contemporaries like Allan Nevins, many historians have declared it a defeat. Numerous other authorities are opposed to them in that opinion. It would be tedious to list all the varying views. Many who have called the battle an American victory have qualified their findings by emphasizing that it was dearly bought. One official verdict should be noted. Nearly a century after the event, the Historical Division of the Army War College ruled: "General Kearny did not sustain a defeat at San Pasqual."

Curiously enough, Captain Gillespie, although serving under Commodore Stockton and linked with Frémont in all the latter's contention with Kearny, stoutly maintained that San Pasqual was an American victory. A biographer of Gillespie, in disagreeing, stresses the allegedly heavier American casualties, as have many critics. Decision about victory or defeat in any battle has never turned solely on the preponderance of casualties. Several of U. S. Grant's victories were purchased by losses greater than those of the Confederates. Thinking of the same kind afflicts those who argue that because Kearny became immobilized at San Bernardo and had to be rescued by Commodore Stockton's forces, he suffered a defeat. This was no private battle of Stephen Kearny's. American military policy had directed that the Army of the West should push through to San Diego. Kearny happened to be its commander, but the ultimate arrival of his expedition is the test of American victory or defeat.

The defect in reasoning here is another by-product of the animus planted by Benton and Frémont. They were more interested in showing that Kearny reached California with forces too small for effective action and that Kearny, severely mauled on December 6, had to have relief sent him, than they were in the final result. Considering all the arguments concerning the outcome, I am most impressed with Valentine Mott Porter's query in summation. He asks his readers if any defeated army has ever been left in complete possession of the field, their victorious opponents having fled because of the sudden increased effectiveness of the defeated side? He follows this question by observing that many a hard-fought battle has begun with seeming disaster to the side that finally emerged victorious. Andrés Pico certainly so reasoned when, a few years after the fighting, he claimed that he had won a big victory and that only the coming of the large number of marines saved Kearny's command.

Mr. Porter's observation suggests the correct answer. Too many critics have proceeded on the fallacious assumption that the early-morning charges of December 6 constituted a battle complete unto itself. If so, the action at San Bernardo on the seventh was another action. Then the final breakout on the morning of December 11 must have been a separate engagement.

I submit that all of General Kearny's activities from the night reconnaissance of December 5 until the breakout from Mule Hill on the eleventh were essentially one action. What happened on separate days was subordinate to the final result. By this approach we find that the Americans suffered a check on the sixth that came perilously near to defeat. Their march on the seventh and the flight of Pico's forces from Mule Hill was by this reasoning a victory. But because their mobility had been vitally impaired, it was certainly a Pyrrhic victory. If the Californians were the victors at San Pasqual (thinking of the sixth and seventh as one action) how are we to rate their sudden disappearance on the night of the tenth and eleventh and their failure to interfere with the march to San Diego on the eleventh and twelfth? The last shot fired over the heads of the Americans after Lieutenant Gray's arrival was a strange way indeed for victors to behave! I am convinced that the whole San Pasqual campaign—not this or that separate incident of it—must be rated an American victory.

16. *The San Gabriel and the Mesa*

AMERICAN FORCES first occupied San Diego on July 29, 1846. Except for a brief interruption during the October uprising, they had remained in possession ever since. Stockton fortified Presidio Hill shortly before Kearny came to California, and had been preparing to march against the Pueblo de Los Angeles. His agents had found it difficult to secure the livestock necessary for the expedition. The arrival of the battered remnant of the Army of the West temporarily delayed these plans.

Despite his poor physical condition, General Kearny on the day he rode into San Diego began his report of the long march and the fighting at San Pasqual. He finished it the next day, concluding with: "I have now to offer my thanks to Commodore Stockton and all of his gallant command for the very many kind attentions we have received and continue to receive from them." After commenting upon the rugged terrain north of the Gila River, Kearny wrote: "If a tolerable wagon road to its (the Gila's) mouth from the Del Norte is ever discovered, it must be on the south side (and therefore the boundary line between the United States and Mexico should certainly not be north of the 32° of latitude)." Evidently the peace commissioners who negotiated the Treaty of Guadalupe Hidalgo paid little attention to this recommendation. Under it the Gila River was made the boundary for the greater part of its course. Thus the United States was confined to the relatively impassable mountains

233

on its north bank. The Gadsen Purchase in 1853 substantially remedied this defect.

General Kearny seems to have made a surprisingly rapid recovery, considering his great loss of blood. By December 20, Dr. Griffin found only one of his wounds still troublesome. The previous day the General had written Mary Kearny a brief account of the fight with Pico's forces, with these more personal additions: "I know my dear wife that you may be uneasy about me. . . . Let me therefore in the first place tell you that I am moving about as if nothing had happened to me, that my appetite is perfectly good & that I feel but little inconvenience from my wounds. They are healing up much faster than I could have expected . . . do not think that I am worse than I represent myself, for it is not so. I expect in less than a week to be on my horse & as active as I ever was." Then he added news of Mary's brother, Lieutenant William Radford, which he had learned from naval friends: ". . . is quite well—he is . . . in the Bay of San Francisco, about a week's sail from here. I hope to see him ere long." Then followed nostalgic references to the approaching "holy day" of Christmas and the New Year: "May we all live, my dear Mary, to be reunited before the year is past (of course he was referring to 1847). You must take good care of yourself and all of our little ones, so that when I return our numbers will be complete." His last letter from Mary had been dated August 19. Then he recalled the death of "my friend Captain Allen. What great changes have taken place in the Regt within the last 6 months? Phil (his nephew) has been for years sighing for a captaincy. He is now entitled to Company B which was poor Johnston's. . . . Say nothing of this except to Phil himself." His letter then became more intimate. "Kiss all my dear little ones for me. I hope William and Charles are learning fast. Harriet, I am certain is improving & Mary & Lou no doubt, also Puddy (this must have been Ellen Kearny's nickname) Clarence and the youngest (Henry) must occupy your time. I hope that you have some good woman in your nursery to take care of them. Take care of yourself and the young ones. . . ." Then Stephen Kearny reverted to his more practical self: "I wonder how you get on in the management of business &

in your money affairs. I will be able in a month or two to send to you some more pay accounts. . . . Should you . . . have more than you want for use, put it out at 10 per cent for not less than 3 nor more than 5 years. Consult Patterson or Col. Brant & let either of them attend to the business for you. Love again to you and the children."

San Diego was then so remote that the General instructed his wife how to locate it on a map. His tone verged on poetry when he added: "we have the ocean in sight and hear the rolling waves which sound like rumbling thunder."

Because of the scarcity of merchandise in San Diego, the General sent Major Swords to the Sandwich Islands to purchase foodstuffs, clothing, and medical supplies. Drilling went forward briskly in preparation for the advance against Flores and Pico. Sailors had to be made into soldiers overnight. In view of the long marches contemplated, Commodore Stockton planned to mount his force, a novel experience for his improvised army. The successful reinforcement of Stockton by Kearny's force had a disheartening effect on the insurgent bands. Small parties of Californians straggled in from day to day to surrender. Some of these arrivals reported that Andrés Pico had joined General Flores at the Pueblo and that the Americans had retaken Santa Barbara.

One of the first signs of the trouble to come appears in Dr. Griffin's journal on December 20: "Our General has no force at his command and he seems low spirited." In the story of the relations between Kearny on the one hand and Stockton and Frémont on the other, few questions are more clouded than the clash that was now developing. Who was legally the military governor of California? Who commanded the expedition to the Pueblo? What was behind the various offers of that command to General Kearny and his declinations coupled with his later request to take command? Much controversy has arisen over these questions.

Immediately after meeting Commodore Stockton, General Kearny had given him his own instructions from the War Department. He testified at Frémont's court-martial that because of his serious wounds and the slight force under his command, he had refrained from asserting his authority at that time. Stockton testified at the trial that soon after the General's arrival he (Stockton) offered to make Kearny

> . . . commander-in-chief over all of us and offered to go as his aide de camp. He said no—the force was mine and he would go as my aide de camp. This was done in seriousness and sincerity. . . . A few days after I made a formal call on him . . . and made the same offer and received the same answer.

One of his aides confirmed this. Stockton further testified:

> General Kearny . . . handed me his instructions from the War Department. I was simple enough to believe that he had handed them to me that I might be gratified by seeing how fully and thoroughly I had anticipated the wishes of the government and when I returned the papers to him with thanks I sent him copies of some of my own despatches to the government that he as a friend might participate in the pleasure I felt of having in anticipation executed the orders of the government.

Stockton also testified that Kearny's claim to the governorship "amazed" him. "I took the position his orders were predicated on his conquering the country which I had already done except around Santa Barbara and Los Angeles." He termed the series of events since early October a "temporary interruption." These few sentences of the Commodore's testimony resemble the flamboyant proclamations he had fired at the unhappy people of California. Such a cavalier brushing aside of the written orders from his own commander-in-chief, presented by the General, was unbelievable to an officer like Stephen Kearny.

Others beside Commodore Stockton wanted to see General Kearny take the field against the Californians. Captain du Pont wrote:

> On one day he (Kearny) drilled all the troops and as soon as the sailors were through, they were heard to express great admiration for "that old gentleman" and hoped he was going with them. . . . There has been some clashing between General Kearny and the

Commodore. To the latter's arrangements the general has succumbed, being a mild, affable, easy old gentleman of the old school, feeling his preservation due to our forces here and having none of his now left to give him moral support. He had orders to make himself governor of the territory, to establish civil government, etc. which the commodore says he has already done.

Captain du Pont records his first meeting with General Kearny: "I called to see General Kearny on the first day of my arrival (December 27th) and found a most delightful old gentleman of fine erect appearance, cordial and affable. Everyone has taken to him wonderfully." (Kearny was then fifty-two years of age!)

It is hard to realize that the Kearny whom Captain du Pont found so likeable is the same individual described at this time by Allan Nevins as "a grim martinet, a fighter without any mild or ingratiating qualities whatever . . . a stern tempered soldier who made few friends and many enemies, who has been justly characterized by the most careful historian of the period, Justin H. Smith, as 'grasping, jealous, domineering and harsh.' " Certainly Captain du Pont had the immense advantage over Nevins and Smith of personal contact with the man—an acquaintance that was soon to ripen into warm friendship. If General Kearny was not quite as mild and easygoing as Du Pont pictured him, it seems reasonable that neither was he the grim, harsh, and domineering martinet these later writers describe.

Kearny's position at this time has been termed a delicate one. He must have been conscious that his prestige had suffered because of the heavy losses at San Pasqual. He now commanded only a handful of troops, some of them like himself, suffering from wounds. In all probability he owed his safe arrival at San Diego to Stockton and had joined him in the midst of the Commodore's plans to take the offensive with a force nearly all composed of naval personnel. On the one hand military protocol forbade any surrender of his authority; on the other this seemed a poor time to assert it.

Therefore a sense of duty prompted Kearny to write the Commodore on December 22. At a conference the day before, Stockton had told him that he intended as soon as he could to march as far as

San Luis Rey with a part of his forces. He wanted ultimately to advance on the Pueblo, but after "taking San Luis Rey" (evidently he expected he must fight to get even that far), any further advance would depend entirely on the information he might receive about the movements of Colonel Frémont and the enemy. "It might be necessary for me to stop the pass of San Filipe (*sic*) or march back to San Diego."

We can infer that General Kearny had favored a bolder course. If the Commodore could take a sufficient force to oppose the Californians now near Los Angeles and awaiting Frémont's approach from the north, Kearny advised him to march toward the Pueblo as soon as possible. Stockton should either join Frémont or make a diversion in his favor. Kearny felt he must express this in writing:

> I don't think Frémont should be left unsupported to fight a battle upon which the fate of California may for a long time depend. Your troops in advancing might surprise the enemy at San Luis Mission and make them prisoners. . . . I shall be happy in such an expedition to accompany and give you any aid either of head or hand of which I may be capable.

With increasing heat the Commodore replied at once:

> If object of your note is to advise me to do anything that would enable a larger force of the enemy to get in my rear and cut off my communication with San Diego and hazard the safety of the garrison and the ships in the harbor, you will excuse me for suggesting I can't follow any such advice. My purpose is still to march for San Luis Rey as soon as I can get the dragoons and riflemen mounted which I hope will be in two days.

(Did Commodore Stockton seriously fear that an enemy force "larger" than his contemplated expedition of over six hundred could cut him off from San Diego? With the broad Pacific only a few cable lengths away, how could his ships be placed in the slightest jeopardy by Californians who did not possess a solitary skiff?)

Probably these questions made General Kearny smile grimly as he reminded Stockton on December 23 that he had made his whole advice conditional:

238

If you can take from here, etc. [referring to the proposed movement of troops], repeating . . . what you stated to me yesterday . . .
I have only to remark that if I had so understood you, I certainly
would not have written my letter to you of last evening. You certainly
could not for a moment suppose I would advise or suggest to you
any movement which might endanger the safety of the garrison
and the ships in the harbor.

General Kearny seems to have outfinessed Commodore Stockton
in this correspondence. It was one thing for Stockton to announce
timid half-measures orally. He may even have spoken in vague,
general terms. Whether deliberately or unconsciously, Kearny had
now made his naval opposite reduce to writing plans which the
General was convinced were unsound. I believe this correspondence
answers the questions earlier posed in connection with the command
of the expedition. That is the only logical explanation for the about-
face performed by General Kearny immediately afterward. He was
convinced that if the Americans were only able to march some forty
miles to San Luis Rey and then retreat to San Diego, their prestige
would hit a new low from which it might never recover. At Stockton's proposed destination they would be several miles inland with
no harbor accessible, and worse off than where they were now. They
would also be too far south to aid Frémont if he were in trouble.
No one knew his whereabouts or strength. With the forces of Flores
and Pico concentrated around the Pueblo, a junction with Frémont
in all probability could only be effected by engaging those Californians. Thus the pressure would be removed from Frémont if,
unaided, he was too weak to oppose Flores and Pico.

We do not know when Kearny again saw Stockton. It must have
been quite soon. According to the famous letter signed "Justice,"
printed in the *Missouri Republican* on June 14, 1847, Kearny's
recommendation of a march to the Pueblo to support Frémont "was
roughly refused for two days and Frémont was denounced by Commodore Stockton." (This letter has been attributed to Lieutenant
Colonel Cooke.) It seems more than mere coincidence that on the
same day when the Commodore had insisted he would stop his
advance at San Luis Rey, a General Order was issued by Stockton's

adjutant: "Forces composed of . . . artillery, Dragoons, Companies A & B California Battalion . . . and . . . sailors and marines . . . will take up the line of march *for Los Angeles* on Monday 28th 10 a.m." [The italics are mine.]

The expedition did not move on the twenty-eighth, but Kearny met Stockton once more that day and again produced his instructions from the War Department about setting up a civil government in California. Sometime between the twenty-third and the twenty-eighth he must have concluded that regardless of the delicacy of his position, his country's interests demanded that he take command. In his report to the War Department on January 17, 1847, he wrote:

> I have to state the march of troops from San Diego to Los Angeles was reluctantly consented to by Commodore Stockton on my urgent advice that he should not leave Colonel Frémont unsupported to fight a battle on which the fate of California might for a long time depend.

By now I believe General Kearny was anxious to correct his regrettable mistake in refusing the command.

His letter to the War Department, just quoted, indicates that the two officers conferred at least once before the twenty-ninth. According to Stockton's testimony, he expected until the morning of the twenty-ninth that the General would serve as his aide-de-camp. As they were making ready to depart, Kearny inquired who was to command the troops:

> I told him Lieutenant Rowan of the "Cyane." . . . He gave me to understand he would like to command and after a conversation I agreed to appoint him. I sent immediately for Rowan and assembled the officers near at hand and told them that Kearny had volunteered to command the troops, that I appointed him to command but I retained my own position as commander in chief.

Kearny as commander of the expedition, Stockton as commander-in-chief; confusion and question inevitably spring from such similar titles. It is not too surprising that ever since December 29, 1846, historians have argued about who commanded on the march to Los

Mule Hill, showing the stone battlements built by Kearny's dragoons while they awaited reinforcements after the battle with the Californians at San Pasqual, December, 1846. In the present century, the Historical Division of the Army War College ruled: "General Kearny did not sustain a defeat at San Pasqual."

Commodore Robert Field Stockton, whose troops rescued the Army of the West at Mule Hill, was commander-in-chief of the march to Los Angeles; Kearny was commander. This was but one of many conflicts between the two men over who held authority in California.

Angeles and at the Battles of the San Gabriel and the Mesa. Bancroft concludes quite reasonably that this argument is less important than the over-all controversy between the two officers. He did not regard either man too favorably. Yet on this point he felt that Kearny's instructions from the President unquestionably gave him the right to assume the command whenever he felt that military necessity demanded. Bancroft made the additional point that under War and Navy Department regulations, General Kearny outranked Commodore Stockton. The latter's rank was only the equivalent of an army colonel's.

It is interesting to read the distinction Kearny himself made between the titles. Toward the end of Colonel Frémont's court-martial, a member of the court asked the General whether he had admitted the superior rank of Stockton or yielded precedence to him. He answered:

I did not. . . . I found Commodore Stockton acting as governor and commander in chief in the territory on arriving in San Diego. . . . He gave me the command of his sailors and marines . . . told his officers to look upon me as their commander. . . . During our march his authority and command though it did not extend over me, or over troops which he had himself given me, extended far beyond where we were moving. It extended to the volunteers stationed at Nueva Helvetia, Sonoma, Monterey and I think some few in San Francisco and it extended also over the California Battalion of mounted riflemen under Colonel Frémont's command which I had not then claimed. Though I had instructions with me of the President . . . yet I did not until Jan. 16, 1847 attempt to avail myself in full of them.

At the court-martial and in the newspapers immediately after the capture of the Pueblo, army and navy officers warmly disputed over who was in command. Loyalty to their particular branch of service actuated all these officers. Emory, who had become Kearny's adjutant, testified that Kearny gave all the orders, either personally or through himself as adjutant. Later Emory admitted he had at least once obeyed a command from Stockton and had heard that the Commodore had given others. Undoubtedly Kearny and Stockton each issued commands. Sometimes their orders conflicted. John Bidwell later recalled such instances: "I as quartermaster received orders from both and obeyed both so far as I could," he said; "Stockton was determined to command. A conflict was growing between the two." Bancroft here sides with Stockton. Kearny, he felt, was wrong in saying he had never been under Stockton's command. "His subsequent effort to ignore Stockton's real position in the campaign must be attributed to a wish to strengthen himself for the coming controversy (i.e., over the governorship) and later to the spirit aroused by that controversy."

Whether General Kearny was right or wrong, Bancroft's reasoning is sound concerning the reason the General took the position he did. In addition I feel that his underlying motive was to stiffen the Commodore's resolution and forestall the chance that he might prematurely halt the expedition. As its commander, even with his title clouded, Kearny was in better position to push on for Los Angeles and a junction with Frémont than he could hope for as a mere aide to Stockton.

Despite these underlying differences, the column finally got under way on the morning of December 29, 1846; the band from the *U.S.S. Congress* marched in the lead. In addition to the naval personnel, the few remaining dragoons were commanded by Captain Turner. Captain Gillespie had recovered sufficiently to lead the volunteers. Commodore Stockton's small bodyguard was under Kit Carson. Sailors, marines, dragoons, volunteer riflemen, scouts, and skirmishers totaled 563 men and 44 officers. Despite Commodore Stockton's efforts to mount his force, only Gillespie's volunteer riflemen finally set out on horseback. Because the dragoons were a mounted organization, the Commodore had offered Captain Turner his choice of animals. Turner reported that none of the horses was fit for dragoon service and his command would give a better account of itself afoot.

The Stockton-Kearny expedition took much the same route (in reverse) that the General had followed into San Diego. Just as the Army of the West had longed to meet the enemy months before, so now a lust for combat pervaded the ranks. But carts broke down and packs slipped and spilled off mules and oxen so that progress was slow and tiresome. The weather was variable—rain, beautiful sunshine, and freezing nights. The mountains to the east were covered with snow; the plentiful rains had mantled the lower hills and meadows with sprouting grass and wild oats. The New Year's Eve camp was at the San Bernardo rancheria, familiar ground of painful memories to many in the column.

The Commodore and his staff found quarters in the Snook ranch house. Dr. Griffin observed that Stockton "has a fine large tent well supplied with table furniture and bedstead I am told—while our old Genl has nothing in the world but his blankets and bear skin— and a common tent—one pack mule for himself, Capt. Turner and servant."

From San Bernardo the little army marched to the San Luis Rey Mission. The surrounding vineyards and orchards marked its valley as a land of plenty. While prowling around their camp, some of the sailors discovered several casks of wine. These were quickly broached and widely sampled. The drinking bout ended in a raid on a near-by band of sheep, many of which were borne to camp. The next morning a council of the junior officers resolved on disciplinary measures with the "cat" (cat of nine tails). Here, report says, General Kearny entered the scene—that harsh, stern martinet whom we have heard so often condemned:

General Kearny had, by reason of the suavity of his manners and the good reports of the Dragoons as to his kindness of heart, become as great a pet with the sailors as even Bobby himself (Commodore Stockton), when the matter was first blown that the Minor Council had resolved to serve out some dozens with a "cat," a delegation was appointed to wait on him and solicit his interference in the affair. They accordingly went to his quarters at break of day, made known their errand and received from him a quiet promise that he would attend to it. Accordingly the old fellow watched the moves, and as they were about to proceed to the guard-room to administer the morning dose, he caused the bugler to sound the call, assembling all the officers in his quarters. They of course went, post haste, and one of them carried in his hand the "cat."

When they were all assembled, the General, without saying a single word, walked up to the gentleman who held the "cat," and taking it from his hand, enquired what he called that article. "This, sir, is the cat," was the answer. "What use do you put it to?" "It is to punish the men when they infringe upon the rules of discipline." "But, do you mean to say you whip men with so barbarous a thing as that?" "Yes, sir," "Oh," said the General, "that is bad, very bad." and coolly taking out his knife, he commenced cutting it to pieces, at the same time remarking, "Gentlemen, if your 'Jack Tars' cannot be governed without the aid of so murderous an instrument as this, I'll have you know that my Jacks (and while I command here they are mine) shall never be degraded by my orders, and I request as a *favor*, that none of you will ever attempt to lay the 'cat' upon the back of any man without my particular orders." This was a stumper; they pocketed the affront and sneaked away slightuously (*sic*) ashamed of themselves.

There seemed no question in anyone's mind on this occasion over who commanded these men and had the last word concerning their discipline.

Near Los Flores scouts reported that Frémont was approaching Los Angeles from the north and that Andrés Pico had marched with six hundred men to oppose him. The Commodore sent a messenger to Frémont by sea to advise the Colonel of his coming. Stockton cautioned the Pathfinder about the superior horsemanship and tricky tactics of the Californians. He feared their successes against Mervine and Kearny had emboldened them. Stockton haughtily refused to deal with negotiators sent by Flores under a flag of truce. In announcing this decision without consultation with General Kearny, he was consistent with his claim that he was commander-in-chief. (One of these messengers was William Workman, a prominent pioneer of Los Angeles.)

On January 7, while some distance west of Santa Ana, enemy horsemen were sighted ahead and on either flank. The scouts reported the Californians intended to fortify themselves on the banks of the San Gabriel. They had sworn to defend the line of the river to the death. According to Dr. Griffin:

That morning . . . I accompanied the old Genl around to every division of the force on the field. The old fellow I believe had been informed that we would certainly have a fight that day. He appeared in fine spirits and was particularly gay—he made a short speech to each corps as he passed, he did not fail to remind the men of the day, that it was the 8th of January (anniversary of Jackson's victory at New Orleans) and that we had a right on that day to flog anything that we might come in contact with—that after the fight that the Jack Tars would have a good long yarn to spin . . . and we would have a good fat bullock for our supper.

An American settler named Forster had joined the march and explained that the direct route into the Pueblo was via the lower ford of the river. Stockton wisely listened to Forster, and when the march was resumed on the morning of the eighth, it changed course. Forster had warned that Flores' command was ambushed in the willows and tall mustard near the lower ford. Now by swerving in a northwesterly direction, the Americans headed for the crossing of the San Gabriel at Paso del Bartolo, also known as the Pico Crossing or by its Indian name *Curunga.*

A short geographical explanation is in order. The San Gabriel River of 1847 was not the stream of that name today in the region east of the Pueblo. At that time the present Río Hondo carried the waters of the San Gabriel. Twenty years after the battle, heavy floods cut a new channel to the east and continued southward to the ocean. The old stream bed became known as the Hondo. It is difficult to pinpoint the location of Paso del Bartolo. Few rural areas of southern California have undergone more changes in a century. The stream courses have been lined with concrete. The Metropolitan Water District's vast settling grounds occupy much of the region. When several railroad embankments and bridges are added, it is hard to visualize the area in 1847. Only one certain landmark remains: the steep bluffs along the westerly bank of the present Río Hondo. Undoubtedly these are the heights up which the Americans charged at the Battle of the San Gabriel. Almost surely the Californians' battle line approximated the location of Bluff Road today.

The exact spot where Stockton's artillery crossed the river is questionable. On the northeast corner of Bluff Road and Washington Boulevard, close to the bridge over the Río Hondo, two small field guns flank a bronze plaque to mark the battlefield. Undoubtedly the battle was fought between this monument and the Whittier Boulevard crossing; probably close to the latter.

On January 6, General Andrés Pico, while near the San Fernando Mission, learned that the Americans were on the march. That day and the next he rushed his cavalry to the lower or Los Nietos ford of the river. Here, as Forster had warned, they waited in the heavy growth along the San Gabriel for Stockton and Kearny to approach. The Californians also had scouts, and early on the eighth some of them apprised Flores of the enemy's changed direction. The Americans came in sight of the Paso del Bartolo between two and three o'clock in the afternoon of the eighth. Some of Pico's and Flores' men barely reached the ford in advance of them. By the time Stockton and Kearny rode to the front of the column to survey the crossing, about five hundred of the enemy had taken positions on the bluffs skirting the river. These heights rose from forty to fifty feet above the bottom lands. They lay from four to six hundred yards west of the stream. At the time the San Gabriel was about one hundred yards wide, flowing knee-deep over quicksands and thickly bordered with underbrush. From the east bank the approach was level.

As the first of the Americans came within range, sharpshooters on the bluffs opened fire. The Californians could be seen posting their artillery along the heights commanding the ford. The two commanders formed their line of battle with Gillespie's riflemen in the advance as scouts followed by the dragoons and the sailors from the *Cyane*. Four of the artillery pieces came next with the marines and more sailors. The small baggage train kept the center while the rear guard with the two remaining guns drove the cattle before them. It was agreed that the Commodore would direct the artillery fire while the General led the infantry. One hundred of the Californians trotted across the river to charge the vanguard. A brisk fire from the skirmishers quickly drove them back. Then the Mexican artillery roared its defiance. The noise and flashes were impressive, but the grape and round shot fell short of the oncoming army. Jets of spray rose from the river as the missiles fell harmlessly. Flores had only a little good powder remaining after the battle on the Dominguez ranch. The insurgents' homemade substitute was of such poor quality as to cripple their artillery.

General Kearny now ordered the guns unlimbered so that the Californian batteries might be silenced. Seeing this operation from a distance, Commodore Stockton dispatched a messenger to countermand the order. He wanted the guns taken across the river where they could be served at closer range on the western bank. When they were halfway over the General saw their wheels sink in the quicksands and sent word to Stockton that this made safe passage impossible. The Commodore spurred to the scene, jumped from his horse, and impetuously seized the ropes on one of the guns. "Quicksands be damned! Come on boys, follow your Commodore!" he cried. (John Bidwell said Kearny bit his lips in suppressed rage; Bancroft thought this an exaggeration.) As Stockton floundered waist-deep in the swirling waters, all the artillerymen grabbed the ropes on the nine-pounders. The balky mules were plunging about aimlessly as the carriage wheels constantly sank deeper. It was a critical moment, for the group around the guns in the river were under sharp fire from the enemy's artillery. Probably only the miserable quality of the powder prevented heavy casualties among the Americans. In a few minutes, by dint of much splashing and straining by many hands, the guns were hauled from the treacherous sands onto the farther bank. It was a risky enterprise that could have brought disaster.

Swiftly the nine-pounders were unlimbered. "Steady, boys," cried the excited Commodore, "don't waste a shot." He helped sight and fire the first gun at the largest of the Californians' fieldpieces. Stockton was primarily a gunner, and his accuracy was such that the shot smashed the carriage into splinters and rendered that cannon useless. The brisk fire maintained by these pieces was visibly thinning the ranks of the defenders and made a cover for the column as it crossed the river. General Kearny, standing near the Commodore, distributed his infantry up- and downstream under the protection of the bank while those behind splashed over the ford. Finally, with a pistol grasped in each hand, he called to Stockton, "I am now ready for the charge," and in a louder voice with arm upraised, rallied his infantry with: "Forward, my Jacks, charge," and away went tars, marines, and dragoons toward the heights. Stockton in turn advanced his guns up the shelving bluffs. Excited by the roar of the artillery and the tumult in the river, the charging Americans cheered and shouted as they raced forward with fixed bayonets. The sight and sound struck panic in the ranks of the enemy, who were already demoralized by the concentrated fire of the artillery. The men directly facing the column broke and fled, leaving the disabled gun behind them. When the Americans were halfway to the top of the bluffs, some of the mounted rancheros charged around the column and attacked both the rear guard and the left flank of Kearny's forces. The threat to the rear was quickly repulsed. Kearny met the flank attack by forming a square of two of the battalions. The Californians, while individually brave, seemed to lack leadership and were quickly driven off. Immediately afterward more of the enemy were seen galloping toward the right flank. Kearny reformed his square to meet that new threat, but the foemen veered away out of range. The General now ordered his right wing to charge the hill. This maneuver was executed with more cheers and a rush over the crest, only to find to the amazement of all that no enemy remained on the heights. A little dust and some galloping horsemen signified the Californians' retreat. In about an hour and a half the San Gabriel had been crossed and its west bank secured.

After their retreat the foe pitched camp across the rolling plains in sight of the Americans. It was useless to pursue such well-mounted opponents without cavalry, so the victors camped on the field they had won. Now and then through the night the pickets exchanged shots with prowlers, but no general attack disturbed the Americans.

Early on the ninth a Californian galloped up with a white flag and reported that Frémont was at San Fernando, only eight leagues from the Pueblo. Everyone expected him to press forward and perhaps meet his countrymen in Los Angeles. Flores and his camp had vanished overnight. Both Stockton and Kearny addressed the expedition that morning. The former still glowed with the exuberance of victorious combat, but the General spoke temperately. He congratulated the sailors under him for their soldierly conduct, said he had been told sailors could not be managed without the "cat" but he was prepared to give the lie to that assertion, that he wanted no better men than these to march all over Mexico. Then he outlined his plans for the day's advance. They would cross a great plain where the enemy's cavalry could operate to advantage. He proposed to form his men in a hollow square with cattle and provision train in the center (really a moving corral). He admonished the men to remain firmly in ranks, with no straggling nor breaking out. They must be ready to resist the cavalry charges that were to be expected. Hearty cheers were given both speeches.

The march commenced at nine in the morning. It crossed the mesa between the San Gabriel and the Los Angeles rivers. The Commodore indulged his love of music by having the band lead the way with its martial strains. Scattered horsemen of the enemy hung on the flanks. Soon their main force could be seen. Flores had drawn up his command in the shape of a horseshoe as if to outflank the advancing Americans.

As they came within range the Californians opened artillery fire on the front and right flank. Most were wild shots that plowed up the ground between the opposing armies or whistled harmlessly overhead. Spent missiles wounded a few of the men and felled some cattle and oxen. These were an annoyance so the column halted long enough for the American artillery to return the fire. A quarter of an hour's brisk exchange of shots silenced this threat, and the march was resumed. Then Flores resolved on a charge. It headed for the front of Kearny's square, consisting of the marines and the dragoons. Once more the Californians were using their lances. The General ordered his men to hold their fire until he gave the command. On galloped the rancheros, three rows deep, lances set and hooves thundering—one minute half a mile away, then closing rapidly until only one hundred paces separated the combatants. Then Kearny's voice rang out: "Ready—aim—pick your men, boys—fire!" and all along the front of the square a sheet of flame spurted with a sharp crackle. Again he shouted: "Front rank, kneel and prepare to resist cavalry—rear rank, load." As the second order was obeyed the advancing horsemen reined up, staggered, and reeled like drunken men. The shower of lead had been too deadly. Before the smoke cleared, the Californians turned and fled. Many riderless horses galloped madly away. Here and there bodies of men and horses lay on the grass of the mesa; the wounded were being hurriedly snatched up and carried off by their companions still able to ride. "Forward!" the General commanded and the column moved on. In the distance the rebuffed enemy could be seen reforming his diminished line. Soon it separated; one detachment galloped around to charge the left flank, the other converged on the right. Flores' men had had their fill of the front of that square; maybe its sides were defended by less resolute fighters.

One of the guns roared the signal for these simultaneous charges. It could have been a critical moment for the Americans compelled to face the enemy from two directions. But Kearny remained cool and ordered his men to hold their fire until less than fifty yards lay between them. Then as he shouted "Fire!" another leaden rain burst forth to the right and left. Sailors were now doing the firing so Kearny called to them: "Steady, my Jacks, steady. Keep your ranks, load again. Give 'em hell!" Two full rounds were discharged this time, and as before, the charges suddenly halted and a wildly disordered and broken line of riders dashed off with such wounded as they could rescue. Small groups of cavalry assailed the rear with the same result. Finally Stockton's cannon fired a round of grape to complete the rout. Away trotted the discomfited rancheros; here and there they could be seen reclaiming saddles and bridles. In a little while the last of them disappeared in the hills off to the right, and with them went the last hostile shots at the American occupation of California.

By three in the afternoon it was evident that entry could be made into Los Angeles without difficulty. The town was visible but it was known to contain great stocks of wine and *aguardiente*. From previous experience in attempting to control such a force after the toil and heat of battle, it seemed preferable to camp below the Pueblo. Entry on the morrow would allow a whole day to effect an orderly occupation. The column therefore crossed the Los Angeles River and camped on its west bank some three miles below the town.

The American casualties in these two short but sharp engagements were surprisingly light. One sailor was killed at the San Gabriel and nine men were wounded. One of these died the next day. No Americans were killed in the action on the mesa, but five were wounded, among them Captain Gillespie, so recently severely mauled at San Pasqual. Fortunately this wound was slight. The Californians' losses were variously reported. At the time the Americans thought the enemy had suffered heavier casualties; horses often appeared rider-less because the rancheros purposely hung low on one side of their animals while retreating. Estimates range from about a score killed and wounded to more than double that figure. Most of Flores' forces were very young *caballeros* aroused by the patriotic zeal of their women. Many of the older men knew the province lacked resources to wage war and that their undisciplined bands could not prevail against the United States. Especially at the mesa, the youths fought as a point of honor; since the passage of their "impassable" San Gabriel they held faint hope of victory.

The Battle of the Mesa was fought in the vicinity of the present Union Stock Yards in Vernon, an industrial suburb of Los Angeles. In the parking area in front of the Stock Yards Headquarters Build-ing, just east of Downey Road, a boulder monument commemor-ates the battle. As if to echo the old controversy, only Commodore Stockton's name appears as the American commander. The omission of any reference to General Kearny is both unjust and untruthful. Regardless of the over-all command, he certainly headed the daunt-less square of sailors, marines, dragoons, and volunteers who re-peatedly broke the last charges of the *caballeros*. Moreover, had it not been for Kearny's insistence that the expedition push on to Los Angeles, the Battle of the Mesa might never have been fought.

Even Stockton himself, in a grandiose report of the whole cam-paign dated January 11, 1847, said he had been "aided by General Stephen W. Kearny with a detachment of sixty men on foot from the First Regiment of U. S. Dragoons and by Captain A. H. Gil-lespie with sixty mounted riflemen." Again at the court-martial he testified: "The witness (Stockton) was wholly and solely responsible for the success of the expedition but he takes great pleasure now in saying that he was efficiently sustained by the gallant and good conduct of General Kearny and all the officers and men under his command."

After the Americans went into camp on the evening of the ninth the enemy was seen emerging from the hills. Some four hundred horsemen and four pieces of artillery passed near the Pueblo, while sixty more moved down the river to the left and rear of the Americans. Were they on their way to attack Frémont or waiting for nightfall to resume battle with Stockton and Kearny? The Americans had no way of knowing that Flores and a number of his officers had fled up the Arroyo Seco toward present-day Pasadena. As a precaution against any night attack, sentries were strengthened. Some alarms were sounded but no fighting occurred. At nine o'clock on the morning of the tenth William Workman and two others under a flag of truce proposed the peaceful surrender of the Pueblo, provided property and persons would be respected. This was agreed to, but with mental reservations about General Flores. His previous violation of his parole was still remembered, and when the column moved into Los Angeles, it went in combat formation with weapons prepared for action.

The route taken was from the river to Main Street near the old Celis house, where the Los Angeles City Hall now stands. Thence with all their flags flying and the band playing the Americans passed north along Main Street to the Plaza. Many black looks and muttered threats greeted the conquerors. From near-by heights men brandished their guns and hurled curses. This sort of welcome, while no surprise, inspired vigilance. Two hundred men and two of the artillery pieces were at once stationed on a hill overlooking the Plaza. (This was Fort Hill, the site of future Fort Moore.) Here Captain Gillespie proudly raised the flag over his old quarters. As rapidly as the officers could find suitable barracks for the rest of their force, they were quartered near the Plaza.

The more respectable inhabitants were peaceably disposed, but rowdies and irresponsibles deliberately created trouble wherever possible. One of these rascals knocked another Californian from his horse. The assaulted man was alleged to be a *vaquero* for the Americans. Several Americans rushed to the man's rescue and shot the offender. The tumult drew General Kearny to the scene. He roundly censured the sailors and dragoons for firing without orders—and then for their poor marksmanship in not killing the scoundrel outright! Two other rioters were slain by the guard. With so much liquor available, drunkenness soon became widespread among the invaders. Assembly was blown and the sentries were increased to forestall trouble.

On his first evening in Los Angeles, General Kearny wrote to Lieutenant Colonel Frémont to apprise him of the events of the past three days. The General was worried about Flores and the cavalry that had ridden away the day before. He asked for information about Frémont's own position as regarded the enemy and whether he needed aid of any kind. In the next few days he wrote twice again to Frémont, brief, informal—and friendly—notes. Kearny feared the first might be intercepted. He was apprehensive, too, lest the peculiar combat tactics of the *caballeros* might make trouble for Frémont's mounted riflemen. He learned that they did not carry sabers and warned Frémont not to charge the Californians. From his experience with their deadly lances he knew it would be fatal to charge them without sabers.

Victory had only deferred, not lessened, the friction between the two commanders. On January 12, the Commodore brought it out in the open in a General Order which he signed as governor and commander-in-chief and handed to Lieutenant Emory as acting adjutant general for Kearny. The order, written in Stockton's ebullient manner, congratulated the members of the expedition on the battles of January 8 and 9. Emory carried it to General Kearny and asked if he should read it to the troops. The General answered with a blunt negative.

On the eleventh a torrential rain probably helped check the unruly element. General Kearny directed Emory to select a site for a fort that could contain 100 men and command the town and its principal approaches. Many inhabitants came in to pledge allegiance. The Americans vainly sought information about Flores. Rumor alleged he had gone to fight Frémont and would return to besiege the Americans. Later it was more reliably reported that the defeated General had fled to Sonora with 150 men and the best horses and mules they had hastily assembled. Andrés Pico had been left in command of the remaining Californians.

The morning of January 13 brought puzzling news to Kearny. Commodore Stockton sent him a dispatch from Frémont (possibly received the night before) that on the twelfth he had entered into an armistice with Andrés Pico. This had occurred at Cahuenga. Because of his uncertainty that Frémont had received his notes, Kearny became very uneasy. He wrote to Stockton that he felt he should take 250 or 300 men and join Frémont. The word "armistice" carried alarming connotations. Frémont, in ignorance of the events of the last three days, might agree to withdraw to the north. The General also dashed off a third more guarded note to Frémont, indicating his anxiety. The Commodore did not share Kearny's apprehension.

Neither had long to wait. Stockton soon received a second dispatch that the Lieutenant Colonel on his own responsibility had accepted the surrender of General Pico and signed a capitulation with him that same morning. Under it a general amnesty was granted the Californians for past offenses, including all parole violations. The enemy had surrendered their two pieces of artillery and agreed to make no more war on the Americans. Now it was the Commodore's turn to be upset. He was furious at this subordinate who had taken such extreme measures without deigning to consult his commanding officer. Kearny seems to have felt relief at this news of Frémont's safety. The latter's action, while admittedly irregular, was in keeping with the administration's declared policy of friendly treatment of the Californians. Kearny may well have reasoned that Stockton was partly to blame because of his uncompromising refusals to treat with the rebels. That had certainly driven them into Frémont's more conciliatory arms.

Hard on the heels of the messenger bearing the Treaty of Cahuenga, Colonel William H. Russell of Frémont's staff rode into Los Angeles and called on the General. (They had known each other in the Middle West.) General Kearny and Captain Turner, who roomed together near the Plaza, invited Russell to have supper with them. A long conversation followed and the visitor stayed overnight. Captain Turner shared his bed with their guest. At the court-martial the defense attempted in rather silly fashion to make something sinister of this hospitality. Frémont's own questions strongly insinuated that unusual efforts (such as plying Russell with liquor) were put forth by the hosts to prolong the conversation and "pump" Russell. All that persistent cross-examination of Kearny could develop was that he retired and fell asleep before Russell and Turner stopped talking and went to bed. This apparently had so dampening an effect on the defense that when Captain Turner was later examined, no reference was ever made to the midnight conversation—or drinking—with Russell.

This visit with Russell seems to have been a pleasant one. The three men had participated in many thrilling events. This was Russell's first chance to hear about the conquest of New Mexico. He was much interested in the civil administration the General had set up there. The visitor inquired whether the General objected to the treaty at Cahuenga. Kearny said he did not though others were not happy about it. Under questioning he admitted that Stockton disapproved the capitulation. Russell later testified that the General told him the Commodore was unfriendly both to himself and to Frémont. Russell also said the General cautioned him to be on his guard in any discussions with Stockton. (The General may well have made these remarks for, although there were sharp discrepancies in the testimony of these two witnesses about other occurrences, Kearny never disputed these particular statements by Russell.) During the visit on the night of the thirteenth, Kearny unquestionably expressed a high opinion of Colonel Frémont, saying he was glad the latter was in California because of his eminent qualifications to render good service there, especially through his knowledge of the Spanish language and the manners of the people.

The next morning Russell rode back to meet Colonel Frémont and carried with him many ideas that profoundly influenced his superior's subsequent conduct. Russell met Frémont only a few miles from the Plaza. The night before Frémont had written General Kearny that he and his volunteers were nearing the Pueblo.

17. *"Who Is Governor of California?"*

DURING A HEAVY RAINSTORM on January 14, John C. Frémont rode into Los Angeles at the head of his California Battalion of four hundred men and six pieces of artillery. Two of these had just been taken from the rebels. One was the howitzer Pico's men had captured at San Pasqual.

In Monterey some months before, the battalion's commander had laid aside his army uniform. For the long hours of riding, he found the loose buckskin clothes of the frontiersman more practical. Knife and pistol hung ready in his belt. A broad-brimmed slouch hat shielded him from the dazzling California sun and gave some protection from rains. His followers were a heterogeneous lot: sailors, American settlers from the Sacramento, hunters, trappers, and wanderers to whom the battalion had offered adventure. The men had not discarded uniforms; they had never owned any. Like Frémont, they were arrayed in very unmilitary garb. One common characteristic was a worn and ragged appearance. Like him, too, they were all bronzed and bearded, caked with dust, mud, and sweat. These irregulars were excellent horsemen and good riflemen, disciplined by the challenge of this unruly land. The strict obedience exacted by Frémont was observed because their lives might depend on it.

The populace of the Pueblo and the victors of San Gabriel and the Mesa watched them ride into the Plaza with curiosity. These were the men who had humbled vainglorious Andrés Pico. These gaunt, weather-beaten riders had seized his cannon and lances and dispersed his *caballeros*.

A certain melodramatic flavor attaches to John C. Frémont's entry into Los Angeles. Stockton and Kearny had reoccupied it after beating the insurgents in two battles. Frémont had had no part in those victories. But as rather an effective checkmate, he without the spilling of any blood had accepted the enemies' surrender and their promise to fight no more. General Kearny gazed curiously at Colonel Frémont. He had not seen him since the day when he had supplied the young explorer with a twelve-pound howitzer in St. Louis. He had talked since with Senator Benton and his family about the adventures of their engineer. Kearny remembered how smartly attired had been the John C. Frémont of 1843. Now Jessie Frémont's husband was yonder "bearded pard" who looked more the mountain man than even Kit Carson.

The General wrote to Benton that same day to assure him that Lieutenant Colonel Frémont had just arrived with his command, "perfectly well and has gained great credit . . . . Will you please in my name congratulate Mrs. Frémont upon the honor and credit gained by the Colonel and with my best wishes for her and all your family." In his later philippic against Kearny, the fiery Benton gave this letter a sinister sound as part of a plot to lull the Colonel's family to a sense of false security. We must remember that the letter was written two days before the first breach between the officers.

Kearny rejoiced that the American forces in California had united with over one thousand rugged men to overcome all opposition. The General may have had a more personal reason for his interest in Frémont's appearance. The mounting friction with Stockton made Kearny anxious to reinforce his own meager command with these four hundred volunteers. Some historians have suggested that such reasoning lay behind the several informal and friendly notes which Kearny dispatched to Frémont in quick succession after the General's arrival at the Pueblo. Certainly much depended on Colonel Frémont's co-operation.

Later in the day Frémont called upon the General. At his court-martial, the Lieutenant Colonel referred to that visit in significant language: "On my entrance into Los Angeles with my battalion, I went direct to the quarters assigned it . . . then *reported* in person to Governor Stockton and afterwards *called* on General Kearny." (The italics are mine; it is plain that Colonel Russell's report of the *status quo* in Los Angeles was bearing fruit.) Kearny did not then know that his visitor had already seen the Commodore. The circumstance is mentioned now because the distinction Frémont then made between these two senior officers of the army and navy underlay all his future relations with both of them.

On July 24, 1846, while Frémont was a captain of topographical engineers of the United States Army, Commodore Stockton had commissioned him a major in the California Battalion of Mounted Riflemen. This was a naval unit that Stockton had just created, composed of Bear Flaggers and other volunteers. Thenceforth Frémont supposedly acted as an officer of this naval command, and Commodore Stockton continued to regard him as such during his operations in California. However, let us note that on October 27, 1846, a commission reached Major Frémont from the United States Army making him a lieutenant colonel of the army's regiment of Mounted Rifles. (A wholly separate unit from the naval battalion of somewhat similar name organized by Stockton.) It is equally important to observe that when Frémont wrote General Kearny on January 13, he signed himself "J. C. Frémont, Lieutenant Colonel U. S. Army and military commandant of the territory of California," and not as a major in the naval battalion.

The call that Lieutenant Colonel Frémont made upon General Kearny on January 14 probably began pleasantly enough with an exchange of civilities between men who had long known each other. Colonel Frémont had learned from Russell that the General's attitude toward him had seemed friendlier than Commodore Stockton's. Kearny informed his caller of his own instructions from the President to take command of the land forces and establish civil government in California as he had done in New Mexico. Undoubtedly he also mentioned that months before he had received "a letter from my friend, Colonel Benton, telling me that I was to be the civil and military governor of the territory." (His statement at the court-martial coupled that letter with the famous orders of June 3 and 18, 1846.) The General must have quickly realized that it weakened his position to have to admit that Stockton was still acting as governor. He now found himself on the defensive toward a subordinate. A restless, ambitious man like this young officer was only too quick to seize upon the situation. Commodore Stockton had already proposed to make Frémont governor. The latter felt he had just added to his prestige by the Treaty of Cahuenga. Almost within his grasp were the laurels of conqueror of California and its first appointed governor. Now this Brigadier General plainly took a different view of affairs that threatened to dim the glory that John C. Frémont felt was his. Sensing this, General Kearny on January 16 had Emory send the commander of the battalion an extract from the instructions given Kearny on June 18, 1846, and called attention to this provision: "These troops, and such as may be organized in California, will be under your command."

At the court-martial General Kearny maintained that the California Battalion came under his command from the time Colonel Frémont reported his arrival to him on January 13. Therefore Emory's letter now directed: "No change will be made in the organization of your battalion of volunteers or officers appointed in it without his (General Kearny's) sanction or approval being first obtained." (Rumor said Gillespie was to succeed Frémont in the command of the battalion.) On the sixteenth the General formally wrote Stockton his objection to the latter's proposed institution of a civil government in California. This duty, he pointed out, the President had entrusted to Kearny himself. If the Commodore's authority was from the President, Kearny would cheerfully acquiesce in his actions. If not, the General demanded that he cease further proceedings in the matter.

This letter touched off the explosion long threatening. Commodore Stockton from his first conversations with General Kearny in San Diego had maintained that the latter's instructions from the President were contingent in character. They read: "*Should you* conquer and take possession of New Mexico and Upper California or considerable places in either, you will establish temporary civil

259

government therein." (The italics are mine.) Stockton maintained that before Kearny arrived in California, he, Stockton, had already "conquered" the territory. Therefore, he argued (and Frémont and Benton forever after endorsed his position), the General's instructions had become nullified and obsolete before his arrival—"a glaring case of orders suspended by events and no longer in force" as Frémont later phrased it. Stockton in effect insisted that "should you" meant "if you personally." The opposite school of thought construed "should" as meaning "when" or "after our forces have conquered," etc. Even though the Polk administration and the court-martial's verdict ultimately upheld General Kearny's interpretation of his orders, it is most unfortunate that Secretary of War Marcy used language involving such doubtful semantics.

There were fundamental weaknesses in the Commodore's position which a century of controversy has not removed. How could he—and Frémont—seriously maintain that California had been conquered before December 1, 1846? All the southern part of Upper California had been retaken from the Americans with the exception of San Diego. From Monterey south, Mexican authority was unquestioned. Even Monterey was insecure; close to the town armed Californians kidnapped Consul Larkin in November. It took hard campaigning and three battles—in all of which Kearny played a leading role—to reduce the greater part of the territory's population to submission. All American activities after Gillespie's expulsion from Los Angeles in September until the Treaty of Cahuenga on January 13, 1847, meant nothing if they were not acts of conquest against the enemy. Equally unreasonable was Stockton's claim that a civil government of his creation was in "successful operation" before Kearny's arrival. Since October, 1846, it had been only a government on paper. The Commodore had enacted some laws and appointed certain officials. Washington had been notified of these facts, but the people of California were not being governed by them.

Nothing can be more unfair than the Stockton-Frémont-Benton reiteration that General Kearny brought too small a force to conquer California and had to be rescued by the Commodore. It was impudent when we remember that Kearny's force was reduced in size only because of the "wretched despatches" from Stockton carried by Kit Carson.

Students of California history have long sought the reason for Commodore Stockton's stubborn refusal to recognize the President's instructions. Champions of John C. Frémont have to maintain that Stockton acted with proper authority. Otherwise they leave Frémont defenseless against the charges of mutiny and insubordination. They build their case on the Navy Department's order dated July 12, 1846, to Commodore Sloat, Stockton's predecessor. This order bore a date several weeks later than General Kearny's and so, the argument goes, superseded his. After directing Sloat to occupy various ports in California, it said "This will bring with it the necessity of a civil administration. Such government should be established under your protection, etc." There lies our conflict. Both orders authorized the senior army and naval officer to perform the same act. One flaw in Stockton's chain of title vitiates all his actions relating to civil government. *Commodore Stockton never received nor had knowledge of this order while he was the senior naval officer in California.* He relinquished the post of governor in favor of Frémont on January 22, 1847, and sailed for Mexico. By the time he returned, Commodore Shubrick, sent out to replace Stockton, had assumed command. The last orders which Stockton or Sloat had received said nothing about establishing a civil government. It developed at the court-martial that Commodore Shubrick brought the July 12 orders with him in January. He had received them at Valparaiso and showed them to General Kearny on February 10, 1847—some three weeks after Stockton's departure from San Diego. The "conflicting instructions" were never a reality at the only place where their conflict could confuse anyone.

While most of Frémont's admirers have defended him because of these "conflicting instructions," Allan Nevins in his later biography adopts a different approach:

It has been objected that while the order was sent, Stockton did not actually receive it before his departure from California. But the powers which it explicitly conferred had been already conferred by

261

implication in the previous orders and he had acted on that theory. What wonder that each commander honestly thought that he had an exclusive right to erect and control the new civil government of California?

Even Stockton did not claim such implied powers. At the court-martial he testified: "My right to establish the civil government was incident to the conquest, and I formed the government under the law of nations." That seems a weak excuse for refusing to recognize express orders from the President which Kearny exhibited to the Commodore. Even if he had relied on implied powers, how can it be argued that express instructions of a later date can be superseded by mere implications from earlier orders? That way lies anarchy.

At Frémont's court-martial, his erstwhile secretary of state Russell gave some strange testimony about Stockton's authority. When he had visited the Commodore on January 13, Russell told him he had seen Kearny's instructions and asked if Stockton had anything that would "countervail" them. Stockton replied that he had full sealed instructions not to be opened until he reached a certain point but would not exhibit them "like slaves did their papers," and that he had no fear of his power being impaired by Kearny's instructions. While this sounds bombastic, it must be remembered that some of Russell's contemporaries did not take him very seriously.

Stockton answered Kearny's demands of the sixteenth by briefly reiterating that the General's instructions had been negated by events before his arrival. Then he declared open war:

> I will only add that I cannot do anything, nor desist from doing anything, or alter anything on your demand, which I will submit to the President, and ask for your recall. In the meantime you will consider yourself suspended from the command of the United States forces in this place.

Because it was written in anger, this could be construed as an admission by Stockton that Kearny *had* been in chief command of all the American forces, as it does not limit the suspension to any portion of them. Obviously, Stockton had no authority to suspend a brigadier-general from any army command. Yet at the court-martial, the Commodore with colossal condescension said of Kearny: "I permitted him to take with him all the United States troops belonging to the army and only retained my own sailors and the battalion."

On January 17, General Kearny sent a brief note to Frémont requesting that he see him "on business." As soon as he arrived, the General asked whether he had received his communication of the previous day. Frémont replied ("with a touch of defiance," says Allan Nevins) that he had written a reply but left it with an assistant to be copied. In a few moments Kit Carson came in with the letter. Frémont picked up a pen, signed the paper, and handed it to the General. The latter asked his caller to be seated while he read the letter.

It gave Stephen Kearny one of the greatest shocks of his life. After referring to the General's directions regarding his battalion, Frémont said:

> I found . . . on my arrival at this place . . . Commodore Stockton . . . exercising the functions of civil and military government, with the same apparent deference to his rank on the part of all officers (*including yourself*) as . . . in July last. I learned also in conversation with you, that on the march from San Diego . . . you entered upon and discharged duties implying an acknowledgment *on your part*, of supremacy to Commodore Stockton. I feel therefore, with great deference to your professional and personal character constrained to say that, until you and Commodore Stockton adjust between yourselves the question of rank, where I respectfully think the difficulty belongs, I shall have to report and receive orders, as heretofore, from the Commodore.

Again the writer signed himself "Lieutenant Colonel, United States Army and Military Commandant of the territory of California." The italicized words indicate how Frémont seized upon the weakest links in the General's armor. Again Kearny doubtless regretted his refusal of Stockton's offer of the command. Like Banquo's ghost, it would not down.

Although the General must have seethed with indignation at such disregard for military discipline, his reaction affords us one of our best insights into his true character. Kearny gave his account of the whole episode while on the witness stand at the court-martial, and Frémont did not challenge that part of his testimony. The General stated:

> I told Lieutenant Colonel Frémont that I was a much older man than himself, that I had great regard for his wife, and great friendship for his father-in-law, Colonel Benton, from whom I had received many acts of kindness, that these considerations induced me to volunteer advice to him, and the advice was, that he should take that letter back and destroy it, that I was willing to forget it. Lieutenant Colonel Frémont declined taking it back, and told me that Commodore Stockton would support him in the position taken in that letter. I told him that Commodore Stockton could not support him in disobeying the orders of his senior officer, and that, if he persisted in it, he would unquestionably ruin himself. He told me that Commodore Stockton was about organizing a civil government and intended to appoint him as governor of the territory. I told him Commodore Stockton had no such authority, that authority having been conferred on me by the President of the United States. He asked me if I would appoint him governor. I told him I expected shortly to leave California for Missouri; that I had previous to leaving Santa Fé asked for permission to do so, and was in hopes of receiving it; that as soon as the country was quieted I should, most probably, organize a civil government in California, and that I, at that time, knew of no objection to my appointing him as the governor. He then stated to me that he would see Commodore Stockton, and that, unless he appointed him governor at once, he would not obey his orders, and left me.

The older officer's forbearance was amazing and more than tips the balance against Justin Smith's indictment of him as "grasping, jealous, domineering and harsh." It is astonishing that Kearny could even consider important preferment for the man who had just defied him. Quite as marked is the picture of Frémont as audacious, impetuous, and with a bold disregard of consequences. A strange man indeed, this topographical engineer, who could calmly discuss the governorship (even if he did not actually bargain for it) with the superior whom he had just refused to obey.

In the long argument he filed in his own defense, Frémont indignantly denied the charge—implicit in Kearny's testimony—that he had bargained for the governorship. The General certainly indicated that Frémont had weighed a present appointment by Stockton against a deferred one from Kearny. Frémont admitted that the governorship had been discussed, and produced his own letter of February 3, 1847, to Senator Benton, in which he wrote: "Both offered me the commission and post of governor; Commodore Stockton, to redeem his pledge to that effect immediately and General Kearny offering to give me the commission in four or six weeks." According to Frémont, the General offered him the position; General Kearny testified that Frémont asked for it. Every student of the affair must finally reach his own conclusions. Bancroft felt the letter to Benton strongly supported Kearny's position. Allan Nevins on the other hand accepts Frémont's denial as valid; he was "frequently hot-headed but never base." Nevins supports this view by the too-well-founded case against the reliability of General Kearny's memory. Several instances of this occurred during the court-martial. It is due to Kearny to note that his lapses of memory seemed most genuine and not convenient excuses. A good memory would have better served the General's cause.

Benton and all of Frémont's other champions naturally joined in the denial that there was any bargaining over the governorship. But while that remains a question of veracity, no one ever disputed the fact that Kearny gave Frémont full opportunity to withdraw the fatal letter and erase the incident. That shines forth as the act of a kindly man not easily moved to anger.

Only John C. Frémont viewed it in a different light. Bancroft very tellingly pointed out the defect in character here revealed. In his argument, Frémont accused General Kearny of condoning an alleged act of disobedience. By offering to let Frémont reclaim and destroy his incriminating letter, the General had become a party to any offense involved. If there was one, it was his duty to

265

report it to the proper authorities and bring the guilty (Frémont) to justice. Bancroft's logic is devastating; while General Kearny might be technically at fault, "dishonor in such cases pertains not to the officer who shows such leniency but to the recipient who uses it against him."

When he was cross-examined at the court-martial, the General recalled that during this conversation Frémont expressed a great desire that Kearny have a personal interview with the Commodore. General Kearny expressed a willingness for such an interview but would not ask for it. Frémont maintained that he could have arranged such a conference, that Stockton was willing to hold one, and that only Kearny's unannounced departure from Los Angeles prevented it. Frémont was inaccurate on this point. Stockton did have definite advice of Kearny's expected departure. We shall see them passing each other en route to San Diego without the Commodore making any attempt at conversation. After the treatment to which the General had been subjected, he certainly could not have been expected to show these two officers any special courtesies.

It is essential to a good biography that its author show some partiality for his subject. While striving to be fair, Allan Nevins honestly displays such sentiment for Frémont. But it is hard to accept his analysis of the famous letter of January 17, 1847—"a decisive though tactful refusal to obey Kearny's commands." An army officer's reaction to that judgment might be violent. Maybe if Dale Carnegie had been born a century earlier, he might have advised John C. Frémont on how a military subordinate can tactfully refuse to obey his superior officer. Nevins' judgment of this same point in his later biography is well considered: "In all this Frémont was ill-advised. After all, since he was now back in the army, Kearny was his superior officer. Stockton should have counseled him to obey the General or at least try to reach an agreement with him."

Oddly enough, Bancroft, although believing that Frémont actually bargained with Kearny for the governorship, decided in his favor on the letter of refusal (although favoring Kearny as opposed to Stockton):

. . . his action in disobeying Kearny's orders or rather in leaving the two chiefs to settle their own quarrel must, I think, be approved. . . . Like Stockton he merits no praise for earlier proceedings. He had perhaps done even more than the commodore to retard the conquest. His mishaps as a political adventurer call for no sympathy. But his cause was identical with that of Stockton who had adopted his views, had saved him from a position that might have been dangerous, had given him his commission, had approved his irregular acts at Cahuenga and depended upon his own support in his assumption of authority. There is or should be honor even among filibusters. For Frémont to have deserted his patron at the last . . . would have been dishonorable and treacherous. . . . Kearny was in the right and Stockton in the wrong. Kearny in obedience to instructions from Washington had marched to California, had cooperated with the naval officers in conquering the country and was entitled to the chief command.

Captain du Pont recorded his view of this triangular dispute:

The Commodore having refused to treat with Pico, the latter when driven back went to attack Frémont, or rather to give him the honor of receiving his sword. I do hope the Commodore will wear his honors meekly. His general order I have seen (Stockton's report of the actions on the 8th and 9th, etc.) Although a little exaggerated, it is the best of his publications. But it contains a grave omission. General Kearny's name does not appear where it was so much his due. I learned by a (lieutenant's) private letter that . . . the old gentleman is very sore about it. So soon as he has forces collected I believe the navy will be confined to its appropriate sphere. . . . It is a fitting time now for Stockton to leave with honor. . . . I think the appointment of Frémont wrong and unnecessary. The Commodore takes the ground it is a civil appointment similar to that of our governors of territories and the United States officers commanding troops have no communication with them. I said to him: "But Frémont cannot hold on then to his army commission as it is contrary to our Constitution to hold two!" *Evidently this was a point that had been overlooked by all.* [The italics are mine.]

Captain du Pont was the first to call attention to John C. Fré-

267

mont's astonishing acrobatic feat. He was a lieutenant colonel in the army so far as title and emoluments were concerned or when it otherwise served his purpose, but when a brigadier general issued an order displeasing to him, he was serving under a naval commission issued by Commodore Stockton to Major Frémont! Not the least surprising phase of this situation is that Stockton, of all persons, had remained ignorant for nearly three months of Frémont's changed status. Strangest of all is that Frémont, despite his vaunted "loyalty" to the Commodore, had in all that period not troubled himself to mention his new commission to Stockton. Many biographers and historians have made quite a case of this loyalty to Stockton. In most instances they have overlooked or disregarded the stubborn fact that in January, 1847, Frémont was serving under an army, not a naval, commission. None of them has ever rationalized the simultaneous possession of the two commissions. I am unaware of its counterpart in all our history.

Frémont probably went directly from his interview with General Kearny to call upon the Commodore. The latter's commission to Frémont as "governor and commander-in-chief of the territory of California until the President of the United States shall otherwise direct" was actually dated January 16. At the same time Stockton named Colonel Russell secretary of state. Gillespie had been slated for that role but preferred to become major of the California Battalion. He also appointed a legislative council of seven prominent citizens to meet in Los Angeles on March 1 to consider necessary legislation. This council never actually came into being.

General Kearny apparently learned very quickly of the issuance of the gubernatorial commission, for on that same seventeenth he wrote Commodore Stockton two letters. The first concluded:

> As I am prepared to carry out the President's instructions to me, which you oppose, I must, for the purpose of preventing collision between us, and possibly, a civil war in consequence of it, remain silent for the present, leaving with you the great responsibility of doing that for which you have no authority and preventing me from complying with the President's orders.

268

The second letter merely informed the Commodore "that I intend to withdraw tomorrow from this place, with the small party which escorted me to this country"—certainly not an unannounced departure.

On the same day General Kearny also wrote to the Adjutant General a letter which was to have fateful consequences. It enclosed copies of the General's orders to Colonel Frémont, the latter's refusal to obey the General, and Kearny's first letter to Stockton of January 17, and said:

> . . . I am not recognized in my official capacity, either by Commodore Stockton or Lieutenant Colonel Frémont, both of whom refuse to obey my orders or the instructions of the President; and as I have no troops in the country under my authority, excepting a few dragoons, I have no power of enforcing them.

It is interesting to read an opinion of General Kearny written by an American civilian in Los Angeles at this time. He described him as "very polite, genteel and mild in his manner with no pomp or show, listening with patience to every one." Internal evidence points to U. S. Consul Thomas O. Larkin as the writer.

About ten o'clock on the morning of January 18, General Kearny rode out of the Plaza with some fifty dragoons. Officers Emory and Turner accompanied him. Dr. Griffin was also in the party and gloomily predicted that they would all be massacred before they reached San Diego because the Californians were not living up to the surrender terms and were preparing for another uprising:

> If it does (happen) every bit of it is to be attributed to Frémont's thirst for glory, and Stockton's—I won't say what—but I only wish I could marry a Senator's daughter. I might then set at defiance the orders of my superiors and do as I pleased. Of course as affairs are now Kearny has no forces at his command, and must submit. . . . General Kearny has been most outrageously used by Frémont and Stockton, they are both men of political influence, and of course they will go scot free and in all probability throw the whole blame on Kearny.

The little detachment was low in equipment as well as morale. The men's shoes were badly worn; some had none at all. They suffered greatly on the first day's march. Because he was sick and had badly blistered feet, one of the soldiers rode the General's horse. Like any private, Kearny himself made this entire march of 145 miles on foot. Trudging along the rough road, the General talked freely with his adjutant, Lieutenant Emory. He had plans for the latter to embark with dispatches for Washington and wanted him to know that he would take matters into his own hands when he had a sufficiently strong force to exact obedience. For the present he must bide his time.

During that day's march, a messenger brought word that Commodore Stockton was eight miles behind Kearny's party and asked them to wait for him. Later he and his staff arrived and spent the night at San Juan Capistrano. Most accounts of Stockton's movements state that he left Los Angeles soon after General Kearny and went to San Pedro to embark. This must have referred to his sailors and marines, for Captain du Pont, on noting his arrival at San Diego, said Stockton came with an escort of thirty men. Under the strained relations existing, the Commodore would hardly have requested the General to wait had he marched with all his command. The unsettled condition of the country must have induced Stockton to seek the protection of Kearny's larger force. Quite evidently there was no fraternizing at San Juan. The next day the Commodore's party passed the General's, with "nothing more than a passing salute."

A little later the dragoons encountered Congressman Willard P. Hall, bringing important news. Colonel Cooke and the Mormon Battalion were now near Warner's Ranch. Hall observed a very weary file of soldiers covered with dust and sweat, and with bruised and bleeding feet. Hall was riding a good horse. When he saw Kearny marching on foot, he said, "Take my horse, I am younger than you and will walk." "No, I thank you," the General responded, "I am a soldier and can walk better than you as I am accustomed to it." Soon after General Kearny reached San Diego on January 23, he ordered Cooke to march his battalion there. Cooke with 350

Mormons arrived on the twenty-ninth. He brought the General a letter from Mrs. Kearny.

Cooke's well-deserved gratification over the success of his long march was tempered by the disquieting news of Frémont's behavior. In his eyes this was one of the most heinous offenses an army officer could commit. The General directed Cooke to quarter his battalion at the San Luis Rey Mission and await further orders. As the next ranking officer in California he would in Kearny's absence exercise full authority. Both officers had in mind the disturbed conditions in the territory. They realized that discontented natives might be encouraged by the well-known dissension among the Americans to attempt another uprising.

In writing the Adjutant General on the thirtieth, Kearny regretted that the Mormon Battalion's paymaster had brought no specie with him. The General pointed out that cash could not be obtained in California for his drafts on the government except at a prohibitive 20 per cent discount. To the Secretary of War he wrote on the same day:

> I intend leaving here tomorrow in the Ship Cyane for Monterey & San Francisco to examine those places & the country above here, and decide where to station Col. Stevenson's Regt. of Volunteers, & Capt. Tompkins Compy of Arty (which I hope may shortly arrive here).

General Kearny unburdened himself to Secretary Marcy:

> The people of California are quiet at this time, but how long they will remain so, is very uncertain. Should Gen'l Castro, Gov'r Flores, or any other Mexican officer return here with 2 or 300 Mexicans or Sonorians, I have no doubt, but the People would again rise & give us much trouble—they have been badly managed & domineered over by the Volunteers raised in the Sacramento & below and their feelings are decidedly hostile at this time to the Americans, & our Government in consequence of it. Our senior officers too have pursued, as I think, towards the Californians, an imprudent course & far from conciliatory, so that they are quiet

271

now from fear, not from love of us. Such quiet may easily be disturbed.

It will most probably be necessary to keep in California (even if Peace is this day made with Mexico) for a year or two to come at least 1000 men after the end of the war, & unless a force is raised expressly for the country, as I have previously suggested, volunteers should be sent here by sea, bringing their stores, provisions, money, etc etc with them—We cannot depend upon raising volunteers here, & a march by land is so long & fatigueing that men & animals require some months' rest after their arrival. . . .

[General Kearny then detailed the troubles with Stockton and Frémont which we have just reviewed.]

. . . In my opinion it was all wrong. We want at this time a steady & firm military government to punish promptly the disturbance of the Peace.

. . . Is it possible that a Naval & a Military officer can find countenance in Washington or in the U.S.A. for such conduct? I will not believe it! . . . I rely upon the Presdt. & upon yourself for justice! I have endeavored to preserve a steady & prudent course and from patriotic motives & to prevent our own countrymen from being arrayed against each other in this part of the country, have even given way to others, who I thought & still think were fools & madmen, and prepared to go to any length, without reflecting upon the consequences, to carry their point.

I shall, as I now propose, when I have examined the country, establish my Head Quarters at Monterey, during my continuance in California—But I still hope to receive from you permission to return to Missouri the ensueing summer or Fall, provided the Peace of the country is firmly established & placed beyond the fear of interruption.

We are indebted to Captain du Pont for our knowledge of the *U.S.S. Cyane*'s cruise from San Diego to Monterey with General Kearny and his staff as passengers. Her commander's journal for February 17 reads:

I sailed from San Diego on January 31st having with me General Kearny, and staff . . . and the Consul (Larkin). I was pleased to have them and as they are still with me (or rather the General is) you may infer we have not quarreled. On the contrary I believe

Army Colonel John C. Frémont was appointed governor of California and given a naval commission by Stockton. He refused to obey Kearny's commands, and was later convicted of mutiny and disobedience by a military court-martial.

For many years before Missouri Senator Thomas Hart Benton's (pictured above) son-in-law, Frémont, was court-martialed as a result of charges preferred by Kearny, the two older men enjoyed a warm friendship. But their relationship ended in one of the most tragic enmities of American history.

it has been a matter of real enjoyment to us both. . . . On arriving at Monterey after an eight days passage it was gratifying to see the "Independence" there. . . . he (Kearny) was in every way charmed with the arrival of Commodore Shubrick. . . . Shubrick on learning of Kearny's presence on the "Cyane" sent for him and fired a thirteen gun salute. They had dinner, the old general was delighted and seemed to forget the discourteous treatment he had received elsewhere.

(According to testimony at the court-martial, Commodore Shubrick was aboard the *Lexington*. Both ships were there on the *Cyane's* arrival.)

One passenger aboard the *Lexington* was a young artillery lieutenant named William Tecumseh Sherman. In his *Memoirs* he recalled a picturesque incident of Kearny's arrival:

Because of rumors of a quarrel between Kearny and Frémont, the younger officers could be heard to inquire "Who the devil is Governor of California?" One day while on board the "Independence," a war vessel was reported in the offing. The ships exchanged signals—it proved to be the "Cyane," Captain Du Pont. A boat was sent from the "Independence" to the "Cyane". . . . Lieutenant Wise, Montgomery, Lewis, William Chapman and others were on deck as the boat returned with a stranger in the stern sheets clothed in army blue. Kearny wore an old dragoon coat and army cap to which he had added a broad visor cut from a full dress hat to shade his face and eyes against the glaring sun of the Gila region.—Chapman exclaimed: "Fellows, the problem is solved, there is the grand vizier (visor), by G——d! *He* is Governor of California. All hands received the General with great heartiness. Between Kearny and Shubrick existed from that time forward the greatest harmony and good feeling.

Shubrick soon afterward wrote that he felt particularly fortunate in having "so gallant an officer as Kearny."

Echoes of the Kearny-Stockton controversy had appeared in the January 28 issue of the *Californian* published in Monterey. The article had been strongly critical of General Kearny for the Battle

273

of San Pasqual and included a slur at Captain Mervine for his reverse at the Dominguez Rancho. It gave all credit for the victories at the San Gabriel and the Mesa and the recapture of Los Angeles to Commodore Stockton. Evidently this did not sit well with many readers, and in the issue for February 13 appeared a spirited reply. General Kearny was praised and severe exception taken to "the great injustice both to General Kearny and Captain Mervine."

What was happening in southern California where General Kearny had found himself powerless to exercise authority? Commodore Stockton had reached San Diego on January 22, about the time his forces came by sea from San Pedro. He reported to Washington that the civil government he had organized was once more successfully operating. With his sailors and marines again aboard their vessels, he was about to leave for Mexico. That day or the next he sailed south. Word had reached him that a French schooner was landing guns on the coast and that a General Bustamante with some fifteen hundred Mexicans was marching north. Stockton cruised south some 120 miles without finding an enemy. In a longer report to the Navy Department on February 4, he detailed his difficulties with General Kearny and urged the recall of Kearny "to prevent the evil consequences that may grow out of such a temper and such a head." According to his own admission, Stockton exercised no authority in California after this departure from San Diego. On January 22, Frémont as governor proclaimed order and peace restored, authorized the release of all prisoners, and directed civil officials to resume their various duties. In the south he was generally recognized as governor for several weeks.

Consistent with his announced defiance of General Kearny's orders, in quick succession Frémont took various steps to reorganize the California Battalion. He had learned much about the temper of the Californians. Not only was his attitude more conciliatory than it had been in the north, but it was a vast improvement on the highhanded courses pursued by Stockton and Gillespie. Americans were critical of his leniency, but the same policy made him many friends among native Californians around the Pueblo.

Frémont in the next few weeks made heavy purchases of cattle on government credit and borrowed money for sundry expenses. His most ambitious project perhaps was the purchase of White or Bird Island (now Alcatraz) in San Francisco Bay. He purchased this in the name of the United States on his promise to pay five thousand dollars. These transactions of the pseudo governor were to plague him and his creditors for many weary years.

Commodore Shubrick proved to be a man of energy and practical sense. He was unaware of Kearny's presence in California when he arrived at Monterey. Accordingly on January 2, thinking Colonel Frémont the senior army officer in the territory, he wrote him in friendly vein, expressing a desire to co-operate with the land forces. Frémont, replying on February 7, brought Shubrick down to date concerning his differences with General Kearny. He closed with a plea for whatever funds the Commodore could advance to relieve his financial embarrassment. Before this reply was received, Shubrick had learned the facts and wrote Kearny a similar letter.

At Monterey, General Kearny exhibited to Commodore Shubrick his instructions of June 3 and June 18. Shubrick readily admitted the General's right to command all troops in California. His disapproval of the courses pursued by Stockton and Frémont was quite evident. He then showed Kearny the Navy Department's orders of July 12 addressed to Commodore Sloat, which Shubrick had received at Valparaiso. These of course directed Sloat (or his successor) to organize a civil government after California was taken. On reading them Kearny cheerfully stated that he stood ready to afford the Commodore any assistance in his power. Shubrick's temperament was very different from Stockton's. He desired a peaceful settlement with "Governor" Frémont and was in no hurry to assert rights under orders then seven months old. He and Kearny agreed it was best to await more explicit instructions from Washington which might be expected shortly.

Kearny was happy to learn that other passengers on the *Lexington* were Captain Tompkins and an artillery company. Its first lieutenants were Edward O. C. Ord and William T. Sherman, whom we have already seen in Monterey. Another officer with this detachment was Lieutenant Henry W. Halleck of the engineers. The rank and file numbered 113. Lieutenant Sherman had government funds in his custody, and the General secured part of them. He had not seen any specie for many harried months. Kearny rejoiced too in the ample supply of clothing brought by the artillery company, and promptly sent half of their reserve apparel to the nearly naked dragoons he had left in the south.

On the eleventh Captain du Pont's *Cyane* with General Kearny on board sailed from Monterey for the north. Captain Turner and Lieutenants Halleck and Warner accompanied the General. These short voyages with Captain du Pont were doubtless among the few pleasant experiences Kearny enjoyed in California. He was a good sailor, his associates were congenial, and the fare was a great improvement over the meager rations available ashore and a farther cry from the rigors of Mule Hill!

After the *Cyane* departed, Commodore Shubrick advised the Navy Department of all the recent developments. One sentence bears quoting: "With regard to the civil government of the territory . . . measures have been, in my opinion, prematurely taken by Commodore Stockton, and an appointment of governor made of a gentleman who I am led to believe is not acceptable to the people of California."

On February 13, as the *Cyane* was about to enter San Francisco Bay in thick weather, a bark was seen near at hand. It proved to be the naval storeship *Erie*, commanded by Captain Henry Turner's brother Charles. The swifter *Cyane* drew away from the other ship as it entered the yet unnamed Golden Gate and came to anchor in Yerba Buena cove. The *Warren* and the *Savannah* were already in the harbor and saluted the General with thirteen guns. The *Erie* signaled that it had Colonel Richard B. Mason on board. He was dangerously ill. As the *Erie* carried no medical officer, Captain du Pont immediately sent his own surgeon to attend him.

Soon afterward one of the *Cyane*'s boats rowed General Kearny over to the *Erie* to call on his old associate of the First Dragoons. When he returned, Du Pont described him as "radiant with the news that Colonel Mason had given him." The latter had brought dispatches from Washington. The most important of these was a letter from Winfield Scott, General-in-Chief of the Army, dated November 3, 1846. Here was the long-awaited verdict from the government. Scott complimented Kearny for his success in New Mexico and anticipated similar results in California. He instructed him to erect defenses for the Bays of Monterey and San Francisco, as well as other important points he might select in the area. The letter specifically referred to the California volunteers organized by Commodore Stockton and directed that they be mustered into the army.

General Scott reiterated that "the senior officer of the land forces" was to be the civil governor of the province! Kearny was cautioned not to declare the formal annexation of the province; that must depend upon the government of the United States. After he had occupied all necessary points in Upper California, established a temporary civil government therein, and was assured of the country's tranquility and safety from danger of reconquest by Mexico, General Kearny was authorized to turn over to Colonel Mason all his duties and return with a sufficient escort of troops to St. Louis. General Scott believed that Lieutenant Colonel Frémont was still in California. "Should you find him there, it is desired that you do not detain him, against his wishes a moment longer than the necessities of the service may require." Harmony and co-operation with the naval forces were urged.

Mason had also handed to the General a copy of a letter from the Secretary of the Navy to Commodore Stockton, dated November 5, 1846. It acknowledged the Commodore's report of July 28 and his proclamation to the people of California. After complimentary references to what he had accomplished during the previous summer, it advised him that Commodore Shubrick had sailed for California in September and would assume command upon his arrival:

The President has deemed it best . . . to invest the military officer commanding with the direction of the operations on land and with the administrative functions of government over the people

277

and territory occupied by us. You will relinquish to Colonel Mason
or to General Kearny if the latter shall arrive before you have done
so, the entire control over these matters.

In these two letters, Kearny read the unequivocal answer to the
whole dispute between himself and Commodore Stockton and Colonel Frémont. In the strange politico-military drama of Kearny's
stay in California, that hour with Mason on San Francisco Bay
marks the turning point. December had been a month of mortal
anguish; January, apparently the nadir of his fortunes. Until this
moment he could never be wholly certain that he would be upheld.
Now he knew; he faced more weary months of trial and vexation
but uncertainty was gone. His commander-in-chief had told him
what to do; now he approved what Kearny had done. Kearny could
resume his habit of undertaking the next task confronting him.

Captain du Pont rejoiced with the General that he was "now
supreme in California. . . . I think he is worthy of the trust. He
is a man of energy and good sense and has made the same favorable
impression that Commodore Shubrick has with every one." Du
Pont's journal of February 19 and 20 sets forth the best explanation available to us of the famous "conflicting" instructions:

> The history of things at home is curious in relation to Cali-
> fornia. The General who shows me and tells me everything has
> put me au fait of the matter . . . as to the secret springs of action.
> The first authority to form a civil government was given to Gen-
> eral Kearny and set aside by Commodore Stockton. Then followed
> instructions to that effect to Commodore Sloat. Commodore Shu-
> brick had similar ones when he sailed but the moment old Sloat
> reached Washington and the government learned Stockton was
> left here, authority was immediately transferred back to General
> Kearny. But for fear he should not have arrived, Colonel Mason
> was dispatched with the appointment of governor. It is evident
> the War and Navy Department respectively had great fears lest
> Colonel Stevenson on the one hand and Commodore Stockton on
> the other should have control of things in California. They de-
> serve credit for their foresight and the very opportune arrival of
> clear and emphatic instructions. These I have seen. Stockton was

278

gracefully bowed off by Mr. Mason (Secretary of the Navy), told he may . . . return in the "Savannah."

Lieutenant Henry B. Watson of the marine corps was also a passenger on the *Erie* and brought orders from the Secretary of the Navy to the naval command, very similar to General Scott's to Kearny. Soon after his arrival a boat from the *Savannah* took him down the bay to Santa Clara whence he proceeded on horseback to Monterey to deliver his dispatches to Commodore Shubrick.

The diminutive *California Star* of Yerba Buena in its issue of February 20 reported Kearny's arrival at the Bay and said:

> General Kearny is a mild, amiable and intelligent man, plain and unassuming and possessing great experience both in military and civil government affairs. He is eminently qualified to discharge the important duties assigned to him in this country by the President. We understand that he came here vested with full powers after the conquest of the country to organize the civil government and that *since his arrival despatches have been received from Washington City not only renewing the authority originally invested in him but granting him additional powers.* . . . [The italics are mine.] We have not been able to ascertain whether General Kearny will act as Governor himself or whether he will appoint some other person to that office.

(The *Star* was probably the first to publish this news.) The *Star* also quoted from the *New York Daily Globe* of November 7: "He ranks very high as a bold, indomitable, energetic and accomplished officer who has the head to contrive, the hand to execute and the heart to brave every difficulty."

One of the most persistent criticisms of General Kearny has been his failure to inform Colonel Frémont about this confirmation of his authority. It is true that the General did not himself advise his unruly subordinate. But that is very different from Frémont's insistence that he was never informed and knew nothing about the new orders.

There is abundant indication that Frémont must have learned

the facts by early March. Major Gillespie wrote from Los Angeles on March 5 that Frémont "had received some newspapers by couriers who came down lately but has not favored our eyes with a sight of them." It is unreasonable to suppose that any correspondent who took the trouble to send him papers would have failed to include the February 20 issue of the *California Star*. Could it have been that the Governor was reluctant to let his associates know of this decided setback? Other letters of the period comment on the "latest instructions" from Washington. Gillespie himself by April 1 mentioned Kearny's "last instructions"—it being plain that he meant the orders of November 3 and 5. Late in March, according to Allan Nevins, Larkin told Frémont "for the first time" in Monterey of the November 5 order. Certainly by then— if not considerably earlier—Frémont was on constructive notice that General Kearny had been fully upheld in Washington.

At the court-martial General Kearny was asked whether he communicated the instructions of November 5 to Lieutenant Colonel Frémont. He answered stiffly that he was "not in the habit of communicating to my juniors the instructions I receive from my seniors, unless required to do so in those instructions." That answer has been often cited against the General. Allan Nevins has called it "a base act." I agree that Kearny could have supplied a better reason for his silence, but after two weeks of the trial, his nerves were frayed and his patience exhausted by the badgering tactics of the defense. He could have answered that he knew the information had been promptly furnished Frémont by others.

Since men's characters are being judged by their answers, let us look at Frémont's record on this subject. In the long argument submitted by him near the end of his trial (Appendix No. 4 at p. 365 of the Proceedings) the accused in the most solemn manner reiterated his denial of any knowledge of Kearny's new orders. The document even capitalized part of one sentence as if to emphasize that denial: "the instructions of the 5th of November . . . *which was never communicated to me and of which I remained totally ignorant till since the commencement of this trial*. Neither General Kearny, Commodore Shubrick or Commodore Biddle communicated them to me." (p. 413 of the Proceedings).

It would be easy to apply an uglier word than "base" to that allegation. In addition to all the circumstantial evidence we have just reviewed, it has been generally overlooked that the language in the charges against Frémont directly contradicts him on this point. The seventh specification of the charge of mutiny (p. 12 of the Proceedings) reads:

> Frémont . . . having been officially informed by W. Branford Shubrick . . . in a letter dated U.S.S. Independence Monterey February 23, 1847 in the following words: "General Kearny, I am instructed, as the commanding military officer in California and invested by the President with the administrative functions of government over the people and territory."

The same letter is quoted again, both in the fourth specification of the second charge and the fourth specification of the third charge (pp. 22 and 27 of the Proceedings).

Note that Frémont did not confine his denial to not having *received* any communication; the officers named had never *communicated* the orders to him. If he did not receive Shubrick's letter of February 23, why did he (reinforced by two able and vigilant lawyers) overlook this perfect opportunity to challenge the statement reiterated in the three specifications?

From this review of the record, it seems certain that soon after Lieutenant Watson delivered his dispatches to Commodore Shubrick in Monterey, the latter wrote the February 23 letter to Frémont. Allowing over a week for the letter to reach Los Angeles, Frémont must have had the facts before him by March 6 or 7. Shubrick either told Kearny of this letter or let him read a copy of it on his return from San Francisco a few days later. Since Kearny's own knowledge that Shubrick had informed Frémont has become important, a letter which the General wrote to Commodore Biddle on April 11 is evidence in his behalf (that was long before anyone had charged him with dereliction in the matter). At that time Biddle inquired of Kearny about a shipping license Frémont had issued as governor on March 9. The General replied that Frémont had no right at that time:

... to consider himself Governor of California except what he may have derived from Stockton and he well knew that the President of the United States had assigned that duty to myself, *having been officially informed* of that fact by Circular of March 1st signed by Commodore Shubrick and myself before your arrival here (a copy of which was sent to him) *and by letter from* Com. S. of February 23rd." [The italics are mine.]

But what a stickler for punctilio this Lieutenant Colonel Frémont! He refused to obey the orders of a brigadier general bearing specific instructions from the President of the United States. The simultaneous possession of army and navy commissions did not embarrass him; nor did his silence toward Stockton about his lieutenant colonelcy trouble him. But when General Kearny's authority was confirmed by Washington, then he, John C. Frémont, had to be personally informed by General Kearny or he would go through life asserting that he had no knowledge of these facts. This misrepresentation has led most students of the episode to believe that General Kearny deliberately concealed the knowledge from Frémont to entrap him into more compromising acts.

While on this subject, why has no unfriendly comment been directed at Commodore Stockton? Frémont as governor was a figure solely of his creation. Since loyalty to Stockton was supposed to have motivated Frémont's refusal to obey General Kearny's orders, was it not incumbent upon the Commodore to see that his appointee was notified of this change in their fortunes—a change that could be calamitous for John C. Frémont? We know definitely that a little over a month after the arrival of the orders of November 3 and 5 Stockton was told of them by Commodore Biddle. Even if that was his first knowledge, there is no evidence that he then or later ever bothered to apprise Frémont of their existence. Is it not odd that only Stephen Kearny could arouse the indignation of Frémont's champions?

On the fifteenth one of Captain du Pont's guests at dinner on the *Cyane* was Edwin Bryant. He was presented to General Kearny and has left us one of the best descriptions we have of him at this period:

> . . . about five feet ten or eleven, his figure all that is required of symmetry. The features are regular, almost Grecian, the eyes blue and with an eagle like expression when excited by stern or angry emotions but in ordinary social intercourse the whole expression of his countenance is mild and pleasing and his manners and conversation are unaffected, urbane and conciliatory, without the slightest exhibition of vanity or egotism. He appears a cool, brave and energetic soldier, a strict disciplinarian without tyranny, a man in short determined to perform his duty in whatever situation he may be placed, leaving the consequences to follow in their natural course.

The next day Bryant rode with the General and his officers to the Presidio to inspect the old fortifications. No garrison had been stationed there for several years. Once more Kearny found himself at the familiar task of locating forts and planning construction work. His practiced eye was quick to see the commanding position of Punta del Cantil Blanco (better known now as Fort Point) and the pressing necessity of replacing the ruinous Castillo de San Joaquin by a fortification capable (in the mid-nineteenth century) of barring entrance by an enemy. While the massive walls of Fort Winfield Scott (now dwarfed by the giant tower of the Golden Gate Bridge) were not commenced until several years after Kearny's death, that inspection tour in February, 1847, marked the inception of plans for fortifying the harbor.

On the twentieth the General was rowed over to the *Warren* for a visit with Lieutenant William Radford. This was the first time in several years that Stephen Kearny had seen his brother-in-law. After mentioning the General's dinner on the *Warren*, Captain du Pont wrote:

> The old gentleman is reading at my elbow. . . . When he came back he told me he had just told Radford he must go back to his *home* on board the "Cyane." My intercourse with him and all his

officers has been very pleasant. They drop in my cabin of an evening, read the papers and discuss, etc. and being men of education it is improving as well as agreeable. . . . In the new order of things about to take place, no one falls so flatly and irretrievably as Frémont and I feel very sorry for him.

Du Pont, while blaming Frémont for the evils he had brought down on himself by his rash conduct, clearly foresaw the tragic events that were to darken General Kearny's last days:

> The General is very awkwardly placed too in reference to him (Frémont) but seems never to falter in matters of duty. The only friend the General has in the political world is Colonel Benton and he appears a true one. He showed me last night several letters from him (Benton) . . . keeping him informed from Washington of everything concerning himself a little in advance of the Department, his promotion, the President's satisfaction with his operations in New Mexico and promising a brevet major General's commission after he is done with California. They have been long intimate and the Colonel's daughter, Mrs. Frémont, is warmly attached to the General. This makes matters trying enough.

(How strangely these last words read in the light of our knowledge of Senator Benton's later great enmity for Stephen Kearny!)

Evidently the favorable impression Edwin Bryant had formed of Kearny was reciprocated, for on the twentieth the General appointed him alcalde of San Francisco.

Before we terminate this account of Kearny's visit to San Francisco, mention should be made of two long letters Henry Turner wrote to his wife on February 21. He told her of recent events in California in his most uninhibited style:

> Commodore Stockton . . . having shown himself wholly unfit for such a station . . . we of course were delighted to find his authority at an end and a person much more capable and much more gentlemanly had arrived to relieve him. . . . this was in the highest degree gratifying to the General . . . for never were people more

disgusted and dissatisfied . . . with the misrule practiced under the Stockton administration.

In the second letter Turner discussed at much greater length Kearny's difficulties with Stockton and Frémont:

Both of them (i.e., Stockton and Frémont) should be tried by court-martial but whether either will be or not is very uncertain. What I communicate to you . . . you must keep entirely to yourself as the matter is destined to create a great deal of talk in the country and the less we say about it the better . . . . I am sorry to say that I do not think the General displayed his usual firmness and decision of character in dealing with Frémont . . . . The General is swayed too much . . . by what he supposes will be agreeable to Benton. I am sick, tired, and disgusted with such a state of things and were it practical I would leave the General and join my company but that I cannot do without leaving him at a time when more than any other he needs support.—I know the General will be severely attacked for his temporising course in relation to Frémont . . . . Were I to behave as Frémont has done he would cause me to be put in irons and would pursue me with a bitterness that would drive me to desperation. . . . He says he will prefer charges against Frémont and cause him to be tried but I do not believe it. . . . if he does, he will not be tried by a court-martial. . . . were it anyone else he would be dropped from the rolls without a trial. . . . Commodore Stockton's conduct out here has been extraordinary. . . . I entertain the most contemptuous opinion of the man; he is a low trifling, truckling politician regarded with as much contempt by the officers of the Navy as those of the Army . . . . Commodore Shubrick's arrival is the subject of general rejoicing; both (Stockton) and Frémont have become the most unimportant people in the Territory. The papers of the country are beginning to attack them with the greatest virulence. . . . so far as Commodore Stockton was concerned, it would have been infinitely better for us to have fallen into the hands of the enemy to have been treated as prisoners. . . . he is doing his utmost to undermine us at home by conniving at the reports for publication of our battle at San Pasqual.

Captain Mervine gave a dinner in General Kearny's honor on board the *Savannah* during his stay at the Bay. Soon afterward

Mervine received orders from Commodore Shubrick to bring the *Savannah* to Monterey immediately. The same messenger brought a letter to General Kearny. The Commodore had read the instructions brought by Lieutenant Watson and hoped he would see the General soon. Shubrick assured Kearny that the latest orders placed the affairs of the territory where the Commodore wished them. Mervine's sailing seemed a fine opportunity for General Kearny to return to Monterey. Therefore Captain du Pont personally took him over to the *Savannah* in his gig on February 22. "Before quitting my cabin," Du Pont wrote, "he expressed in a very handsome, frank and cordial manner his thanks for my hospitality." Adverse winds and erratic navigation delayed the *Savannah*'s arrival at Monterey until the morning of February 26.

Kearny and his staff made Consul Larkin's house in Monterey their headquarters. Larkin's letters show they were "paying guests." Previous officialdom had blandly accepted hospitality without thought of remuneration. There is some evidence that there may have been friction in the household. One young friend of the host complained that there was "too much Big Company."

It is possible that General Kearny visited San Francisco about the middle of April, 1847. When Bancroft was amassing information for his monumental history of California, he employed many researchers. Their index-summarys of the documents studied are in the Bancroft Library. Among them is a note reading: "General S. W. Kearny arrived in S. F. about 15th April by sea." The source given is "Larkin doc. V.80." In the Larkin papers, Documents 79 and 81 are in their proper place but 80 is missing. It was missing when photostats were made of the documents in the thirties. We can only surmise its nature or further content. No other record I have found refers to such a trip, and General Kearny's heavy correspondence for this period was all dated Monterey. The source, though fragmentary, is too responsible to ignore.

If Kearny visited San Francisco after his return to Monterey in February, the incident recounted in John Henry Brown's *Early Days of San Francisco* may have taken place then. That pioneer innkeeper was careless about dates. He writes that during the early part of 1847:

> Governor Mason arrived at Brown's Hotel from Monterey. He was very fond of billiards, and invariably played with me from ten to eleven o'clock in the morning. . . . on one occasion, while we were playing billiards, the following persons met in the room: General Kearny, Commodore Biddle, Captain Mervine, Captain Hull and Commodore Stockton.

One senses many inaccuracies. Mason was not governor until after Kearny had started for the States. Stockton spent most of that spring in San Diego or on the Mexican Coast. The picture of Kearny and Stockton enjoying an idle hour together watching a billiard game is a bit thick. But when Kearny was in San Francisco in February, Mason was too sick to be playing billiards and Stockton was certainly not then in that vicinity. These make up some of the ill-fitting fragments of the jigsaw puzzle of history.

Immediately on General Kearny's return he and Commodore Shubrick counseled about their new instructions. They agreed that the best way to promote the general tranquillity was to make a joint declaration clearly defining their respective fields of authority. Such a "Circular" was issued on March 1, at Monterey, printed in both English and Spanish. Monterey was to be the capital of California. After promising in the name of the President to "all whom it may concern" peace and protection from foreign foes and internal commotions, it stated that the commander-in-chief of the naval forces would regulate the ports and import trade. To the commanding military officer was "assigned the directions of operations on land—and—administrative functions of government over the People and Territory." The circular was published in the few newspapers of the territory, and copies were posted in public places up and down the province. Once again civil government had come to California, this time with the distinct blessing of the President of the United States. Now Stephen Kearny was indeed governor of California.

18. *"A Bright Star in Our Union"*

AFTER THE PROCLAMATION of the joint circular of March 1, General Kearny's hours were occupied with both civil and military duties. He was governor of California and also commander of the Tenth Military District which had just been established. This was like his experience in New Mexico except that the population was scattered over a larger territory, and there were overtones of John C. Frémont's continuing opposition.

One of Kearny's first steps was to issue a proclamation to the people of California, signed by him as "Brigadier General U.S.A. and Governor of California." The proclamation was published in the *Californian* of March 6, 1847. "The President of the United States having instructed the undersigned to take charge of the civil government of California," he stated his "ardent desire to promote . . . the interests of the country and the welfare of its inhabitants." The proclamation pledged respect and protection for the religious rights of the inhabitants. The persons and property of all quiet and peaceable inhabitants were to be protected from foreign and domestic enemies. The United States planned to provide a free government as soon as possible. Californians would have the right to elect their own representatives to enact their laws. The territory's existing laws would continue in force and the present officials would temporarily retain their posts, provided they took an oath of allegiance. The inhabitants were absolved from all allegiance to

288

Mexico and promised American citizenship. When Mexico had forced war upon his country, the General pointed out, the United States had had to occupy California to forestall its seizure by some foreign power. Admittedly some excesses had occurred, but he promised reimbursement for any proven losses. The General exhorted everyone to work with him for the peace and quiet of the land. The proclamation appeared in both English and Spanish.

Most of the criticisms and countercharges launched against Kearny by Frémont will not stand close scrutiny. One that requires some attention is that his proclamation of March 1, 1847, violated the terms of the Treaty of Cahuenga. Even though Frémont lacked authority to enter into that capitulation, his superiors decided to accept it. Since they benefited by whatever advantages flowed from the treaty, they were morally bound to recognize its obligations.

To summarize the capitulation, the Californian forces under Andrés Pico agreed to surrender the arms and artillery in their possession, to withdraw to their homes, submit to the laws of the United States, and not again take up arms during the present war. They were to assist in bringing about peace and tranquillity. Frémont agreed to protect the lives and properties of the surrendering parties and all other residents. Any Californian or Mexican citizen who wished to do so was free to leave the country. An important clause was "equal rights and privileges shall be enjoyed by the Californians as the citizens of the United States of North America."

Kearny's proclamation enlarged upon the rights of the Californians. However, it threatened punishment for offenders against its provisions; the capitulation did not. While Frémont hinted darkly at the unrest caused by the proclamation, only one provision in the capitulation seems clearly in conflict with it. That was Article 3rd, "that until peace is made . . . no Californian nor Mexican citizen shall be compelled to take an oath of fealty." As we have seen, the proclamation of March 1 provided that existing officeholders could continue to function if they took oath to support the Constitution of the United States.

Obviously any Mexican official who wished to retain his station had an obligation under Kearny's instrument which was not required by the capitulation. No other citizen was affected. It was

absurd to contend that any dissatisfaction concerning this require-
ment among the few officials involved could have started another
insurrection. If General Kearny realized that this "violated" the
Treaty of Cahuenga, he must have justified it on the grounds that
his instructions of June 3, 1846, expressly directed such action. As
between the orders given him and Frémont's irregular treaty, he
could not have hesitated very long. Actually, as we saw in the case
of New Mexico, Kearny went farther in promising American citizenship to the Californians than was approved by Washington; his
proclamation was certainly an extension rather than a limitation of
anything guaranteed at Cahuenga.

On that busy March 1, Kearny also sent Captain Turner south
with department Orders No. 2, to be handed to Lieutenant Colonel
Frémont in Los Angeles. He was addressed in his capacity as commander of the Battalion of California Volunteers. Frémont was instructed to bring to Monterey, as soon as possible, all papers in his
possession pertaining to the government of California. Kearny also
wrote:

> I have direction from the general-in-chief not to detain you in
> this country against your wishes, a moment longer than the neces-
> sities of the service may require, and you will be at liberty to leave
> here after you have complied with these instructions and those in
> the "orders" (No. 2) referred to.

Orders No. 2 contained three directives: first, the California Battalion was to be mustered into the federal service at once; thereby
its members could be paid in a regular manner. Second, should any
of the volunteers be unwilling to continue in service, they were to
be conducted by Frémont to Yerba Buena via Monterey and there
discharged. Third, Lieutenant Colonel Cooke was to supervise the
southern military district and to command, in addition to the Mormon Battalion, Company "C" of the First Dragoons and the California Volunteers. Kearny also sent Frémont copies of the War
Department's orders establishing the 10th Military District and
the joint circular he and Commodore Shubrick had issued.

Kearny advised Cooke of his new duties. The General warned

that Cooke's was the most important part of the territory and exposed to dangers of invasion from Sonora. The pass near Warner's Ranch should be well guarded. Kearny emphasized the necessity of placing "a very discreet officer" in charge of the forces in Los Angeles to insure humane and just treatment of the populace. On the same day General Kearny relieved Major Gillespie of duties with the California Battalion and ordered him to report in person to the commanding officer of the marine corps in Washington. Gillespie promptly withdrew from the battalion but delayed his departure.

It is difficult to understand the policies pursued by the Navy Department in the Pacific during the Mexican War. We have seen Commodore Sloat succeeded by Stockton. The former's illness occasioned that. Then Shubrick succeeded Stockton in late January, 1847. Now on March 2 the *Columbus* suddenly sailed into Monterey Bay with Commodore James Biddle, who outranked Shubrick and had orders to take over command. General Kearny wrote Captain du Pont in San Francisco about Biddle's succession. Du Pont wrote that the General had been:

> . . . since he left me . . . a most attentive and kind correspondent. The very points I wish most to hear he always touches upon. . . . If you get all my letters you will see the changes we have had to contend with out here. Commodore Sloat, Commodore Stockton, Commodore Shubrick and now Commodore Biddle, all in seven and a half months . . . . Then the farce of Frémont's governorship with General Kearny in the country. Then comes Colonel Stevenson anticipated by Colonel Mason. The Californians think that we cannot be much better than Mexico for they connect the appearance of every new commander-in-chief with the result of some new revolution. They are, however, delighted with the General's last proclamation which has made a decided hit.

When the struggle involving Stockton and Frémont was added to the dizzy procession of commodores, no wonder that the population felt bewildered about their American conquerors. General Kearny's relations with Biddle seem to have quickly assumed the same friendly and co-operative character as those enjoyed with Shubrick.

On March 5 the *Thomas H. Perkins* entered San Francisco Bay with Colonel Jonathan D. Stevenson and three companies of his Seventh New York Volunteers. Four more companies arrived on the nineteenth and three on the twenty-fifth. Colonel Stevenson apparently had been told that he was to be civil governor of California. Fortunately he asserted no claim nor did it create any friction between him and Kearny. At last General Kearny had been adequately reinforced. As soon as he learned of Stevenson's arrival, he wrote him to come to Monterey with all but one company. A total of three companies were to garrison the San Francisco Presidio. The heavy ordnance and stores brought by Colonel Stevenson were to be kept aboard ship at the bay because of the lack of proper warehouses.

Because of his familiarity with the territory, General Kearny obtained from Consul Larkin recommendations upon the most advantageous distribution of the New York regiment. These involved defense against both Mexico and the wild Indians and protection of the all-important harbor of San Francisco. In dispatching the various companies to their locations, Kearny was careful to emphasize the necessity of "a mild and conciliatory course towards the Californians. They have been greatly excited. They are now quiet and our object is to keep them so. I recommend frequent social intercourse between your command and the inhabitants in the vicinity of your station."

Residents of California in 1847 nursed a deep-seated grievance with which the General had to contend. It was responsible for much ill will toward him even after he left the Pacific Coast. Kearny's letter to Commodore Biddle on March 10 sums up the matter. Fourteen discharged volunteers had filed pay claims with the naval authorities. Biddle, as a late arrival, was wholly unfamiliar with the matter and referred it to Kearny. The latter answered that these men had served under a marine corps officer at rates of pay verbally fixed by Commodore Stockton. A bill of $1,050 had been rendered for rations of these volunteers. The General pointed out that these men had been recruited without his orders and not in accordance with any existing law. Their rate of pay was actually greater than the eleven dollars per month authorized by statute. With perhaps intentional irony, Kearny wrote that he believed "the matter probably concerns those who hired or authorized hiring these men." He understood that about $325,000 was claimed against the United States government in California arising from Stockton's administration or the acts of his appointees. Kearny, himself, had not authorized one cent of it and would not direct its payment because "such payments would not pass the Auditor's office."

The volunteers had real cause for complaint. Most had made material sacrifices. They could not be expected to know the statutory limitations affecting their compensation, or to check the authority of the officers who hired them. The merchants, ranchers, and other residents who provided goods and services for the government stood in the same position. The correspondence of prominent Californians, including Larkin and other merchants, is full of complaints because of the long delay in adjustment. Gillespie and others of the California Battalion joined in such recriminations. Many of these creditors waited for several years to get their money. The whole episode is a disgraceful blot on the American acquisition of California. The expansive mood of Manifest Destiny had outpaced its sense of responsibility as well as its fiscal machinery.

It is ironic to find some of these critics slower to recognize Kearny's right to govern than they were to blame him for the nonpayment of accounts. It is hard to see how any exception can be taken to the position assumed by the General in his letter to Biddle. Many of the debts had been incurred months before his arrival, and he was the last man in California likely to have been a party to any of the financial operations of Messrs. Stockton and Frémont. How in fairness could he be held responsible for the payment of their accounts, which in all too many instances were tinged with varying degrees of irregularity? One glaring example was a certificate issued by Colonel Frémont for $6,975 for six hundred head of beef cattle, allegedly purchased to feed the California Battalion. Its members never received the cattle, which came into the possession of Abel Stearns who used them for breeding purposes. The excessive rates of pay claimed by the volunteers were also an awkward detail. True, Commodore Stockton in agreeing to such wages had probably taken a realistic view of local conditions, but the proper man to convince Washington of that fact was Stockton—certainly not Kearny. Despite the obvious equities of the situation, both Frémont and Benton later charged that Kearny's nonpayment of these debts was largely responsible for the threats of insurrection around Los Angeles about which Frémont sounded repeated alarms. Benton and Frémont always neglected to specify the funds with which General Kearny could have paid these bills.

This reference to Benton recalls a letter written by Kearny to some eastern correspondent on March 17. In his violent attack on Kearny in September, 1848, the Senator quoted from it:

> Please say to Mrs. Frémont that I yesterday heard by a man from Los Angeles that Colonel Frémont was quite well. I have instructions from General Scott not to detain him against his wishes in this country. I think it probable he may start about the 1st of May and cross the mountains. But this is a conjecture of mine as I have not seen him since mid-January nor heard from him directly.

Benton made the most of what might be interpreted as equivocal language in the light of our later knowledge that General Kearny had determined to file charges against Colonel Frémont sometime after their last interview in January. I am not sure why Kearny wrote as above. On its face the opportunity to send the Frémonts word about the Colonel was a natural enough courtesy. We know that the threatened breach of the long intimacy with Benton and his daughter hung like a dark cloud over Kearny. Maybe a letter in the old mood seemed to push back the cloud.

With the American occupation, the little village on San Francisco Bay began to prosper. Both townspeople and seafaring men foresaw its future importance. While General Kearny was there in February, a public meeting had stressed the need of wharves and the filling in of the mud flats in front of the settlement. The Governor had been petitioned to grant the tidelands to the town. On

March 10 he issued a decree granting to the town of San Francisco the government's rights in the beach and water lots between Rincon and Clark's points, except those lots needed by the army and navy. The tract was to be divided and sold at public auction to the highest bidders for the benefit of the town.

The legality of Kearny's conveyance of the water lots to San Francisco has been questioned along much the same lines as his promulgation of the Kearny Code in New Mexico. Regardless of any technical irregularity, the result curiously parallels Kearny's experience at Santa Fe. The public weal was served, and the outcome justified the steps taken. Where rules and precedents were lacking, his *ad hoc* decisions displayed both courage and common sense befitting a statesman.

Stephen Kearny never had any legal training, but more than once he had to exercise judicial functions. His natural instinct for justice and equity proved a good substitute for formal preparation. Without time to codify laws and harmonize them with American standards, and without any courts beyond the very limited field of the local alcaldes, Kearny as governor was like a mariner without a chart or compass. Under such circumstances he wins our admiration in his practice of one broad principle that would have done credit to a seasoned jurist—the doctrine of *status quo ante bellum*.

For example, in the highly delicate field of relations with the Catholic church and its clergy, within a few days he decided both for and against the church. Four of the missions were threatened by trespassers and claimants of their church lands. The Governor issued a proclamation on March 22 that these properties must remain in the hands of their present priestly custodians until the courts could later determine the rights of any adverse claimant. Any trespassers were to be forcibly removed. On the other hand, the priest at Sonoma had brought an action before the local alcalde to dispossess a man who was in actual possession of property claimed by the church. This individual based his rights on a Mexican title which the alcalde believed was baseless. He rendered judgment to the church. Governor Kearny ruled that this question of title must await decision by judicial tribunals not yet in being. Since the defendant was in actual possession of the premises at the time of the

295

American occupation, he annulled the judgment. In handling another appeal, Kearny reiterated the principle which guided him in numerous cases on which he passed as Governor of California: "I believe justice and good faith require that so far as is in our power, we fulfill engagements entered into by authorities who preceded us and without inquiring into their expediency if not contrary to law."

Part of the daily routine of Kearny's administration was necessary public correspondence and the appointment of new officials. It would be tedious to detail them and the Governor's rulings on numerous appeals from the alcaldes' decisions. Many times these rulings reiterated some fundamental principles: first, cases previously decided by earlier authorities were not to be reopened because of the change in sovereignty; second, intricate questions such as land titles must await the setting up of more formal tribunals.

Kearny opposed premature attempts at lawmaking. Commodore Stockton had called a legislative council to meet on March 1, but the Governor canceled the meeting since a group with no legal basis could serve no useful purpose and could not enforce its decisions. General Kearny as governor was no respecter of persons. John Warner of Warner's Ranch was one of the influential citizens of southern California. The alcalde at San Diego reported that Warner, although a party to a case before him, had refused to obey the decree handed down by the alcalde. Kearny wrote the official: "If he (Warner) remains refractory, you are authorized to call upon the military officer most convenient to you for men to enforce your decree." When Warner, himself, appealed, the Governor curtly told him to obey the orders of the alcalde.

Kearny actually fathered the United States mails in California, for on March 19 he established the first regular mail service between the north and south. While only a semimonthly run in the beginning, it marked the first fixed schedule. Every Monday a soldier would start on horseback from San Francisco, and another, from San Diego. They would meet at San Luis Obispo, exchange mail pouches, and start back to their respective stations where they were due to arrive the next Sunday. Kearny also recommended to Washington that a mail service be established from the head of the Sacramento Valley to San Diego. (Lieutenant Edward M. Kern in September, 1846, while in command at Sutter's Fort, had established a weekly mail service between that point and Sonoma; apparently this was soon discontinued.)

Raids by the wild tribesmen repeatedly disturbed the peace. The General was forced to send small detachments of troops about the countryside to hold them in check. He also appointed several Indian subagents to watch over the natives. Some of these officials were leading residents like Captain Johann Sutter and General Mariano Vallejo. Greatly to his regret, Kearny narrowly missed meeting Vallejo during his visit to San Francisco in February. Soon after appointing him, the General sent Vallejo a carbine with his compliments. In acknowledging its receipt Vallejo promised to return it. Kearny reassured him, "I intended it as a present—as a small mark of the high respect I entertain for you and beg that you will retain it as such." Instead of "your obedient servant" as General Kearny usually closed his correspondence, he signed this letter "your friend."

In one appointment Kearny, in co-operation with Commodore Biddle, boldly improvised where neither law nor precedent could solve a problem. Legalists may find it interesting to review the action of these two officers in setting up a Court of Admiralty at Monterey with Walter Colton as its judge. They had no color of authority, but Mexican prizes rotting in California ports demanded attention, and the General and Commodore again proved that "living law" can fill a need for which "positive law" is inadequate.

Not until March 15 did the *Savannah's* departure for New York give Kearny opportunity to answer General Scott's memorable letter of November 3, 1846. He reported the steps taken to fortify San Francisco at a cost of a few thousand dollars. Other sites on the bay required larger expenditures which he would not commence until appropriations had been made in Washington. He had sent Lieutenant Halleck to San Diego on a similar mission. Replying to Scott's plea for harmony between the army and navy, Kearny bluntly told him:

I take no censure upon myself for the interruption of that harmony which should have existed here and am confident that you, the War Department and the Executive will fully exonerate or acquit me! There is no possibility of any further difficulty as long as Commodore Biddle or Shubrick remain in command of the naval forces on this station.

Kearny hoped to start back for the States about July 1.

By the same *Savannah* mail went one of the most outstanding letters Kearny wrote while on the Pacific Coast. He outlined to the Adjutant General his bold and prophetic vision of the future of California, expressing gratification at the substantial reinforcements received:

I infer from that that the Territory will never be returned to Mexico and it should not be! Should it be restored Mexico could not hold it three months. The people in the Territory, Californians as well as emigrants, would resist Mexican authority and there would follow dissensions, quarrels and fighting between them until humanity would compel our government to interpose a strong arm to put a stop to such a civil war and to take the country again under her protection. The Californians are now quiet and I shall endeavor to keep them so by mild and gentle treatment. Had they received such treatment from the time our flag was hoisted here in July last, I believe there would have been but little or no resistance on their part. They have been most cruelly and shamefully abused by our people, by volunteers (American emigrants) raised in this part of the country and on the Sacramento. Had they not resisted they would have been unworthy the name of men. If the people remain quiet and California continues under our flag, it will ere long be a bright star in our union. The climate is pure and healthy, physicians meeting with no encouragement as its inhabitants are never sick. The soil is rich and there is much unsettled land that will admit of a dense population. California with Oregon is destined to supplant the Sandwich Islands and will furnish our six hundred whaling vessels and our twenty thousand sailors in them, besides our Navy and our troops with the breadstuffs and most of the other articles they are to consume. At present the population is small, most probably not exceeding twelve thousand of whom about one fifth are emigrants. A very few years will add greatly to the latter class. Besides these there are about fifteen thousand Indians, nearly one third being called Christian Indians who speak Spanish and subsist in great measure upon horses and cattle that they steal from the farms. The Christian Indians are laborers and servants of the country and are held if not in bondage like our own slaves, at least very much like it. For the preservation of the peace and quiet now so happily existing in California and to protect the people from the Indian depredations upon them, there should be kept in the Territory for some years to come about a thousand soldiers. They should be enlisted expressly to serve here. . . . We can get no recruits here.

Captain Turner saw Frémont in Los Angeles on March 11 and delivered Kearny's dispatches. The next day Frémont promised to go to San Gabriel to muster the California Battalion. Turner continued on to San Luis Rey to deliver his dispatches to Cooke. A letter from there to Julia Turner about his interview with John C. Frémont warrants quotation:

> Notwithstanding this officer on a former occasion positively declined obeying the orders of General Kearny, he quietly submits now and promptly acts on the instructions I handed him. Commodore Biddle's arrival on the coast has thrown consternation among all the evil doers and they show a disposition to work well in the traces.

On March 14, as Cooke had not received any report of the muster of the California Battalion, he wrote Frémont urging prompt action. On March 17 a reply came from Frémont's Secretary of State Russell. Turner was shocked to find how premature had been his elation when he wrote Julia. Once more John C. Frémont had refused to obey General Kearny's orders. Of course Russell was euphemistic in the words of refusal:

> . . . the volunteers . . . decline without an individual exception to be mustered into the United States service, conformable to Order No. 2. . . . The governor (Frémont) considers it unsafe at this time, when rumor is rife with a threatened insurrection, to

299

discharge the battalion, and will decline doing so. . . . he regards his force quite sufficient for the protection of the artillery and ordnance stores at . . . San Gabriel.

Captain Turner immediately started north, not stopping to call on the changeable-minded pseudo governor while passing through Los Angeles. By hard riding he reached Monterey in five days.

No detail of Frémont's checkered career in California is harder to rationalize than these events of mid-March, 1847. His conduct in declining to obey Kearny in January can be explained on the grounds that he was answerable only to Commodore Stockton. But on March 12, Captain Turner handed him besides Orders No. 2 a copy of Kearny's and Shubrick's joint circular of March 1. If he did not already know that Stockton had been replaced, he knew it now. Hence the sole basis for his earlier refusal had disappeared. His mood of quiet submission to authority as described in Turner's letter indicates he realized the changed conditions. What happened to him between March 12 and 16? "Either [he was] insincere or had changed his mind," was Turner's explanation. The peril of a threatened insurrection alleged by Russell sounds like a trumped-up excuse. Ever since the treaty of Cahuenga, there had been rumors of new uprisings. But these were just as evident on the twelfth of March as on the sixteenth. Nothing occurred in the intervening four days to increase the risk of trouble. If the pretext given by Russell on March 16 was flimsy, all of Frémont's champions in over a century have failed to improve upon it.

Allan Nevins in his earlier biography says: "Of course Frémont refused to obey this demand for the papers" (overlooking the other order to muster the Battalion). Nevins argues that Frémont knew nothing of the government order of November 5 and believed Kearny was using bluster and threats to depose him from the governorship. When he wrote his later *Pathmarker*, Nevins felt less certain of Frémont's position—"Naturally, but very unwisely, Frémont refused to obey the demands for the papers." As previously pointed out, Frémont by the middle of March must have known of the orders of November 3 and 5. It is hard to see how he could dismiss the joint circular of March 1 as "bluster and threats." Not only Kearny but Shubrick had signed it. Any reasonable man should have believed these two officers acted on clear authority and that Orders No. 2, issued by one of them, merited very respectful attention.

A letter written by Frémont on March 15 to Captain Richard Owens affords convincing evidence that we are no longer dealing with an officer merely perplexed about the conflicting orders of two superiors. The letter stated that official duties required Frémont to visit the northern district of the territory. In his absence Owens was to command the California Battalion and maintain as much order, vigilance, and discipline as he felt could be prudently enforced. Two other orders warrant full quotation:

2nd *You will make no move whatever from San Gabriel in my absence,* unless to repel an actual invasion, or *obey the order of any officer that does not emanate from me.*

3rd You will take the best possible care of the *public arms and munitions belonging to the command and turn them over to no corps without my special order.*

I have italicized the parts of this letter that read more like the language of a clan chieftain or guerrilla leader than of a lieutenant colonel of the United States Army, as Frémont signed himself.

This later defiance of General Kearny's orders by John C. Frémost seems even a sounder basis for the charge of mutiny than his disobedience of January, 1847. Impulsiveness may have contributed to that conduct, but this latest assertion of sole and final authority was deliberate and premeditated.

After receiving Russell's letter conveying Frémont's negative answer about the muster of the California Battalion, Lieutenant Colonel Cooke started for Los Angeles. The First Dragoon Company and four companies of the Mormon Battalion marched with him, and they arrived early on the morning of March 23. Captain Gillespie met the detachment on the edge of the Pueblo and informed Cooke that Frémont had just gone north to see General Kearny.

The next day Cooke rode out to San Gabriel with Lieutenant Davidson and Dr. Sanderson to see the California Battalion. A little over two hundred of the volunteers were encamped under Captain Owens. Considerable ordnance was in their custody. In the course of their inspection Lieutenant Davidson recognized the two mountain howitzers which he had so laboriously hauled from Santa Fe to California. General Kearny had directed Cooke to return these two fieldpieces to the dragoons. Colonel Cooke informed Owens that he was sending mules to San Gabriel that same day to haul the howitzers to Los Angeles. Captain Owens immediately declared he had received positive orders not to permit the removal of any of the arms in his keeping. When Cooke indignantly asserted his instructions from General Kearny and his senior rank in the district, Owens doggedly stood his ground. He had never seen the joint circular nor Orders No. 2, so Cooke read them to him and demanded that he recognize the authority of the government of the United States. Owens coolly replied that he considered Colonel Frémont the chief military authority in California. Colonel Cooke with rising exasperation appealed to every motive of patriotism, loyalty, and duty. All he could elicit from the stubborn captain were Frémont's recent orders. Owens permitted Cooke to read them but would not even let him make a copy, and declared that because of his orders he would not obey General Kearny nor the President of the United States himself!

Colonel Cooke returned to Los Angeles seething with indignation. Cooke reported the situation to General Kearny on the twenty-fifth. He added his conviction that the proposal to muster the volunteers into the federal service had never been fairly presented to them. Frémont had not even made the promised trip to San Gabriel to lay the proposal before the battalion. The representative he had sent probably gave the matter only perfunctory attention. Cooke considered the members of the battalion "generally as good citizens, but cruelly and studiously misguided and deceived." Every fiber of his being spurred him to the most drastic action. On strictly disciplinary grounds, he could have justified any punitive steps. All too probably that would have ignited civil war between the volunteers and the Mormons. It could have set off another insurrection and a reconquest of poor, embattled California. That no such sequel followed Frémont's and Owens' mutinous denial of Cooke's authority proves that General Kearny had used rare judgment in selecting his southern deputy. Cooke carried on under sore provocation just as Kearny must have known he would—and as he, himself, would have done under like circumstances. Concluding his report, Cooke gave vent to his feelings:

> The general's orders are not obeyed! My God! to think of a howitzer brought over the deserts with so much faithful labor by the dragoons; the howitzer with which they have four times fought the enemy, and brought here to the rescue of Lieut. Colonel Frémont and his volunteers, to be refused to them by this Lieut. Colonel Frémont and in defiance of the orders of his general! I denounce this treason, or this mutiny . . . Mr. Russell left here with an express party for the States a few hours before my arrival. He was sent . . . by Lieut. Colonel Frémont. . . . it is said here he went to take a petition . . . signed by some of the Californians in favor of Lieut. Colonel Frémont.

That assiduous troublemaker Owl Russell had been active in exciting the populace around Los Angeles about the coming of the Mormon Battalion. At Frémont's court-martial he testified:

> I saw repeatedly armed parties of Californians, that it was generally understood had for their purpose of organizing, the intention of attacking the Mormons. This occurred between the 15th and 22nd or 23rd of March when I left the country. . . . I was told by respectable and influential Californians that the people were generally exasperated, and would probably rise if the Mormons came among them.

There were numerous Missourians in the California Battalion. In the 1840's, Missourians and Mormons generally held each other in very low esteem. Undoubtedly there was some real animosity among the people toward this sect, but, just as surely, designing persons in southern California fanned the core of bad feeling and exaggerated its gravity. John C. Frémont, in the light of his own

303

ambitious and headstrong course, found the Mormons a thorn in his flesh. Speaking of their arrival, Cooke's biographer says:

> Its commander was faithful to Kearny, and the Mormons to Cooke. . . . a battalion of men who feared neither Californians nor trappers, obeying only God, Brigham Young and Philip St. George Cooke.

General Kearny's opinion of these members of his army appears in Du Pont's journal:

> The General and I have just had a talk about the Mormons. (Kearny) having been long stationed in the West is high authority relating to this most objectionable community to my present knowledge of them. He says they are a very sinning people but that they have also been much sinned against. His impression is that if let alone they will gradually slide back into an ordinary condition, that persecution has kept them together.

The next appearance of the unpredictable Lieutenant Colonel Frémont showed him in his most spectacular role. At daybreak on the morning of March 22 he rode out of Los Angeles at breakneck speed toward Monterey. Don Jesus Pico and a negro servant, Jacob Dodson, accompanied him. Each man led two extra horses as spare mounts. The first day they made the incredible distance of 120 miles and slept in their blankets by the roadside north of Santa Barbara. On March 23 they even exceeded this record by 15 miles and reached San Luis Obispo. By the third day the maddening pace had slowed to a total of 70 miles when darkness overtook them in the Salinas Valley. Another 90 miles of the hardest riding brought them into Monterey by mid-afternoon on March 26.

This sensational feat has probably never been equaled and is one of the dramatic rides of history. A colossal spectacle in the best Hollywood tradition, it cries for assists from Technicolor and Cinemascope. Paul Revere from his galloping horse had shouted that the redcoats were coming. John Jouett had spurred his steed to warn Thomas Jefferson that Tarleton's raiders were after him. But those bursts of speed, regardless of how momentous their reasons, had been for short distances compared with this mad, grueling race of over four hundred miles. Surely its cause had to be even more heroic to match the supreme efforts of the three horsemen. Just why did John C. Frémont so punish horseflesh, himself, and his companions?

To quote his own explanation at his court-martial:

Men, armed to the teeth, were galloping about the country. . . . The whole population was in commotion and everything verged towards violence and bloodshed. For what cause? The approach of the Mormons, the proclamations incompatible with the capitulation of Cahuenga, the prospect that I was to be deposed by violence, the anticipated non-payment of government liabilities and the general insecurity which such events inspired. . . . I determined to go to Monterey to lay the state of things before General Kearny and gave all the orders necessary to preserve tranquillity while I was gone. I then made that extraordinary ride.

Even Frémont's most understanding biographer would not buy that! Allan Nevins very sensibly points out:

It was not necessary for Frémont to go in person and had there really been danger his duty would have been to stay vigilantly with his Battalion in Los Angeles. He knew that perfectly well. The chief reason for his ride beyond a doubt was that he wished to find out in person his real status. Another reason very likely lay in his worry over the possibility that Kearny would influence the government against paying the heavy debts he had incurred.

Frémont's most unfriendly critic could hardly deflate this ride more completely. Bancroft, much closer to the event, took the same view. The stubborn fact remains that no revolt ever occurred. No one has ever offered a reason why Frémont did not send Kearny a report by any one of several trusted lieutenants available to him.

When this young Lochinvar out of the south drew rein before Kearny's headquarters, Thomas Larkin conducted him to the General. Apparently they merely exchanged greetings that first evening. In a separate interview Larkin informed Frémont of the "latest orders" from Washington. Nevins believes he advised Frémont to come to terms with the General. The next morning Larkin made an appointment for Kearny to see Frémont.

Frémont always claimed that the General received him with disrespect and discourtesy. Colonel Mason was closeted with Kearny when his caller entered the room. Frémont wished a private interview. Kearny answered that Colonel Mason would later succeed him, so there could be no conversation on public affairs that Colonel Mason should not hear. Frémont's temper was very short, and he retorted that perhaps the General had Mason there to take advantage of some unguarded expressions he might make. Kearny flushed and told Frémont his reply was offensive but surely he had not come there just to insult him. Frémont remained silent. Suddenly he blurted out his resignation as an officer of the army. General Kearny sternly replied that he would not accept it. The two men glared at each other, and then Kearny reminded his caller of the orders that Captain Turner had delivered to him. Before he would hold further conversation, Kearny demanded a definite answer. Did Frémont intend to obey those orders? The Colonel hesitated irresolutely. Stern-faced but controlled, Kearny told him to reflect well upon the matter; his answer would be most important. If he wanted an hour or even a day to consider it, he might have it. Frémont made no reply and left the room.

In about an hour he returned and bluntly announced that he would obey the orders. The General's lips relaxed into a half-smile. "I am gratified to hear that," he said, "very gratified indeed." Kearny then told Frémont to return to the southland and immediately embark his battalion at San Pedro for Monterey. Frémont agreed to do this but demurred that he, himself, was a poor sailor and always suffered greatly from seasickness. The General quite readily modified his order. Frémont could return overland to Monterey after he had promptly conducted the battalion to the ship that would be sent south by Commodore Biddle. As soon as this arrangement was concluded the Colonel took his departure. With his two companions he made the return journey to Los Angeles at the same terrific speed. The round trip had covered only eight days. Seventeen horses were expended in seventy-six hours of hard riding. Surely this feat lacked justification.

Frémont asserted at his court-martial that he visited General Kearny in Monterey to see if he "would provide for the payment of arrearages of the government incurred while he was governor." Kearny denied that this matter was even discussed. He added that he never knew the object of Frémont's call upon him; it had often been a subject of speculation by himself and others. What had become of the rumors of another insurrection and the menacing approach of the Mormon Battalion? These must have evaporated in the heat of Frémont's anger at Mason's presence.

Bancroft believed that Frémont's manner and words in this interview formed the turning point in their controversy. They may very well have determined Kearny's later course and the accusations he made against the Colonel. Bancroft also thought that Kearny's tone toward Frémont was most annoying to the latter's pride. When we recall his first outburst over Colonel Mason's presence in the room, it is hard to see how much more forbearance could have been expected of the General. His patience had already been severely tried, and his caller certainly had not given him "the soft answer that turneth away wrath."

One circumstance not mentioned in this discussion is most significant. This interview occurred just three days after Captain Owens refused Cooke's demand for the howitzers. General Kearny could not then know of this added flouting of his authority. Frémont did not tell him of the astonishing orders he had given Owens when he was planning this visit. Frémont did not actually know what had happened at San Gabriel on the twenty-fourth, but he was certainly aware that he had planted the seeds of trouble. Repeatedly, in their review of these events, various writers have censured Kearny for withholding information or for lack of frankness, but here we are confronted with a suppression of facts more extreme than any alleged lapses by Kearny. Frémont interpreted Colonel Mason's presence in the room as distrust on Kearny's part. Although he himself had just concealed information of vital importance, his honor could still be wounded by fancied slights!

The day after Frémont galloped out of Monterey, General Kearny directed Colonel Mason to proceed to southern California to inspect all troops there. On March 28 he wrote Colonel Frémont of

Mason's coming and of the powers conferred upon him—"any instructions he may give you will be considered as coming from myself." The letter then directed Frémont to complete any unfinished business he had in Los Angeles, "as it may be necessary for you to proceed from here to Washington." He was to send to Monterey any members of his topographical party not wishing to remain in California. "In twelve days after you have embarked the volunteers at San Pedro I desire to see you at this place." Colonel Mason sailed for Los Angeles on the twenty-eighth. Kearny hoped Mason's presence in the south would exert a salutary influence.

Colonel Mason reached Los Angeles in early April. Frémont had preceded him on March 29. From Bancroft's account it would seem that Cooke was with Mason when the latter met Frémont soon after his arrival. From the outset their relations were strained. This time it was Cooke's presence that grated on the ever-sensitive Frémont. Mason repeated General Kearny's orders about the muster of the volunteers and demanded delivery of all government artillery, arms, supplies, and horses. Mason next visited the California Battalion at San Gabriel. Once more its members refused to be mustered into the United States service. The Colonel ordered Frémont to discharge the battalion forthwith and at last secured possession of the artillery, which was placed in charge of the Mormon Battalion in Los Angeles.

A few days later Mason sent his orderly to Colonel Frémont's headquarters with a written request to deliver various civil and military records. Three times the orderly presented himself at Frémont's quarters. Three times the sentry turned the orderly away without even announcing him. Colonel Mason was exasperated at such flagrant discourtesy. When after a long interval Frémont presented himself, Mason handed his caller the letter with visible anger. Frémont answered with equal heat and the two men nearly came to blows. The next day Frémont sent Colonel Mason a reply accompanied by a "few papers pertaining to the Battalion which I can at present find." He explained that many documents connected with his acts as governor had been forwarded to the States.

Mason sent for Frémont again on the fourteenth. This time he had to dispatch two messengers before any attention was paid his summons. When at last the hard-to-find Lieutenant Colonel appeared, Mason questioned him about the horses belonging to the government. Only a few had been delivered to Kearny's Quartermaster. Mason demanded that Frémont account for a large herd which the latter had reserved to carry his topographical party to the States. This was the last straw. Frémont burst forth in angry recriminations. Colonel Mason loudly exclaimed "None of your insolence or I will put you in irons." Frémont froze for a second and then demanded an apology. Mason shouted that he would be personally responsible for his language. Frémont turned on his heel and stalked out of the room.

Not long afterward Major Reading of the Battalion called upon Mason. On behalf of Frémont, he demanded an apology. Mason stiffly refused, so Reading presented Frémont's challenge to a duel. As the challenged party, Mason was entitled to name the weapons, and he soon chose double-barreled shotguns loaded with buckshot— about as lethal an instrument as man has ever devised. Frémont always asserted afterward that Colonel Mason was renowned in army circles as an expert with this firearm and that he was unfamiliar with its use.

By the fifteenth Mason's temper had cooled sufficiently for him to realize that if two high-ranking officers of the United States Army were to fight a duel at that uneasy time, American interests could be irreparably damaged. Accordingly he sent Frémont a note that the duel must await both men's return to Monterey. Mason planned to be there very soon and expected that Frémont would shortly follow.

We lack a complete record of the next development in this quarrel. Bancroft infers that General Kearny learned of it in Monterey and wrote both Mason and Frémont from there. Allan Nevins and Cardinal Goodwin treat the episode in similar fashion. On the other hand, Wagner and Bashford allege that Kearny came to Los Angeles and in a talk with Frémont forbade the duel. Actually the General did not reach Los Angeles until nearly a month after the challenge. I am sure that he did not sit idly by for so long a time. I believe he learned of it in Monterey and took immediate action there. In all of General Kearny's voluminous correspondence in California there are no copies of his letters to Mason or Frémont on this subject, nor any mention of the threatened duel. We do not know when Colonel Mason reached Monterey. He left Los Angeles a few days after the fourteenth and wrote his report of the trip to Kearny in Monterey on the twenty-sixth.

Kearny must have been greatly disturbed. He knew only too well how American prestige would suffer from such a duel. We know that he wrote both men demanding that the duel be indefinitely postponed. Allan Nevins is most fair in his judgment of the two principals: "it must be said that the challenge did Frémont anything but credit and that Mason showed much more cool sense and prudence than he in the matter." Bancroft as well as Wagner and Bashford censured General Kearny for the course he pursued, saying he should have caused both officers to be arrested and held for trial in strict compliance with military regulations.

This is further proof that Kearny was more concerned with the spirit than the letter of the law. He foresaw damage before the event and then forestalled its occurrence. Had he arrested the offenders, he would have raised another series of ills. Mason was his highest-ranking officer and had been nominated as his successor. His arrest just now would have badly damaged American interests. Frémont had become the perennial problem-child of Kearny's administration and had certainly given plenty of provocation for his arrest. But a challenge to a duel growing out of a hot-tempered quarrel would have been the worst possible reason for arresting him. It would have made him a martyr. General Kearny exercised excellent judgment and followed the course of action least harmful to the public interest.

As for the duel itself, Frémont accepted Mason's postponement on the latter's promise that the meeting would be held as soon as possible. After the General's veto, nothing more could come of it in California, but it still remained "unfinished business." As late as 1850, Mason invited Frémont, then in Washington, to come to St. Louis to fight that duel. Frémont ignored the request and not long afterward Mason's own death ended the quarrel.

The mustering out of the California Battalion proceeded slowly;

the last of the volunteers was not discharged until April 19. Three weeks after Frémont had told Colonel Mason that his business would be finished in two or three days, he still lingered in Los Angeles. True, he had various accounts to certify and other tag ends of official business, but he showed far more deliberation than was his wont. Later his excuse was that General Kearny's orders had not seemed urgent. (It will be recalled that Kearny on March 26 had definitely allotted him twelve days for these duties.) Moreover with an apparently straight face he alleged the hazards of travel as another reason for tarrying; but the roads had not been too dangerous for his eight-day journey in late March. This was only mid-April!

Colonel Mason's report disclosed an interesting method Frémont had devised to relieve his straitened financial condition. Although regulation of customs was within the jurisdiction of the navy, on March 20, Frémont, still calling himself governor, authorized the collector of the port at San Pedro to accept in payment of customs duties the evidences of debt of the California Battlion at 30 per cent discount. Merchants having customs to pay could make a neat profit by buying the battalion's paper at a heavy discount and using it in payment of their customs obligations. The only catch was whether the federal government would countenance such legerdemain. Actually, Secretary of State Buchanan did refuse to honor many such drafts. Because the San Pedro collector had been led into this mistake "by the acts of others," General Kearny allowed him to take credit for the government paper heretofore received for customs. But both he and all other collectors were admonished to accept nothing but specie, treasury notes, and drafts in the future. Once more we find Kearny upholding sound financial procedure.

On April 23, Kearny received a letter from Secretary Marcy dated January 11, 1847. This dealt with the question of American citizenship for peoples of conquered territory. While the war continued, lands occupied by American forces could not be considered permanently annexed. Authority to exercise civil government would not be restricted. "As to Upper California it is presumed no doubt can arise, but it may not be so clear as to lower California." Washington was assuming that actual possession of the latter territory would be accomplished.

Kearny on April 28 replied to Secretary Marcy that these were his first instructions referring to Lower California. He had immediately applied to Commodore Biddle for assistance in carrying out the orders. He had planned to send one or two companies of the New York Volunteers to seize La Paz. But before they could be started, he had been compelled to suspend these preparations because of disquieting news brought by Mexicans from Sonora. Again the shadowy General Bustamante threatened to take substance. He was reputedly now preparing to reconquer California. General Kearny did not credit the reports, but they had caused much excitement among the Californians. As a result he was having to reinforce his garrison in Los Angeles. In all of Upper California, Kearny had 1,059 troops. The General wisely felt that the security of Upper California was all-important and that Lower California was a secondary objective. He must defer its occupation until quiet was restored in the lands already conquered. He hoped that would be very soon. The Mormon Battalion's term of service would expire in July. The New York regiment had enlisted only for the duration. Wages of laborers and mechanics were so high in California that the army could not count on any re-enlistments, nor on recruitment from immigrants. It was therefore important that more troops be sent from the East to preserve quiet and secure the possession of the two Californias. General Kearny mentioned his perennial Indian problem and recommended that the government supply his department with suitable gifts to conciliate the natives. He had high praise for Cooke and the Mormon Battalion. California now seemed tranquil. If it continued in that state he proposed to avail himself of the permission given by General Scott to leave Colonel Mason in command and start for Missouri; "and, should the war with Mexico not be ended, ask for employment in the field under the General or any other of my senior officers."

In another letter Turner unburdened himself to his ever-discreet Julia:

> . . . the General leaves here in a few days for the Pueblo to correct some of the abuses that have been practiced by Lt. Colonel Frémont. This officer has not yet been arrested and I suppose will not be. . . .

The whole army is disgusted with General Kearny's course in relation to Frémont but don't you speak of the matter. . . . I defend the General as well as I can.

In the middle of April, Major Swords arrived in Monterey to resume his duties as quartermaster. From the beginning of his administration, General Kearny had favored the restoration to their owners of the horses, saddles, and other equipment that had been seized by the volunteers. In a sparsely settled land almost solely dependent on the horse for transportation, this vitally concerned every resident. Up and down the territory a great many "public horses" were in possession of army units, while many roamed at large. Usually these were animals that had been purchased or more often appropriated without compensation by Frémont's battalion or had come to be regarded as government property. Some were branded "U.S." or "F," but many were unbranded. It became Swords' duty to return to their rightful owners such of these animals as could be identified and to care for those not so claimed. These could be useful in the further service of the army. General Kearny's plans to return to Missouri would call for a large band of mules and horses.

About this time Swords wrote:

I have got along with the General much better than I ever did before—the truth is—he is now discovering my good qualities— ahem, and takes me into his cabinet counsels, so I know all that is going on. . . . all (is) in commotion here at this time. General K. with Col. Stevenson and two of his companies are just embarking on board the "Lexington" for the Pueblo. . . . Frémont by last account was still there and while he remains there cannot be quiet in the country. . . . What course the General will pursue . . . I don't know but I hope he has found by this time that indulgence towards Frémont only encourages him in his open defiance of orders.

The *Lexington* sailed from Monterey on May 4. A short time before his departure Kearny asked Lieutenant Sherman to go on the journey as his aide. Congressman Willard Hall was another passenger. When the *Lexington* dropped anchor off San Pedro, small boats carried the officers through the kelp to the beach. General Kearny took Sherman's arm as they ascended the steep bluffs overlooking the roadstead. In his memoirs, Sherman remembered the heated discussions among the junior officers at Monterey about what General Kearny would do with Frémont. Some thought that he would be tried and shot for mutiny in wartime; others, that he would be carried home in irons. "All agreed that if anyone else but Frémont had put on such airs and acted as he had done, Kearny would have shown him no mercy for he was regarded as the strictest sort of a disciplinarian."

General Kearny's entry into the Pueblo on May 10 was greeted with a twenty-one-gun salute. Less than four months previously he had ridden out rebuffed and frustrated. His two opposites in the January argument must have been keenly aware of the contrast. One was sulking aboard his ship in San Diego; the other, as Sherman put it, "held his court in the only two story frame house in the place." The General found the town quiet and not concerned with the recent rumors of fresh invasions from Mexico.

Kearny and his aide found quarters with Lieutenant Colonel Cooke at the home of Nathaniel Pryor, the Kentucky clockmaker, south of the Plaza between First and Commercial Streets. Kearny sent Sherman to summon Frémont. Contrary to his usual habit, the Lieutenant Colonel promptly appeared, "dressed much as a Californian with a peculiar high broad-brimmed hat with a funny cord." Kearny repeated his orders that Frémont immediately go to Monterey to await their early departure for Washington. His caller demurred that he had 120 horses and wanted to make his way with his exploring party to General Scott's army in Mexico where he could rejoin his regiment. The General "brusquely refused," according to Frémont. The latter then requested leave to go directly east himself from Los Angeles. Again Kearny's answer was a firm negative.

Frémont always complained that this refusal violated General Scott's direction that he "not be detained against his wishes a moment longer than the necessities of the service may require." Superficially that was true. But a lot of water had flowed under the bridges since General Scott wrote on November 3. Lieutenant Colonel Frémont had repeatedly refused to obey orders, had denied his superiors' demands for the delivery of the army's artillery, and had almost fought a duel with General Kearny's second in command—all this in an enemy province in time of war! General Kearny undoubtedly felt it his duty to keep such a turbulent officer under close surveillance.

The General finally extracted from Frémont a promise to leave immediately for Monterey. Kearny must have believed him for that evening he wrote Captain Bailey of the *Lexington* that he would be ready to sail north five days later. He told Bailey he had received an express from Santa Fe that would hurry him back to Washington. (This must have been the news of the insurrection and massacre at Taos.) Captain Bailey was another salt with whom General Kearny was on friendly terms. His letter closed with its most important news: Lieutenant Colonel Frémont was about to leave for the north. Actually he rode out of Los Angeles under Kearny's watchful eyes on May 12.

If one of the renowned wits of early-day Los Angeles is to be credited, General Kearny about this time averted a very different sort of duel. At a dance General José Antonio Carrillo commented most sarcastically that a certain Mormon captain danced like a bear. The Mormon fancied himself a great dancer and challenged his traducer to a duel. Carrillo had commanded the Californians at the battle of the Dominguez Rancho and accepted the challenge with alacrity. Kearny, so the story goes, intervened. The principals and their friends met at Pryor's for the negotiations. Kearny persuaded Carrillo that he owed the captain an apology. The latter's friends insisted it must be in writing. Carrillo finally promised to deliver the written amends the next day. Carrillo's peace offering in Spanish was translated as follows:

I am a native of California. I love my country and stick up for it. The bear is my countryman so I love the bear. I now apologize to the bear for suggesting that the redheaded captain danced like a bear. The injury is to the bear because the captain could not dance half so well. José Antonio Carrillo.

315

Naturally this enraged the Mormon even more than the original slur, and he insisted on a fight. All the others were so amused that they laughed the poor man out of the room, and nothing more was heard of that duel.

On May 10, General Kearny inspected the Mormon Battalion. It was paraded before him and Colonel Stevenson and drew his warm praise. According to one of its members, the General "spoke of us in the highest terms, so high I thought it flattery. He promised to report our conduct to the President and in the halls of Congress and give us the justice we merited." Another Mormon recorded "that General Carney (*sic*) first inspected us and said that we were a good looking set of fellows." What seemed like flattery may have been part of the General's "sales talk" in trying to persuade the battalion's members to re-enlist. His appeal produced disappointing results. The men were anxious to join their coreligionists who were beginning to arrive at the Great Salt Lake. The General promised Cooke's Mormons some new clothing. A call was also made on the battalion for volunteers to escort Kearny when he returned to Missouri. Despite their unwillingness to sign up for a long term of service, sufficient volunteers were found for the overland journey.

During his brief stay in Los Angeles, Kearny wrote to both the Adjutant General and the Secretary of War. To the former he reported: "I find the people of this part of California quiet, notwithstanding some rumors to the contrary, circulated and I fear originated by some of our own officers to further their own wicked purposes. I leave here tomorrow for Monterey and will close my public business there as soon as possible and proceed to St. Louis via the South Pass." He hoped to reach his destination by August 20 and would await orders there for his future movements. "I shall be prepared to go at once whenever my services may be needed." Frémont, he wrote, had been sent to Monterey to close his California affairs before leaving for Washington. "His conduct in California has been such that I shall be compelled on arriving in Missouri to arrest him and send him under charges to report to you." The letter to Secretary Marcy was to the same effect: "False and wicked rumors . . . which there is good reason to fear have been and are originated and kept in circulation by some of our own officers (naval and military)." Kearny also promised to send a portion of the New York regiment to take possession of towns in Lower California as proposed in the Secretary's instructions of January 11.

Kearny wrote one other letter while in Los Angeles which has been repeatedly cited against him. It does not appear in his letter books and official files, nor have I seen it quoted in full. While under cross-examination at the court-martial, he was asked by Frémont himself: "Did you write . . . in May last to Colonel Benton to inform him of your design to arrest Lieutenant Colonel Frémont?" Kearny answered: "I wrote to Colonel Benton in . . . May from Los Angeles, telling him that the conduct of Lieutenant Colonel Frémont had been in opposition to my orders and those of the War Department. Delicacy prevented me from saying further to Colonel Benton on the subject."

Even more savagely than in the case of the message which Kearny had sent to Jessie Frémont about her husband's health, Benton denounced this letter as intended to deceive Frémont's unsuspecting family about his peril. It lent color to the charge that the General arrested Frémont without warning to forestall his defense and prevent his obtaining needed witnesses and records. In the absence of its actual text one cannot fully appraise this communication. There is too little basis for a charge that General Kearny's intentions were anything but honorable.

General Kearny, Lieutenant Colonel Cooke, and Willard Hall embarked the *Lexington* on May 14. She did not drop anchor in Monterey Bay until May 27. Good news awaited her passengers. General Taylor had just won a big victory over Santa Anna. The latter had suffered five thousand casualties and eight thousand desertions. He had been driven back to Mexico City with the remnant of his army. General Scott had also captured Veracruz. It seemed possible that by this time Mexico had sued for peace.

The day after his arrival Kearny wrote Commodore Biddle that "the southern portion of this territory is now like the remainder of it, quiet, and there is no probability of that quiet being disturbed by the Californians unless instigated by others." He then informed the

Commodore of the government's wish to seize Lower California: "I am now prepared to send two companies (about 120) New York Volunteers now at Santa Barbara if you will furnish a vessel to transport them and remain with or near them. I believe troops should be landed at La Paz or San Jose (on the eastern (*sic*) shore of the Gulf of California) or both places." In closing Kearny told Biddle that he planned to start to Missouri in a few days and that Colonel Mason would succeed him.

On May 30, Kearny advised Lieutenant Colonel Burton at Santa Barbara to embark his two companies on the *Lexington*. He told Burton to carry six months' provisions. Burton was apprised that during March and April, Captain Montgomery had taken possession of San Lucas, San Jose, and La Paz with sailors from the U.S.S. *Portsmouth*. The General recommended either La Paz or San Jose as the landing place for the expedition, but left the final decision to Burton after he and Captain Bailey had conferred at the scene. He closed the letter with a caution that well summarized his philsophy as a soldier:

> It is understood that the people of Lower California have not the power if they possess the disposition to resist your coming, but you must not on that account allow the discipline of your soldiers to relax but hold them at all times ready to resist or make an attack. The best means of preserving peace is to be prepared for war.

Kearny's last letter to the Adjutant General from California was written at the same time and closed by reiterating: "I shall be ready for any duty which may be assigned to me." It must be emphasized that General Kearny four times in May, 1847, invited orders for whatever active duty his superiors might designate. Notwithstanding this unusually full record of his willingness to serve in the war, Senator Benton, during his thirteen-day diatribe in 1848, accused him of "returning to St. Louis to spend the remainder of the war in peace with his family." This despite the fact that months before Benton made the speech, Kearny had gone to Mexico, served in various capacities in the theater of war, and been invalided home by what proved to be his fatal illness. It would be hard to select a more

318

perfect instance of Benton's vitriolic bias—a bias so profound as to cast doubt on any utterance he made involving his quondam friend Stephen Kearny.

Frémont with members of his topographical party rode into Monterey on May 29. Soon afterward General Kearny ordered the group paraded before him to effect the immediate discharge of any members who wished to remain in California. Frémont maintained that this method of mustering out the party was employed solely to humiliate him. Kearny also directed that Frémont himself remain inside the town and not at the camp his engineers had set up in the outskirts. That seems relatively more harsh than the line-up of the topographers for a very necessary formality. Frémont resented also the General's refusal to allow him to send for his engineering assistants, Kern and King, who were supposed to be near San Francisco. He was also directed to deliver his surveying instruments to Lieutenant Halleck as the senior engineering officer in California. Each of these orders was galling to the proud and temperamental explorer who so long had been a law unto himself. Perhaps some of them were unnecessary limitations, but before judging Kearny too severely, it must be remembered that he was dealing with a man who had proved he would take an ell if given an inch. The surest way to prevent new mischief was to circumscribe his field. One of Frémont's many complaints was that General Kearny did not tell him he intended to arrest him. Despite his brilliant mind, Frémont seemed strangely lacking in perception. These restrictions should have been an unmistakable warning to expect arrest. Kearny stood singularly alone, criticized by friend and foe alike. Some echoed Frémont's complaint that he was not warned of his impending arrest. Others claimed he was already a prisoner when he left Monterey for Missouri. Yet Kearny was being privately criticized by his own subordinates because he did not arrest Frémont.

Archibald Gillespie reported to Commodore Biddle in Monterey on May 26. According to the marine officer's testimony at Frémont's court-martial, Biddle told him "that he had nothing to do with me, and that I could return to the United States when I pleased."

Gillespie and Commodore Stockton were already planning an overland trip to the States, and Gillespie in preparation sent three men to Sutter's Fort with six fine horses and twelve mules. He planned to join them a day later. While returning from shore to his quarters on the *Congress* one evening, an officer brought him a peremptory message from Commodore Biddle that he "should not quit the town until further orders." Gillespie considered this an unwarranted reversal of their previous understanding and, though the hour was late, went on board the *Columbus* to remonstrate with Biddle. Colonel Mason was just then leaving the vessel. Commodore Biddle told the marine "that he had received a note from General Kearny and that I must remain in Monterey until further orders; that he wished to avoid difficulty between the army and navy." The Major protested that if General Kearny had any charges to prefer against him, he wanted to know so that he could answer them. Biddle did not wish to argue the matter and dropped an allusion to the house Gillespie had in the Pueblo. The Major replied that he could not see what his private affairs had to do with his embarrassing detention. This ended the immediate discussion. During the time of his enforced delay, marauding Indians seized the Major's animals on the road to the Sacramento Valley. They were rescued by one of the guards, but Gillespie blamed his detention for the narrowly averted loss. After four days he was informed by Commodore Stockton that the latter "had obtained Commodore Biddle's permission for me to leave and that Commodore Biddle required that I should give my word of honor." Thereafter Gillespie departed for the Sacramento Valley to overtake his party and procure supplies for the journey with Stockton. They left the Sacramento a month after General Kearny's party.

Gillespie testified that he had always believed that Kearny induced Biddle to detain him because he did not want him to visit the Sacramento Valley nor to return to the United States ahead of Kearny. Gillespie felt the General's objection arose from the Major's intimate connection with Stockton and Frémont during their differences with Kearny.

During the court-martial the General gave quite a different account of the incident. While in Los Angeles in May he had learned that Gillespie had just rented quarters there for the ensuing six months. On the night of May 30 he was informed by Colonel Mason that Gillespie was planning to leave the next day for San Francisco or the Sacramento or both. Mason feared Gillespie's appearance in that region might excite the residents. Kearny replied that if he was apprehensive, Mason should so inform Commodore Biddle. He supplemented this by an informal note to the Commodore saying the best way to preserve the prevailing peace in California was not to permit Gillespie to move about the country. The General claimed he did not know the marine officer was planning to go east until much later. Because Gillespie had rented a house in Los Angeles, Kearny had supposed that the Major intended to return to the south-land after visiting the Sacramento Valley.

The members of the court-martial accepted Kearny's explanation. Frémont did not strengthen his attempts to discredit him by charging that the General had also interfered with the departure of several naval officers likely to be witnesses for Frémont. Kearny testified that he had actually requested Commodore Biddle to allow one of these officers to accompany him to Missouri. Kearny thought highly of this particular lieutenant and regretted that Biddle refused his consent. That circumstance seems to have been lost sight of in the condemnation of Kearny. A biographer of Gillespie's charged that the General "lamely defended his actions by the traditional army practice of passing the buck." None of these critics mentions that when Kearny testified about this episode he had been ill, part of the time too ill to attend the sessions. Since General Kearny knew that he, himself, would be on his way to the States within a few hours after his conversation with Colonel Mason, it was hardly "buck passing" to have him concerned by Mason's apprehensions about Gillespie. Mason was to assume all Kearny's responsibilities, so it was natural for the General to listen to his views. What grounds had Mason for apprehension about Gillespie's travels in northern California?

Frémont's champions have emphasized that he was quite popular in California with Americans and Californians alike. In March, 1847, Owl Russell had carried east a petition to the government signed by numerous residents of southern California. It had been easy to secure signatures for Frémont's reinstatement to power and glory. It was true that he was very well liked throughout the south, but in northern California it was a different story. Most of the unpaid volunteers lived in that area, as did the majority of the creditors for supplies furnished the battalion and for Frémont's administration. Both groups were bitter. Frémont had been the government to these men. He could not pay them nor does blame attach to him for that inability, but impoverished frontiersmen with money due them are not prone to logic nor patience.

Therefore when a similar petition was circulated for signatures in the bay region, it produced an angry clamor. This resulted in a heavily attended mass meeting in San Francisco on July 14, 1847, to consider Frémont's conduct and his claims to be named governor by the President. A committee was formed "to investigate and publish all reliable instances of his misconduct; and meantime the meeting protested against his being chosen as their governor." (This agitation was never so much as hinted at during the court-martial, and I cannot recall seeing a word about it in any of the writings of Frémont's admirers.) Of course this meeting occurred some six weeks after Colonel Mason voiced his alarm, but feelings of this character do not culminate overnight; and, beyond a doubt, reports of the unfriendly sentiment had reached Mason's ears by May 30. A letter written Larkin by a well-known San Francisco merchant probably echoes this sentiment:

> Being informed Colonel Frémont is about to leave there for the United States which I am indeed sorry to hear and not having the pleasure of seeing him for the adjustment of my accounts, consequently I remit you a copy and that will empower you to regulate them with him and in my name. . . . You will also please say to the Colonel that *I wish nothing more of him nor do I wish to injure him in any way about what is passed between himself and me.* [The italics are mine.]

An itemized bill for $5,609 accompanied this letter.

The native Californians in the north had also not forgotten nor forgiven the unprovoked murder of the elderly Berreyesa and the two young De Haro brothers at San Rafael less than a year earlier. The victims were related to many prominent Californians. Of all Frémont's actions in California, these killings had the least justification. Some of the stain attached itself to Kit Carson. He was always unhappy to hear the execution mentioned. Frémont's lofty "I have no room for prisoners" may have sounded Napoleonic at the time he doomed the three men, but it lingers as a sadly tarnished memory of his adventurous life.

Lieutenant John M. Hollingsworth of the New York Volunteers, who had no part in the controversial events of the period, commented in his journal during May, 1847, that Frémont had "ruled like a despot, with an iron arm, the band of men about him—of lowest grade and worst of characters . . . (he) permitted acts of cruelty and injustice that will ever be a stain on American character." This officer, who had met General Kearny on the *Lexington's* cruise to San Pedro, quoted the General that one of these acts had been a cold-blooded murder and that Frémont knew and could have prevented it. (This may well have referred to the Berreyesa-De Haro affair.)

An officer like Major Gillespie was bound to be closely associated in men's minds with any disfavor in which they held Frémont. He actually witnessed the Berreyesa-De Haro tragedy but was not in any way involved. Colonel Mason—and General Kearny—may or may not have been justified in the degree of apprehension they expressed to Commodore Biddle; but unquestionably there was a well-defined sentiment abroad in the land against Frémont and the officers closest to him.

What did Gillespie mean by saying "Commodore Biddle required that I should give my word of honor?" Oddly enough, no one sought an explanation while he was on the witness stand. An unsigned memorandum of two pages, probably in Gillespie's own handwriting, repeats the story of his detention but adds some details. Here are the concluding lines of the memorandum: "I was permitted to leave Monterey, first pledging my word of honor not to say anything (here the word "against" has been scratched out) about Gen'l Kearny for the performance of which Commodore Stockton went my security." If, as charged by Frémont, Kearny, Mason, and Biddle conspired to hold Gillespie so that he could not be a witness for the Lieutenant Colonel (which the members of the court-martial refused to believe) why was he allowed to go on his way after only four days? Why was his word of honor, backed by a pledge from Commodore Stockton, required? If it was to prevent his ultimately testifying, it did not succeed. His appearance as a witness seemed unopposed and his testimony uninhibited. No adequate explanation has ever come to light.

Edwin Bryant had decided to return to the States. General Kearny gladly invited him to become one of his party. Bryant first resigned his post as alcalde of San Francisco, and Kearny replaced him with George Hyde. Thomas O. Larkin, doubtless to assist his overworked house guest, wrote Bryant that the General and his party, including Lieutenant William Radford of the navy, were to leave Monterey on the thirty-first for Captain Sutter's via the San Joaquin. If Bryant wanted to join them, they would probably be at Santa Clara the second day following. Radford had considerable leave due him and conceived the idea of accompanying his brother-in-law. The trip promised a welcome break from the routine of sea duty, so he applied to Commodore Biddle for permission to go. Biddle did not favor long overland journeys by his officers. Probably his cordial relations with General Kearny were the deciding factor for he acceded to the request, with the canny proviso that the trip should be at Radford's own expense. There were grounds for this caution; receipts in Major Gillespie's papers show that the cost of the journey that he and Stockton made that same summer exceeded $12,000.

Captain du Pont heard of Kearny's departure with real sorrow. The General had once interrupted the Captain while he was writing to his wife: " 'Tell Mrs. Du Pont I shall be passing through Wilmington next fall and I shall most surely go out and see her.' I have told him I would hold him to his promise." Later the Captain wrote: "With General Kearny my association has been . . . agreeable—indeed as I have before told you one of the most pleasing incidents of my cruise has been the friendly acquaintance which has sprung up between us." At sea on June 23 the *Portsmouth* brought him late news from California's capital. Reminding Mrs. du Pont of the General's proposed visit, he wrote:

General Kearny with a large staff had . . . started on May 31 via South Pass and took Frémont with him—said to be arrested on arrival at Fort Leavenworth. A court-martial is inevitable but will injure both arms of the service and benefit nobody. Yet I don't know how the government can act otherwise. . . . He (Kearny) is a frank unostentatious soldier of good sense, affable manners, kind hearted without stiffness or reserve. Do not be worried about his accommodations or fare. He is no epicure, has roughed it very much —in fact has "no nonsense about him."

One of the General's last interviews was with his landlord. Larkin handed him a letter in which he appealed to Kearny to do whatever he could in Washington for the government's many creditors in California. Larkin was only too correct in his position that "the claimants performed services and made advances with good will and readiness; had every reason to expect that their demands would be approved of and paid by the United States government." He pointed out that merchants of the best credit, because of inability to collect what the government owed them, were compelled to pay 2 per cent a month for any loans. Many recently arrived emigrants who had helped seize California were now penniless. "I would therefore press on you the importance of . . . an early interview with President Polk . . . urging immediate action in the premises."

Stephen Kearny's mind must have been filled with many memories when he led his escort out of Monterey on the morning of May 31. The year just ended had been the stormiest that he had yet experienced. His ninety days as governor had been crowded with memorable incidents. When he commenced his administration, California, with the exception of a limited area around Los Angeles, was without any real government. Rumors and alarms agitated the population. His task of bringing peace and tranquillity had been made more difficult by his predecessors. Frémont's continued assertion of authority long after its source had been removed had greatly complicated matters. It seems little short of miraculous that ninety days of Kearny's rule brought so much order to a vast territory so lately given over to chaos. Possibly the General weighed the debits and credits of his efforts as he rode toward San Juan Bautista across meadows prodigally sprinkled with wild mustard, lupines, and poppies. He could take pride in his record as the first military governor of California. He had been signally successful in completing one more task for the republic to whose service his life was dedicated.

19. *Saddle Leather and Statecraft*

THE GENERAL HAD PLANNED to travel via the Carquinez Strait to Sutter's Fort and so avoid crossing many streams. On June 2, however, it was decided that the strait offered the greater hazard. The heavy discharge of the rivers into Suisun Bay made a swift current at Carquinez which could only be ferried with difficulty at ebb tide. There were sixty-four men in the column. Besides a number of privately owned animals, their livestock totaled 172 "public" horses and mules. With the limited boats available, nearly a week would be lost in the passage of such a cavalcade. Therefore the General decided to cross the Coast Ranges and travel north to Sutter's. Since the change of direction was made near "Gilderoy's" ranch, the party undoubtedly followed the route of present Highway 152 over Pacheco Pass. Many wild horses, antelope, and other game were grazing on the luxuriant grass as they entered the San Joaquin Valley. Captain Turner, the official diarist of the expedition, described the weather as clear and pleasant.

They were enjoying the most beautiful of California's seasons—springtime, with its lush verdure before the hillsides browned with the heat of summer. Numerous streams slowed their progress. The winter of 1846–47 had broken records for heavy snowfall in the Sierra Nevada, and now melting snows filled every river as it tore down to the bay. On June 4 the travelers found the San Joaquin had flooded a wide area. In fording, the men had to carry their packs on their backs to keep them dry. Although the nights were chilly for the season, mosquitoes infested the camps. Rivers were icy cold. Both men and horses had to swim several crossings as they were too deep for the animals to ford.

One boat was swamped on the Tuolumne on the seventh, and the greater part of Major Swords' baggage was lost. All the spare mule shoes and horseshoe nails sank in the river. Expert Indian swimmers aided the soldiers in ferrying their packs. By the tenth the weather had grown exceedingly hot. At the Mokelumne, Cooke played in even harder luck than Swords. A skin boat capsized, dumping into the river all of Cooke's possessions save the clothes he wore. His journal of five hundred pages was carried away in the swirling waters. Its loss would have been irreparable. Fortunately after quite a long interval it was recovered by some of Captain Sutter's Indians (it must have had a waterproof covering). The circumstance offered Senator Benton the excuse for one of his unfair insinuations—that, because of something embarrassing to Kearny in Cooke's journal, the mishap had been conveniently arranged! The ultimate publication of the journal revealed nothing of the kind.

On June 13 the American Fork was crossed, and a campsite was made about two miles above Sutter's Fort. Two days were spent jerking beef and making other preparations for the journey. More horses were procured from public bands in the vicinity. It was not expected that these would complete the trip to Fort Leavenworth, but they were taken along to relieve the mules in crossing the mountains. Later they would perhaps be killed for food. In connection with these horses, a seemingly minor incident was later given surprising attention. Near the Cosumnes, a messenger from Frémont directed the General's attention to a band of public horses. Swords commandeered them by Kearny's orders. Some were turned over to Frémont's representative. The latter complained of the division made and because Swords did not give him a receipt for the horses. By the time this was solemnly inquired into at the court-martial, an impression was created of irregular conduct and of wrongs presumably done the unknown owners of the horses. It is hard to see why so much time had to be devoted to examination, cross-examination, and a paper filed by the accused about such a trivial issue.

Members of the California Battalion, including some Walla Walla Indians, called upon Frémont while near Sutter's Fort to ask for their pay. He ordered payment made in government or public horses. Perhaps this incident somehow was involved with the animals taken by Major Swords.

The day he arrived, Kearny and several of his officers rode over to the trading post to pay their respects to Johann Sutter. A salute was fired and the tiny garrison paraded in the General's honor. The next night Captain Sutter entertained them at dinner. Kearny told his host that he liked the location of the fort and thought the government might buy it together with a small parcel of surrounding land.

Kearny may well have brushed shoulders at Nueva Helvetia with a man destined to achieve unique fame. In Captain Sutter's diary, the last entry before the record of Kearny's arrival mentions "Mr. Marshall" and his work on a flour mill for Sutter at Brighton. Five weeks after the General's departure, Sutter and James A. Marshall were to leave the fort to select a site for a sawmill in the foothills—a mill destined to become one of America's most famous landmarks. Compared to a discovery Marshall would soon make there, all that had previously occurred in California would seem but a curtain raiser.

On that same June 14, Frémont once more applied to Kearny for permission to return to the United States with a small party at his own expense. The letter reminded Kearny of the direction given by the Commander in Chief that Frémont be allowed to leave California at his pleasure. (He seems never to have realized that his own insubordination had absolutely negated that permission. When granted, the administration did not know of his disobedience and insubordination. The administration had a right to expect the distant commander to exercise discretion in following it. That was exactly what Kearny did.) Frémont pointed out that with his knowledge of the country, a few men could reach the states forty or fifty days ahead of the General's party. (Complete candor would have made Frémont add that he could employ this extra time in building his defenses against the trouble awaiting him.) Briefly Kearny refused the permission. His note informed Frémont that he planned to leave

329

the camp near Sutter's on the sixteenth and directed the Lieutenant Colonel to be at the General's camp some fifteen miles distant on the evening of that day "and to continue with me to Missouri."

Frémont also twice protested that two members of the topographical party, Edward M. Kern and Henry King, had not yet arrived and would be left behind if the start was made as scheduled. Kearny would not change his plans because of anyone's late arrival. At the court-martial the Kern-King incident was cited as further evidence of Kearny's efforts to deprive Frémont of witnesses. Throughout his career Kearny had been noted for the rapidity with which he invariably moved with his detachments. Yet Frémont argued that the General's swift travel across the mountains now was further proof of his base motives!

Several days later Frémont again made application to separate from the General's party, giving as his reason his wish to explore and map a new and shorter route to California across the Great Basin for the benefit of emigrants. Kearny would not alter his decision.

Captain Turner's journal lists the personnel of the expedition that headed north from Sutter's Fort at three o'clock on the afternoon of June 16. In addition to General Kearny and the officers— Majors Cooke and Swords, Captain Turner, Lieutenant Radford, and Assistant Surgeon Sanderson—there were the Mormon escort and several discharged dragoons and engineers as well as Lieutenant Colonel Frémont with his topographical party. Congressman Hall also traveled with the General. Nearly a score of servants were in the column. Turner lists "Mr. Murphy, guide." According to some authorities, William O. Falton or O'Fallon, "the Irish trapper of California," a huge man known to his fellow mountaineers as "Big" or "Le Gros" Fallon, was Kearny's guide across the Sierra Nevada; but I feel Turner's statement must be accepted. The party totaled sixty-four men. The twenty-eight in Frémont's group usually marched a mile or two in the rear and made a separate camp at night. Many writers state that Kearny ordered Frémont to observe this plan of march. I have never found a written order to that effect; it could have been a verbal direction. The alleged instructions to follow in the rear of the column and camp apart were more of the many indignities of which Frémont complained. At least once, Fré-

330

mont charged, he was brusquely commanded to abandon a location he had chosen and camp at another spot.

The men with the General's own detachment cooked their meals and camped in what Cooke called "convenient small messes." Only the minimum of communication was maintained between the two divisions of the column. Actually the separation of the two groups seems a sensible and practical one. With the tension existing between the leaders, enforced association for well over two months might have resulted in serious friction. It certainly would have been most unpleasant for everyone. It is hard to conceive why marching behind the Mormon escort was in itself an indignity.

Thirty-three miles of travel on June 17 brought the cavalcade to Johnson's Ranch on the Bear River three miles east of present-day Wheatland in Yuba County—"the last house we expect to see this side of Fort Hall," wrote Sergeant Jones of the Mormon escort. Johnson's Ranch was the western end of one of the first trails beaten into California by trappers of the Hudson's Bay Company. Some of the earliest immigrants followed their route, and many eastbound travelers chose it as their starting point. Edwin Bryant and a servant had left San Francisco on June 2 and met General Kearny at Johnson's. From Bryant the General heard for the first time of Major Gillespie's plan to take the overland trip to the States.

On the eighteenth the expedition, now numbering sixty-six, began the ascent of the Sierra. A few years later enthusiastic promoters were to lay out the site of the city of Kearney (misspelled, of course) on their last campground in the valley. Like many such ambitious projects, no trace of the budding metropolis remains. Those first hours in the foothills and lower mountains must have been exhilarating. After the heavy winter every open slope was carpeted with a profusion of wild flowers. Comparatively few immigrants had yet entered the country, and the scattered aborigines had been but little disturbed. The forests not yet slashed by ax and saw, the river canyons yet unravaged by placer mining or blasted for railroad rights of way, Kearny and his companions beheld the California mountains in their pristine beauty.

The journals reflect only mild appreciation of the scenery because uppermost in every mind was the wish to reach home speedily. It is easy to trace Kearny's route—up Bear River and past the site of North Bloomfield, thence to the headwaters of the Yuba and American where the first patches of snow were reached. By the twenty-first these had become deep drifts. The men wore handkerchiefs over their eyes to ward off snow blindness. The fresh sunny air of the lower, flower-clad slopes had given way to the chill and gloom of lingering winter among the thick, dark pines.

Hours of laborious travel at length brought them to the awesome Cannibal Camp on Donner Lake. There they gazed upon the half-ruined cabins and broken fragments of wagons littering the snow, where a party of eighty hapless souls had been forced to abandon their journey. Skeletons, some intact, others in hideous fragments, were scattered among the pathetic remnants of the immigrants' baggage. Accustomed though they were to war and desolation, every man shuddered at the somber spectacle. General Kearny directed Major Swords and a detail to inter the remains. Then he ordered the cabins burned together with all grisly reminders of the horrible events of the preceding winter.

The question of who erased from the face of mother earth the evidence of the Donner tragedy is admittedly not of first importance. Yet in justice to General Kearny and for the sake of truth, the record needs to be corrected. Captain Turner wrote: "The Gen. directed Maj. Swords to collect these remains & inter them." Swords, himself, in reporting to the Quartermaster General said: "We collected and buried the remains of those that had perished from hunger." Sergeant Jones was even more explicit: "The General called halt and detailed five men to bury the deserted bodies that lay on the ground. . . . Col. Frémont passed us here, the first time we have seen him since we left Fort Suter (*sic*). After we had buried the bones of the dead . . . we set fire to the cabins." Here are the records written on the spot or recorded soon afterward by the official chronicler of the expedition and two other diarists. All were eyewitnesses and two of them actual participants in the melancholy task. It should be especially noted that the last quotation includes the words "Col. Frémont *passed* us here." [The italics are mine.] Nothing in Jones' narrative indicates that Frémont took part in the grim labors. I only call attention to these facts because Allan

Nevins writes: "Frémont paused to destroy all traces which might operate to discourage emigrants burning the broken wagons, ox yokes and other sad relics."

I believe Nevins' source was the narrative of William Alexander Trubody, who died in 1933 at the age of ninety-four. Five years earlier, according to Charles L. Camp, the eminent historian who edited his account, Trubody wrote his recollections of his overland journey from Missouri to California in 1847. It reads: "We camped one night at the Donner camp where so many perished the winter of 1846. Frémont on his way back east destroyed everything he could that might be a discouragement to future travelers—wagons, ox yokes and anything and everything that would burn were given to the flames." The similarity of Trubody's language to Nevins' is unmistakable.

In a paragraph preceding this quotation Trubody recalled meeting Frémont on the Big Sandy River (Captain Turner's journal places the Kearny expedition on the Big Sandy on July 23). Frémont spent the evening with the emigrants, among whom was the Trubody family. The explorer gave these travelers advice on how to cross the mountains safely and cautioned them against delays like those that had ended so tragically for the Donner party. A footnote quotes Trubody as saying Kearny was not well liked by these emigrants. He had invited them to come to see him at his camp so was considered "offish and high-hat" while Frémont "was very sociable and good to the emigrants." *He* went to see *them*.

Trubody was under eight years of age when he made this epic trip. The party in which he traveled could not have reached Donner Lake until well over a month after it met Frémont on July 23. All that this small boy could have known about who interred the bodies and burned the cabins was what he or his elders may have heard from Frémont at the Big Sandy campfire, or from the wagon party as it toiled westward. John C. Frémont had a flair for the dramatic and for tales of adventure—especially his own. May I hazard the guess that in recounting the tragedy that befell the Donners, whose grisly remains he had passed a month before, he saw no harm in embellishing his narrative by naming himself a principal at the final sepulture? I am sure Allan Nevins would agree that the recollections of a boy under eight, written over eighty years later, cannot be credited against the accounts of three separate eyewitnesses and participants, recorded soon after the event. Neither Turner's journal nor Jones' diary has ever been published so may never have come to Nevins' notice.

The journey down the Truckee, across the waterless barrens to Mary's River (now the Humboldt) and up that stream was devoid of striking incident. By July 13 the expedition, having crossed to the Snake, found itself on the main Oregon Trail. Fort Hall was reached on the fifteenth but could not furnish needed supplies. Horse meat would have been resorted to had not a westbound emigrant train opportunely appeared. Its animals were so thin from their long haul that the owners were glad to sell enough surplus to lighten their loads. On July 24 the column surmounted the South Pass. General Kearny was retracing his 1845 trail and felt that he was nearing home. Buffalo and antelope were so plentiful that food ceased to be a problem. Lieutenant Radford possessed the only shotgun in the party, and his sage hens, grouse, and other game enriched the messes.

Methodically Captain Turner counted the emigrant trains. What he thought was the year's last caravan passed Kearny's column on July 28. Turner's list totaled 941 wagons; over 3,500 men, women, and children; and horses, mules, cattle, and sheep running into many thousands. Most of these trains were bound for Oregon.

On the twenty-ninth the Mormon escort were cheered when they encountered a small group of their brethren. These men were an advance guard of the main migration who had been sent ahead to prepare buffalo meat for the throngs that followed. General Kearny was back among his Plains Indians. On August 2 west of Fort Laramie he held a council with some Sioux chiefs. Here and along the road eastward many a brave remembered Shonga Kahega Mahetonga. Persistency was one of John C. Frémont's virtues. At Fort Laramie he once more applied to General Kearny for leave to take a separate route home with his party. Again permission was refused. Two days later the column met the main Mormon wagon train of more than three thousand souls, heading for its promised land. The

334

leaders told the General they had abandoned the idea of going to California. The Great Salt Lake was now their goal.

At nine o'clock on the hot morning of August 22, General Kearny and his cavalcade drew rein on the familiar parade ground at Fort Leavenworth. Major Swords estimated they had traveled an amazing 2,152 miles from Monterey in eighty-three days. The 1,905 miles from the Sacramento had been covered in just sixty-six days, every one of them spent in travel. By Major Cooke's calculations, they had averaged 33 miles per day. An unknown newspaper correspondent wrote an eyewitness account: "The Well Beloved Old General Looked Natural as Life and was Welcomed back by his friends and they fired a Salute of 13 guns. . . . he is a Grate [sic] Soldier one who knows No Fear Nor feels No fatigue . . . he is looked on as a Protector and a friend to the inhabitants of this Post."

Almost immediately after their arrival Kearny summoned Frémont to the office of Lieutenant Colonel Clifton Wharton, the commander of Fort Leavenworth. Kearny had written out a formal order which he requested Colonel Wharton to read aloud when Frémont reported. The latter was directed to deliver to the officers of the post the horses, mules, and other public property in possession of his party. He was to verify the amounts due each member under him, so that all might be paid. Then came the fateful climax of the order: "Lieutenant Colonel Frémont having performed the above duty will consider himself under arrest and will then repair to Washington city and report himself to the Adjutant General of the Army." A study of the original order in the General's letter book is a mute commentary on the emotional strain under which the writer was laboring; the handwriting and signature are far more cramped and shaky than those on the adjoining pages!

Frémont's reception at Fort Leavenworth and the manner of his arrest were more of the alleged indignities heaped upon the Lieutenant Colonel. He complained that none of the officers at the post, with the exception of Colonel Wharton, addressed a word to him or extended him any of the courtesies usually shown a travel-worn arrival. He blamed these shortcomings on Kearny's influence. One is forced to conclude that Frémont found all the formalities of military discipline distasteful unless he gave the orders and received

335

the salutes. His honor and sensibilities were so frequently offended that their recital becomes repetitious.

The Lieutenant Colonel should have been very grateful that this arrest had been so long delayed. For months his conduct had provided the General with plenty of excuses, had he been anxious to arrest him. A headstrong man like Frémont might have made the theatrical gesture of demanding an immediate trial. Ordinarily an officer arrested for mutiny in enemy territory in time of war is speedily tried. Had Kearny been actuated by the mere desire to punish the slights offered him, nothing would have better served his purpose than a prompt arrest and trial. A court-martial is made up of officers senior, junior, and of the same rank as the accused. What chance would John C. Frémont have stood with a court composed in part of Mason, Cooke, Swords, Turner, and Sherman? Moreover, had he been tried in California, he could not have had the benefit of the able counsel who defended him in Washington. Because he was performing a most unpleasant duty and not an act of revenge, General Kearny waited until the return of the accused to the United States ensured Frémont the advantage of a more neutral court. Considering the strong feeling repeatedly expressed against the accused by army officers in California, that forbearance on the part of General Kearny may well have saved Frémont's life. Neither realization nor appreciation of that fact was ever displayed by those most vitally concerned.

It has been repeatedly asked—why did General Kearny persist in filing charges against John C. Frémont? As well as any man living, he knew the powerful enemies and the storm and bitterness this would create. On the personal side he had the strongest motives to deter him—intimate family friendships and his own sense of obligation to Senator Benton. By overlooking the personal affronts, he could not only preserve treasured ties but save himself the endless vexations attendant upon a prosecution of the charges.

The last letter from Captain du Pont, from which we have quoted, holds the answer. Du Pont dreaded the scandal and passions of a court-martial, but he did not know "how the government can act otherwise." Stephen Kearny had a deep sense of duty. In carrying out the instructions of his Commander in Chief, his authority had

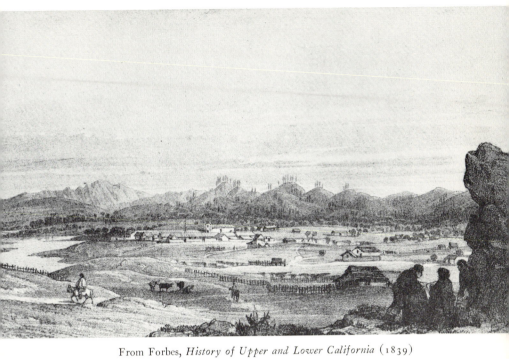

From Forbes, *History of Upper and Lower California* (1839)

A lithograph of the Presidio and Pueblo of Monterey, Upper California, where Kearny spent his brief tenure as governor of California.

Mrs. Philip Kearny, nee Susanna Watts, mother of the General, posed for this oil portrait by Samuel F. B. Morse sometime early in the last century.

been challenged and his orders disobeyed. If such contempt and insubordination were overlooked, it was not General Kearny who
would be harmed. The whole American system of orderly government would immediately be in jeopardy. If today a subordinate
could with impunity disobey the commands of his superior officer,
refuse to deliver government arms, and then fail to report in person
to his commanding officer when directed to do so—if any one officer
could repeatedly so offend and not be held to account, then what
would become tomorrow of the morale and authority—not only of
the army—but of the sovereign government it served? General
Kearny found this challenge infinitely more compelling than even
the claims of friendship. The integrity of the army which he had
served for thirty-five years was in the balance; no option was left him.

On that same August 22, before the dust of his column had fairly
settled in the road, Kearny wrote to the Adjutant General. The first
sentence of the letter referred to Frémont's arrest with a typically
impersonal formality that did not even name the accused: "I enclose
herewith a copy of an order this day issued by me at this Post." The
letter referred briefly to his arrival at Fort Leavenworth that morning. He would proceed forthwith to St. Louis and in a few days to
Washington, "where I shall be ready to receive the orders of the
War Department." I have a photostat of this letter; it could serve
as a model for neatness and penmanship, although the writer had
just alighted from his horse after a ride of more than 2,100 miles.

General Kearny, accompanied by Major Swords and Cooke and
Captain Turner, boarded the steamer *Amelia* the day after he rode
into Fort Leavenworth. Several of Kearny's children had been born
there. It had long been his home. Fate was to decree that he was
now leaving it for the last time. On their way downstream, Cooke
inquired whether he would be needed at the court-martial that now
seemed inevitable. The General thought that the evidence would be
mainly documentary and that Major Cooke would not be called.
The travelers reached St. Louis late in the evening of August 25.

It must have been deeply disappointing to Kearny to find that
his wife was absent from home because of illness in the family. News
of his return quickly spread, and a group of prominent citizens
planned a public dinner in appreciation of his great services. Kearny,

337

while most grateful for the honor, regretted that he could not accept because of his early departure for Washington. Missourians, however, were very conscious of the vast territory that had just become American soil, and eager to salute the man who had played so prominent a role in those dramatic conquests. Hastily a reception was arranged in the ladies parlor of the Planters' House, where many of the General's friends gathered on August 27 to pay their respects. He was sorry that Mrs. Kearny's absence prevented him from receiving them at his own residence.

Another pleasant incident of his return was the receipt of a letter informing General Kearny that on July 5, 1847, he had been unanimously elected an honorary member of the New York State Society of the Cincinnati (the organization of the officers of the Continental Army and their direct descendants). Considering that he was the scion of two prominent Tory families of New York and New Jersey, General Kearny had a right to feel honored. The General stayed only four days in St. Louis and was in New York on September 10. A reporter wrote: "He looks remarkably well, notwithstanding the effect life in camp has had in giving a silvery grey color to his locks. General Kearny is a Jerseyman—a true Jersey blue." He arrived in Washington on the morning of the eleventh.

It is timely now to review some happenings at the nation's capital. On April 30, 1847, the Secretary of War had brought to the President dispatches just received from Kearny. Conscientious James K. Polk noted in his diary: "An unfortunate collision has occurred in California between General Kearny and Commodore Stockton in regard to precedence in rank. I think General Kearny was right. It appears that Lieutenant Colonel Frémont refused to obey General Kearny and obeyed Commodore Stockton, and in this he was wrong." Four days later President Polk read the January dispatches Stockton had sent by Lieutenant Gray and those of Kearny carried by Lieutenant Emory. "Upon the full examination of the correspondence of both, I was fully satisfied that General Kearny was right and that Commodore Stockton was wrong. Indeed both he and Lieut. Colonel Frémont in refusing to recognize the authority of General Kearny acted insubordinately and in a manner that is censurable." Polk laid these reports before his Cabinet. All of its members concurred in his views, but as to Stockton and Frémont, "all agreed as I did that they were both gallant and meritorious officers and all regretted the occurrence. None of the Cabinet censured General Kearny. The two former have subjected themselves to arrest and trial by court-martial but as all collision has probably been since that time avoided, I am disposed not to pursue so rigorous a course."

The Secretary of War felt that in replying to General Kearny, he should approve his conduct. The Secretary of the Navy objected because that would seem to censure Stockton. He preferred that no opinion be expressed and that the matter be passed over as lightly as possible. That was the final decision reached. The President agreed, with some mental reservations. In a fashion typical of politics, consideration was deferred. Reading between the lines, one detects the fervent hope that the administration could avoid offense to either side. Perhaps time would spare it that embarrassing duty.

After five weeks' delay the Cabinet determined to send dispatches to both General Kearny and the naval commander on the Pacific station. (Polk was understandably vague about who the present commander was.) Kit Carson, who had recently come to Washington, was entrusted with these messages. These latest instructions would show Kearny in the right and Stockton and Frémont in the wrong concerning authority to command the land forces. It seems ironic to find Polk's Cabinet still solemnly passing on a controversy in California on June 8, when two of the principals to that argument were already on their way to the States and the third (Stockton) was about to follow.

The public, too, was becoming aroused about the brawls in California. The Benton-Frémont influence had not had time to disseminate its propaganda, and a part of the public had formed very definite opinions. One of Larkin's correspondents wrote:

What battles General Kearny and his worn-out troops fought with the troops of Flores. . . . all people here censure the Commodore for the position he has taken against Kearny. It admits not of question on which side was right and the most astonishing thing is that Commodore Shubrick did not immediately put Stockton in his proper place. The valiant Commodore stands very low in the estimation of

339

his countrymen and has done so for many years. He is considered a blustering, hypocritical would-be important being, but when sifted there is found no substance in him.

On June 14, Jessie Frémont accompanied by Kit Carson called at the White House. Carson had brought letters from Frémont to his wife and Senator Benton. Mrs. Frémont was plainly disturbed about her husband's status and requested the President to retain his services in California (to her that unquestionably meant continuing him as governor). Polk replied that Carson would carry dispatches to General Kearny when he returned to the Pacific. It would be left to Colonel Frémont's option whether he remained in California or returned to join his regiment of Mounted Rifles in Mexico. Mrs. Frémont had hoped for more, but this was as much as the President chose to say to her.

On July 22, Polk and his Cabinet became even more detached from present realities. Kearny and Frémont were then crossing the Rockies, and the latter in another month would be under arrest. Yet in Washington mail had just been received from General Kearny and Commodores Shubrick and Biddle that led the statesmen to think all the controversy was behind them.

One man was not so easily satisfied. Thomas H. Benton on August 17 had just returned from the Midwest and called upon President Polk. Sometime previously the Senator had demanded that a court of inquiry be organized to deal with the California affair. Polk's diary said: "I replied that I had read his communication but that it had not been deemed necessary to take any action upon it. I told him that there had been some difficulties between the officers in California . . . and that I hoped it might not be necessary to institute any trial by court-martial." Benton instantly tried to twist this to Frémont's advantage: "I am glad to hear from you . . . that there has been nothing in Frémont's conduct which requires a court-martial in his case." Cautious James K. Polk could not let this pass and most earnestly told Benton that he was not expressing any opinion at this time. He hoped the matter would not end in a court-martial, but if it did a certain contingency might force him to take official action. Therefore he could not with propriety express any opinion in ad-

340

vance. Benton assured the President that he understood that the latter could make no commitment. Later he declared that he proposed to move in the Senate for a full investigation "of the whole California business." Polk resented this as an implied criticism of his administration and told the Senator to go ahead. He had nothing to fear from such a step. After a long discussion, Polk noted in his diary that Benton "was evidently much excited but suppressed his feelings and talked in a calm tone."

Events had gone beyond the control of either man. Five days after this interview General Kearny arrested Frémont at Fort Leavenworth.

Apparently the first thing Kearny did after his arrival in Washington on the morning of September 11 was to pay his respects to President Polk. The two men had never met before. Polk reported their interview:

> While the Cabinet was in session Brigadier General Kearny . . . called. . . . I received him in my office and introduced him to my Cabinet. . . . I received him kindly for I consider him a good officer. He has performed valuable and important service in his late expedition to New Mexico and California. He remained but a few minutes. I invited him to call again.

Kearny returned on the sixteenth. Polk wrote:

> I had a conversation of more than an hour with him in relation to his late expedition to California and to the affairs in that country. He is a good officer and an intelligent gentleman. He gave me much valuable information in relation to affairs in California and the military operations in that country. No conversation took place in relation to his recent difficulties with Commodore Stockton and Lieutenant Colonel Frémont. Colonel Frémont is under arrest, charges having been preferred against him by General Kearny and I preferred not to converse with him on the subject. I did not introduce the subject and I was glad that he did not. My conversation with him was a pleasant and interesting one.

Apparently Frémont tarried longer en route to Washington than

Kearny, for only on September 17 did President Polk hear of his arrival. Senator Benton's other son-in-law, William Carey Jones, called at the White House to report that Frémont wished to be absent for a few days to visit his sick mother in South Carolina. Jones quoted him as wanting a speedy trial and said he would be ready in thirty days.

On the eighteenth Frémont's case was the sole topic at the Cabinet meeting. The President asked Secretary Marcy to report on whether a court-martial rather than a court of inquiry was indicated by an examination of the charges. A week later Frémont himself called upon the President "but made no allusion to that fact (his arrest) or to his case while in conversation with me." In due course the Secretary of War informed the President that the charges filed necessitated a court-martial. Accordingly, on September 27, one was ordered convened at Fortress Monroe, Virginia.

In his letter of September 20, Kearny called the Adjutant General's attention to the outstanding services of Major Cooke in leading the Mormon Battalion to California. He particularly stressed Cooke's acts at Tucson, where he "drove off a considerable Mexican force which was collected to oppose his progress." He recommended that Cooke be brevetted a lieutenant colonel. Captain Turner and Lieutenant Emory were also given special mention with the recommendation that each be brevetted a major. About the same time General Kearny wrote to Captain Turner. The General had just concluded a long conference with the Secretary of War about his charges against Frémont. It was expected that witnesses would be summoned from Missouri, and Kearny asked Turner to hold himself in readiness to come to Washington.

Allan Nevins says that General Kearny hastened to Washington because he was "alarmed by Benton's anger and the growing storm." Benton's correspondence at this time amply justifies the statement. His first letter to Frémont, after he read the charges, pronounced them "absurd" and said acquittal would be "easy enough." He was indignant at various stories published in New Orleans, Louisville, St. Louis, and Pittsburgh papers written apparently by officers recently arrived from the Far West. He complained because Frémont had not been given sufficient credit for his deeds in California. A few days later his fury increased to the point that he wrote his son-in-law: "We shall demolish him (Kearny) with all ease and overwhelm him with disgrace." He denounced the General, too, for bringing witnesses with him from California and was bitter about some anti-Frémont speeches Willard Hall had made since his return: "We will finish his career in Missouri. . . . You will have to employ counsel, it will be more nominal than otherwise as I shall do the work. . . . I shall be with you to the end if it takes up the whole session of Congress." A day later Benton exulted: "I am perfectly at ease. You will be justified and exalted. Your persecutors will be covered with shame and confusion. The proceeding through which you have gone is bitter. . . . You may be at ease. The enemy is now in our hands and may the Lord have mercy upon them for I feel as if I could not."

Benton's attitude of righteous indignation was not shared by everyone. Letters received by Thomas Larkin said:

> People censure Colonel Frémont generally. . . . His recent letter to the War Department is couched in language arrogant and unbecoming and has done him no good. I hope he will come out of the fire unscorched but fear rapid promotion and popular applause has turned his head. . . . General Kearny has returned and the Benton party are endeavoring to get up a strong excitement against him for his arrest of Frémont, but the country at large will sustain him.

Benton's anger continued at boiling point. On October 22 he again called on the President and portrayed a long series of events in California which he insisted had to be investigated and exposed. He felt the present charges against Frémont were not broad enough to permit the thorough disclosures which he wished. Therefore Frémont in a few days would demand of Secretary Marcy that other charges should be preferred against himself so as to make the investigation more complete. Not for the first—nor for the last—time, Senator Benton's zeal for his son-in-law was actually working against the accused. Like many men of power, Benton was prone to threaten dire things when he could not have his way. He now told the President that if the full investigation he demanded was not instituted, he would file charges against four other officers and demand their court-martial. General Kearny of course led the list, followed by Captain Turner, Lieutenant Emory, and Major Cooke. Polk's diary states that the Senator:

> . . . became excited and exhibited much deep feeling on the subject. . . . I was careful to say as little as possible but listened attentively. . . . I finally said to him that I would act justly in the matter, that I regretted the whole affair but had no agency in producing the difficulty. He said he knew I would act justly. He left in good humor toward me as far as he expressed himself in relation to any act of mine in the matter.

President Polk was keenly aware, however, that their relations hung on a delicate balance; the Senator would be satisfied with nothing less than virtual submission to his own views. Both men were Democrats. Any serious breach between the President and a leading Senator of his own party could be disastrous to Polk's administration.

Matters unrelated to the Frémont case complicated the President's problem. A son of Senator Benton's chose this particular moment to request a military commission. In Polk's opinion, his only qualification was his father's position. The President refused and the young man left abruptly muttering threats and profanity. Not long before, Polk had declined two other requests for federal posts made by the Senator's son-in-law Jones. That very day Benton demanded certain things of Secretary Marcy which could not be granted. In a troubled spirit, Polk wrote:

> I have always been on good terms with Senator Benton but he is a man of violent passions and I should not be surprised if he becomes my enemy because all his wishes are not gratified. . . . I am resolved that Colonel Frémont shall be tried as all other officers are tried against whom charges are preferred. I will grant him no favors or privileges which I would not grant to any other officer even though I should incur his displeasure and that of his friends by refusing to do so.

Before October ended William Carey Jones had joined his father-in-law as one of Frémont's defense counsel. The Senator and Jones sent the *Washington National Intelligencer* (according to them, "the only paper in the city . . . which publishes ample reports of the trial of Lieut. Colonel Frémont") a copy of their complaint to the Adjutant General about letters in the press which they charged had been written by Major Emory and Lieutenant Colonel Cooke. Largely because of those newspaper articles, counsel represented that their client should be tried for numerous other alleged offenses, such as having commenced hostilities against the Mexican authorities without instructions from his government before he learned of the outbreak of war, for all of his conduct during said hostilities, and particularly for raising the California Battalion, for the pardon of Don Jesus Pico, and for the Treaty of Cahuenga. Even the challenge to a duel given Colonel Mason must be investigated "for the good of the service."

The Adjutant General in a letter to Messrs. Benton and Jones on October 27 took the very sensible view that no evidence had been lodged with his office in support of the additional charges which Frémont and his counsel wished to have preferred against him. For once that official departed from the diplomatic language of officialdom and quite bluntly told Frémont's counsel that "it is certainly not to be understood that you believe them (the new charges urged by Benton and Jones) to be well founded. . . . it appears that incumbering the record with such charges would be useless, not to say improper." The Adjutant General also demolished the charge that Frémont had not had time to summon witnesses, prepare his defense, etc. The accused had advised the War Department that he would be ready for trial in thirty days. The date fixed for the court-martial was more distant than that. If the accused now needed longer time, or required the presence of witnesses at remote locations, let him name such witnesses and request the longer time.

One of the oft-repeated grievances of Frémont was that somebody in the War Department, if not Kearny himself, broadened the latter's single charge of mutiny into three charges, with several specifications in support of each. This complaint is the more amazing when we find first Benton and then the accused himself urging and in fact demanding that many other charges be added! Other charges were later added, but they were not the ones the defense requested. Allan Nevins may well be correct in his opinion that Frémont might very likely have escaped conviction on the single charge of mutiny. But he and his counsel clamored so loudly for more charges that two more were added. Unhappily for the defendant and his overzealous father-in-law, those two were: disobedience of the lawful command of his superior officer and conduct to the prejudice of good order and military discipline.

At the Cabinet meeting on October 26 the Frémont case was again the chief business. The claim of the accused that he be tried on all the additional grounds was not well received. More reasonable was his request that the place of trial be transferred from Fortress Monroe to Washington. To quote Polk about this Cabinet meeting: "As Senator Benton manifests much excitement on the subject, it was resolved that the Cabinet meet again to consider the answer to be prepared by the Secretary of War." Then with strange naïveté Polk wrote: "I know of no reason why this case should produce more interest or excitement than the trial of any other officer charged with a military offense . . . . I think he (Benton) is pursuing a mistaken policy so far as Colonel Frémont is concerned."

One's sympathy goes out to the harried President when he wrote: "I will do my duty in the case without favor or affection . . . it will be very difficult to avoid giving offense to Senator Benton. . . . I shall have the consciousness of having done my duty to the public and justice to Colonel Frémont and more than that I cannot do." Probably these vexations were uppermost in Polk's mind when he wrote in his diary on November 2, 1847. That date was not only his birthday, but also marked the opening of John C. Frémont's trial—one of the most famous courts-martial in American history: "I am fifty two years old today—have passed through two-thirds of my Presidential term and most heartily wish the remaining one-third was over for I am sincerely desirous to have the enjoyment of retirement in private life." Perhaps he was even ready to agree with Henry Clay whom he had defeated in the Presidential election of 1844. Clay had said, "I would rather be right than be President."

20. Witness on Trial

THERE HAVE BEEN MANY REFERENCES in this narrative to "the proceedings of the court-martial in the trial of Lieutenant Colonel John
C. Frémont." If thereby the author may have seemed to anticipate
the story, it was because those proceedings were the best and sometimes our only source of knowledge of numerous events. Frequently
incidents that were trivial in themselves attained importance because
of their inclusion in the official record. In dealing with the court-
martial now, repetition will be avoided as far as possible. This chapter is intended not to chronicle what went on in the courtroom between November 2, 1847, and January 31, 1848, but to bring into
focus the writer's study of the testimony. Bernard De Voto has rendered a very searching judgment on many previous accounts of the
trial: "Recent treatments of Frémont have *consulted* but not *studied*
it (the proceedings)." [The italics are mine.]

In one sense the attention paid Frémont's court-martial by American historians is justified. Stephen Kearny's life exhibited some of
the characteristics of Greek tragedy. Conscientious performance of
duties had won recognition in the pattern of the conventional American success story. But in the fall of 1846—to revert to our dramatic
figure—it suddenly seemed that some malevolent force intervened
and attempted to overthrow the work of more than a half-century
of living. So implacably was this man harassed during the last two
years of his life that a Euripides would have suspected the agency

of the Fates or Furies. Since a drama demands a climax, the trial of Frémont marked the culmination of the struggle.

The order of September 27 had named Fortress Monroe, Virginia, as the place for the court-martial. Senator Benton railed that it was "an island in the sea" deliberately chosen for its inaccessibility by Frémont's enemies to make his defense more difficult. Not a shred of evidence indicates that Kearny had any part in its selection. No official opposition developed, and by order of October 28 the arsenal at Washington was designated for the trial.

Brigadier General G. M. Brooke was named president of the court, and Captain J. F. Lee, the judge advocate. Twelve other officers composed the bench of judges—three colonels, five lieutenant colonels, and four majors. They met at noon on November 2, in the old Washington arsenal. It was a large, shabby, wooden structure, but the chamber assigned for a courtroom would only hold two hundred persons. It had a high, domed ceiling with windows near the roof that provided a gloomy light appropriate to such somber proceedings.

The accused and his counsel sat before a side table. Among the spectators was Jessie Benton Frémont, wearing a wine-colored costume and a bonnet of burgundy velvet. Her sister, dressed in bright blue, sat beside her. In this hall where lights and shadows fell aslant the rows of spectators, gold braid glittered on the dress uniforms of the officers in attendance. General Kearny, of course, headed a group of witnesses for the prosecution, looking "solemn, stern and inflexible" according to one reporter. By contrast, the accused "appeared as if writing at his campfire in the mountains." Captain Turner sat with General Kearny. The charges were read by the judge advocate. The accused formally pleaded "not guilty."

Previous mention has been made of Irving Stone's novel *Immortal Wife*, the story of Jessie Benton Frémont. Hers was an exciting career; she took part in many thrilling adventures. Mr. Stone is admittedly an entertaining writer. It is not because of any lack in his narrative or descriptive powers that I sound a note of warning about this book. But one who wishes to know the true story of John C. Frémont's troubles with General Kearny, and particularly a factual account of the court-martial itself, should not seek them in the pages of *Immortal Wife*. It tells a melodramatic tale, but in several particulars its trial scene is quite at variance with the recorded facts.

In an earlier chapter, comment was made on the dramatic license taken by Mr. Stone about the howitzer incident in St. Louis in 1843. He uses the same device later in the novel. He has Jessie Frémont seek out General Kearny shortly before her husband's trial. Seven or eight pages are devoted to their very tense and emotion-charged interview. Mrs. Frémont pleads with the General to drop the prosecution. He tries to show her that his duty outweighs his personal feeling and refuses. He reminds her somewhat accusingly of how guilty both she and her husband were in the matter of Colonel Abert's intercepted letter about the borrowed howitzer. She reproaches the General with the memory of their long friendship. Both make some speeches that sound authentic; Mr. Stone has carefully studied his characters. However, he makes the General so inflexible and obdurate that I suspect the novelist imbibed too deeply of the weird brew concocted by Benton, Justin Smith, and the 1856 Frémont campaign biographers. To my knowledge there is no reference to such an interview in any other book nor in any letters or official papers of the period. The meeting of General Kearny and Mrs. Frémont could have happened without any written record being preserved, but this writer is more than doubtful that it ever occurred.

My skepticism is the greater because a few pages later Mr. Stone introduces entirely fictitious incidents into the trial. Abundant written records run directly counter to the novel. Describing the opening session of the court-martial, he says Kit Carson was present in the courtroom. Several pages later he has Frémont, in the conduct of his own defense, call Carson to the witness stand. Carson then testifies to a certain episode that was actually in dispute between Kearny and Frémont. Carson of course corroborates Frémont. This is not dramatic license but a falsification of history. In the 447 pages of the official record of the court-martial, there is not one line of testimony by Christopher Carson on any subject whatsoever. Carson was not even present. On page 231 of the proceedings appears a statement by Frémont himself about certain activities of Carson in which the accused says: "The fact of Mr. Carson's present absence in California having been proved . . . ." Recalling Mr. De Voto's strictures on "recent treatments of Frémont," it would seem that we are here confronted with an instance where the court-martial proceedings were neither consulted nor studied.

If anyone still doubts Carson's absence from Frémont's trial, let him read the scout's autobiography edited by Milo Quaife. In this narrative, Kit accounts for his whereabouts throughout the fall and winter of 1847–48 in careful detail:

> We arrived at Los Angeles in October (1847) and from there went to Monterey to deliver the despatches to Colonel Mason, the officer in command . . . . I passed the greater part of the winter in charge of a detachment of twenty-five men guarding the Tejon Pass. . . . In the spring I was again ordered to Washington as the bearer of despatches.

A footnote states he left Los Angeles on May 4, 1848. Catherine Coffin Phillips in her life of Jessie Benton Frémont states that Carson was present in the courtroom, though she does not place him on the witness stand and cause sworn testimony to issue from his mouth. Mr. Stone acknowledges Mrs. Phillips as one of his sources and apparently accepted her erroneous assertion of Carson's presence.

Returning to the trial itself, the first (and original) charge of "mutiny" had eleven specifications supporting it. The second charge of "disobedience of the lawful command of his superior officer" had seven, and the third charge of "conduct to the prejudice of good order and military discipline" had five specifications. The twenty-three specifications fill that same number of closely printed pages. The second and third charges were based on some of the specifications enumerated under the first charge. To summarize them all, the charges started with Frémont's refusal in January to recognize Kearny's authority and to obey him then. Among several other specific acts of disobedience was the astonishing order given Captain Owens "to take orders" from no other officer and to refuse delivery of the howitzers. Frémont's repeated failures and ultimate refusal to muster out the California Battalion were cited, as was his own failure to proceed to Monterey despite repeated orders from General Kearny.

It would seem that all that was necessary at the trial was to prove or disprove these facts and determine whether they constituted offenses. Kearny was justified in predicting to Cooke that the evidence would be largely documentary. The proceedings are filled with copies of letters and orders directly bearing on the matters at issue. Even though events had belied Captain Turner's prophecy that Benton's influence would prevent Frémont's arrest or trial, that same influence—or fear of it—had its effect on the members of the court. From the outset they allowed the defense unparalleled latitude, so that it departed from the written evidence and wandered far afield to impugn the motives of the prosecution.

To quote Bernard De Voto's penetrating summation of the case:

They (the court) permitted Fremont and Benton . . . to turn a military trial into a political circus. . . . Here at a trial designed to assess his actions on the fringe of empire, was created a figure of pure advertising. . . . A creature of oratory and newsprint . . . . It was enough to convince innumerable people born since the advertising stopped and its proprietors died, so that you will find it in the instruction given our children. The report of that trial is a case study in the dynamics of reputation.

On the first day, the president of the court announced that application had been made to admit reporters. The accused quickly waived any benefits which the exclusion of the reporters might have meant to him. Frémont must have found it difficult to preserve a dignified demeanor; he and his counsel would have moved heaven and earth to insure the presence of newspapermen. The court solemnly declined to sanction or approve publication of its proceedings, but did not exclude the reporters.

The fourth estate did not take the court's ruling too seriously. Comments in both news and editorial columns reflect the public's reaction. As the trial dragged on, the tone of most of these articles changed radically. In the beginning, many were moderate, even neutral, in the views expressed as: "It must be understood that no charges have been preferred against any of these officers (Kearny, Frémont or Stockton) for a dereliction of duty. Probably no three officers ever had such dangerous, difficult duties to discharge. It is a mere difference in a claim of rank . . . . Colonel Frémont is a most scientific and valued officer." Another said: "As it is said that General Kearny has never undertaken anything in which he has failed, there would be small chance for Frémont, if it were not known that he, too, has been successful in everything he has undertaken, which makes the case exceedingly interesting." Four days later the same reporter wrote: "We believe that the testimony of General Kearny cannot easily be invalidated. He is proverbial in the army as an unimpeachable soldier. Still the rebuttal evidence of Commodore Stockton will go to show if we mistake not that he, and not Frémont, is the officer responsible for the exercise of authority assumed by Frémont in disregard of the remonstrances of General Kearny."

Kearny as the prosecution's first witness identified the many documents in the case—his own instructions from the War Department, his orders to Lieutenant Colonel Frémont, and the latter's various letters to him. Then he briefly related his famous interview with Frémont on January 17 when the latter declined to obey him.

In cross-examining the General, Frémont presented the first of many formal written addresses. He argued that since the accused had acted under Commodore Stockton's orders, the Commodore was really being tried in the person of Frémont. The defense announced that it was going "to impeach the motives of the prosecutor (Kearny) by showing his acts and conduct towards me during a period of six months and twenty-one days of time and over a distance of about three thousand miles of traveling."

From that moment Frémont and his counsel adopted the well-known military principle that the best defense is a bold offensive. They shifted attention from the charges against the accused, and with only infrequent and faltering protests from the judge advocate or court, proceeded to place General Kearny on trial. He had to defend almost everything he had done from the moment he met Kit Carson at Socorro. Not only did this deflect the limelight from Frémont's own actions, but it placed General Kearny at a great disadvantage. Frémont was no mean advocate of his own cause and in addition had two wily legal minds to reinforce him. Kearny, since nominally only a witness, had no counsel. Having expected that the trial would largely depend on the written documents, he was not prepared for the tactics of the defense. The judge advocate could have come more aggressively to his aid but seemed never to realize that the defense had boldly seized the initiative. Conscientious Captain Lee was merely correct and plodding in a situation that demanded courage and assertiveness.

Before General Kearny left the stand that first day he found himself plied with questions such as: When did he decide to arrest Frémont? When did he tell him of his intention? Why did he not inform Senator Benton of his purpose? What force had he planned to take to California before he met Kit Carson? What proportion consisted of the Mormon Battalion? Why did he reduce the size of that force? Why did he go on to California after meeting Carson? Why had he countermanded the orders given Carson by Stockton and Frémont to carry their dispatches to Washington?

In a trial of John C. Frémont, what relevancy was there to such questions as: On entering California, did General Kearny encounter a detachment from Commodore Stockton, etc., etc.? Where and when did he meet it and who commanded it? Did he engage in an action with the Californians before he got to San Diego, and how large was their force? Then followed the question to which the others had all been leading: "Did you lose cannon in that action, and *was it afterwards recovered* and by whom?" [The italics are mine.] Tardily a member of the court objected to the irrelevancy of this question.

At the next session Frémont dilated at great length on an army's grief at losing a cannon and its exultation on its recovery. Although he, the accused, had retaken Kearny's lost howitzer at Cahuenga, Kearny had not formally reported that fact to the government. This "showed the state of his temper towards me." Thus, with artfully twisted logic, Frémont argued that such prejudice on Kearny's part gravely undermined the validity of any charges brought by the General against him. Never did the accused show the remotest connection between the question he had put to Kearny and the offenses with which he, himself, was charged. Amazingly, none of the court

353

seemed to notice that omission. Though allowing the question, the judge advocate advised the General that the inquiry about the lost cannon imputed official misconduct to him. Under the rules, Kearny could object to it.

Repeatedly it has been said that General Kearny was a poor witness, but on this occasion, certainly no one could criticize him. His answer to Captain Lee's cautionary advice was straightforward: "There is no question which the accused can put to me, but what I shall be most willing and most free to answer." He proceeded to tell how during the heat of battle, the mules became unmanageable and dashed off with the howitzer into the Californian ranks. After the Treaty of Cahuenga, Frémont had informed the General that he had taken two cannons from the Californians, but never by word or letter had he identified them to Kearny. Even now the latter only knew by rumor that one of them was the howitzer lost at San Pasqual. Presently the accused asked whether the General had seen the lost howitzer in front of Frémont's headquarters in Los Angeles? Did not the General ask him about the guns there? One of the specifications to the first charge referred to Frémont's refusal to give up two cannons, "brought by the 1st Dragoons from Fort Leavenworth, and then at San Gabriel." Hoping to embarrass the General, the accused asked him to explain what cannons were referred to and how they had gotten from Fort Leavenworth to San Gabriel. Now the General pointed out for the first of many times that he had not drawn the present charges nor the alterations made in them.

For over a week the slanted questions continued—with veiled meanings, with hints reflecting not only on the General's judgment but at times even on his basic integrity as a soldier. Even the scant references to the acts of which the accused was charged carried imputations against General Kearny's part in them. Long hours of such tactics were bound to arouse the anger of the witness. One must conclude that was the deliberate intention of the defense.

During the second week Frémont filed another lengthy paper. It argued that since Kearny got into difficulty at San Pasqual and had been rescued by Stockton, it naturally followed that the General had not come in accordance with his instructions to conquer the territory. Stockton had already done so, else how could he have succored

Kearny? Moreover, Kearny had departed from his instructions to take an army to California when he reduced it to a small escort. (*There was no mention about whose premature and mistaken dispatches had influenced his decision.*) Frémont even argued that Kearny only went to California because he wished to be its governor! At this point General Kearny respectfully requested permission to comment that he had gone there pursuant to instructions given him by the War Department on June 3 and 18, 1846, as well as by the letter from Colonel Benton previously mentioned. Laboriously the defendant reasoned from these premises that since the General had not come to conquer as instructed, and had not conquered the country, the justification for all his orders to Frémont was removed and thus those orders had become invalid.

It was a long and tenuous thread of argument. Its reiteration increases our wonder that the court did not snap it asunder well before the end of January, 1848. Even greater is one's amazement that down to this day, Frémont's champions rail about the unfairness of the trial and the prejudice of the court against him. Unfair it certainly was, but the unfairness was in the rough handling of the prosecution's chief witness. Instead of showing prejudice *against* Frémont, the court through several sessions leaned over backward to give free rein to the defense. The press sensed the influence of Benton. One reporter observed:

Colonel Benton is never so pleased as when his hands are full of business; and the heavier the task, the more it is to his liking. In this case of Fremont he is positively in clover . . . . He is ever ready to take up the "glittering spear and shield" when his country or his friends, or his family demand it . . . . If you touch his friends, you bring the old war horse down on you.

Only on the eighth day did Captain Lee warn the defense that he would insist that the cross-examination be confined "to matters which relate to the case under trial." By that time the questions propounded by the defendant had become encyclopedic.

While General Kearny was wary and at times appeared to advantage by reminding the judges of the basic soundness of his position—the orders of his own superiors—the long harassment visibly told upon him. He made his first serious error when questioned about Frémont's call upon him in Los Angeles on January 17, 1847. He was asked about a letter delivered to his quarters just after Frémont entered the room. Who was the person who brought it? The General replied that he did not know the person, had never seen him before nor probably since.

Quickly the adroit inquisitor seized this advantage: "Was it not Mr. Christopher Carson?" The General answered "I think not." Later Frémont had no difficulty in proving that the bearer of the letter *was* Carson. The defendant made the most of this slip. Kearny knew Carson well so the denial sadly reflected upon his memory. In an argument filed near the end of the trial, Frémont drove the point home that General Kearny had here exhibited "an infirmity of memory almost amounting to no memory at all." In all fairness we admit that Kearny suffered a lapse of memory—but whether the messenger was Kit Carson or not was entirely immaterial to the issues. This incident became an argument against reliance on Kearny's other uncorroborated testimony. Three days later the General's own striving for accuracy strengthened the feeling that his memory was unreliable. At the opening of each session, the proceedings of the previous day's hearing were read. On this occasion Kearny sought to modify a negative answer by adding "to the best of my recollection."

Even this was not so damaging as his forgetfulness two days afterward. In an earlier chapter, it was shown that Kearny knew that Commodore Shubrick had written Frémont on February 23, 1847, about the November 5 instructions, and that the General specifically mentioned that circumstance in a letter to Commodore Biddle. Now *he* not only admitted that he had not informed Frémont of the new instructions, but failed to recall either Shubrick's letter or the references to it in his own letter to Commodore Biddle, and in the official charges against Frémont.

Memory, reason, and judgment have limits of endurance. We must conclude that the constant heckling and badgering of the witness had undermined the General's self-possession. If the defense did not deliberately aim at such a result, it appears that generations before Nazis and Communists perfected techniques of torment, General Kearny was the victim of very similar tactics.

Over a month later, denial by another witness helped to confirm the unwarranted impression with posterity that no one ever told Frémont of the "new orders" from Washington. Owl Russell, while on the stand for the defense, was asked whether Shubrick, Biddle, Kearny, "or any other person" had informed Frémont that Kearny had been confirmed in command of both military and civil authority. As Frémont's secretary of state, Russell himself should have known of Shubrick's letter of February 23, but unaccountably, he answered in the negative.

Philip St. George Cooke had been about to depart from Veracruz for the front when orders reached him to return to testify in the court-martial. Here was the prosecution's best witness to the cannon episode at San Gabriel. His account was the most damning proof that Frémont was guilty under all three of the charges. His cross-examination, if conducted with any semblance of propriety, must have confined itself chiefly to the field of Cooke's direct testimony. Instead, the accused was soon asking when Cooke learned of Kearny's plan to arrest Frémont, when was he told that he was to be a witness, had he ever written anything in the newspapers about the case, was he the author of a letter signed "Justice," published in the *Missouri Republican*? This long "Justice" letter was read into the record, but Cooke was not permitted to answer the question. The author of "Justice" (very probably it *was* Cooke) had stated facts but plainly expressed his disapproval of Frémont's conduct. The court's action barring Cooke from answering about the authorship of the letter may have been legally correct, but the effect was blundering since the letter had been read. Under the ruling Cooke had no opportunity to verify the facts alleged in the letter, but the defense was supplied with ample basis for asserting there was a plot to slander Frémont by clandestine publications.

With similar guile, Cooke was asked in cross-examination if he had tried to secure Frémont's post with the regiment of Mounted Rifles. There was not a shadow of truth in this allegation. The question was plainly irrelevant so Cooke was not permitted to clear

357

his good name by entering a denial. Thus did the defense manufacture material for the case they were trying, with the public as the jury, where John C. Frémont would be cast in the role of a persecuted hero, assailed by sinister forces behind General Kearny.

For six days the defendant roamed at will over many areas. That portion of the proceedings fills twenty-four pages of the record, yet one must search closely for matter relevant to the charges of which he stood accused.

In the same spirit, the defense summoned Lieutenant Colonel Emory in order to charge him with having written letters injurious to Frémont. Some of these had been signed by Emory. The court would not permit questions about these communications, but still the defense managed to read three of them into the record. Only one bore Emory's signature. Despite repeated rulings against such questions, Frémont continued to probe the authorship of each letter. Once, before the court could rule against the question, Emory admitted he had signed a certain communication. Regardless of the court's adverse rulings, this made good propaganda for the defense in its charges of a conspiracy against the Pathfinder. Emory was also asked many questions that cast a doubt on General Kearny's authority to command in December, 1846, and January, 1847.

The few surviving personal letters of Kearny include one to his brother-in-law Lieutenant Radford on November 28. He expressed the hope that the court-martial would soon be over. He told William he would remain in Washington until after the court adjourned:

> ... to see that Colonel Benton shall not exercise any undue influence to set aside the verdict of the court if unfavorable to his son-in-law. The difficulty between Commodore S(tockton) and myself has been adjusted. I wrote to him asking if he alluded to me in his letter of November 3rd to the editors of the "Republican." He replied that he did not. We have since that time twice met in the street and we salute each other. He says the affair between us is amicably and honorably adjusted to both parties. Colonel Benton will be very disappointed in the testimony of Commodore S as I think when he hears it. I have been led to believe that it will be much more against the defense than in its favor.

From old files of New Orleans and St. Louis papers we can piece together the facts about that letter in the *Missouri Republican*:

Commodore Stockton . . . reached St. Louis on (November 4th) as we learn from the "Republican" of that city. . . . The editors of the "Republican" had an interview with the Commodore and extract a portion of the impressions they derived from him on some disputed points. Commodore Stockton in the conquest of California acted upon his own responsibility. He claims that this was accomplished before the arrival of General Kearny and . . . that the conditional powers vested in General Kearny were inoperative . . . . The "Republican" appends the following from the Commodore written in the worst taste, in our opinion. The insinuations in it derogatory to General Kearny will meet with no sympathetic response from the country. We are compelled to give it as a part of the history of the times, but for the Commodore's sake we wish the letter had not been written:

Steamboat Meteor,
Nov. 3, 1847.
Editor Missouri Republican—I have not yet seen the papers but I am informed that it has been stated in yours, as well as in other newspapers in the United States that I was not commander-in-chief of the U. S. forces in California. My reply to the editor of the Californian whom it turned out, was the mere cat's paw, with the accompanying letter and by all the staff officers then in California, settled the matter there.

I now send the same paper to you and request that you will produce the same result here.

My respect for the Government and the people of the United States will not permit me to characterize such unworthy attempts in the manner they deserve, but those who have been guilty of misrepresentation will not go unwhipped of justice.

I have been forced quite unwillingly before the public in self-defense, and if it should so be that the misstatements, by which the second in command has been converted into commander in chief, have not arisen from any malus animus, but simply from a confusion of ideas on the field of battle, nevertheless I will be excused for having written this letter without further information on the subject because I wish the people of Missouri, who have treated me with so much

359

consideration and kindness, should be informed that I have nailed
one falsehood to the counter, and that I intend to back up all I have
said or written or others have said or written on my authority.

Faithfully your obedient servant,
R. F. Stockton.

The letters herein referred to are much more offensive to General
Kearny than this one but go to sustain the same positions.

In the *Republican*'s interview with the Commodore, he dwelt at
length on the story of the tender and refusal of command before the
march from San Diego to the Pueblo, and all the ensuing events
which we have earlier reviewed. Commodore Stockton reduced the
whole controversy to the single question of who commanded on the
march. He all but ignored the far more important issue of the right
to form a civil government in California—who had been vested with
and later confirmed in that authority by the President.

Two interesting letters among Archibald Gillespie's papers un-
doubtedly relate to the *rapprochement* alluded to in General
Kearny's letter. One is unsigned and undated, addressed to L. C.
Levin:

> Rumors being in circulation in relation to a settlement of the mis-
> understanding between Commodore Stockton and General Kearny,
> that you have been acting as the friend of both parties, will you do
> me the favor to state what has transpired if at liberty to do so so that
> I may be prepared to meet any misstatement. My position near Com-
> modore Stockton will I trust be my apology for this request.

Under date of December 4, 1847, L. C. Levin wrote Gillespie from
Washington:

> In answer to your letter of this day's date, asking to be informed
> concerning an interview between Commodore Stockton and myself,
> when I called on him in relation to his St. Louis letter of the 5th ult.,
> I beg to inform you that Commodore Stockton stated to me that the
> letter alluded to was intended to be applied and did apply to one and
> all persons who denied that he, Commodore Stockton, was Com-
> mander-in-Chief on the march from San Diego to the Ciudad de

Los Angeles and also during the battles of the 8th and 9th of January, or denied that he had sent orders or messages to General Kearny both on the march and in the battles or that the General had not complied with such orders or messages. That he, Commodore Stockton would not move one hair's breadth from the position assumed in that letter. I replied that General Kearny would not deny those things. The Commodore then said that his denunciations were altogether hypothetical and that if General Kearny would admit what he, Commodore Stockton, had contended for in that case, his letter of the 5th could of course have no reference to General Kearny. I then said to Commodore Stockton "suppose a letter acknowledging all you ask were sent to you by General Kearny, would you receive it in the spirit in which it is written?" He replied, "Mr. Levin, I must be approached in a friendly spirit such as you have brought with you and not in any belligerent attitude." I then said "if I should be the bearer of a letter from General Kearny and that letter should be an acknowledgment of all you ask, will you then say that you did not allude to him in your letter of the 5th?" He said "No" but that he would say that his letter can have no reference to General Kearny. I was the bearer of a satisfactory letter from General Kearny to Commodore Stockton and took from Commodore Stockton a satisfactory reply to General Kearny. [There is nothing in these papers that identifies L. C. Levin.]

During several days on the stand as a witness for the defense, Commodore Stockton proceeded to recite the history of the war in California. Much of his testimony had no bearing on the charges against Frémont. A Honolulu correspondent of Larkin's had called the Commodore "a bladder of wind." The court evidently shared this view for with growing impatience it urged that he get to the point. The relevant features of his testimony were, first, that he was commander in chief on the march from San Diego to Los Angeles and that General Kearny commanded the troops in the battles of January 8 and 9, "subject to the orders of him, the witness, as commander-in-chief on the field of battle as well as on the march." The second point testified to by Stockton should have forever silenced the noisy insistence that the "conflicting instructions" explained all the controversy between Kearny and Frémont, and therefore excused any irregularities in the latter's conduct. When asked whether he ever received the July 12, 1846, instructions sent by the Secretary of the Navy to Commodore Sloat, Stockton testified: "I have no recollection of having received these instructions." Lastly (and this too has been generally overlooked), when asked if he communicated the Navy Department's instructions of November 5, 1846, to Frémont, the Commodore replied without explanation or apology, "I did not."

As the sessions dragged on into the New Year, it is amazing to find more than eleven pages of the proceedings given over to Frémont's arguments over a question asked of Colonel Russell about his late night visit with General Kearny and Captain Turner on January 13. Comic opera could hardly improve on the question itself: "Please state whether you slept with or near General Kearny and whether the conversation in relation to Lieutenant Colonel Frémont . . . was kept up after lying down?" After nearly a full day of argument, the court ruled that it had no bearing on the trial!

Is it any wonder that one reporter wrote:

> This investigation is getting to be perfectly ridiculous. The court made a terrible fuss the other day and expelled a reporter because he happened to insert the word "merriment" in his report in relation to some sensation of the court upon a certain question being propounded to them. If this decision was correct, they will have to expel all the reporters, and the public as well; for really everybody is beginning to look upon the whole affair as perfectly absurd—so completely ridiculous and pettifogging has the affair now become. A quarrel which any two persons might settle in ten minutes, has occupied a body of respectable men . . . for an equal number of weeks and nothing has as yet been done.

Some of the press, too, was showing a growing impatience with Senator Benton's role:

> We can sympathize with his motive, even while we doubt the policy of his course, or condemn his exclusive devotion to family interest.— By some devoted and influential friends of Frémont, his daily presence at the court-martial is looked upon as rather a source of regret than a reason for congratulation. It is considered as intended to over-

awe—at least to influence—the decisions of that body. His manner is too abrupt, the tone of his voice too vivacious, his general bearing too little condescending, for such an assembly of men—all of whom have been accustomed to exercise more authority than he would ever undertake to assume.

On January 3 the record noted General Kearny's absence because of illness. He was in attendance again the next day. The prosecution had decided to recall him for more questioning. Scenting trouble, Frémont inquired of the judge advocate about who had written some questions the latter was preparing to ask. A paper filed by the defendant shortly afterward indicated Frémont believed that Kearny had composed the questions to be put to himself. The next day the president of the court admonished the defendant that it considered this question to the judge advocate "highly improper." In this strained atmosphere General Kearny, not yet fully recovered from his illness, returned to be questioned by the judge advocate concerning Gillespie's detention by Commodore Biddle at Monterey. Gillespie had told his version a few days before. In cross-examination the defendant twice insinuated that the General had framed the query. Each time the court disallowed his question.

Prolonged arguments over various points built up to an explosive climax on January 8. General Kearny asked to be heard. Striving to control his emotions, he said:

> I consider it due to the dignity of this court, and the high respect I entertain for it that I should here state that, on my last appearance before this court, when I was answering the questions propounded to me by this court, the senior counsel of the accused, Thomas H. Benton, of Missouri, sat in his place, making mouths and grimaces at me, which I considered were intended to offend, insult and to overawe me. I ask of this court no action on it, so far as I am concerned. I am fully capable of taking care of my own honor.

The audience gasped and the judges shifted uneasily. The very atmosphere was electric. The prosecution's chief witness, harried and badgered for weeks and now visibly ill, had turned on his tormentors. He had flung down the gauntlet in public to one of the doughtiest fighters of his age. Benton, who at sixteen had started his career as a duellist and had once fought a savage duel with Andrew Jackson, was at bay. His murderous wrath was evident to everyone. Catching his breath, the president of the court realized that he must not let the situation get out of hand. Assuming a calmness he was far from feeling, he said he very much regretted the charge made by General Kearny. He had not observed the Senator's behavior. He proceeded to read one of the Articles of War that prohibited the use of menacing words, signs, or gestures in the presence of a court-martial under penalty of punishment.

The massive Benton arose impressively. On the first day of the proceedings he said General Kearny had insinuated that Colonel Frémont had intentionally destroyed certain correspondence. Then, boomed Old Bullion, the General "had fixed his eyes upon Colonel Frémont . . . insultingly and fiendishly at him." One of the court interrupted: "Remarks reflecting upon the integrity of our proceedings are not . . . admissible." The Senator recognized that the court had power to punish but declared he must first be heard. Since the hour of adjournment was near, General Brooke as the presiding officer seized this chance to terminate the discussion, but allowed Benton to finish his statement. The Senator said that he had made up his mind if General Kearny "should attempt again to look down a prisoner, I would look at him. I did this day . . . look at General Kearny when he looked at Colonel Frémont, and I looked at him till his eyes fell—till they fell upon the floor." He protested the great respect he had for the court and sat down.

The president replied that he had observed General Kearny look toward Colonel Frémont during the trial not with an insulting expression but with what he thought was one of kindness and politeness. Kearny remarked: "I have never offered the slightest insult to Colonel Frémont, either here as a prisoner . . . or anywhere, or under any circumstances whatsoever." With this the tumultuous session adjourned.

Thomas H. Benton's unrestrained advocacy of Frémont had injured the latter's cause with some influential newspapers:

We must say, that from our personal observation, General Kearny has deported himself in court with a dignity, a grace and propriety that attracts general admiration. The manner of General Kearny was, in truth, the subject of general remark, and the self-possession with which he bore his severe and protracted cross-examination was a subject of public approval. We are a friend, also, of Colonel Benton. Altogether we like the man. . . . From the beginning of this trial . . . he has constantly increased the difficulties of the court, he has acted in a manner incompatible with the progress of the trial, and disadvantageous to the defence. He has acted as though he considered the court as a sworn tribunal of the enemies of the accused and not as impartial judges of the case. He has acted as if determined to exhaust the patience of the court or to reduce it to submission. The court on the other hand . . . has acted with a patience of investigation and a diligence . . . really commendable and worthy of the experienced officers composing the Board.

It is not surprising that this correspondent found drama in these proceedings:

We request those literary persons who are fond of Dickens, to read something today in our columns, which far outstrips the Pickwick papers . . . . It is a scene between Lieut. General (*sic*) Benton and Brig. General Kearny on the Frémont Court Martial. It is a most capital thing of the kind and we trust that some of our writers will dramatise it and bring it out at the Bowery or Chatham Theatre, immediately.

Contrary to this reporter's view, there was far more tragedy than comedy in the situation. Old friendships dissolved in hatred, a major figure on the national stage conducted a private war with deadly fury—these things called for the genius of a Greek tragedian or Shakespeare in the bitter mood of Timon of Athens. Shortly afterward, the same paper commented:

If the most bitter enemy of Mr. Benton had represented him as acting in this manner, he could hardly select a more cruel mode of attack, but . . . Mr. Benton . . . has reported himself as having acted in this rude, gross and ungentlemanly manner. Our correspondent observes that Colonel Benton had recommended General Kearny for appointment in California. This places Mr. Benton in a very bad light, if he could have looked to subserviency to himself from General Kearny, because of his recommendation. . . . While Mr. Benton gives license to his tongue to wound the feelings of a gentleman, he guarantees himself from all punishment for such conduct by giving it out that he will not fight. Is this the conduct of a brave man? . . . No one can admire such conduct, society itself would be destroyed if men thus ceased to act in the character and deportment of gentlemen.

Other newspapers also censured Benton's manners:

Many say that he will meet General Kearny if summoned to the field; but this is an error. Mr. Benton, at the time of his marriage, put himself under a pledge not to fight another duel. Again, it has been said that Colonel Frémont would take up the matter; but General Kearny has expressly disclaimed before the court any intention at any time, to insult Lieut. Colonel Frémont, and thus there can be no difficulty between them.

By this time at least one of the newspapers washed its hands of the whole affair:

We request our reporter at Washington to pick up his hat and leave the Court Martial . . . for it is not worthy of any further reporting. We entertain the highest respect for every member of that body . . . but we think this investigation has degenerated into one of the smallest and silliest pieces of trifling we have ever seen.

However, most of the historians of the period emphasize that a great segment of the press was fiercely partisan to the defendant. According to Thomas Kearny, biographer of General Philip Kearny, some of Frémont's champions descended to depths of vituperation and misrepresentation that have never been surpassed by American journalism. The author gives no citations for these references, and my research has not discovered their sources. The Know-Nothing party at that time was in its heyday and appealed to the militant anti-Catholicism then rampant. According to Thomas Kearny, the General was roundly abused, despite the plain fact of his Episcopalian faith, as an Irish immigrant and rabid papist.

By January 11 the defense had presented all its testimony but requested time to correct the record and prepare its concluding statement. Adjournment was taken to January 24, when Frémont commenced the reading of his long argument. (It fills eighty-one pages of the official proceedings.) His reading concluded on the twenty-seventh. During those last days the courtroom was crowded to capacity. Jessie Frémont and many of her personal friends were there. She had attended twenty-three sessions of the trial. Senators, public officials, and numerous representatives of the press thronged the room. Until the thirty-first, the court deliberated in private while everyone impatiently awaited the verdict.

Reporters are keen observers and sometimes accurate forecasters. One of them wrote: "The court . . . will condemn Colonel Frémont and the President will pardon him." During the deliberations another newsman risked a prophecy: "It is generally supposed that the decision of the Court is that Colonel Frémont is guilty of the charges specified and that he is broken. The President, it is said, is so much afraid of Mr. Benton that he will restore or promote his son-in-law. Democracy is a beautiful thing for big folks, but nobody has any business to be poor."

On January 31, 1848, the full court found John C. Frémont guilty of all three charges and of every one of the specifications under each charge. It sentenced the accused to be dismissed from the service.

Some of the court's remarks command our special interest because this narrative has given so much attention to the famous "conflicting instructions": "The court has found nothing conflicting in the orders and instructions of the Government; nothing impeaching the testimony on the part of the prosecution; nothing in fine, to qualify, in a legal sense, the resistance to authority of which the accused is convicted."

Sick and wearied in body and mind after the long ordeal, there was balm to Stephen Kearny in the concluding paragraph in the remarks accompanying the verdict: "The attempt to assail the leading witness for the prosecution has involved points not in issue, and to which the prosecution has brought no evidence. In the judgment of the court, his honor and character are unimpeached." The presiding officer and six other members of the court recommended that the President exercise clemency toward Frémont because of his earlier important professional services and because they were impressed with the embarrassing circumstances in which Frémont had been placed between two officers of superior rank.

The drama was now transferred to the White House. The verdict and sentence were considered by the Cabinet on February 12, 1848. The members all advised that Frémont not be dismissed. Could the President approve the verdict and yet remit the sentence? Polk, himself, doubted whether the crime of mutiny was proven by the record, although everyone agreed that Frémont was guilty of disobedience to orders. Opinions differed so the Cabinet delayed immediate action. The Secretary of State and Attorney General shared Polk's view that mutiny had not been proven. They wanted the President to disapprove the sentence. The Secretaries of War and Navy and the Postmaster General recommended approval but remission of the penalty. Illness prevented one member's attendance. Secretary of State Buchanan termed Kearny "pusillanimous" in yielding to Stockton. Secretary of War Marcy retorted that since the General had no forces to compel obedience, he had acted with great forbearance and propriety.

President Polk remained firm in his opinion that mutiny had not been proven but was equally sure the other two charges had been established. He would approve the sentence but remit the penalty. He would order Frémont released from arrest, direct him to resume his sword and report for duty. The verdict was so endorsed by the President on February 16. In his diary Polk did not overstate matters: "The decision in this case has been a painful and responsible duty. I have performed it according to my lights and am satisfied with what I have done."

James K. Polk may have been satisfied but John C. Frémont was not. He even broke on this point with his father-in-law. The latter favored acceptance of the President's clemency although forever afterward he denounced the verdict, the judges, and the prosecution.

From a mezzotint engraving in the Library of Congress;
taken from an original daguerreotype engraved by
J. B. Welch for *Graham's Magazine*
Courtesy U.C.L.A. Photographic Department

Major General Stephen Watts Kearny, during the period of the Mexican
War. He had been in command at Veracruz in 1848, but an illness
necessitated his return to Jefferson Barracks.

From a portrait by M. J. de Franca
Courtesy Mrs. Gerald Mihm

Mary Radford Kearny, devoted wife of the General, bore him eleven
children and outlived him by more than half a century.

Benton must have reviled himself when he realized that had he not insisted that more charges be filed, Frémont might now stand acquitted under the sole charge of mutiny. Smarting under the verdict, the convicted man declared he had done nothing to merit the finding, therefore he could not accept clemency and so admit the justice of the decision. Instead he resigned his commission on February 19.

Allan Nevins seems to share Frémont's disapproval of Polk's action: "Polk acted . . . with . . . narrow legal rectitude . . . and lack of any large generosity." I cannot agree with him. The easy and popular course, the smart thing politically, would have been to disapprove the verdict under all charges. James K. Polk, in this instance, rose above politics and acted against his own interests. There are times when duty demands legal rectitude, times when generosity would only condone flagrant insubordination. President Polk was actuated much as General Kearny was when he arrested Frémont. Each chose the hard and unpopular alternative, and because of these decisions the United States Army—and the nation it serves—have had a loftier tradition of discipline and obedience.

The public was by no means unanimous in its disapproval of the verdict. During the trial one of Larkin's correspondents had shrewdly predicted: "He (Frémont) will undoubtedly be condemned but not punished though he ought to be to the full extent of the law and Stockton also." Writing again the following fall, the same man bluntly declared: "Frémont as you know was condemned by the Court Martial and guilty too . . . . Beware of him, he is not all he has been cracked up to be."

One observation about the court itself seems in order. For over a century the assertion has been almost unchallenged that West Point influence prompted the prosecution of Frémont. (Sometimes "persecution" has been the word.) We commented earlier that General Kearny was not a West Pointer. Apparently none of the critics has investigated the status of the judges at the court-martial. Of the fourteen officers involved, nine were not West Pointers, but five were graduates of the United States Military Academy. In terms of the judges the score is nine to four—Captain Lee, the judge advocate, was a graduate of West Point. *All* the officers of higher rank were non-West Pointers, so any fair-minded observer must believe the West Point influence was far less than has long been popularly supposed. Otherwise we must conclude that one lieutenant colonel, three majors, and a captain were able to dominate the minds of a brigadier general, three colonels, four lieutenant colonels, and a major.

Bernard De Voto properly described this court-martial as "a case study in the dynamics of reputation." There the legend was created of a modern knight errant who was being persecuted by a jealous clique of West Pointers, resentful and conspiring to rob him of his laurels because they were dull plodding figures who lacked the spark to fire men's imaginations. Guilty of insubordination? Perhaps that was technically true, but one commentator shrewdly noted that Americans in the 1840's did not view insubordination as a very serious offense. Cardinal Goodwin in a keen analysis said that the defendant at the time of his sentence did not appreciate the prominence given him by the trial. However, Frémont must have soon observed that front-page stories were making him the hero of Western exploration. He was coming to personify Manifest Destiny. To expansion-minded Americans that meant he could have done no wrong.

Ere this belief had cooled in sober afterthought, Benton would make the welkin ring for thirteen days with his attack upon General Kearny, unparalleled for savage invective and reckless mendacity. Men who could believe Kearny half the villain portrayed by Benton were bound to admire Frémont the more. From this long perspective it is hard to decide which of the assaults on Kearny had the more enduring effect on his reputation. Was it the slurs at the court-martial, or Benton's denunciation before the Senate? A recent biographer of Philip St. George Cooke was only too correct when he wrote: "So successful was he (Benton) that Stephen Kearny's reputation was permanently damaged by his libels." If the present work can substantially repair that undeserved damage, it will have achieved its purpose.

Bancroft's unique place among California historians justifies quoting his estimate of the court-martial:

It was the . . . aim of Frémont and his friends to make the trial cover the entire field of California annals in 1846–47 so far as those annals were favorable to himself . . . They were disposed to make much of the errors and belittle the efforts of other officers . . . . For the jury they had in view, those questions not permitted to be answered, unsupported implications and arguments on what was to be proven by testimony not admitted were quite as effective as legitimate evidence . . . . It cannot be denied they won a victory—that the verdict of popular sympathy was in Frémont's favor. In that phase of the trial, the prosecution could do nothing but limit the extent of irrelevant testimony. Could they have known, however, and proved the facts revealed in this volume respecting the true character of Frémont's and Stockton's part in the conquest from the beginning, they would have had an easy road to victory over the pretending conquerors.

The hero-myth built around Frémont in 1848 has persisted to this day. Popular sympathy for the underdog dies hard. One writer a few years after his trial achieved the acme of understatement: "(Frémont) at Fort Leavenworth . . . was arrested by General Kearny, tried and condemned to lose his commission on account of some alleged breach of military discipline." This mood lived on into the Presidential campaign of 1856. Its pamphleteers and biographers of course warmed over everything that would arouse the public's emotion for their candidate. Like the stump orator, the political penman is never embarrassed by facts. Perhaps because Frémont was defeated in the election, these superheated enthusiasms lingered longer. There is always something appealing about the central figure of a lost cause. The official mistakes chargeable to the successful candidate cannot embarrass the panegyrist of his opponent. Writers partial to the Frémont legend proliferated. By the eighties they were grinding out this sort of travesty:

When he (Kearny) found Frémont already in place appointed by Stockton, he *applied* to Shubrick for the position. According to some authorities Shubrick and Kearny planned a method of disposing of Frémont by issuing a proclamation to the people *purporting* to be from President Polk . . . . This was a very sharp plan on the part of these two as it gave them the collection and disposition of the State funds . . . . Frémont with true courage was not to be intimidated by proclamations and held his office until March 11 when an *unjust* order from Washington came commanding him to muster his battalion into the regular service. [The italics are mine.]

That is a typical sample of the weirdly distorted "history" from which the next generation learned how great was John C. Frémont. Recently we have had the benefit of a close-up view of the man from a companion of his explorations. Charles Preuss was Frémont's cartographer on his first, second, and fourth expeditions. His journal has just been translated from its original German, and is a day-to-day account written on the spot and apparently never edited. Even allowing for obvious prejudice, Mr. Preuss describes Frémont as very unstable, obstinate, and temperamental. Terms such as "childishly passionate," "foolish lieutenant," and "that simpleton" frequently recur. According to Preuss, Frémont was a vain and moody individual prone to claim credit not due him.

Oddly enough, Frémont's mishaps and failures long after Stephen Kearny's death seem not to have dispelled the mirage of his heroic achievements. His fourth expedition, the winter after the court-martial, ended in such death and disaster as would have completely discredited any other explorer. His early Civil War days in Missouri were anything but successful. Even if adverse conditions beyond Frémont's control mitigated those failures, his defeats in West Virginia were of his own doing. His malodorous career as a railroad financier would have ruined an otherwise fine reputation, yet despite this more than dubious record, schools are still being named for the hero of a romance almost as imaginary as that of King Arthur. Only a few years ago a new municipality was incorporated out of several suburban areas in one county in California. With the wide world to choose from, the city fathers christened it Frémont, although the location is not connected with any incidents in his life, and it is highly possible he never set foot in the area. It would be interesting to compile a census of all the schools, parks, streets, and geographical landmarks named for this hero of a nineteenth-century myth.

In contrast is this sad commentary on human prejudices. Some years ago a granddaughter of Admiral William Radford (brother of Mary Kearny) made a strenuous effort to have a California mountain named for General Stephen Kearny. A relative wrote me that her attempt failed because "the Frémont faction was still too strong" in the state of which General Kearny was the first military governor.

21. Taps

General Kearny went to New York a few days after President Polk approved the verdict. That was destined to be his last visit to the land of his forebears. Shortly a letter arrived from the Adjutant General's office, directing him to go to Veracruz and join the main army in Mexico. It will be remembered that from California and later from Fort Leavenworth, Kearny had advised the War Department of his wish to be assigned to service in the field as soon as he had completed his duties in California. One letter had expressed willingness to go "wherever my services may be required," and the instructions received in New York directly answered this application.

The General immediately returned to Washington and was given orders to travel to Veracruz via Cincinnati and St. Louis in order to confer with recruiting officers. At Jefferson Barracks he was to assemble and send to Mexico as large a detachment of recruits and officers as he found immediately available for duty in the field. These tasks probably consumed some time since the General did not reach New Orleans until the end of March. Two letters tell of the stir created in that city by Kearny's arrival. A testimonial signed by many "prominent citizens" who "solicit your attendance at a public festival . . . wish to express their sentiments towards the commander of the Army of the North. [By what strange confusion had the heroic Army of the West had its course of empire altered?] and conqueror of New Mexico and California."

374

The proprietors of the St. Charles Theatre requested General Kearny to attend as guest of honor the first performance in New Orleans by the famous actress, Miss Julia Dean. The invitation expressed the "universal wish to behold the man who has so very essentially added to the splendour of the American Arms." General Twiggs was also to attend. General Kearny's brother-in-law must have accompanied him as far as New Orleans, for the invitation included Captain Radford. His stay in the Crescent City was of brief duration as, in company with Colonel A. H. Sevier, the American minister to Mexico, he arrived at Veracruz on April 7. There he found orders from the commanding general in Mexico City making him the commander at Veracruz, and hence its military governor. General Kearny immediately provided a strong escort to conduct Colonel Sevier to Mexico City.

Reporting his arrival, Kearny called the War Department's attention to its instructions that he "join the main army in Mexico." He was anxious to proceed to Mexico City himself, and the Adjutant General's office concurred. General Kearny had succeeded a Colonel Wilson who had commanded at the seaport before his arrival. Wilson was still available to resume his duties, and the Secretary of War suggested to Major General W. O. Butler, now commander in chief at the front, that Kearny join his forces. Word reached him that Butler felt it very desirable to have a general officer in command at Veracruz. If peace ensued there would be a large movement of troops through that port, but he would reconsider the matter if hostilities were resumed. Probably it seemed an unimportant detail to the command at Mexico City. For Stephen Kearny, however, it was to have tragic consequences.

The issue of peace—or war—was at this moment most uncertain. On September 14, 1847, after heavy fighting, Mexico City had been occupied by the American Army. Santa Anna had resigned as president, and the government of the defeated republic fell into chaos. Trist, the American envoy, had difficulty finding any responsible official with whom to negotiate. A peace treaty was drafted on February 2, 1848, and an armistice was finally agreed to on March 4 and 5. The United States Senate approved the treaty on March 10. However, at the time General Kearny assumed command at Veracruz, the Mexican government had not yet acted upon it. The General reported on April 9 that the Congress then trying to meet at Querétaro was making little progress. It was still short fifteen deputies and three senators of the number required to take legally binding action.

The populace throughout the occupied regions was uneasy. The armistice had brought only a lull in a land disrupted by war and beset by guerrillas who usually were nothing but bandits. This lawless element preyed far more upon their own countrymen than upon the American invaders. Such was the background of Kearny's first days at his new post. Although robberies and other outrages were frequent along the road connecting the capital with the Gulf, no untoward incident marred the peace in Veracruz. Not all the evildoers were Mexicans. Early in April, Kearny helped in the pursuit of an absconding American judge. The most pressing problem after the General's arrival was the disquietingly large number of sick soldiers at Veracruz. The unhealthiest season of the year was rapidly approaching. Major General Butler urged that all sick and wounded unlikely to make a quick recovery be shipped back to the United States as fast as transportation was made available. A week after he took charge, General Kearny was able to report that he had sent home about 170 such casualties and returned a siege train no longer needed in Veracruz. Every few days ships brought more recruits into the city, and these had to be dispatched to the main army.

The General learned that fifty-three new volunteers of a Louisiana battalion were confined in the Castle of San Juan de Ulloa for mutinous conduct. Investigation convinced Kearny that the prison had cooled these unruly spirits. Their promises to obey orders in future seemed genuine, and he therefore directed their release. Three days later a letter from the Secretary of War stated that he and the President desired the mutineers returned to duty. The General was glad to reply that he had anticipated their wishes.

While engaged in these routine tasks, Kearny soon became a victim of the unhealthy climate. Some twelve hundred Americans died at Veracruz between April and December, 1847, mainly victims of yellow fever and dysentery. The first intimation of the General's illness is in a letter his adjutant, Major J. H. La Motte, wrote to his wife on April 22: "The scourge that was so destructive last season will not it is thought be so fatal this . . . . Among the cases is General Kearny though his was not a severe case and he is getting better . . . . General Kearny has nearly recovered from his late attack."

Evidently Major La Motte was overly optimistic for two weeks later a letter to Kearny from General Butler's adjutant in Mexico City closes: "The General has understood unofficially that you have been sick since your arrival at Vera Cruz and he desires me to say that if your health requires it and you wish to do so, you can leave your station and come to this city. Should you leave, it is hoped you may be able to leave the command in the hands of an officer of experience." The bad news also reached Washington, for on May 9 the Adjutant General addressed General Butler in his own hand, urging him to carry out the Department's original plans for Kearny. It ended on an anxious note: "General Kearny has been very sick at Vera Cruz. I write in great haste." Then on May 12, Major La Motte wrote his wife: "General Kearny has been ordered to report to the imperial city and I am going with him at four P.M. tomorrow." Prior to his enforced trip to the healthier uplands of Mexico, Kearny probably had a brief visit with his old comrade in arms, Major General Winfield Scott. The latter had been recalled to the States and departed from Veracruz on May 1.

General Kearny arranged for Colonel Wilson to resume command at Veracruz on his departure. Evidently his journey to the capital was at a leisurely pace, for General Butler addressed him at Puebla on May 20. Mexico had approved the Treaty of Peace the day before, and Butler directed that all recruits be held at Puebla until further orders. General Kearny himself was to continue on into Mexico City. General Butler was busy with preparations for the evacuation of the Mexican capital and the ultimate departure of all the American armies from Mexico. When Kearny arrived on May 23 he was made military governor of Mexico City.

Butler's plan was to have the retiring troops start for the coast in separate divisions. The first began its march on May 30. The remaining divisions followed at two-day intervals. Jalapa was the point of concentration. Its location on the edge of the temperate

377

plateau made it a healthier stop than Veracruz. Only when transports actually arrived at the seaport were the regiments marched down into the steaming tropics. This precaution was necessary because in early May nearly one-fifth of all the forces under General Butler were on the sick list.

During the evacuation General Kearny commanded the second division of the regular army, which left Mexico City on the morning of June 6. Kearny's was next to the last unit to depart from the capital. The number of soldiers comprising the second division does not appear in the record, but it is quite possible that it was the largest body of troops ever under General Kearny's immediate command. With brief stops at Perote and Jalapa, Kearny was soon back at the coast. It required several days for him to embark all of his division, and he himself did not leave Veracruz until the evening of July 11. The ship on which he sailed arrived at New Orleans on July 17.

General Kearny's Mexican tour of duty lasted only three months and ten days. He saw no fighting and was responsible for no important policy decisions. Nothing but the performance of colorless routine occupied his time. Compared with a shorter period of service in New Mexico and one twice as long in California, this episode indeed seems anticlimactic. But we cannot write it off as such. The opportunity to win laurels was missing in both Veracruz and Mexico City, but Kearny's evil genius still had more woe in store for him. He carried home a grim reminder of Mexico. Yellow fever had claimed him for its own. He seemed to make a partial recovery, but the ordeal left seeds of some tropical malady. Several contemporaries described it as vomito. Even today amoebic disorders contracted in the Torrid Zone baffle medical science. A century ago all physicians were helpless before them.

The letter to the Adjutant General in which Kearny reported his arrival at Fort Leavenworth in August, 1847, was in neat, firm handwriting. The similar advice of July 18, 1848, telling that he had reached New Orleans was in the faltering script of a very sick man. It said he was leaving immediately for Jefferson Barracks. On arrival there he found orders making him once more a department commander with headquarters at that post. General Kearny assumed command of the Sixth Military Department on July 30, 1848. The vigor with which he had undertaken similar tasks in 1842 was now sadly missing. Officers who had long known him were startled by his loss of weight and sallow complexion. The whites of his eyes were a lackluster yellow, and instead of his customary erect military bearing, his shoulders sagged wearily.

At least he was home once more. Mary and his children were an added comfort now. A very real sacrifice exacted of every professional soldier is the enforced absences from his loved ones. His wife noticed his changed condition with alarm. To most of his children their father was a tall figure in uniform whom they only dimly recalled. (Two of the older boys were attending school in the East at this time.) Mrs. Kearny had special reasons for apprehension for in a few months she was to bear another child. She had long hoped that her husband would be with her. Now it seemed that he, himself, would require nursing. Her heart quailed as she contemplated the suddenly uncertain future.

At first the General tried to make light of his illness. Surely in a few days he would be able to resume his old activities. The circle of family friends who called to pay their respects shared his wife's concern as did the surgeons of the Medical Corps at the Barracks.

As the worry grew, one bit of news momentarily cheered the sick man. President Polk had sent to the Senate his nomination of Stephen Kearny for the brevet rank of major general, "for gallant conduct at San Pascual and for meritorious conduct in California and New Mexico." But soon even the joy in this recognition was soured by an answering outburst from Senator Benton. In the months since Frémont's sentence, Benton's hatred for General Kearny had only smouldered. Now this nomination triggered such an explosion as had never before been witnessed in the United States Senate. In an attempt to block confirmation of the President's nomination, Benton spewed forth his wrath for thirteen days. Once more he paraded all the facts most favorable to Frémont which had been adduced at the court-martial, while also dredging up much that had been excluded as irrelevant.

This outpouring of venomous hate fills sixty-three of the large, closely printed pages of the *Congressional Globe*. In previous chapters mention has been made of this speech. One extract well indicates its unbridled violence. Benton declared that while General Kearny was reviewing Frémont's party at Monterey, the General referred sarcastically to Frémont's comments that some of his horses were tenderfooted and needed shoeing for the journey to Missouri. Then, shouted the Senator:

> Frémont's hand, unobserved by any except Captain Owen who was near him, went up to his pistol in the holster. Happy had it been for Kearny, if he had drawn it and blown out his brains. It would have saved him from that black cloud of infamy which is now settling down upon him like the dark shades of night in the vale of death and which is soon to hide him forever from the view of all honorable men. Happy had it been for Kearny if he had then been killed! Unhappy for Frémont if he had killed him! But as that young man never made a mistake under any circumstances no matter how sudden or critical the occasion, so he made none then. The unconscious hand withdrew from the deadly weapon and Kearny lived to consummate his plots against Frémont.

As typical of Benton's reckless exaggeration, he stated that the elevation of Lake Tahoe is 8,000 feet (actually it is 6,225) and that San Francisco and Sacramento are nearly four hundred miles apart (less than one hundred miles separates them). In both instances the effect of the larger figures was to enhance the magnificence of Frémont's achievements.

Benton was one of the giants of the Senate. In vision and in the courage with which he met strong opposition he showed himself a statesman. He rendered great service to the republic and particularly to the West. Yet his stature in the long perspective of history is diminished because of this speech against Kearny. Despite the great influence he wielded in the upper chamber, despite his threats to filibuster, he could recruit no respectable support. When Benton had finished, the Senate voted to confirm the nomination! He must have realized that the vote against his harangue was a rebuke. How large was that vote? It seems strange that the official printed record of the Senate does not give it. "Nomination confirmed" appears in the journal as it would have read had there been no opposition. Did some influence exerted by the fiery senator from Missouri prevent the permanent recording of the extent of his defeat?

Such an attack was bound to react against its author. A Washington friend wrote Larkin: "Benton is considered as a sour, disappointed man and some even doubt his sanity. Certainly there is no more unpopular man in this city and his family are equally disliked." When writing his *Thirty Years' View* some time after Kearny's death, Benton made some wholly inadequate amends to the dead soldier's memory. He reiterated that the charges on which Frémont had been tried (Benton was still calling them "preposterously wicked . . . [they] were not the work of General Kearny but had been altered from his." He once more blamed West Point influences and "the clandestine sources of poison publications against (Frémont) which inflamed animosities and left the heats which these engendered to settle upon the head of General Kearny. Major Cooke and Lieutenant Emory were the chief springs of these publications." Benton referred to these paragraphs as "justice to the dead," but they sound more like very grudging admissions to appease his own guilty conscience.

On September 7, 1848, the Adjutant General's office issued a brevet major general's commission to Stephen Watts Kearny. Ordinarily that promotion would have brought great rejoicing to the Kearny household. But preceded by Benton's vilification of the General, the honor and recognition had too much the flavor of apples of Sodom. Kearny was a reserved and sensitive man. Benton's barbs sank deep and increased his despondency. Other officers might have unburdened themselves by letters to the newspapers to pillory their detractors. Even had his health permitted, Kearny could not have brought himself to such steps. It was a soldier's duty to perform the tasks assigned him without public expressions of either glorification or defense. Not a letter remains in which he expressed protest or resentment. Bernard De Voto voiced the thought of many historians that Benton's malice helped kill General Kearny. Major Swords denied this. Writing to Dr. Griffin after Kearny's death, he said: "He had the dysentery, the consequences of the yellow fever at Vera Cruz. Old Benton will swear he killed him which is not the case as his speech was kept from the Gen'l for fear of irritating him."

One would like to think that Swords was correct and that Stephen Kearny in his last days was spared the travail of that abuse, but from the widespread references to it in the press, that seems unlikely.

His figure was missing now from the parade ground at Jefferson Barracks. The regimental returns from that post for September stated that Major General Kearny was dangerously ill and that the physicians despaired of his recovery. The General's wife would not give up hope. A temporary rally encouraged her to write to some of the Kearnys in Newark that her husband was improving. This brought particular joy to Stephen's brother Philip. He, himself, had been dangerously ill but seemed to mend when he heard better news of Stephen. (Philip was to survive him by about six months.) He was so loyal to his younger brother that he discontinued his subscription to one of the Newark papers because "it has been afraid to support Stephen and has been silent." His daughter shared her father's devotion for in replying to Mary's letter, she wrote: "Tell dear Uncle, *if you* dare, that I say *he* has made such a name for the Kearny family, it will go down in history. I look upon *him* as *the ancestor* of the family."

Evidence that Stephen Kearny was still affectionately remembered by the dragoons at Fort Leavenworth reached the stricken man in September. I. L. Schnell, the "principal musician of the First Dragoons," sent him a musical tribute which he had composed and dedicated to General Kearny, "commemorative of your campaign to Santa Fé and California in which your *distinguished* skill and bravery in a campaign that is without a parallel, have won for you and those gallant officers and men under your command as much fame and glory as they have been honorable and beneficial to our common country."

Many years later a cousin of Mary Kearny's, William Clark Kennerly, recalled how as a young man of twenty-four he became the General's close companion during that fall of 1848. Kearny was taken out to stay at Persimmon Hill, the home of the Kennerlys. Perhaps his own house so full of children disturbed the sick man. Kennerly remembered that: "In the fine autumn weather the doctor wanted him to be in the country; so, when he began to tire of our place, I drove him on a round of visits to the country homes of our different relatives, remaining several days or perhaps a week where he found most interest." Strangely enough the ailing soldier's favorite spot in that hospitable neighborhood was the home of Major Meriwether Lewis Clark, his long-ago rival for the hand of Mary Radford. Here he seemed most comfortable and contented.

An incident of this period has been frequently recounted with varying interpretations. Probably we will never know the whole story. Realizing that his days were numbered, General Kearny sent a message by his physician to Jessie Frémont, requesting her to visit him. The son born to her in late July had recently died. Mrs. Frémont's response to the General's message is best told by one of her biographers:

> Perhaps if she had realized that he was on his death-bed, she would have felt different; but with the conviction that her child had been a victim of her own frightful anxieties and with its loss too fresh in mind, she sent word that she was sorry to learn of General Kearny's illness, but that no good could come of an interview, since a little grave lay between them.

We can only surmise what moved Kearny to send for his old friend. Some writers have believed he felt contrition for his course toward Frémont and wanted to ask forgiveness of his wife. Perhaps he did wish to explain his side of the controversy and do what he could to repair the breach in their friendship. For a man of his reserved nature, even his request that Mrs. Frémont visit him was a difficult gesture. Its rebuff must have sorely grieved the invalid. The pathos of this attempt at some degree of reconciliation still moves us. The warmer heart seems to have been his who extended the hand rather than hers who thrust it aside. Bernard De Voto, in mentioning this episode, called the lady beautiful but closed with Abraham Lincoln's word for her—"virago."

Irving Stone in *Immortal Wife* saw the drama in this situation and, in making the most of it, stretched dramatic license past the breaking point. The novelist has an army sergeant visit Jessie Frémont in western Missouri. The sergeant, one O'Leary—with a brogue—represents himself as a veteran of Kearny's march to California and claims to be the General's friend. (No name of O'Leary appears on the rosters of the dragoon companies that accompanied Kearny to the Pacific.) The sergeant has come in great haste because the General is dying. He bears a note which declares Jessie was right and General Kearny wrong. The trial was a deadful mistake. The writer asks her to come back so he can beg her forgiveness for the harm he has done her and her family. If she cannot come, will she not please send a message of forgiveness. If a character in fiction ever made a good deathbed repentance, this is it. The missive borne by lachrymose Sergeant O'Leary is calculated to fill our eyes with tears, as when the villain confesses his crimes on the last page of a novel.

But did General Kearny ever write such a message? This short letter is certainly unlike any written by Kearny that this author has ever seen. Its abject confession that he had been wrong in his whole course toward Frémont is violently out of character. No officer after more than thirty-five years of faithful service could so repudiate his own actions and standards. Dear as reconciliation with an old friend might have been, Kearny would not have sought it by denying the basic principles of his whole life as a soldier.

If the original of this purported letter exists, it would command an exceptional price among collectors. Before bidding high for it, however, they should be sure it is genuine. They should pay particular attention to the subscription of this letter. It is signed "Your old and devoted friend, Stephen Watts Kearny." The writer has examined in letter books, microfilms, photostats, and typescripts both originals and copies of hundreds of letters by General Kearny, including a dozen or more of a purely personal character. Almost invariably he signed "S. W. Kearny." One very early letter used "Step. W. Kearny." In a few cases with his family, he used merely the initials "S.W.K." Even as solemn an instrument as the will which he executed in these same last days was signed "S. W. Kearny." Never have I seen a letter signed "Stephen Watts Kearny"!

Mr. Stone closes his version by having Mrs. Frémont state that forgiveness was impossible because of the open grave between them. Actually the novelist is less kind to his heroine than the biographer.

He makes her coldly obdurate even though she knew the General was dying.

Ere we take our final leave of this turbulent family, mention must be made of the continuing animosity of John C. Frémont himself. Cardinal Goodwin's book contains a curious story that Frémont made a special trip to St. Louis in December, 1847, for the sole purpose of challenging Kearny to a duel, but that he found the latter was on his deathbed. An error is apparent here. In December, 1847, General Kearny was in attendance at the court-martial in Washington. In the same month a year later (if the error is in the year) he was dead.

The story seems confirmed by the following old newspaper clipping preserved for generations in the General's family. Unfortunately the name and date of the publication were not saved, but the context indicates it appeared in St. Louis soon after the General's death:

Gen. Kearny—Col. Frémont.—An article appeared in a paper of this city, shortly after the death of Gen. Kearny, announcing that, before that event, a message was communicated from Col. Frémont to Gen. Kearny, of a conciliatory character, and some credit has been claimed for Col. Frémont for his magnanimity in this matter. The annexed Card has reference to that publication. It may be stated, in this connexion, that Col. Benton has published a statement, in which he denied that Colonel Frémont ever sent such a message as was made the foundation for the paragraphs, in the "Herald of Religious Liberty;" and he adds an important fact, until now unknown, that Col. Frémont visited St. Louis with the intention of challenging Gen. Kearny to mortal combat.

A Card

An article appeared in the "Herald of Religious Liberty" of the 9th November past, relative to the attitude existing between the late General Kearny and Lieut. Col. Frémont. The author of that communication has spoken unadvisedly or by false intelligence. I am authorized by Mrs. Kearny and his immediate attending physician, Dr. Wm Hammond, of the Army, to say, that no such message, or any other, relative to General K. and Lieut. Col. Frémont was ever delivered. Surgeon Wheaton of the Army brought such a message as

385

*coming from Col. Brant: it was delivered to Mrs. Kearny by him
and there it rested.*

JOHN D. RADFORD.

Colonel Brant was a long-time resident of St. Louis with whom
General Kearny had social and business contacts. This card raises
almost as many questions as it does answers. The record does not
mention any breach between the General and Colonel Brant. It is
not even clear whether the message from Brant had anything to do
with Frémont. However, when Frémont returned to St. Louis in
September, 1847, a card appeared in a local newspaper inviting those
who wished to call upon him to do so at Colonel Brant's residence.

Charles Preuss would not have found it hard to believe that Frémont journeyed to St. Louis to challenge Kearny to a duel. At Fort
Vancouver in 1843, when Frémont and his assistants expected to be
invited to a dinner where ladies would be present, the explorer
strongly urged that Preuss cut off his beard to make himself pre-
sentable. When the cartographer rejected the idea, Frémont became
very angry and threatened to challenge him to a duel.

Frémont and all that his name implied was unimportant now to
the stricken General. He was not afraid to die. His sole remaining
concern was to provide for the future of his family. Before he had
marched out of Fort Leavenworth for California, he had made a
will. He reread this testament but felt he could not improve upon
its provisions. Probably because no one had witnessed his signature
in June, 1846, he concluded to re-execute the will. On October 12,
he asked his brother-in-law John Radford and his physician William
Hammond to witness it.

During the month of October, the Kearny household experienced
the strange and poignant juxtaposition of birth and death. On the
fifteenth Mrs. Kearny was delivered of another boy at Jefferson
Barracks. Out at Meriwether Clark's country seat, the sick man
smiled wanly when told he was again a father. In view of all the
abuse and slander so recently heaped upon her husband's name,
Mary Kearny paid him probably the finest tribute in her power.
She gave this youngest of her children the name which his father

386

had always borne with such dignity and honor. Back in Newark brother Philip, with his penchant for family names, must have approved most heartily. Undoubtedly the thought of his little namesake brightened the General's last days.

About six o'clock on Tuesday morning, October 31, 1848, Stephen Watts Kearny breathed his last in the home of Major Clark.

Two steamboats lashed together came up the river early on the morning of Thursday, November 2, from Jefferson Barracks. The *Luella* and the *Herald* carried nearly seven hundred of the 7th and 8th regiments of United States Infantry who were to march in the funeral procession of General Kearny. His was the largest and most impressive funeral that St. Louis had ever witnessed. A military escort conveyed his remains to St. George's Episcopal Church on Locust Street. Services were conducted by the Right Reverend Bishop Hawks.

At their conclusion, a full military band with muffled drums led the solemn procession. Immediately preceding the casket rode a troop of the First Dragoons under the command of Colonel Sumner. Members of the clergy and the Army Medical Corps came next. The General's favorite charger followed the casket with boots reversed in the stirrups. Carriages conveyed the family, close relatives, and six pallbearers. Several civic military companies followed. Next marched a long file of volunteers who had served under General Kearny, together with military, naval, civil, and diplomatic officers of the United States and the state and city governments. The long parade moved slowly down Olive Street and thence by Fourth and Broadway to the private cemetery at the estate of Colonel John O'Fallon, a nephew of General William Clark, located on what would now be Eighth Street, north of Franklin Avenue. Interment was in the O'Fallon family vault. (In 1861 the General's remains were removed to Bellefontaine Cemetery.)

On November 6, 1848, the War Department issued General Orders No. 57, announcing the death of Brevet Major General Kearny. It declared: "His character and bearing as an accomplished officer were unsurpassed, and challenge the admiration of his fellow citizens and the emulation of his professional brethren." Pursuant to these orders, the Adjutant General's office instructed all military posts in the Sixth Military Department, lately under command of the deceased, to fire thirteen-minute guns at twelve noon and display the national colors at half-staff. For thirty days the officers of the army were directed to wear the usual badge of mourning.

A few months later the legislature of New Jersey passed a memorial resolution honoring this illustrious Jerseyman. The handsomely engrossed scroll was signed by the Governor and sent to the General's widow.

Typical of many sincere though less formal tributes was a letter written by Kearny's late adjutant in Mexico from a post on the Río Grande: "Early in my military career it was my good fortune to serve under him, and afterwards too . . . . The government will find an officer to take his post but not to fill his place. Kearny is gone!"

In reporting his dangerous condition a few days prior to his death, a Louisville paper had said of him: "He is and justly regarded as a model soldier, a model gentleman and a model citizen."

Both Stephen Kearny and his wife were typical of the early Victorian age. With its formalities and reticences, it was natural for the General not to discuss his personal business with his wife. Therefore Mary Kearny was decidedly worried for a brief period after her husband's death about what would become of her and the nine children. Her son Charles, not then fifteen, tried to reassure her by saying he would quit school and go to work. Fortunately it soon developed that General Kearny had made ample provision for his family, and she and her children were able to continue their former manner of living. His will which was filed for probate in St. Louis on November 21, 1848, left all of his estate to his wife. It urged that when she should make her own will, she give "a fair and equitable portion" to each of their children, but suggested that the girls receive larger shares than the boys to protect them from want.

We can only surmise the extent of the General's estate, since the probate court in St. Louis now has no record of it. Mary Kearny continued to live in St. Louis for more than half a century. She always resided in a rented house as her husband was opposed to ownership of a home. Probably this grew out of the hard experience of an army officer accustomed to being moved from post to post on short notice. One of her great-granddaughters recalls a visit when she was a little girl and remembers her "as an old lady . . . to whom the maids brought breakfast in bed, and who took me driving with her in the afternoons in an open surrey, driven by the colored coachman. She had two Irish maids who had been with her for many years."

A grandniece, too, remembers Mrs. Kearny: "She was plump and laughed with keen enjoyment of her brother (Admiral Radford's) and other gentlemen's witticisms and her well-arranged white side curls shaking as she laughed or talked with animation." William Radford's marriage occurred only a few weeks after Stephen Kearny's death. Because of the strict mourning then customary, his bride was not allowed to wear her beautiful wedding dress and lace veil at their nuptials.

On December 2, 1870, a pension was awarded the General's widow in the amount of $30.00 per month for life, dated back to 1861. In her eighty-eighth year, on June 27, 1899, Mary Radford Kearny died in St. Louis. A St. Joseph, Missouri, newspaper stated that she left a "snug fortune" to her children, one of them a prominent resident of St. Joseph. Another clipping described her as "very wealthy . . . having in trust a large fortune which will be inherited by her grandchildren, the children of Major (Charles) Kearny of this city. It was bequeathed by his sister who died several years ago." (I am unable to determine which of Mrs. Kearny's daughters is referred to; three of them predeceased their mother.)

Such eminent writers as Justin Smith and Allan Nevins, as well as the more fanatical Frémont partisans, have definitely projected General Kearny's personality as harsh and unattractive. If that accurately described him, it is surprising that so many of his contemporaries were very quickly drawn to him and formed lasting friendships after only short acquaintances. Their brief association at Santa Fe won him the devotion of young Susan Magoffin. Captain S. F. du Pont, very much a man of the world, was unrestrained in his enthusiasm for the new friend he had made in General Kearny. Secretary of War Marcy's opinion almost echoes Du Pont's:

389

"General Kearny is a sound man and I have great confidence in his judgment.... It is a long time since I have seen a man whom I have liked so well on short acquaintance as General Kearny." The same sentiment was expressed by an uncle of Mrs. Kearny's: "We all received with unfeigned sorrow the account of the lamented death of General Kearny. I do not know any person in whom I felt a stronger interest from the short acquaintance I had with him."

Months later out in California, Walter Colton noted:

> The intelligence of the death of General Kearny has been received here with many expressions of affectionate remembrance. During his brief sojourn in California his considerate disposition, his amiable deportment and generous policy had endeared him to the citizens. They saw in him nothing of the ruthless invader but an intelligent, humane general largely endowed with a spirit of forbearance and fraternal regard .... They took leave of him with regret and have received the tidings of his death with sympathy and sorrow.

Edwin Bryant wrote:

> It is not my province to extol or pronounce judgment upon his acts . . . no man, placed under the same circumstances, ever aimed to perform his duty with more uprightness and more fidelity to the interests and honor of his country; or who, to shed lustre upon his country, ever braved greater dangers or endured more hardships and privations, and all without vaunting his performances and sacrifices.

These and many other estimates of Stephen Kearny by his contemporaries convince me he was a far more human and attractive figure than has been generally believed. Certainly he was anything but an exhibitionist. He was essentially a man who thought deeply, kept his own counsel, and then acted upon his orders and convictions. Such an individual cannot be appraised at a glance.

Despite the stern demands upon a soldier, he displayed compassion for the weak and helpless again and again throughout his career. Mercy and justice were always evident in his councils with the savages. In all his dealings with them, no barbarous slaughter nor needless destruction of villages and livestock were ever committed by his command. In this respect Stephen Kearny shines in sharp contrast with many of the Indian fighters who followed him.

What is his place in our history? He was not one of our greatest military leaders. We can be very sure he never pictured himself in such a role. Yet his contribution was basic and far-reaching. He was a soldier who possessed a natural bent for exploration and was no mean diarist. Although not an engineer, he built more frontier posts than any contemporary.

During more than a decade when the United States was militarily weak, he protected a long, exposed frontier from Indian attack. With fantastically small but mobile forces he maintained peace with warlike savages so numerous that we can still wonder by what miracle they did not overwhelm the few soldiers who opposed them. That Kearny accomplished so much without any large-scale battles robs his achievement of some of its glamor. Only when the numbers are studied—the handful of dragoons compared to the thousands of red warriors—does the analysis reveal the hidden heroism of the situation. At the risk of repetition, a major factor was the matchless training and discipline practiced by this officer.

Because of the charge that Kearny was too severe a disciplinarian, the opinion of one of America's greatest commanders seems particularly pertinent. Ulysses S. Grant as a young lieutenant first saw Kearny at Jefferson Barracks in the early 1840's and wrote of him:

> . . . one of the ablest officers of the day . . . under him discipline was kept at a high standard but without vexatious rules or regulations. Every drill and roll call had to be attended but in the intervals officers were permitted to enjoy themselves . . . leaving the garrison, and going where they pleased without making written application . . . so that they were back for their next duty.

More than any other individual Kearny can be called the father of our cavalry system. Students of military history credit the élan and performance of our dragoons in the Mexican War to both the tactics and the thorough indoctrination given them by Kearny. Even though he was never within hundreds of miles of any of the fiercest fighting in old Mexico, he certainly had a share in the victories there.

On the mere score of physical areas encompassed by his activities, his record is striking. Thirty years ago a Colorado newspaper columnist wrote of his long march to the South Pass in 1845, followed a year later by the epic achievements of the Army of the West:

> If we advance with General Kearny from Santa Fe . . . to the conquest of California and return with him during the summer of 1847 overland . . . to Fort Leavenworth, we will find that this inveterate marcher of men, who added a third to the territory of the United States, incident to his progress *four times traversed within two years substantially a third of the breadth of the United States.* [The italics are mine.]

It is worth noting that in his thirty-six years of military service, Stephen Kearny visited—usually on horseback, by keelboat, or afoot —every present continental state of the American Union west of the Mississippi with the exception of Washington, Oregon, and Alaska. (On his eastbound journey in the summer of 1847 he may either have crossed the edge of Utah or very narrowly missed it.) With the exception of the extreme southeast and some of New England, his duties caused him to visit all the rest of the country. Hardly any American of his time had traveled so widely within his own land in a manner so calculated to acquaint him intimately with it.

His labors in New Mexico and California revealed qualities of statesmanship distinct from purely military capacity. He brought law and order to large regions of the present United States which had known very little of either blessing under their previous governments. In one respect he was indeed unique. He was the military governor of two of our commonwealths, New Mexico and California, and of two great foreign cities, Veracruz and Mexico City.

Viewed in this light, I submit that his proper place in history is that of the forerunner of a small but very devoted and distinguished group of what I will term America's pro-consuls. Leonard Wood, William Howard Taft (with his service in the Philippines), George W. Goethals, and Arthur and Douglas MacArthur—these men followed in the footsteps of Stephen Watts Kearny.

Certainly it was an ill day for the United States when General Kearny was sent to Veracruz. What a tragedy to lose such a man at the age of fifty-four! His reputation, experience, and judgment would have made him invaluable to the government during the next decade. Serious Indian problems in the 1850's would have fared the better for his wise attention. By that time few officers could have equaled his knowledge of Indian affairs or commanded the trust and respect which most of the tribes felt for Shonga Kahega Mahetonga. It is idle to speculate on what might have been any man's destiny if Death had stayed its hand. However, we are safe in assuming that so valuable and dedicated a public servant as Stephen Watts Kearny would have made further impressive contributions to the United States of America.

Appendix A

Instructions from the War Department to Colonel S. W. Kearny:
(Confidential)

WAR DEPARTMENT,
WASHINGTON, JUNE 3, 1846.

SIR: I herewith send you a copy of my letter to the governor of Missouri for an additional force of one thousand mounted men.

The object of thus adding to the force under your command is not, as you will perceive, fully set forth in that letter, for the reason that it is deemed prudent that it should not, at this time, become a matter of public notoriety; but to you it is proper and necessary that it should be stated.

It has been decided by the President to be of the greatest importance, in the pending War with Mexico, to take the earliest possession of Upper California. An expedition with that view is hereby ordered, and you are designated to command it. To enable you to be in sufficient force to conduct it successfully, this additional force of a thousand mounted men has been provided, to follow you in the direction of Santa Fé, to be under your orders, or the officer you may leave in command at Santa Fé.

It cannot be determined how far this additional force will be behind that designed for the Santa Fé expedition, but it will not probably be more than a few weeks. When you arrive at Santa Fé with the force already called, and shall have taken possession of it, you may find yourself in a condition to garrison it with a small part of your command, (as the additional force will soon be at that place,) and with the remainder press forward to California. In that case you will make such arrangements, as to being followed by the reinforcements before mentioned as in your judgment may be deemed safe and prudent. I need not say to you that in case you conquer Santa Fé, (and with it will be included the department or State of New Mexico,) it will be important to provide for retaining safe possession of it. Should you deem it prudent to have still more troops for the accomplishment of the object herein designated, you will lose no time in communicating your opinion on that point, and all others connected with the enterprise, to this department. Indeed, you are hereby authorized to make a direct requisition for it upon the governor of Missouri.

It is known that a large body of Mormon emigrants are *en route* to California for the purpose of settling in that country. You are desired to use all proper means to have a good understanding with them, to the end that the United States may have their cooperation in taking possession of, and holding that country. It has been suggested here, that many of these Mormons would willingly enter into the service of the United States, and aid us in our expedition against California. You are hereby authorized to muster into service such as can be induced to volunteer; not, however, to a number exceeding one-third of your entire force. Should they enter the service, they will be paid as other volunteers, and you can allow them to designate, so far as it can be properly done, the persons to act as officers thereof. It is understood that a considerable number of American citizens are now settled on the Sacramento river, near Suter's establishment, called Nueva Helvetica, who are well disposed towards the United States. Should you, on your arrival in the country, find this to be the true state of things there, you are authorized to organize and receive into the service of the United States, such portion of these citizens as you may think useful to aid you to hold the possession of the country. You will in that case allow them, so far as you shall judge proper, to select their own officers. A large discretionary power is invested in you in regard to these matters, as well as to all others in relation to the expeditions confided to your command.

The choice of routes by which you will enter California will be left to your better knowledge and ample means of getting accurate information. We are assured that a southern route (called the caravan route, by which the wild horses are brought from that country into New Mexico) is practicable; and it is suggested as not improbable, that it can be passed over in the winter months, or, at least, late in autumn. It is hoped that this information may prove to be correct.

In regard to the routes, the practicability of procuring needful supplies for men and animals, and transporting baggage, is a point to be well considered. Should the President be disappointed in his cherished hope that you will be able to reach the interior of Upper California before winter, you are then desired to make the best arrangement you can for sustaining your forces during the winter and for an early movement in the spring. Though it is very desirable that the expedition should reach California this season, (and the President does not doubt you will make every possible effort to accomplish this object,) yet if, in your judgment, it cannot be undertaken with a reasonable prospect of success, you will defer it, as above suggested, until spring. You are left unembarrassed by any specific directions in this matter.

It is expected that the naval forces of the United States which are now, or will soon be in the Pacific, will be in possession of all the towns on the sea coast, and will co-operate with you in the conquest of California. Arms, ordnance, munitions of war, and provisions, to be used in that country, will be sent by sea to our squadron in the Pacific for the use of the land forces.

Should you conquer and take possession of New Mexico and Upper California, or considerable places in either, you will establish temporary civil governments therein; abolishing all arbitrary restrictions that may exist, so far as it may be done with safety. In performing this duty, it would be wise and prudent to continue in their employment all such of the existing officers as are known to be friendly to the United States, and will take the oath of allegiance to them. The duties at the custom-houses ought at once to be reduced to such a rate as may be barely sufficient to maintain the necessary officers, without yielding any revenue to the government.

You may assure the people of those provinces that it is the wish and design of the United States to provide for them a free government, with the least possible delay, similar to that which exists in our territories. They will then be called on to exercise the rights of freemen in electing their own representatives to the territorial legislature. It is foreseen that what relates to the civil government will be a difficult and unpleasant part of your duty, and much must necessarily be left to your own discretion.

In your whole conduct you will act in such a manner as best to conciliate the inhabitants, and render them friendly to the United States.

It is desirable that the usual trade between the citizens of the United States and the Mexican provinces should be continued, as far as practicable, under the changed condition of things between the two countries. In consequence of extending your expedition into California, it may be proper that you should increase your supply for goods to be distributed as presents to the Indians. The United States Superintendent of Indian Affairs at St. Louis will aid you in procuring these goods. You will be furnished with a proclamation in the Spanish language, to be issued by you, and circulated among the Mexican people, on your entering into or approaching their country.

You will use your utmost endeavors to have the pledges and promises therein contained carried out to the utmost extent.

I am directed by the President to say, that the rank of Brevet Brigadier General will be conferred on you as soon as you commence your movement towards California, and sent round to you by sea, or over the country, or to the care of the commandant of our squadron in the Pacific. In that way cannon, arms, ammunition and supplies for the land forces will be sent to you.

Very respectfully, your obedient servant,

W. L. MARCY,
SECRETARY OF WAR.

Colonel S. W. Kearny,
Fort Leavenworth, Missouri.

War Department,
Washington, June 18, 1846.

Sir: By direction of the President, I have given to the bearer hereof, Colonel James W. Magoffin, a letter of introduction to you, and trust you will derive advantage from his knowledge of the country in which you are to carry on military operations, and the assistance he may afford in securing supplies, &c.

I have nothing of importance to add to the despatches which have been already forwarded to you. Since my last letter it has been determined to send a small force round Cape Horn to California. The arms, cannon, and provisions, to be sent to the Pacific, will be accompanied by one company of artillery of the regular army. Arrangements are now on foot to send a regiment of volunteers by sea. These troops, and such as may be organized in California, will be under your command.

More than common solicitude will be felt here in regard to the expedition committed to you, and it is desired that you should avail yourself of all occasions to inform the government of your progress and prospects. The President desires your opinion, as early as you are in a situation to give it, of the practicability of your reaching California in the course of this autumn, or in the early part of next winter. I need not repeat the expression of his wishes that you should take military possession of that country as soon as it can be safely done.

I am, with great respect, your obedient servant,

Wm. L. Marcy,
Secretary of War.

To Colonel S. W. Kearny

Appendix B

Portraits and Personal Relics

PERSONAL MEMORABILIA of General Kearny can be found in various museums, principally in Missouri, New Mexico, and California. There are several portraits. The two best known are of the Mexican War period. One is a large oil painting hanging in the quarters of the Missouri Historical Society in St. Louis. Mrs. Kearny is reported to have ordered it painted by an unknown artist about the time that her own portrait was done by De Franca in 1857. If so, the artist must have used an existing miniature or engraving for his model. Mrs. Kearny bequeathed this portrait to the Society upon her death. The second is a mezzotint engraving in the Library of Congress, taken from an original daguerreotype engraved by J. B. Welsh for *Graham's Magazine.* Like the oil painting owned by the Missouri Historical Society, this has been reproduced in many books and magazines and is perhaps the best-known likeness.

Mr. Cresson Kearny of Montrose, Colorado, has two most interesting and little-known portraits. One is an oil painting (by an unknown artist) of Stephen Kearny as a first lieutenant, in the uniform worn by officers during the War of 1812. According to an expert on army apparel, it must have been painted about 1812 or 1813. While Kearny would have then been only eighteen or nineteen years of age, the face is that of a somewhat older man. The

399

other portrait owned by Mr. Cresson Kearny is a miniature that probably antedates the Mexican War pictures above described, although it is much later than the oil last mentioned. From some features common to both pictures, I suspect that the unknown painter of the Missouri Historical Society portrait may have used this miniature as a model.

The Missouri Historical Society also owns the General's diaries. These and many letter books and letters were presented to the Society by Charles Kearny, the General's second son. With them he gave the coat worn by his father when colonel of the First Dragoons, with spurs and a cartridge belt that he wore during the Mexican War.

The New Mexico Historical Society was presented with an oil portrait of the General by his daughter, Mrs. Western Bascome (Ellen Kearny) of St. Louis. I believe this is now hanging in the old Palace of the Governors in Santa Fe. From descriptions this portrait seems to be of the Mexican War period.

Henry Kearny, a grandson (son of Clarence), presented this same Society with one of a pair of cap and ball pistols carried by General Kearny on his march to the West. It is marked "H/ or R/ Young & Co. New York." Henry Kearny gave the companion pistol to the old Custom House in Monterey, along with a four-barrel pepperbox revolver belonging to his grandfather.

A pair of gold epaulets worn by General Kearny as part of his dress uniform is displayed in the quarters of the Society of California Pioneers in San Francisco.

Notes on Sources

THESE NOTES bear the following code references:

AI: *Annals of Iowa,* published by Iowa State Department
              of History and Archives, Des Moines.
BL: Bancroft Library, University of California, Berkeley.
CHS: California Historical Society *Quarterly,*
              San Francisco.
CSL: California State Library, Sacramento.
HL: Huntington Library, San Marino, California.
HR: House of Representatives, Washington, D. C.
HSSC: Historical Society of Southern California,
              Los Angeles.
LC: Library of Congress, Washington, D. C.
MHS: Missouri Historical Society, St. Louis.
MKC: Papers from Estate of Mary Kearny Cobb, a
              granddaughter of General Kearny.
NA: National Archives, Washington, D. C.
NJHS: *Proceedings* of New Jersey Historical Society,
              Newark.
NMHR: *New Mexico Historical Review,* Albuquerque.
PJK: Mr. Philip J. Kearny of New Haven and New York
              City, a great-nephew of General Kearny.
SHSI: State Historical Society of Iowa, Iowa City.
UCLA: Library, University of California at Los Angeles.

BACKGROUND: Bernard De Voto, *The Year of Decision—1846* (Boston, Little, Brown & Company, 1943), 230, 305, 466 f. (hereinafter referred to as De Voto).

CHAPTER I—*Birth—Ancestry—School Days*

BIRTH AND ANCESTRY: Reverend W. Northey Jones, M.A., *History of St. Peters Church in Perth Amboy, New Jersey, 1698–1923* (n.p., 1924), 340, 343, 347 f., 360, 369 f. (hereinafter referred to as Northey Jones); Charles Smith, *The Antient and Present State of the County and City of Cork* (Dublin, 1750), Bk. II, Chap. III, 242–43; Thomas Kearny, *General Philip Kearny, Battle Soldier of Five Wars, Including the Conquest of the West by General Stephen Watts Kearny* (New York, G. P. Putnam's Sons, 1937), 33; Kearny Family Bible, Stephen Watts Kearny Collection, MHS. Carroll Storrs Alden, *Lawrence Kearny, Sailor Diplomat* (Princeton, N. J., Princeton University Press, 1936), 8 (Lawrence Kearny was a half-first cousin of Stephen Watts Kearny); Whitehead, *Early History of Perth Amboy* (no page cited, book itself not available, but quoted by PJK); *New Jersey Archives, Second Series*, I, 48 n.; NJHS Vol. II, New Series 4, pp. 113, 334–38; PJK, letters from, on birth and ancestry, August 7, 1951, October 31, 1951, September 3, 1955, September 22, 1955, October 17, 1955; MKC, genealogical papers found among effects.

GENEALOGICAL ERRORS: Ralph Emerson Twitchell, *A History of the Military Occupation of the Territory of New Mexico—1846–1851, by the Government of the United States* (Denver, Colorado, Smith Brooks Company, 1909), 203 (hereinafter referred to as Twitchell); William Hyde and Howard L. Conrad, *Encyclopedia of History of St. Louis* (New York, Louisville, etc., The Southern History Company, 1899), II, 1154; J. Thomas Scharf, *History of St. Louis* (Philadelphia, L. H. Everts & Co., 1883), I, 386; Cardinal Goodwin, *John Charles Frémont: An Explanation of His Career* (Palo Alto, Stanford University Press, 1930), 149–52 (hereinafter referred to as Goodwin); PJK, letter from, on spelling of name, October 31, 1951; photographs of Kearny tombstones in Ireland supplied by PJK.

BOYHOOD: NMHR, Vol. V, No. 1 (January, 1930), 20 *et. seq.*
EDUCATION: Letters of Milton Halsey Thomas, curator of Columbiana, Low Memorial Library, May 26, 1955, and September 27, 1955; James Madison Cutts, *The Conquest of California and New Mexico* (Philadelphia, Carey and Hart, 1847), 14; PJK, letters to MHS, January 22, 1934, and to author, December 1, 1955, and January 13, 1956; letter of Secretary of Princeton University, November 25, 1955; William J. Petersen, "Kearny in Iowa," in *The Palimpsest* (August, 1931); Eudora Smith, "Stephen Watts Kearny as a Factor in the Westward Movement, 1812–1834," unpublished thesis presented in partial fulfillment of requirements for the degree of Master of Arts, Washington University, St. Louis, Mo., June, 1923. Information supplied by PJK about final accounting of estate of Philip Kearny III (1733–98) in note to author, January 13, 1956.
HISTORICAL ERRORS: Allan Nevins, *The West's Greatest Adventurer* (New York, Harpers, 1928), II, 345, 376; Frederick S. Dellenbaugh, *Frémont and '49* (New York, G. P. Putnam's Sons, 1914), 363 (hereinafter referred to as Dellenbaugh); Thomas Kearny, "Kearny and Kit Carson as Interpreted by Stanley Vestal," NMHR, Vol. I, No. 1 (Jan., 1930), 1.

CHAPTER II—*The School of the Soldier*

MILITARY COMMISSIONS: In Kearny Collection, MHS; Francis Bernard Heitman, *Historical Register and Dictionary of United States Army* (Washington, D. C., Government Printing Office, 1903), Pt. 2, p. 586.
CAMPAIGN IN NORTHERN NEW YORK AND BATTLE OF QUEENSTON HEIGHTS: Glenn Tucker, *Poltroons and Patriots* (Indianapolis, Bobbs, Merrill Company, 1954), I, 179–92; *National Cyclopedia of American Biography* (New York, J. T. White & Co., 1893–1906), XIII, 140; Fayette Robinson, "Biography of Major-General Stephen Watts Kearny, USA," *Graham's Magazine* (Philadelphia), Vol. XXXV, No. 1 (July, 1849), (hereinafter referred to as *Graham's Magazine*); Twitchell, 203; Kearny, *Battle Soldier*, 27.
PRISONER OF WAR: *Graham's Magazine;* Hyde and Conard, *St.*

Louis, II, 1154; letters of 1st Lt. Stephen W. Kearny to Adj. Gen., March 29, 1813, in NA; letters of Capt. S. W. Kearny to Secretary of War, April 6, 1813, and April 19, 1813, in NA.

LATER WAR SERVICE: J. Frost, L.L.D., *The Mexican War and Its Warriors* (New Haven and Philadelphia, H. Mansfield, 1848), 281; Kearny, *Battle Soldier*, 42; St. Louis *Republican* (November 3, 1848); *Graham's Magazine*.

FOURTH OF JULY ORATOR: Letter of Stephen W. Kearny to Ravaud Kearny, July 8, 1819, in Kearny Collection, MHS.

POSTWAR SERVICE: Kearny, *Battle Soldier*, 42 and *passim;* Thomas Kearny, "General Stephen Watts Kearny," NJHS, Vol. II, New Series (1926), 90.

WESTERN FRONTIER IN 1819: *American State Papers. Documents Legislative and Executive. 1st Session of 16 Congress to 2nd Session of 18th Congress, incl.*, Military Affairs (Washington, D. C., Government Printing Office), II, 33; letter of John C. Calhoun, secretary of war, to Chairman of Military Affairs Committee, HR (December 29, 1819), also p. 324; Hiram Martin Chittenden, *American Fur Trade of the Far West* (New York, F. P. Harper, 1902), II, Pt. 3, Chap. II, 568–70, 574.

ADJUTANT TO COLONEL HENRY ATKINSON: Orders Ninth Military Department, June 25, 1820; MHS.

JOURNAL OF THE MAGEE EXPEDITION: Valentine Mott Porter, "Preface to the Journal of Stephen Watts Kearny," MHS, Vol. III (1908–11), 8 *et seq.;* NJHS, Vol. II, New Series (1926), 90–91.

CHAPTER III—*The Yellowstone Expeditions—1819–25*

STEPHEN W. KEARNY's JOURNAL (Magee Expedition): MHS, Vol. III, 14 *et seq.*

"WESTERN ENGINEER": Elvid Hunt, *History of Fort Leavenworth, 1827–1937* (2d ed., Fort Leavenworth, Kan., Command and General Staff School Press, 1937), 12.

DR. JAMES' JOURNAL OF MAJOR LONG's EXPEDITION: R. G. Thwaites, *Early Western Travels* (Cleveland, Arthur H. Clark Co., 1905), XV, 1880–90; XVII, 12, 42, 82–85.

SERVICES AND PROMOTIONS: Mendell Lee Taylor, "The Western

Service of Stephen Watts Kearny, 1815–1848," NMHR, Vol. XXI, No. 3 (July, 1946), 171 *et seq.* (hereinafter referred to as Mendell Lee Taylor); Kearny Collection, MHS; letter of Capt. Stephen W. Kearny to Gen. D. Parker, Washington, D. C., November 17, 1820, and from Bvt. Maj. S. W. Kearny to Brig. Gen. T. S. Jesup, Washington, D. C., August 26, 1824 (copies furnished courtesy Ward S. Parker, Creve Coeur, Mo.).

DEATH OF MOTHER: Northey Jones, 348; Kearny Collection, MHS.

STEPHEN W. KEARNY'S JOURNAL (Yellowstone Expedition): Unpublished diary, Sept. 17, 1824–May 10, 1826; Kearny Collection, MHS; 19 Cong., 1 sess., *Exec. Doc. No. 117* (November 23, 1825); *Report by Brig. Gen. Henry Atkinson of Yellowstone Expedition of 1825*, 5–15; Chittenden, *American Fur Trade*, III, 608–17.

CARTOGRAPHY: Carl I. Wheat, *Mapping the Transmississippi West* (San Francisco, Institute of Historical Cartography, 1958), II (hereinafter referred to as Wheat, II): Maj. S. H. Long map, facing p. 80; H. S. Tanner map, facing p. 95; Steiler map, facing p. 149. David H. Burr, "Map of the United States, July, 1839," large facsimile in Dale L. Morgan and Carl I. Wheat, *Jedediah Smith and His Maps of the American West* (California Historical Society, 1954).

CHAPTER IV—*The Winnebago War and Fort Crawford*

LIFE AT CANTONMENT BARBOUR AND FORT ATKINSON: Unpublished diary of Stephen Watts Kearny, 1824–26, Kearny Collection, MHS.

BELLEFONTAINE: *Journal of Stephen Watts Kearny*, Kearny Collection, MHS, Vol. III, 105 n.

CONSTRUCTION OF JEFFERSON BARRACKS: Mendell Lee Taylor, 172.

WINNEBAGO WAR: Lyman C. Draper, ed., *Collections of State Historical Society of Wisconsin*, V, 123–58, 178–204; XIV, 65–102 (hereinafter referred to as Draper). Moses M. Strong, *History of the Territory of Wisconsin* (Madison, Wis., State Printer, 1885),

115–22; letter of Maj. S. W. Kearny to Col. John McNeil, Hillsborough, N. H., November 14, 1827, in Kearny Collection, MHS.

COMMAND AT FORT CRAWFORD: Peter Lawrence Scanlan, M.D., *Prairie du Chien—French, British, American* (Menasha, Wis., George Banta Publishing Company, 1937), 134, 138; Bruce E. Mahan, *Old Fort Crawford and the Frontier* (Iowa City, Iowa, State Historical Society of Iowa, 1926), 123–24, 260; Draper, V, 238 n.; Surgeon General's Report, August 1, 1832, NA; letter files, 1832, Adjutant General's Office, NA.

BRUNET AND STREET LITIGATION: Mahan, *Old Fort Crawford*, 143; HR, 22 Cong., 1 sess., *Reports of Committees, No. 437* (April 9, 1832), Vol. III; Scanlan, *Prairie du Chien*, 147; George D. Lyman, *John Marsh, Pioneer* (Chautauqua, N. Y., Chautauqua Press, 1931), 114.

CONSTRUCTION OF NEW FORT AT PRAIRIE DU CHIEN: Scanlan, *Prairie du Chien*, 137; letter of Zachary Taylor, Baton Rouge, January 19, 1848, to Col. J. P. Taylor, in Zachary Taylor papers, MSS Division, LC.

KETTLE MASSACRE AND WINNEBAGO TREATY OF 1830: Draper, V, 144–46.

ACCIDENT ON PARADE GROUND: *Graham's Magazine*.

CHAPTER V—*The Course of True Love*

COURTSHIP AND MARRIAGE: William Clark Kennerly, *Persimmon Hill* (Norman, University of Oklahoma Press, 1948), 54–56, 58, 60, 87, 107–109 (hereinafter referred to as Kennerly); John Bakeless, *Lewis and Clark: Partners in Discovery* (New York, William Morrow & Co., 1947), 447; Sophie Radford de Meissner, *Old Naval Days* (New York, Henry Holt & Co., 1920), 16, 87 (hereinafter referred to as *Old Naval Days*): letter of Mary Kennerly Taylor to Eva Emory Dye, n.d., among effects, MKC; General Kearny's Bible, in Kearny Collection, MHS; information supplied by Mrs. Richard Arthur Bullock of St. Louis, great-granddaughter of General Kearny.

THE FRONTIER IN 1830: Louis Pelzer, *Marches of the Dragoons in the Mississippi Valley* (Iowa City, SHSI, 1917), 1 (hereinafter referred to as Pelzer): Otis E. Young, *The West of Philip St. George Cooke, 1809–1895* (Glendale, Calif., Arthur H. Clark Company, 1955), 14 (hereinafter referred to as Young): Colonel George Croghan, *Army Life on the Western Frontier: Selections from the Official Reports Made between 1826 and 1845*, ed. by Francis Paul Prucha (Norman, University of Oklahoma Press, 1958), xiii, 11 (hereinafter referred to as Croghan).

FORT TOWSON, 1824–30: Grant Foreman, *Pioneer Days in the Early Southwest* (Cleveland, Arthur H. Clark Company, 1926), 61 (hereinafter referred to as *Pioneer Days*); Grant Foreman, *Advancing the Frontier* (Norman, University of Oklahoma Press, 1933), Preface and p. 83 (hereinafter referred to as *Advancing the Frontier*).

EXPEDITION UP RED RIVER AND REBUILDING FORT TOWSON: Unpublished diary of Stephen Watts Kearny, 1831–42, in Kearny Collection, MHS; *Advancing the Frontier*, 83, 86 n.

SPEECH TO CHOCTAWS: See Kearny diary mentioned under last caption.

CHAPTER VI—*The First Dragoons*

ORDERED TO NEW YORK CITY: Letter of Ann Kearny Van Horne to Rev. Ravaud Kearny, March 31, 1832 (courtesy PJK); letter of Stephen Watts Kearny to Rev. Ravaud Kearny, July 4, 1832, in Kearny Collection, MHS; letter of Margaret Kearny Walton to Rev. Ravaud Kearny, January 31, 1833 (courtesy PJK).

ORGANIZATION OF FIRST DRAGOONS: Pelzer, 12–14; Young, 67–68, 71; Albert G. Brackett, *History of the United States Cavalry from the Formation of the Federal Government to June 1, 1863* (New York, Harper & Bros., 1865), 35; Louis Pelzer, *Henry Dodge* (Iowa City, SHSI, 1911), 82, 86, 90 f., 150; Valentine Mott Porter, *General Stephen W. Kearny and the Conquest of California, 1846–7* (HSSC, Annual Publications), VIII, 102; James Hildreth, *Dragoon Campaigns to the Rocky Mountains* (New York, Wiley & Long, 1832), 43, 59 f.; Croghan, 177.

DRAGOON'S EXPEDITION AMONG THE COMANCHES AND PAWNEES: George Catlin, *Letters and Notes on the Manners, Customs, and Conditions of the North American Indians* (London, David Bogue,

1844, 4th ed.), II, 38; Harold McCracken, *George Catlin and the Old Frontier* (New York, The Dial Press, 1959), 143–58 (hereinafter referred to as McCracken); *Pioneer Days*, 123–39, 143–52, 164; *Advancing the Frontier*, 44, 152; Kearny, *Battle Soldier*, 42; 1st Lt. T. B. Wheelock, *Official Journal of Colonel Dodge's Expedition* (August 27, 1834), in Report to Secretary of War, *American State Papers*, Class V, Military Affairs, V, 373; Return of Alterations and Casualties of 1st U. S. Dragoons, 1834, War Records Division, NA; *Niles National Register* (Baltimore), Vol. X, Ser. 4, 389, and Vol. XI, Ser. 4, No. 5, 74, 76; Henry R. Wagner, *The Plains and the Rockies, A Bibliography of Narratives of Travel and Adventure, 1800–1865*, rev. by Charles L. Camp (Columbus, Long's College Book Company, 1953, 3d ed.), Nos. 51 and 59 (hereinafter referred to as Wagner-Camp); Philip St. George Cooke, *Scenes and Adventures in the Army* (Philadelphia, Lindsay & Blakiston, 1859), 227.

DRAGOONS' UNIFORM: *Pioneer Days*, 123–24.

CARTOGRAPHY: Josiah Gregg, *Commerce of the Prairies* (Norman, University of Oklahoma Press, 1954), map; David H. Burr, "Map of the United States, July, 1839," in Morgan and Wheat, *Jedediah Smith*, II, 149 n.

THE IOWA COUNTRY: Pelzer, 50–52, 54 f.; Nebraska State Historical Society Publications, Vol. XX, 59. AI, Vol. V, Ser. I, pp. 888, 892; Vol. III, Ser. 3, Nos. 5 and 6 (April–July, 1898), 351, 353, 355–58; Vol. XXVII, Ser. 3, No. 2 (October, 1945), 89–92, 163 f. Return of Alterations and Casualties of 1st U. S. Dragoons, 1836, NA. *Iowa Journal of History and Politics*, Vol. VII, 364, 367, 372; Vol. XI, 72, 342, 345, 354; Vol. XII, 180, 182 n., 183; Vol. XIV, 494; Vol. XXXIII, 206.

VISIT TO WABASHA: "Dragoon Expedition in Indian Talk," *U. S. Military and Naval Magazine*, Vol. VI (1835), 184 (in Edward Everett Ayer Collection of Americana, Newberry Library, Chicago).

PEMBINA PUZZLE: *Graham's Magazine*; *Minnesota Historical Society Bulletin*, Vol. V, 264, and Vol. IV, 396–97, footnote to article by Grace Lee Nute; letters of Archivist in Charge, Old Army Branch, NA, to author, January 2, 1957, and February 9, 1957.

LIFE AT FORT DES MOINES (first): Kearny Bible, in Kearny Collection, MHS; letter of Ann Kearny Van Horne to Rev. Ravaud Kearny, April, 1835 (courtesy PJK); Catlin, *Letters and Notes*, II, 149.

CHAPTER VII—*Shonga Kahega Mahetonga*

COLONEL OF FIRST DRAGOONS: Letter of Col. Stephen W. Kearny, June 20, 1837, in *American State Papers*, Military Affairs, VII, 960 f.; Glenn D. Bradley, *Winning the Southwest* (Chicago, A. C. McClurg & Co., 1912), 173; *Graham's Magazine*; Robert Selph Henry, *The Story of the Mexican War* (Indianapolis and New York, Bobbs, Merrill Company, Inc., 1950), 123 (hereinafter referred to as Robert Selph Henry); Grant Foreman, *Five Civilized Tribes* (Norman, University of Oklahoma Press, 1934), 302 n.; unpublished diary of Stephen Watts Kearny, 1831–42, in Kearny Collection, MHS; Return of Alterations and Casualties of 1st U. S. Dragoons, 1837–1844, NA; Kearny, *Battle Soldier*, 30–31.

PERSONAL FINANCES: Letter of S. W. Kearny to Capt. E. A. Hitchcock, dated Fort Leavenworth, November 13, 1837 (copy furnished courtesy Ward S. Parker, Creve Coeur, Mo., owner of original).

CARBINE MANUAL: Original in NA.

DISCIPLINE AND MORALE: *St. Louis Republican* (November 3, 1848); Croghan, 43 f., 140–43.

FRONTIER FORTS AND PATROLS: *Advancing the Frontier*, 51–53; Nebraska State Historical Society Publications, Vol. XXI, 215; *Army and Navy Chronicle* (Washington, D. C., Benjamin Homans, 1839), New Series, Vol. IX, 285–86; Pelzer, 82–85; *Iowa Journal of History and Politics* (Iowa City), Vol. XI, 345, Vol. XII, 183; letter of Stephen W. Kearny, February 24, 1842, to Ravaud Kearny, Jr., in Kearny Collection, MHS.

CLASH WITH SEMINOLES, AND CHAVEZ MURDER: Cooke, *Scenes and Adventures*, 379–84; Young, 109–10; Col. Henry Inman, *The Old Santa Fé Trail* (New York, Macmillan Company, 1897), 97–99; R. L. Duffus, *The Santa Fé Trail* (New York, Tudor Publishing Co., 1936), 184.

COMMANDER 3RD MILITARY DEPARTMENT (August 4, 1842–September 4, 1845): Letter of Archivist in Charge, Old Army Branch, NA, to author, March 7, 1957.

CHAPTER VIII—*The Stirring of Manifest Destiny*

LIFE AT JEFFERSON BARRACKS: "Speech of J. Franco Chavez," Santa Fe *New Mexican* (August 14, 1903); letter of Stephen W. Kearny to Lt. William Radford, September 20, 1843, in *Old Naval Days*, 113–14; Kennerly, 148.

FRONTIER IN 1843–44: Return of Alterations and Casualties of 1st U. S. Dragoons, 1843, 1844, and 1845, NA.

COOKE-TRENOR QUARREL: Letter of Stephen W. Kearny to Dr. W. Moffitt, Washington, D. C., March 9, 1843, in Kearny Collection, MHS; Young, 107–108.

SNIVELY AFFAIR: Young, 111–27, 132–35; *Pioneer Days*, 300.

LOAN OF HOWITZER TO JOHN C. FRÉMONT: Dellenbaugh, 104; Irving Stone, *Immortal Wife* (Garden City, Doubleday, Doran & Co., Inc., 1945), 89–96 (hereinafter referred to as *Immortal Wife*); letter of Archivist in Charge, Old Army Branch, NA, to author, April 3, 1958.

SUMMER CAMPAIGN TO THE ROCKY MOUNTAINS: Pelzer, 120–33; Sarah J. Cummins, *Autobiography and Reminiscences* (Freewater, Ore., 1914), 27–28; Leroy R. Hafen and Francis Marion Young, *Fort Laramie and the Pageant of the West, 1834–1890* (Glendale, California, Arthur H. Clark Co., 1938), 107, 109 (hereinafter referred to as *Fort Laramie*); Col. Stephen W. Kearny, *Report of a Summer Campaign to the Rocky Mountains*, HR, 29 Cong., *Doc. No. 2*, 210–20; Nebraska State Historical Society Publications, Vol. XX, 132; Young, 165; Cooke, *Scenes and Adventures*, 295, 336–38, 341, 345–46, 348, 362–71; Leroy R. Hafen and W. J. Ghent, *Broken Hand—Life Story of Thomas Fitzpatrick, Chief of the Mountain Men* (Denver, Colo., Old West Publishing Co., 1931), 164–70 (hereinafter referred to as *Broken Hand*); David Lavender, *Bent's Fort* (Garden City, N. Y., Doubleday & Company, Inc., 1954), 244–45 (hereinafter referred to as *Bent's Fort*).

SPEECH TO THE SIOUX: As reported by Lt. Henry S. Turner in HR *Doc. No. 2* cited above; another version is in Overton Johnson and William H. Winter, *Route Across the Rocky Mountains* (Princeton, N. J., Princeton University Press, 1932), 152–54.

KEARNY FAMILY MATTERS: Letter of Philip Kearny, June 22, 1845, to Mary Kearny, in Kearny Collection, MHS; Thomas Kearny, "New Facts about Fort Philip Kearny," *Annals of Wyoming* (Cheyenne, Wyo.), Vol. XII, No. 4, (Oct., 1940), 331.

CHAPTER IX—*The Army of the West: Genesis*

KEARNY AND HIS CHILDREN: Letter of S. W. Kearny, May 5, 1846, to his son Charles (original courtesy Mrs. Richard Arthur Bullock of St. Louis, granddaughter of Charles Kearny).

OLD (2ND) FORT KEARNY AT TABLE CREEK: Nebraska State Historical Society Publications, Vol. XX, 150–51; Vol. XXI, 216.

WAR WITH MEXICO: Justin H. Smith, *The War with Mexico* (New York, The Macmillan Company, 1919), I, 284–88 (hereinafter referred to as Justin Smith); Carl L. Cannon, ed. preface to *Jacob S. Robinson's Journal of the Santa Fé Expedition under Colonel Doniphan* (Princeton, N. J., Princeton University Press, 1932), v, vi (hereinafter referred to as *Robinson Journal*); Ray Allen Billington, *The Far Western Frontier, 1830–1860* (New York, Harper & Bros., 1956), 178.

CREATING THE ARMY: Letters of Col. Stephen W. Kearny to Gov. J. C. Edwards of Missouri, May 27, 1846, and July 2, 1846; same to Adj. Gen., Washington, D. C., May 28, 1846; same to Gen. G. M. Brooke, May 31, 1846; same to George T. Howard, June 4, 1846; same to Anthony Robidoux, June 4, 1846; same to Capt. B. D. Moore, June 6, 1846, diary and letter book of Stephen W. Kearny, in Kearny Collection, MHS; letter of S. W. Kearny to Capt. E. A. Hitchcock dated St. Louis, October 1, 1833 (copy courtesy William O. Bilden, Minneapolis, Minn., owner of original); letters of John Brown of Laclede Rangers to *St. Louis Weekly Reveille* (May, June, and July, 1846); *Journal of Abraham Robinson Johnston* in *Marching with the Army of the West*, ed. by Ralph P. Bieber (Glendale, Calif., Arthur H. Clark Co., 1936), 20 (hereinafter referred to as *Johnston Journal*); *Journal of Marcellus Ball Edwards* in *Marching with the Army of the West,* just cited, 116 (hereinafter referred to as *Edwards Journal*); Robert Selph Henry, 136; *Bent's Fort,* 253, 255; MHS *Bulletin,* Vol. III, No. 4, 128; De Voto, 232; George Rutledge Gibson (Ralph P. Bieber, ed.), *Journal of a Soldier under Kearny and Doniphan, 1846-47* (Glendale, Calif., Arthur H. Clark Co., 1935), 246 (hereinafter referred to as *Gibson Journal*); William Le Moyne Wills, "Reminiscences," Los Angeles County Medical Association *Bulletin,* Vol. LXXVI, No. 3 (1931), 198, quoted in CHS (June, 1954), 123-24, 126; Lt. W. H. Emory, *Notes of a Military Reconnaissance from Fort Leavenworth in Missouri to San Diego in California,* 30 Cong., 1 sess., *Sen. Doc. No.* 7 (reprinted, Albuquerque, University of New Mexico Press, 1951); Charles Burr Todd, *The Battles of San Pasqual* (Pomona, Calif., Progress Publishing Co., 1925), 5-6. Col. John T. Hughes, *Doniphan's Expedition and the Conquest of New Mexico and California* (Cincinnati, 1847); reprinted in Wm. E. Connelly's *War with Mexico* (Kansas City, Mo., Bryant & Douglas Book and Stationery Co., 1907), (hereinafter referred to as Hughes-Connelly). Return of Alterations and Casualties of 1st U. S. Dragoons, 1846, NA.

KEARNY'S INSTRUCTIONS: From Secretary of War, June 3, 1846, and June 18, 1846. See Appendix A, this volume.

CHAPTER X—*The Army of the West: Exodus*

THE MARCH: *Gibson Journal,* 127, 144; *Johnston Journal,* 76, 82 n., 85, 87 n., 88; *Edwards Journal,* 136, 140-42; *Robinson Journal,* 13; unpublished journal of Capt. Henry S. Turner, July 28 and 30, 1846, in Kearny Collection, MHS (hereinafter referred to as Unpublished Turner Journal); Emory, *Notes,* 31; Young, 175-78; Hughes-Connelly, 168, 178; Santa Fe *New Mexican* (August 22, 1903); letter of Christian Cribben, July 16, 1846, in Kearny Collection, MHS; letters of Col. Stephen W. Kearny to Adj. Gen., July 17, 1846, and August 1, 1846, in diary and letter book, Kearny Collection, MHS.

BENT'S FORT: *Bent's Fort,* 258-59; Stella M. Drum, ed., *Down the Santa Fé Trail and into Mexico: the Diary of Susan Shelby Magoffin, 1846–47* (New Haven, Yale University Press, 1926), xiii, xiv, xviii, 45 f. (hereinafter referred to as *Magoffin*).

CHAPTER XI—*The Army of the West: Invasion*

ASCENT OF THE RATON: Letter of Cresson H. Kearny, a great-grandson of General Kearny, March 2, 1957, to author; Justin Smith, I, 289; *Bent's Fort*, 259, 262; *Johnston Journal*, 92; *Edwards Journal*, 142–43; letter of Capt. Henry S. Turner to Julia Turner, August 5, 1846, in Kearny Collection, MHS.

IN NEW MEXICO: *Edwards Journal*, 150, 155; Emory, *Notes*, 49–51.

OATH OF ALLEGIANCE: Edward D. Mansfield, *The Mexican War, a History of Its Origin* (New York, A. S. Barnes & Co., 1849), 81–83.

FLIGHT OF ARMIJO: Young, 180; *Bent's Fort*, 262.

MAGOFFIN AND ARCHULETA: Herbert Bashford and Harr Wagner, *A Man Unafraid: The Story of John Charles Frémont* (San Francisco, Harr Wagner Publishing Company, 1927), 235 (hereinafter referred to as *Man Unafraid*); F. Stanley, *The Grant That Maxwell Bought* (Denver, Colo., World Press, 1952), 8; Paul Horgan, *The Centuries of Santa Fe* (New York, E. P. Dutton & Co., Inc., 1956), 205 (hereinafter referred to as Horgan); Thomas H. Benton, *Thirty Years' View* (New York, D. Appleton & Co., 1856), II, 682–84 (hereinafter referred to as *Thirty Years' View*); Young, 181, 184; L. Bradford Prince, *Historical Sketches of New Mexico from the Earliest Records to the American Occupation* (Kansas City, Ramsey, Millett & Hudson, 1883), 296 (hereinafter referred to as Bradford Prince); *Gibson Journal*, 198.

ENTRY INTO SANTA FE: Santa Fe *New Mexican* (August 22, 1903); Horgan, 197 f.

CHAPTER XII—*Santa Fe*

OCCUPATION AND PACIFICATION: *Gibson Journal*, 214–16, 219; *Edwards Journal*, 165, 170–71, 178; Hughes-Connelly, 225, 244.

KEARNY CODE: Arie Poldervaard, state librarian of New Mexico, in NMHR, Vol. XVIII, No. 1 (January, 1943); letter of Gen. Stephen W. Kearny to Adj. Gen., September 22, 1846, diary and letter book in Kearny Collection, MHS; Justin Smith, II, 218. NMHR, Vol. X, No. 1, p. 52; Vol. XIV, No. 2, p. 166; Vol. XIV, No. 3, p. 230.

GOVERNOR OF NEW MEXICO: Horgan, 211; letter of Capt. Henry S. Turner to Julia Turner, August 23, 1846, in Kearny Collection, MHS; Unpublished Turner Journal, entry for August 23, 1846; letter of Christian Cribben, August 24, 1846, in Kearny Collection, MHS; diary and letter book of Stephen W. Kearny, entry for August 27 and 28, 1846, MHS; *Magoffin*, 70–113, 124–33, 137–42.

DISCIPLINE FOR MISSOURI VOLUNTEERS: Hughes-Connelly, 222 n., 226; *Edwards Journal*, 167.

PROPHETIC LETTER: Letter of Gen. Stephen W. Kearny to Adj. Gen., September 16, 1846, in diary and letter book in Kearny Collection, MHS.

CIVIL GOVERNMENT: Diary and letter book of Stephen W. Kearny, entry for September 22, 1846, MHS; Gen. Kearny's proclamation at Santa Fe, August 22, 1846, announcing annexation and promising protection (copy), Doc. 242, HL; memorial of Santa Fe citizens, September 28, 1846, Doc. 243, Fort Sutter Papers, HL.

PLANS FOR DEPARTURE: Letter of Gen. Stephen W. Kearny to Adj. Gen., September 24, 1846, diary and letter book, MHS; Bradford Prince, 308; *Robinson Journal*, preface by Carl L. Cannon; William A. Kelleher, "The Year of Decision," NMHR, Vol. XXII, No. 1, pp. 12, 16–17.

CHAPTER XIII—*A Fateful Meeting*

DOWN THE RÍO GRANDE: George Walcott Ames, Jr., ed., "A Doctor Comes to California—The Diary of John S. Griffin, Assistant Surgeon with Kearny's Dragoons, 1846–47," CHS, Vol. XXI, No. 3, p. 196 (hereinafter referred to as "Dr. Griffin's Diary"); *Journal of Captain A. R. Johnston, First Dragoons*, in 30 Cong., 1 sess., *Exec. Doc. No. 41*, 570 (hereinafter referred to as *Capt. Johnston*); letter of Capt. H. S. Turner, A.A.A., to Col. Sterling Price, October 2, 1846, in Stephen W. Kearny letter book, MHS; Maj.

William Clark Kennerly, "Memoirs of a Missouri Volunteer," in Kearny Collection, MHS; Kennerly, 184, 190.

MORMON BATTALION: Orders No. 33, Army of the West, Capt. H. S. Turner, A.A.A., October 2, 1846; letter of Capt. H. S. Turner to Capt. Philip St. George Cooke, October 3, 1846, in Kearny Collection, MHS.

JAMES BECKWOURTH AND SANCHO PEDRO: Leroy R. Hafen and Ann W. Hafen, *Old Spanish Trail, Santa Fe to Los Angeles* (Glendale, Calif., Arthur H. Clark Co., 1954), 245–46; T. D. Bonner, *Life and Adventures of James P. Beckwourth* (New York, Harper & Bros., 1931), 327–29; Hughes-Connelly, 322 n.

MEETING WITH KIT CARSON: *Proceedings of the Court-Martial of Lieutenant Colonel John C. Frémont of the Regiment of Mounted Riflemen*, 30 Cong., 1 sess., *Exec. Doc. No. 33*, p. 43 (hereinafter referred to as *Court-Martial Proceedings*); Col. and Mrs. D. C. Peters, *Kit Carson's Own Story of His Life* (Taos, Blanche C. Grant, 1926), 8–9; DeWitt C. Peters, *Kit Carson's Life and Adventures* (Hartford, Conn., Dustin, Gilman, 1873), 281 f.; Charles Burdett, *Life of Kit Carson* (New York, A. L. Burt Co., 1902), 273; Edwin L. Sabin, *Kit Carson Days (1809–1868)* (Chicago, A. C. McClurg & Co., 1919, 273–74; *Broken Hand*, 186; Stanley Vestal, *Kit Carson, the Happy Warrior of the Old West* (Boston and New York, Houghton, Mifflin Co., 1928), 231; *Thirty Years' View*, II, 718; *Man Unafraid*, 248–50; Charles L. Camp, "Kit Carson in California," CHS, Vol. I, 143; Dellenbaugh, 359, 363; Letter of Thomas O. Larkin to Rachel Larkin, December 14, 1846, in *The Larkin Papers*, ed. by George P. Hammond, director of Bancroft Library (Berkeley, University of California Press, 1955), V, 310–13.

COOKE AT TUCSON: *Young*, 209–13.

CARTOGRAPHY: Commander Wilkes' "Map of Oregon Territory, 1841," copy in Morgan and Wheat, *Jedediah Smith*; J. Disturnell, "Map of Mexico," rev. ed., 1847, copy in *The Treaty of Guadalupe Hidalgo* (Berkeley, Friends of the Bancroft Library, 1949), ed. by George P. Hammond, with foreword by Francis P. Farquhar; H. N. Burroughs, *Map of Oregon and Upper California* (Philadelphia, published by S. Augustus Mitchell, 1848 [copyrighted 1845]).

CHAPTER XIV—*The Thousand-Mile Leap*

ORDEAL AND ENDURANCE: De Voto, 349–50; *Capt. Johnston*, 575, 612; Unpublished Turner Journal, entries for October 18, 25, 27, November 8, 1846, and *passim; Gibson Journal*, 6.

CARTOGRAPHY: Col. George Ruhlen, U.S.A. ret., "Kearny's Route from the Río Grande to the Gila River," NMHR, Vol. XXXII, No. 3 (July, 1957), 213–30, and maps.

MANGAS COLORADAS AND APACHES: Emory, *Notes*, Note 67, pp. 100, 201; Will Levington Comfort, *Apache* (New York, E. P. Dutton Co., 1931), *passim;* Frank C. Lockwood, *The Apache Indians* (New York, The Macmillan Co., 1938), 77; letter of Capt. H. S. Turner, A.A.A., to Lt. Col. Philip St. George Cooke, October 18, 1846, in Kearny collection, MHS.

THE PIMAS: Thomas Edwin Farish, *History of Arizona* (Phoenix, State of Arizona, 1915), 135; Unpublished Turner Journal, entry for November 11, 1846.

ARRIVAL IN CALIFORNIA: Letter of Brig. Gen. Stephen W. Kearny to Com. Robert F. Stockton, U.S.N., December 2, 1846; 30 Cong., 2 Sess. (1849), *Sen. Exec. Doc. No. 31*, 26–27; letter of Capt. H. S. Turner, A.A.A., to Lt. Col. Philip St. George Cooke, Dec. 3, 1846, in Kearny Collection, MHS; Arthur Woodward, foreword and notes to "Notes on the Indians of San Diego County" from the manuscripts of Judge Benjamin Hayes in *Masterkey*, Vol. VIII (March, 1934), 141; CHS, Vol. XXI, No. 4 (December, 1942), 355 n.; unpublished report of Capt. Archibald H. Gillespie, U.S. M.C., to Com. Robert F. Stockton, U.S.N., San Diego, December 25, 1846, UCLA (hereinafter referred to as Gillespie to Stockton); Arthur Woodward, *Lances at San Pascual* (San Francisco, California Historical Society, 1948), (hereinafter referred to as *Lances at San Pascual*); "Dr. Griffin's Diary," entries for October, November, and December, 1846.

CHAPTER XV—*San Pasqual*

OFFICIAL REPORTS: Letters of Brig. Gen. Stephen W. Kearny to Adj. Gen., December 12 and 13, 1846; 30 Cong., 1 sess., *Exec. Doc. No. 1*, 513–16; letter of Stephen W. Kearny to Mrs. Mary

Kearny, December 19, 1846, from San Diego, Upper California (original in possession of Cresson H. Kearny, Montrose, Colo., great-grandson of General Kearny); letter of Lt. Archibald H. Gillespie, U.S.M.C. (Com. Stockton had also appointed him a captain in California Battalion, a naval unit), to Secretary of Navy, February 16, 1847, published with an introduction by George Walcott Ames, Jr., in "Gillespie and the Conquest of California," CHS, Vol. XVII, No. 4 (December, 1938), 340–44 (hereinafter referred to as "Gillespie and the Conquest").

REPORTS OF PARTICIPANTS: Emory, *Notes*, 168–75; "Dr. Griffin's Diary, 334–38; Capt. S. F. Du Pont, U.S.N., *Extracts from the Private Journal—Letters of Capt. S. F. Du Pont while in Command of the* Cyane *during the War with Mexico, 1846–1848* (Privately printed in Wilmington, Delaware, 1885), 97–105; *History of Sonoma County* (San Francisco, Alley, Bowen & Co., 1880), 581; William A. Streeter, "Recollections of Historical Events in California, 1843–1878," CHS, Vol. XVIII, No. 2 (June, 1939), 167–68; Camp, *Kit Carson*, 140. "Gillespie and the Conquest," CHS, Vol. XVII, No. 2 (June, 1938); Vol. XVII, No. 4 (December, 1938), 343. Letter dated April 18, 1846, in Sabin, *Kit Carson Days*, 281; Gillespie to Stockton; unpublished notes of William H. Dunne in BL; *Lances at San Pascual*, 79–80; Hubert Howe Bancroft, *History of California* (San Francisco, The History Company, 1884–90), V, 353 (hereinafter referred to as Bancroft); Vestal, *Happy Warrior*, 233–35; Peters, *Kit Carson*, 284.

INDIAN EYEWITNESS: Elizabeth Judson Roberts, *Indian Stories of the Southwest* (San Francisco, Harr Wagner Publishing Co., 1917), 222–24.

CASUALTIES: "*Dr. Griffin's Diary*," 336; *Lances at San Pascual*, Appendix D on p. 63; Emory, *Notes*, 170.

MARCH TO SAN BERNARDO AND MULE HILL: *Court-Martial Proceedings*, 187; Vestal, *Happy Warrior*, 235; "Gillespie and the Conquest," Vol. XVII, No. 4 (December, 1938), 344; *Lances at San Pascual*, 82 n., 83 n.; "Dr. Griffin's Diary," 337, 355 n.

RELIEF PARTY AND MARCH TO SAN DIEGO: Joseph T. Downey (Fred Blackburn Rogers, ed.), *Filings from an Old Saw* (San Francisco, John Howell Books, 1956), 89 (hereinafter referred to as

Filings); Mary Rockwood Peet, *San Pasqual, A Crack in the Hills* (Culver City, Calif., Highland Press, 1949); 49–50; "Gillespie and the Conquest," Vol. XVII, No. 4 (December, 1938), 344; unpublished manuscript of Thomas Crosby Lancey, "Coxswain on *U. S. S. Dale*," UCLA.

Victory or Defeat?: Letter of Chief of Historical Division, Army War College, Washington, D. C., August 17, 1928, quoted in Kearny, *Battle Soldier*, 465. Werner H. Marti, "Archibald H. Gillespie," unpublished doctoral dissertation (June, 1953), UCLA, 152; since published under title *Messenger of Destiny* (San Francisco, John Howell-Books, 1960). Valentine Mott Porter, *Conquest*, 110; letter of William H. Hilton to Maj. E. A. Sherman, October 1, 1906, reporting conversation with Andrés Pico abt. August, 1852, Munk Library of Arizoniana, Southwest Museum, Los Angeles, Thomas Kearny (great-grandnephew), letters and unpublished manuscripts on San Pasqual and all phases of controversy with Stockton and Frémont, in Society of California Pioneers, San Francisco.

CHAPTER XVI—*The San Gabriel and the Mesa*

San Diego, 1846: Du Pont, *Journal—Letters*, 105, 107; Bancroft, V, 355, 419–20; *Court-Martial Proceedings*, 47, 82, 94, 111 ff., 189–91, 241 f., 322; Allan Nevins, *Frémont, Pathmarker of the West* (New York, Longmans, Green & Co., 1955), 305–30.

March to Los Angeles: *Filings*, 90, 92–96; Du Pont, *Journal—Letters*, 99, 106, 112.

Battles of the San Gabriel and the Mesa: "Dr. Griffin's Diary," CHS, Vol. XXII, No. 1 (March, 1943), 42; *Filings*, 99; Col. J. J. Warner, Judge Benjamin Hayes, and Dr. J. P. Widney, *An Historical Sketch of Los Angeles County, California, from the Spanish Occupancy to the Founding of the Mission of San Gabriel Arcangel* (Los Angeles, Louis Leven & Co., 1876; reprinted, 1936), 43.

Casualties: Viola Lockhart Warren, ed., "Dr. John S. Griffin's Mail, 1846–53," CHS, Vol. XXXIII, No. 2 (June, 1954), 105–106 (hereinafter referred to as "Dr. Griffin's Mail"); Bancroft, V, 396; unpublished Thomas O. Larkin papers including letters of

Larkin, August 4, 1847, January 11 and 17, 1847, in BL; *Court-Martial Proceedings*, 108, 199–200.

CHAPTER XVII—*"Who Is Governor of California?"*

KEARNY VS. STOCKTON AND FRÉMONT: Sen. Thomas H. Benton's speech, 30 Cong., 1 sess., Appendix to *Congressional Globe*, 1038 (hereinafter referred to as Benton's Senate Speech); Nevins, *Pathmarker*, 310, 335, 349; Bancroft, V, 427, 431–32; Nevins, *Greatest Adventurer*, II, 349; Du Pont, *Journal—Letters*, 112–17; letter of January 17, 1847, in Mariano G. Vallejo, Docs. No. 34–254, BL.

RETURN TO SAN DIEGO: "Dr. Griffin's Diary," CHS, Vol. XXII, No. 1, p. 45–46; Hughes-Connelly, 349.

ARRIVAL OF MORMON BATTALION: Unpublished diary of Sgt. Nathaniel V. Jones of Mormon Battalion, entry for January 26, 1847, in San Diego Historical Society's Library, San Diego (hereinafter referred to as Jones, Diary); Philip St. George Cooke, *Conquest of New Mexico and California* (New York, G. P. Putnam's Sons, 1878), 193–96, 280; letter of Brig. Gen. S. W. Kearny to Adj. Gen., January 30, 1847, in Kearny Collection, MHS.

VOYAGE TO MONTEREY: Du Pont, *Journal—Letters*, 118–20; William T. Sherman, *Memoirs* (3d ed., New York, C. L. Webster & Co., 1890), I, 46, 51–52 (hereinafter referred to as Sherman); Bancroft, V, 429; Monterey *Californian* (January 28 and February 13, 1847); letter of Charles Edward Pickett to Lt. E. M. Kern, MS No. 102, Vol. XXV, Fort Sutter Papers, HL.

FRÉMONT'S INSUBORDINATION: *Court-Martial Proceedings*, 48–53, 296, 417.

KEARNY UPHELD BY WASHINGTON: Yerba Buena *California Star* (February 20, 1847), CSL; letter of A. H. Gillespie to Thomas O. Larkin, April 1, 1847, in unpublished Larkin Papers, BL; Nevins, *Pathmarker*, 321–22; *Court-Martial Proceedings*, 102; letter of Gen. Stephen W. Kearny to Com. Biddle, April 11, 1847, in diary and letter book, Kearny Collection, MHS (this letter mentions Commodore Shubrick's letter to John C. Frémont dated February 23, 1847).

KEARNY AT SAN FRANCISCO: Edwin Bryant, *What I Saw in Cali-*

fornia (Santa Ana, Calif., Fine Arts Press, 1936), 413, 416 (here-inafter referred to as Bryant); *Old Naval Days,* 163–64; Du Pont, *Journal—Letters,* 121–35, 140 f., 144–46; 31 Cong., 1 sess., *Exec. Doc. No. 17,* 287; letters of Capt. Henry S. Turner to Julia Turner, February 21, 1847, in Kearny Collection, MHS; John Henry Brown, *Reminiscences and Incidents of Early Days of San Francisco* (1845–50) (San Francisco, The Grabhorn Press, 1933), 65.

GOVERNOR AT MONTEREY: Letters of Thomas O. Larkin, March 17, 1847; of Ebenezer Larkin Childs to Thomas O. Larkin, September 25, 1847; of Thomas O. Larkin to A. H. Gillespie, April 27, 1847; and of Thomas O. Larkin to Com. R. F. Stockton, April 13, 1847, in Larkin Collection, BL. Circular by Brig. Gen. Kearny and Com. Shubrick, March 1, 1847; excellent reproduction in *A Navy Surgeon in California, 1846–47, the Journal of Marius Duvall* (San Francisco, John Howell-Books, 1957), opposite p. 92 (herein-after referred to as *Duvall*).

CHAPTER XVIII—*"A Bright Star In Our Union"*

KEARNY'S PROCLAMATION: Original copy in BL; excellent repro-duction in *Duvall,* opposite p. 94. *Duvall,* 91–94.

CHANGES IN NAVAL COMMAND: Du Pont, *Journal—Letters,* 144–46, 152; letter of Thomas O. Larkin to Com. R. F. Stockton, March 15, 1847, in Larkin Collection, BL, pp. 91–94.

STEVENSON'S ARRIVAL: Letter of James P. Arthur to Thomas O. Larkin, March 6, 1847, in Larkin Collection, BL.

INDIAN AFFAIRS: Letter of Thomas O. Larkin to Brig. Gen. S. W. Kearny, March 6, 1847, in Larkin Collection, BL.

UNPAID PUBLIC DEBTS: Benton's Senate Speech, 994.

WATER-FRONT LOTS: Frank Soulé, John H. Gihon, and James Nisbet, *The Annals of San Francisco* (New York, D. Appleton & Co., 1855), 181 (hereinafter referred to as *Annals of San Francisco*).

BIRTH OF U.S. MAIL, CALIFORNIA: CHS, Vol. XXXIII, No. 2 (June, 1954), 120.

TROUBLES WITH FRÉMONT: Letters of Henry S. Turner to Julia Turner, March 16, 1847, March 31, 1847, and May 1, 1847, in Kearny Collection, MHS; letter of Henry S. Turner to Dr. John

S. Griffin, March 14, 1847, in "Dr. Griffin's Mail," XXXIII, 108; Nevins, *Greatest Adventurer*, II, 376 and *passim*. Nevins, *Pathmarker*, 317; Young, 229; letters of Stephen Reynolds to Thomas O. Larkin, March 7, 1847, and of Faxon Dean Atherton to Thomas O. Larkin, March 31, 1847, in Larkin Collection, BL.

FRÉMONT'S RIDE TO MONTEREY: Bancroft, V, 444; Nevins, *Pathmarker*, 320.

KEARNY ON MORMONS: Du Pont, *Journal—Letters*, 134.

COURT OF ADMIRALTY: 31 Cong., 1 sess., *Exec. Doc. No. 17*, 291; Walter Colton, *Three Years in California* (New York, Barnes, 1850), 194.

MARIANO VALLEJO: Letter of Brig. Gen. S. W. Kearny to Gen. Mariano Vallejo, April 21, 1847, in Vallejo Documents, BL.

FRÉMONT AND MASON: Letter of Dr. G. B. Sanderson to Dr. John S. Griffin, April 8, 1847, in "Dr. Griffin's Mail," XXXIII, 112; Jones, Diary, 13; letter of Com. R. F. Stockton to A. H. Gillespie, n.d., Doc. 206 in unpublished papers of Archibald H. Gillespie, Catherine Coffin Phillips Collection, UCLA (hereinafter referred to as Unpublished Gillespie Papers).

RUMORS OF TROUBLE IN SOUTH: Letters of A. H. Gillespie to Thomas O. Larkin, March 5, 1847, and April 1, 1847; Larkin to Gillespie, March 24, 1847; and Larkin to Edwin O. Bryant, April 7, 1847, in Larkin Collection, BL. Cooke, *Conquest*, 299–303; letter of Maj. Thomas Swords to Dr. John S. Griffin, May 4, 1847, in "Dr. Griffin's Mail," XXXIII, 113.

KEARNY GOES TO LOS ANGELES: Sherman, 54–55; letter of Brig. Gen. Kearny to Capt. Theodorus Bailey, n.d., in T. W. Norris Collection, BL; Horace Bell, *On the Old West Coast* (New York, Grosset & Dunlap, 1930), 116–18; Jones, Diary, 15. Unpublished diary of Elijah Elmer, 1st Sgt. Co. "C" Mormon Battalion, 24; original in San Diego Historical Society, San Diego.

LAST DAYS IN MONTEREY: Letter of Brig. Gen. S. W. Kearny to Col. J. D. Stevenson, May 30, 1847, in John D. Stevenson papers, Robert Cowan Collection, UCLA; letter of same to Adj. Gen., May 30, 1847, in Kearny letter book, MHS; Benton's Senate Speech, 979; letter of Thomas O. Larkin to Edwin Bryant, May 28, 1847; letter of same to Brig. Gen. S. W. Kearny, May 29, 1847, in Larkin Collection, BL.

GILLESPIE AFFAIR AND FRÉMONT: Unpublished Gillespie Papers, Docs. 233 and 243; letter of Dr. G. B. Sanderson to Dr. John S. Griffin, May 30, 1847, in "Dr. Griffin's Mail," XXXIII, 117; *Annals of San Francisco*, 194; letter of Jacob Primer Leese to Thomas O. Larkin, May 24, 1847, in Larkin Collection, BL; "Journal of John McHenry Hollingsworth," CHS, Vol. I (July, 1922), 247–48; *Court-Martial Proceedings*, 214–28.

LOWER CALIFORNIA: Letter of Brig. Gen. S. W. Kearny to Lt. Col. Henry S. Burton, May 30, 1847, in Kearny letter book, MHS.

Bancroft's *History of California* provides the best general background for the California period of General Kearny's career. Zoeth Skinner Eldredge, *The Beginnings of San Francisco* (San Francisco, privately published, 1912), and Theodore H. Hittell, *History of California* (San Francisco, N. J. Stone & Co., 1898), while not primary sources contain excellent summaries of the history of the period. In addition, Eldredge's work includes short biographies of most of its figures.

CHAPTER XIX—*Saddle Leather and Statecraft*

MONTEREY TO SUTTER'S FORT: Letter of Maj. Thomas Swords to Quartermaster General, October 8, 1847, 30 Cong., 2 sess., *HR Exec. Doc. No. 1*, 226–36. Capt. Henry S. Turner, unpublished "Journal of Brig. Gen. S. W. Kearny's Return from California in the Summer of 1847"; original in Kearny Collection, MHS (hereinafter referred to as Turner, "Journal"). Johann Sutter, *Diary* (San Francisco, Grabhorn Press, 1932), 39; letter of Johann Sutter to Thomas O. Larkin, June 25, 1847, in Larkin Collection, BL.

MURPHY OR FALLON: Turner, "Journal"; Introduction to Vol. XIV, Fort Sutter Papers, HL.

JOHNSON'S TO DONNER LAKE: Cutts, *Conquest*, 214; Jones, Diary, 17–28; Nevins, *Pathmarker*, 325; Charles L. Camp, "William Alexander Trubody and the Overland Pioneers of 1847," CHS, Vol. XVI, No. 2 (June, 1937), 126, 141 n.; Turner, "Journal."

THE OREGON TRAIL: Dale Morgan, "The Mormon Ferry on the North Platte," *Annals of Wyoming*, Vol. XXI, Nos. 2 and 3 (July-October, 1949).

FORT LEAVENWORTH: Letter of Joseph Hilbus to "Mr. Editor," August 22, 1847, in Kearny Collection, MHS; James H. Wilbur, unpublished journal, entry for May 29, 1847 (original in Willamette University Library, Salem, Ore.; microfilm in BL); letter of Brig. Gen. Stephen W. Kearny to Adj. Gen., August 22, 1847 (original in Kearny Collection, MHS).

RETURN TO ST. LOUIS: Scharf, *St. Louis*, I, 386; *St. Louis Weekly Reveille* (August 30, 1847); letter of Ed. P. Mercellin, M.D., secretary of the N.Y. State Soc. of the Cincinnati, to Brig. Gen. S. W. Kearny, July 6, 1847, in Kearny Collection, MHS.

POLITICS IN WASHINGTON: *New York Herald* (September 11, 1847); Allan Nevins, ed., *Polk's Diary* (New York, Longmans, Green & Co., 1929), 221, 226–27, 242, 252, 254–56, 262, 264–66, 271–75 (hereinafter referred to as *Polk's Diary*); letters of John Coffin Jones to Thomas O. Larkin, June 10, 1847, and October 1, 1847, in Larkin Collection, BL; Nevins, *Pathmarker*, 330; Francis M. Wheat, "Senator Benton Lays His Plans," CHS, Vol. XIII, 150–54; letter of Ebenezer Larkin Childs to Thomas O. Larkin, September 23, 1847, in Larkin Collection, BL; *Washington National Intelligencer* (October 25, November 3 and 6, 1847).

CHAPTER *XX—Witness on Trial*

PRELIMINARIES: *Court-Martial Proceedings*, 1–447; De Voto, 464, 507 n.

KIT CARSON'S ABSENCE: *Immortal Wife*, 144–50, 153–64; Milo Milton Quaife, ed., *Kit Carson's Autobiography* (Chicago, Lakeside Press, 1935), 122 (hereinafter referred to as *Carson's Autobiography*); John Adams Hussey, "Kit Carson at Cajón not Tejón," CHS, Vol. XXIX (March, 1950), 29–38; Catherine Coffin Phillips, *Jessie Benton Frémont: A Woman Who Made History* (San Francisco, printed by John Henry Nash, 1935), 122.

NEWSPAPER REPORTS: *Washington National Intelligencer* (November 23 and 25, 1847); *New Orleans Picayune* (November 16, 1847, and January 9, 1848); *New York Daily Globe* (November 4 and 18, 1847); *New York Herald* (November 4, 8, 10, and December 25, 1847, and January 13 and 18, 1848); *New York Daily*

Tribune (December 15 and 22, 1847, January 15 and 27, and February 2 and 21, 1848). Kearny, *Battle Soldier*, 32.

PUBLIC OPINION: Letters of J. C. Jones to Thomas O. Larkin, December 12, 1847, and October 8, 1848, in Larkin Collection, BL.

VERDICT AND SENTENCE: Polk's Diary, 282, 303; letter of Stephen W. Kearny to Lt. William Radford, November 28, 1847, in *Old Naval Days*, 175–76; Heitman, *U.S. Army*.

AFTERMATH: See Unpublished Gillespie Papers concerning L. C. Levin correspondence; Goodwin, 155; Young, 236; Bancroft, V, 457.

CREATION OF A LEGEND: Henry Howe, *Historical Collections of the Great West* (Cincinnati, Ohio, H. Howe, 1854), 332; George H. Tinkham, *A History of Stockton* (San Francisco, W. M. Hinton & Co., 1880), 119; Charles Preuss, *Exploring with Frémont*, trans. and ed. by Erwin G. and Elisabeth K. Gudde (Norman, University of Oklahoma Press, 1958), *passim* (hereinafter referred to as Preuss); letter of Mrs. Alice Kearny Coyle Torbert of Washington, D. C. (sister-in-law of glacial geologist François E. Matthes), June 4, 1956.

CHAPTER XXI—*Taps*

ORDERED TO MEXICO: Letters of Adj. Gen. to Brig. Gen. Stephen W. Kearny, February 23, 1848, and March 1, 1848, in NA; letter of "Prominent Citizens," New Orleans, March 31, 1848, in Kearny Collection, MHS; letter of Ludlow & Smith to Brig. Gen. Kearny, March 31, 1848, in Kearny Collection, MHS.

VERACRUZ: Letters of Brig. Gen. S. W. Kearny to Adj. Gen., April 9, 1848, and April 15, 1848, in NA; letters of L. Thomas, Asst. Ajd. Gen., Army of Mexico, dated Mexico City, April 6, 1848, to Col. H. Wilson, and April 17, 1848, and May 6, 1848, to Brig. Gen. S. W. Kearny, in NA; letter of Col. Bankhead, Orizaba, April 10, 1848, in NA; letter of Brig. Gen. S. W. Kearny to Secretary of War Marcy, April 13, 1848, in NA; letter of Maj. J. H. La Motte to Mrs. E. La Motte, April 22, 1848, and May 12, 1848, in Kearny Collection, MHS; letter of Adj. Gen. to Maj. Gen. W. O. Butler, May 9, 1848, in NA.

PUEBLA AND MEXICO CITY: Letters of L. Thomas, Asst. Adj.

Gen., to Brig. Gen. S. W. Kearny, May 20, 1848, June 5, 1848, and June 18, 1848, in NA; unpublished letter book of Maj. Gen. W. O. Butler (courtesy its present owner, Mr. Carl Dentzel, director of Southwest Museum, Los Angeles); Justin Smith, II, 220, 252, 438, 476.

NEW ORLEANS: Letter of Brig. Gen. S. W. Kearny to Adj. Gen. dated New Orleans, July 18, 1848, in NA.

BENTON'S WRATH: Benton's Senate Speech, 1009 *et seq.;* letters of Maj. Thomas Swords to Dr. John S. Griffin, September 28, 1848, and November 24, 1848; "Dr. Griffin's Mail," CHS, Vol. XXXIII, 266, 338; letter of Ebenezer L. Childs to Thomas O. Larkin, November 28, 1848, in Larkin Collection, BL; *Thirty Years' View,* II, 716, 719.

MAJOR GENERAL: Letter of Asst. Adj. Gen. to Bvt. Maj. Gen. S. W. Kearny, September 7, 1848, in Kearny Collection, MHS; Mendell Lee Taylor, 184.

SICKNESS: Letter of Susan Kearny to Mary Kearny, Newark, N. J., October 5, 1848 (original courtesy Mrs. Richard Arthur Bullock); letter of I. L. Schnell to Bvt. Maj. Gen. S. W. Kearny, August 31, 1848 (original courtesy Mrs. Bullock); Kennerly, 111; Phillips, *Jessie Frémont,* 130; De Voto, 467; *Immortal Wife,* 204–206; Goodwin, 153; clipping presumably from *St. Louis Reveille* (November 3, 1848), (courtesy Mrs. Bullock); Preuss, 97, 98 n.

BIRTH AND DEATH: Stephen Watts Kearny Bible, MHS; *St. Louis Republican* (November 2, 1848); *St. Louis Reveille* (November 3, 1848).

DATA ON CEMETERIES: Information supplied by MHS and Mrs. Bullock above mentioned.

HONORS: General Orders No. 57, War Department, November 6, 1848, in MKC papers; resolution of New Jersey Legislature (original in MHS); letter of Maj. J. H. La Motte to Mrs. J. H. La Motte, November 26, 1848, in Kearny Collection, MHS; *Louisville Courier Journal* (October 24, 1848), (courtesy Mrs. Bullock); information supplied by Mrs. Bullock, Mrs. Jerry Mihm of Clayton, Mo. (another great-granddaughter), Cresson Kearny (a great-grandson), and Mrs. Horace Torbert (Alice Kearny Coyle Torbert); newspaper clippings (unnamed) from St. Joseph Mo. (n. d.)

Last Will: Original in office of Clerk of the Probate Court of St. Louis, Mo.; copy of Pension Award by Commissioner of Pensions, December 2, 1870 (original in Mrs. Bullock's possession).

Tributes: Letter of William L. Marcy, secretary of war, to Gen. Wetmore, September 24, 1847, in William L. Marcy papers, MSS Division, LC; letter of William Radford (uncle) to William Radford (nephew), dated Morristown, N. J., December 19, 1848, in *Old Naval Days*, 182; Colton, *Three Years*, 375–76; Bryant, 416; letter of Margaret Kearny Walton to Mary Kearny, New York, November 6, 1848 (original in possession of Mrs. Bullock); U. S. Grant, *Memoirs* (New York, Charles L. Webster & Company, 1885), I, 45; Williamson Greenfield, in unnamed and undated newspaper clipping in MKC papers.

Grant, Ulysses S., estimate of Kearny: 391
Grant County, N. M.: 183
Gray, Lt. Andrew F. V.: leads relief party, 225; controversy about, 225; marches to rescue, 226; tries to prevent looting, 228
Great Bend: *see* Big Bend
Great Britain: and War of 1812, 19; and frontier West, 19; boundary disputes with, 67, 83, 88; sea power of, 91; friction with Spain, 128
"Great Red-headed Father": *see* Clark, William
Great Salt Lake: on Disturnell map, 178; goal of Mormons, 316, 335
Green Bay, Wis.: 35
Griffin, Asst. Surgeon John Strather: in Army of West, 112; leaves Santa Fe, 161; version of Socorro meeting, 169–70; opinion on wine, 192; diary of on San Pasqual, 196, 208; service of at San Pasqual, 215–16; report of casualties at San Pasqual, 217f.; tends wounded at San Bernardo, 222; progress with patients, 221; on Mexican losses at San Pasqual, 218–19; leaves Los Angeles with Kearny, 269; quoted on Stockton's tent, 243; quotes Burgess, 225
Guyer, Lt., commands keelboat: 27

Hafen, Leroy: 164
Hailes, Surgeon: on Leavenworth expedition, 60; illness of, 62
Hall, Congressman Willard P.: codification of laws by, 148–49; gets credit for laws, 149–50; brings news to Kearny, 270; passenger on *Lexington*, 313, 317; on return expedition, 330; anti-Frémont speeches of, 343
Halleck, Lt. Henry W.: sails north from Monterey, 276; sent to San Diego, 297; surveying instruments to be delivered to, 319
Hammond, Lt. Thomas C.: reconnoiters canyon, 141; lost opportunity of, 199ff., 204; death of, 209, 214

Hammond, William, witness to Kearny's will: 386
Harney, Lt., commands keelboat: 27
Hawks Rt. Rev. Bishop: 387
Hayes, Judge Benjamin: 218
Hitchcock, Ethan Allen: 76, 113
Holdenville, Okla.: 60
Hollingsworth, Lt. John M.: 323
Horgan, Paul: 144
Horse Chief of the Long Knives: 72
Horsemanship: of Indian women, 23; of Plains Indians, 72; or Mexicans, 208
Horses: for dragoons, 58; treatment of, 65, 74–75, 82; in *caballada*, 187; bought from Mexicans, 188; death of on desert, 189; seizure of from Coronel, 191–92; reason for attacking Pico, 205; importance of to Kearny, 206; demanded from Frémont, 309; returned to owners in California, 313; commandeered for expedition, 328–29
Howard, George T.: 121
Howitzers: fired to entertain Indians, 29; loaned to Frémont, 88; shot on Fourth of July, 96; arrive in camp, 187; at San Pasqual, 212ff.; capture of, 213; surrendered to Frémont, 256f., 353f.; at San Gabriel under Owens, 302, 350; turned over to Mormon Battalion, 308; question of in trial, 350
Hudson, Capt., in charge of Laclede Rangers: 112
Hudson's Bay Company: 67, 331
Hughes, John T., helps codify laws: 149
Hyde, George: 324

Illinois River: 80
Illness: of Kearny at St. Genevieve, 25; of men on Leavenworth expedition, 60ff.; of Kearny at Fort Leavenworth, 84; of Kearny on Santa Fe Trail, 121–22; of Kearny in Santa Fe, 151; of Kearny at trial, 363; of Kearny in Mexico, 376ff.